CATERINA SFORZA

Caterina Sforza (?), attributed to S. Botticelli, painted in the early 1480's.
Courtesy of Staatliches Lindenaumuseum, Altenburg, Thuringia.

Ernst Breisach

—

CATERINA SFORZA

A RENAISSANCE VIRAGO

THE UNIVERSITY OF CHICAGO PRESS

CHICAGO AND LONDON

Library of Congress Catalog Card Number: 67–25511

THE UNIVERSITY OF CHICAGO PRESS, CHICAGO & LONDON
The University of Toronto Press, Toronto 5, Canada

PREFATORY NOTE

SOME YEARS AGO my interest in the political aspects of Renaissance history led me to a study of Romagna. The forces shaping that region's political structure soon lost their abstract quality and became embedded in the complex minds, aspirations, and varied passions of flesh and blood individuals. From the array of fascinating personages living in what Jacob Burckhardt once called "a hotbed of ferocious passions" emerged Caterina Sforza. When I sought to learn more about her I discovered that she had never been made the subject of an original English language biography, and furthermore, that the two main Italian works about her had been written a long time ago (Antonio Burriel's biography in 1795 and Pier Desiderio Pasolini's in 1893). Since Caterina Sforza's biography is not merely interesting as the story of an amazingly adventurous life but also as a mirror in which a whole segment of the Renaissance world is reflected, I decided to write her biography and to do so not only for the Renaissance specialist but for the educated non-specialist as well. For the former there is the assurance that this biography has been scrupulously based on the careful analysis of evidence, and for the latter I have attempted to keep to a minimum the obstructions to reading sometimes found in the style or language of scholarship. I also hope that this biography will be viewed not as an attempt to substantiate one or the other interpretation of the Renaissance but as a contribution to the understanding of yet another facet of the many-sided Renaissance period. While Caterina Sforza may not have shaped the over-all course of events during that period, she certainly was one of its more colorful representatives.

Combined with the satisfaction of a task accomplished, I feel a sense of gratitude toward those who unselfishly have rendered help to my endeavor. The American Philosophical Society generously assisted work on this biography with a grant which made possible one of my research trips to Italy. Western Michigan University provided me with grants for the purchase of source material in microform. A summary note of gratitude must suffice for the librarians and archivists of over twenty-five institutions in the United States and Europe. Their summarily mentioned merits should not be diminished by my special note of acknowledgment to the following: the officials of the Istituti Culturali ed Artistici della Città di Forlì, particularly the Director of the Biblioteca Comunale "A. Saffi," Dr. Walter Vichi; Direktor Dr. H.-C. von der Gabelentz, Staatliches Lindenaumuseum, Altenburg, Thuringia; Director of the Biblioteca Comunale and Archivio Storico, Imola, Dr. Fausto Mancini; Prof. Gina Fasoli, University of Bologna; and Dr. Vincent Ilardi, University of Massachusetts, who graciously permitted the use of his extensive microfilm collection of Italian diplomatic documents. Advice, criticism, and encouragement have come to me from my colleagues Drs. Abbie Copps, Howard Mowen, Frederick Rogers, Robert Friedmann, Cecil Clough, Hermann Rothfuss, and Robert Shafer, and from my wife and fellow historian, Herma Breisach. Mr. Mario Mion kindly helped me in reading proofs.

E. B.

Kalamazoo, Michigan

CONTENTS

ILLUSTRATIONS

I

PAWN
OF
RENAISSANCE
POLITICS

CATERINA SFORZA, illegitimate daughter of the second Sforza duke of Milan, seemed destined for a life of comfortable obscurity as the wife of a low-ranking Renaissance dignitary. Until, that is, Caterina confronted opportunities for transcending such a station of mediocrity and grasped at them, defiant of the dangers and contemptuous of the counsels of doubt. In doing so she transformed confining circumstances into stepping stones on the way to fame. In moments of triumph, of suffering, of fortitude, and of fear she shaped a life often noble, sometimes base, but never pale or commonplace. Caterina became a heroine of the Renaissance rather than a footnote to its history.

The world which surrounded the infant Caterina was the Italy of the early 1460's. An unprecedented measure of tranquillity had been brought to it by the Peace of Lodi (1454), and the subsequent league between Milan, Florence, and Naples widened eventually into a general league of all Italian powers. Since the two events had not issued from a love of peace but from stalemated self-interests, the Italian situation resembled not a state of bliss but an armed truce characterized by constant maneuvering and small-scale fighting in crisis after crisis. Yet with outside powers, particularly France and the Empire, being kept from intervening in Italian affairs either by wars and exhaustion or by internal conflict, the Italian powers managed for a quarter of a century to keep in check their traditional animosities and burning expansionist tendencies and to preserve the status quo.

Few states and few persons basked with such obvious delight in the tranquillity of the Italian situation as did Caterina's home, the duchy of Milan, and Caterina's family, the Sforza. The Peace of Lodi had ended the war in which the Sforza had established themselves as the ruling dynasty in Milan [1]—a well-deserved position, considering the enemies they had defeated. Venice, the aristocratic republic with its far-flung domains and interests in the Levant, was left with some of its most cherished territorial ambitions unfulfilled. The Kingdom of Naples, powerful though hampered by a lack of common purpose between the Aragonese king and mighty feudal barons, had to acquiesce in a re-establishment of a powerful Milan. The Empire, with its grandiose universal claims and its sadly contrasting reality, had fought the Sforza with little more than words and diplomatic missions; now the emperor could do no more than deny the Sforza formal investiture with the imperial possession, Milan. And finally Savoy, the Alpine state, readily made peace, since it had long been used to little gain in its battles against neighboring France and Milan.

The Sforza had prevailed. Their military prowess, diplomatic skill, and perseverance in the face of adversity had been one weapon. They had also benefited from the benevolent neutrality of the papacy, which at that time, in addition to shepherding Western Christians, was an Italian power of the first order by virtue of its lordship over the Papal States. But the money and the friendship of Cosimo de'Medici's Florence had been the most effective second weapon. In the end the Arno republic gained as much as Milan from the Italian tranquillity it had helped to establish. The Medici family, which governed Florence behind a veil of democratic institutions, needed the respite as it entered a period of threat to its supremacy under the aging Cosimo de'Medici, in the 1450's and early 1460's, and his ailing and short-lived successor Piero.

Ten years after seizing power, the first Sforza duke of Milan, the aging Francesco, was beset by few grave problems. Milan, released from the hardships of war, benefited from renewed prosperity. A stream of Milanese products, particularly expensive cloth, embroidery, goldsmith wares, and arms poured from the city out across the Alps, the Apennines, and the plain of the Po River. In addition to all the advantages accruing to the city from its location in an agricultural area of abundant fertility, the urban prosperity produced new wealth and with it new power for Milan. Whatever was left of enthusiasm for the *Aurea Repubblica Ambrosiana*[2] was dampened by the comforts of peaceful life and a gradually strengthening attachment to the Sforza. The Milanese had become fond of their new ruler, who exhibited an unaffected simplicity and folksiness. But the Sforza also knew how to prepare for less favorable shifts of fortune, when popular support might wane and the importance of brutal power increase. Their insight was manifested by the Castello Sforzesco, a building of the 1450's and 1460's. One of Duke Francesco's major concerns, however, over the portents for the duchy visible in the behavior of his oldest son and eventual successor to the dukedom, Galeazzo Maria Sforza, was less easily mitigated.

Galeazzo Maria was born (1444) the son of a famous *condottiere*, who searched for a greater destiny. When the time came to shape Galeazzo Maria's mind and body, Francesco Sforza could give his son an education befitting a prospective duke. A staff of excellent teachers taught the young man with enthusiasm and sternness.[3] Galeazzo Maria responded by achieving an outstanding mastery of Latin, courtly manners, and outward obedience to his parents. In 1455 his marital future was settled by a marriage contract with the Gonzaga family, who had been, and still were, of great value as a shield against Venice. Susanna Gonzaga was to be his wife, but she developed a hunchback and her sister Dorotea was substituted (1457).[4]

In the summer of 1457, the thirteen-year-old Galeazzo Maria began another phase of his education when he visited Ferrara.[5] Two years later his travels became more extensive and led him to Bologna, Florence, Venice, and Mantua, and to a meeting with Pope Pius II. The letters which he wrote to Duke Francesco bespeak a dutiful son doing what was expected of him.[6] They also show how Galeazzo Maria found the freedom and adulation afforded him on such travels entirely to his taste. He grasped little of what mattered in Italian politics, but fully appreciated the trappings of Renaissance courts—the palaces, the gardens, the chase, the dances, and the ladies. While at home he was still treated as an adolescent; the personages at other courts and in other cities saw in him the prospective duke of Milan. Understandably, Galeazzo Maria felt happier away from home. When not traveling, he tended to prolong his stays at Pavia.[7] The beautiful and extensive park of the old Visconti castle, with its plentiful game, tempted him as much as the distance from Milan. Adolescence added its share of restlessness to Galeazzo Maria's always erratic personality. Gradually a circle of young men gathered around him to form part of his own establishment. In their midst he changed from a dutiful son who wrote pleasant letters in a stilted style to his parents into a brash young fellow who took no advice.

In 1460 Galeazzo Maria traveled within the duchy with parental consent—permission, it is true, but already granted reluctantly.[8] Duke Francesco had great misgivings about his oldest son's aimless assertions of independence and about what he considered the ill-befitting company Galeazzo Maria kept.[9] For two years the son ignored such parental protests and tasted the pleasures of mature life without being bothered by its responsibilities. His world was filled with little but the turbulent companionship of friends, the chase in the green areas of the Po plains, dances, and his first ventures with ladies. The fire of sexual desire was kindled when Galeazzo Maria met Lucrezia, the wife of his companion in pleasure, Giampietro Landriani.[10] The kind of companionship Galeazzo Maria and Lucrezia offered each other was not hindered by the lack of mental brilliance on Lucrezia's part, and was significantly enhanced by her beauty, her easily overcome sense of conjugal fidelity, and her husband's refusal to notice anything. Giampietro Landriani did not mind being cuckolded by the future duke of Milan, who would hold significant power of patronage. The first result of the young Sforza's liaison with Lucrezia was a son Carlo (born 1461). Giampietro's claim to Galeazzo Maria's gratitude seemed assured when, probably late in 1462, Lucrezia gave birth to a second child whom Galeazzo Maria readily acknowledged as his daughter.[11] Caterina Sforza entered the world as a lasting memento to the passionate love of a princeling for a beautiful lady. Such sentimental circumstance did not impress the world of propriety and formality which spoke of Caterina as the daughter of "Galeazzo Maria and one of his concubines." [12]

No festivities greeted Caterina's birth and no letters of joy were dispatched to foreign courts announcing the birth, with God's grace, of a new Sforza. Birth in obscurity was followed by a few years during which Caterina grew up in a limbo. Her father was not yet the duke, and his resources for taking care of the product of his passionate pastimes were limited. In addition, months before Caterina's birth, Galeazzo Maria had begun to strive for a better relationship with his parents and was less willing than before to parade the fruits of his sexual liaison before the world. His youthful taste for defiance of his parents had found temporary satisfaction, and he approached them, not as a repentant son, but at least as one more willing to be obedient. While Lucrezia had been bearing his child, he had been clamoring for more meaningful news from the court.[13] He had visited the brothers and the abbot of the Certosa of Pavia for spiritual exercise and advice.[14] Traces of respect for his parents reappeared in his letters.[15] Galeazzo Maria even expressed his willingness to avoid repeating grave errors.[16] But all of this did not really reform his behavior; he merely became more discreet about it. And his affair with Lucrezia continued.

Galeazzo Maria's energies were gradually diverted into a greater variety of activities. Renewed travel occupied a part of his time. Some of these trips brought him together with Dorotea Gonzaga, who was still destined to become his wife. From the time the two met at a wedding in December, 1458, they had exchanged pleasantries in letters.[17] Their relationship was full of irony. Galeazzo Maria and Dorotea acted like persons who were genuinely fond of each other. Theirs was a mutual affection of remarkable tenderness at a time when Galeazzo Maria was finding his pleasures in the arms of Lucrezia Landriani [18] and at a time too when Duke Francesco had decided to drop the Gonzaga marriage in favor of a tie with some more important family. Galeazzo Maria showed no sorrow over the shelving of the Gonzaga marriage plans by his father's deliberate insistence on a medical examination of Dorotea for a possible deformation of the spine. Pride forbade the Gonzaga to permit this, and the marriage became a remote possibility only.[19] Sforza relations with France were, however, carefully nurtured, and Galeazzo Maria was the instrument of that policy. In August, 1465, an expeditionary corps under Galeazzo Maria's command left Milan to assist Louis XI in the struggles connected with the War of the Public Weal.[20] Galeazzo Maria did well; he had military success (although an experienced professional soldier, Gaspare da Vimercate, had much to do with that) and endeared himself to the French king. Then in March, 1466, he had to hurry home. Duke Francesco had died. Galeazzo Maria was the new ruler of Milan.

Milan greeted the young duke with all the pomp and circumstance he could expect; everybody of consequence took part in the welcoming ceremonies. But Lucrezia and Giampietro Landriani were not amongst the well-wishers.[21] Their hour of prominence had come too early, when Galeazzo Maria could not repay favors accorded him. Now that he could, his passion for Lucrezia had cooled. She was still his mistress (and soon pregnant for the fourth time) but increasingly had to share the favors of the young duke with other ladies. Lucrezia's husband had condoned his cuckolding for little gain. Lists of Galeazzo Maria's dependents and *compagnati,* and of gifts to trusted friends, show Giampietro to have been left out.[22] Yet the three-year-old Caterina, a Landriani herself, did not suffer from the eclipse of her mother's and stepfather's influence. She was accepted into the new Sforza household over which her paternal grandmother, Bianca Visconti-Sforza, presided.

Galeazzo Maria took on the responsibility for Caterina's welfare at the same time that he began to rule one of the great powers of Renaissance Italy. Between his concern with state business and his pursuit of private pleasures he had little time for a serious participation in Caterina's upbringing. On occasion, however, he showed his awareness of his father role even in the midst of pressing affairs of war and politics. In 1467, when Galeazzo Maria was in the field in connection with the Colleoni war, he showed himself genuinely distressed by the news of Caterina's sickness. The girl, then four and one-half years old, apparently suffered an attack of one of the numerous diseases to which, in that period, so many infants were lost. Galeazzo Maria's wish to be kept informed about the course of the sickness displayed an urgency beyond that of dutiful interest.[23] Caterina recovered and soon after experienced a decisive change in her life.

Depressions had haunted Dorotea Gonzaga ever since her dream of becoming Galeazzo Maria's wife had been shattered. In 1467 she died. With all possible legal obstacles to a marriage removed, Galeazzo Maria wasted no time in satisfying his desire for a household of his own. The continuation of the Sforza line depended on it, and the prospect of reducing his mother's influence would be enhanced by it. Duke Francesco, in the interest of Italian politics, had been reluctant to consider the ruling families of France and Savoy for dynastic ties. Galeazzo Maria knew no such restraints.[24] During the spring and summer of 1468 negotiations were conducted with the French and the Savoyards.[25] From them came the suggestion that Galeazzo Maria should marry Bona of Savoy, sister of Duke Amadeus IX of Savoy and close relative of Louis XI of France. She was a short and stocky girl with a high forehead, blond hair, an extremely thick neck, and a foreshortened chin.[26] Galeazzo Maria, a connoisseur of women, must have noticed how much she already resembled a matron. But after seeing her portrait drawn by the Milanese artist Zanetto Bugatti he showed the excitement of an infatuated adolescent rather than the detached attitude of the participant in a dynastic match. The proxy marriage was performed; weeks later the spouses met and consummated the marriage. Within months the position of Bianca became untenable.[27] The aged ex-duchess gave up all her attempts to rule with her son and went into voluntary exile to her dowry town of Cremona. On the way to that city Bianca suddenly died (October, 1468). Galeazzo Maria had rid himself of a person whose well-meant interferences he had resented all along. Bona of Savoy became the unchallenged lady of the Sforza household.

Six-year-old Caterina experienced the change of generations in the Sforza family, too. Bianca Visconti-Sforza had been a highly respected figure. The noble lady had given Caterina a sense of security and even of human warmth.[28] Now Bona of Savoy, nineteen years old, attempted to fill the mother role assigned to her. She did so in new surroundings for Caterina, since the Sforza had moved from the Arengo Palace into the Castello Sforzesco shortly after the ducal wedding.

Despite her inexperience and her own struggles with the complications of early marriage, she did well. Carlo, Caterina, Chiara, and Alessandro (Galeazzo Maria's children by Lucrezia Landriani), cherished the gaiety and youthful exuberance of their new stepmother, who gave love even to those who constantly reminded her of her husband's still unbridled sexual escapades. No less attention was paid to the four bastards after

Bona had given birth to the fondly expected heir, Gian Galeazzo (1469). Caterina always thought of her childhood as a
pleasant period and knew that she had to thank Bona for it.
Caterina's father made every decision concerning her life, even
such minor ones as the purchase of shoes and clothing.[29] He
provided well. Yet it was Bona who offered the growing girl the
gentle guidance and warm companionship Caterina longed for
in her splendid but bewildering world. All through her life
Caterina remembered her father with pride, but she felt deeply
grateful to her stepmother.

Caterina's years of carefree playing came to an end when
Bona entered her life. Tutors went to work on the little girl,
introducing her to the rudimentary skills of reading and writing.[30] While Caterina struggled to master the *abecedario,* simple prayers, and some life stories of saints, changes of great
import for her future as a woman were in the offing. Galeazzo
Maria began to use her as a figure in the marital chess game
which the Sforza family played much as the other Renaissance
dynasties did. At one time, Galeotto del Caretto, lord of Finale,
sought to marry into the Sforza family.[31] Caterina was considered but not chosen. She did not remain unattached for long,
however. Galeazzo Maria, in a rather generous mood, permitted a marriage tie between his daughter and the infant Ono-
rato, son of Marcantonio Torelli. The Torelli were not an
exciting choice, but they had been good *condottieri* and trusted
friends of the Sforza family for a long time. Whatever the
reasons for the contemplated union may have been, they do not
matter; the young Torelli never reached adulthood, and Caterina remained available to her father for other plans.[32] Although she was only one of the natural children of Galeazzo
Maria, she still offered a fine marriage prospect for those who
desired a connection with the Sforza court and a substantial
dowry.

Her betrothal disturbed neither the dreams nor the routine
of Caterina's childhood. Indeed, few things did in those years,
not even the event which early in 1471 excited everybody at the
Sforza court. Galeazzo Maria and Bona prepared for a visit to
Florence, "to strengthen the ties with the new *signore,* Lorenzo
de'Medici." [33] Caterina must have longed to join the pompous
caravan which left Milan in May, 1471. It awed not only the

young girl but also the contemporary chroniclers, who recount with ill-concealed disapproval the members of the traveling group. At its head came fifty steeds with saddles of cloth-of-gold, mounted by fifty youths in doublets of cloth-of-gold and silk and displaying silver stirrups. The coaches followed, some of them drawn by four, others by two horses covered with ornamental cloth with silken and golden fringes. The ducal coach was especially splendid with its cloth-of-gold cushions and its horses covered with silver trappings. It was trailed by two thousand horses, two hundred mules, five hundred dogs, a great number of falcons and hawks, buffoons, servants, and forty pipers and tambours.[34] But Caterina, and the other children, including the infant Gian Galeazzo, were left behind.[35] Galeazzo Maria may have been impressed by the hardships of such a trip across the Apennines, or he may simply have deemed it awkward to take his children on a state visit, although he had done so with Caterina and Chiara on a less important occasion in September, 1470.[36] Heavily guarded, the children continued their routine life in the Castello Sforzesco.

The memories and conversations of the members of the Milanese court were still filled with the Florentine adventures when in July, 1471, a message arrived from Rome announcing the death of Pope Paul II. Shortly afterwards, the good news followed that the candidate whom the Sforza had supported, Francesco della Rovere, cardinal of San Pietro in Vincoli, had prevailed in the conclave. So began in earnest the course of developments which would eventually join the still obscure Rovere-Riario and the already powerful Sforza. A mere two years later, repercussions of the papal election of 1471 brought about a decisive turn in Caterina's life.

2

WHILE THE SFORZA were already filling with great self-assurance their place among the celebrated families of *quattrocento* Italy, history seemed bent on by-passing the family of the newly elected pope, the Rovere, and the closely related one of the Riario. These families, whose stellar rise in Renaissance politics was to become Caterina's fortune, lived at the periphery of Renaissance Italy in Western Liguria. Savona, in and around which the Rovere and the Riario had settled, was a quiet and unexciting port, and a marketplace for the peasants who stubbornly won a living from the steep and terraced slopes.

The founder of the Rovere-Riario dynasty was an inconspicuous man, a certain Lionardo della Rovere.[37] Some have called him a fisherman, others a sailor, but all agree that he was a man *di bassissima condizione* ("of low class origin"). Only later, when the Rovere-Riario had fought their way into the glare of celebrity, did writers attempt to gild this poverty by speaking of an old impoverished noble family. Lionardo abounded in children and grandchildren, whose lives were marked by the common mixture of poverty, despair, *joie de vivre,* moderate success and, above all, dreams—dreams of an escape into a life of velvet gowns, banquets, glittering jewels, imposing palaces, and high honors.

One of the dreamers was Lionardo's grandson, Girolamo Riario, a fateful figure in Caterina's life. In the 1460's, Girolamo, a lad in his twenties, with crude features and manners, stalked the streets of Savona. He subsisted sometimes by selling oranges and raisins and at other times by working as clerk at the customs.[38] Cobelli, the chronicler of Forlì, called him a "mediocriter gentilomo." [39]

History would have never counted Girolamo among its figures had it not been for his uncle, that most successful of Lionardo's sons, Francesco della Rovere.[40] Francesco studied at the universities of Pavia, Bologna, and Padua. In other years he earned his livelihood as a tutor to two of his nephews, Piero and Girolamo Riario. It was for Francesco a most happy time, and later proved to be equally beneficial to the two boys.[41]

From then on success never missed Francesco. He excelled in those disputations which were the intellectual delights of his time. Soon he became a hero of the Franciscan order and successively taught as professor at the universities of Padua, Bologna, Pavia, Siena, Florence, and Perugia. But Francesco della Rovere could also forget all theological subtleties and preach a sermon which lifted the heart and quickened the pulse. He began to climb in the hierarchy of his order, first becoming procurator of Rome and then provincial of the Ligurian Province and main speaker for the Franciscans in important theological disputations.

In September, 1467, Francesco della Rovere became cardinal, with the church of San Pietro in Vincoli as his titular church.[42] Soon the evenings filled with learned discussions in Francesco's unpretentious palace were looked upon as high points of contemporary Roman life. After a burst of energy displayed as a reformer, Francesco appreciated the more tranquil existence of a theological scholar. This calm continued until the day when the people of Savona celebrated in the streets because at last a Ligurian had become pope: in August, 1471, Francesco, Franciscan friar and cardinal of San Pietro in Vincoli, became Pope Sixtus IV.[43]

Had the reformer and scholar prevailed in Sixtus IV, Girolamo Riario would have continued as a minor clerk and a peddler of fruit, and Caterina would have married one of the numerous lesser nobles, borne children, and passed through the mainstream of life in the anonymity which never leaves the great number. Because of the two personalities that lived in Sixtus IV, this was not to be. The Franciscan friar was a man of charm, heartfelt charity, and devotion to scholarly pursuits. But in Francesco della Rovere lived also all the coarseness, violence, and possessiveness of a Ligurian peasant. The hour arrived when these forces burst from an amorphous stirring into determined and articulate assertion, an hour which also signaled the beginning of Caterina Sforza's historical career.

The Rome of 1471 fostered the growth of all that later generations would condemn in Sixtus IV. A hotbed of intrigues, a battleground of ever-warring powerful nobles, a place of the ready and murderous dagger and of an excitable and proud populace, Renaissance Rome did not readily tolerate a saintly pope. Yet more fearful, the web of intrigue was spun tightly in the College of Cardinals. One did not murder the pope, but one diminished his rights, isolated him, and, above all, used him. The dreadful loneliness of the Renaissance pope, who held an august office in less than august surroundings, soon overcame Sixtus IV. Under this strain, and tempted by seemingly unlimited wealth and power, the charitable impulses of the Franciscan friar and the natural gratefulness of a joyful man gradually and imperceptibly combined with naked self-seeking, the first signs of political shrewdness, and an early determination to make the papacy a strong political power, arousing in Sixtus IV an overwhelming urge to hand out rewards to supporters and to lavish riches on his relatives.

The first shock of joy at Sixtus' elevation had hardly worn off when the Rovere and the Riario families left their beloved Liguria to follow the enticing call of Rome. Transplanted into the metropolis, they cut strange figures with their Ligurian costumes, their provincial uncertainty, and their dialect full of harsh sounds and X's. They were not disturbed when the Romans occasionally showed hostility to them; they looked with confident greed to their illustrious relative, certain of a share in the newly acquired wealth and power.

Sixtus IV did not disappoint them. His kin, at one time two brothers, four sisters, eleven nephews, and two nieces, received their abundant portion.[44] Not all of them, of course, were equally favored. Some got only a house, a minor benefice, or a powerful word of recommendation. Others, particularly the nephews, who were so valuable as trustworthy advisors, were handed the plums. There was Giuliano della Rovere, a twenty-eight-year old nephew, serious, diligent, able, and terrible-tempered. As early as December, 1471, he received the red hat: a cardinal by his uncle's grace, but one who would later earn distinction for himself, as Pope Julius II.

Another nephew even closer to the heart of Sixtus IV was Piero Riario.[45] With his brother Girolamo he had been a dutiful pupil of Francesco della Rovere, who never forgot the happy hours spent as tutor in his sister's house. Piero too became cardinal, in December, 1471, and for good measure, also archbishop of Florence, Seville, and Mende, patriarch of Constantinople, abbot of S. Ambrogio, and bishop of assorted bishoprics. These offices gave him an annual income of sixty thousand ducats, enough to sustain the government of a moderate-sized Renaissance state, but mere pocket money for Piero. Yet no excess of whatever kind could diminish the love of his uncle for Piero, the Piero who had followed him in becoming a Franciscan, the Piero who had been a close advisor, intelligent, well-mannered, and always cheerful, the Piero who had shown a keen understanding of human weaknesses and their use in the conclave which elevated Francesco della Rovere to the papacy after much backstage maneuvering, the Piero, finally, who, like Sixtus IV himself, was torn between genuine selflessness and the love of luxury and power.

What did the sudden emergence of the Rovere-Riario from obscurity mean to Piero's brother, Girolamo? He had also drifted to Rome when the Rovere-Riario families began to flood Italian history through the channels of the Church.[46] He had, however, not yet been carried to a position of prominence. For the time being it was enough that he had escaped the dreary existence of a scribe. His new station in life was pleasant though not as spectacular as his brother's. Girolamo waited in comfort, much as Caterina Sforza did, for fortune's gifts.

3

WHATEVER GREATNESS GIROLAMO or Caterina would eventually display, the forces which molded their lives at that point gave no hint of it. These originated in the worldly ambitions of a pope, the stubbornness of a woman, and the miscalculation of a duke—forces which altogether lack nobility, but not the power to change destinies.

The world now had a Franciscan pope confronting the realities of the papal position in the late *quattrocento,* realities which were destined to break the pious devotion of men of stronger character than Sixtus IV. Soon the second office of the pope, that of an Italian prince at the head of the States of the Church, became of first concern to him. Rome herself at this time was embarking on a career as a center of culture and power which was eventually to be adorned by a Michelangelo, a Raphael, and others, by the military and political genius of Cesare Borgia, and by buildings rivaling the splendor of ancient Rome.

The subtle change in motive from true Christian charity to self-seeking had appeared first in the pope's unrestrained nepo-

tism. When a few months after his coronation the whole clan of
the Rovere-Riario tasted the sweet fruits of victory, the initial
break in the dike of good judgment opened. Even more decisive
was the turning of the intellectual brilliance and urge for
action of Sixtus IV from reforms and scholastic enterprises to
goals less worthy of a successor to St. Peter. That also was not
long in happening, once the political realities were experienced
and new lessons learned—lessons in political cynicism taught
mainly by Italian princes to the Franciscan friar who tried to
come to grips with the responsibilities of his new high office. He
was, of course, still the head of all Western Christians, princes
and lowly beggars alike, admired, cherished and duly respected.
But whenever Sixtus IV wanted to assert papal power, even
within his own Papal States, he experienced hostility. He saw
smiling faces and friendly letters, but behind the façade were
the shifting of troops, the intervention of conspiring emissaries,
and a quiet flow of money to his enemies.

The princes' display of pious fervor was just as hollow. However, the Ligurian's naïveté and stubborn persistence made him
send legates in all directions to gather support for the crusade
against the Turks which Nicholas V, Calixtus III, Pius II, and
Paul II had planned, preached, and saved for ever since that
day in 1453 when the Moslems stormed Constantinople,
wounding the conscience and shattering the security of Western
Christianity. None of these popes had been able to accomplish
the sacred enterprise. This time the Italian princes could not
even unite on where to hold a congress for planning the war.
Sixtus IV carried out the enterprise with little outside help and
even less result. When the papal force eventually returned early
in 1473, a triumphal parade displayed on its course through
Rome twenty-five Turks sitting on twelve camels, and that was
all.[47] When the excited shouts of the populace died down, the
venerable idea of a holy crusade was given its more than shabby
funeral, and the Turks threatened more gravely than before.

As the months went by and disappointment after disappointment made the nature of politics in Italy ever clearer to Sixtus
IV, prudence gave way. That part of his temperament that
was inappropriate to his spiritual office and until then had
been held in check was no longer restrained. The head of all

Western Christians became a Renaissance prince in aims and methods.

Soon the Rovere-Riario were staking out their claims to a long career of luxury and power. Up to this point the enjoyment of both had depended too much on that lucky strike that had made one of their members pope. Sixtus IV was healthy and robust but advanced in years. Of the plans to perpetuate the acquired lofty position of the Rovere-Riario, Girolamo became a crucial part, although he was still only an instrument, a key which others turned. That he had not received a red hat or any other high ecclesiastical office proved to be a real asset. Girolamo's road into *quattrocento* politics lay unobstructed before him.

The mastermind behind these family aspirations was Piero Riario; Sixtus IV merely supplied the authority and a pliable mind. The role of leading papal strategist and diplomat suited Piero's passion for planning, manipulating, and plotting. These activities were inspired by his love for power, a passion matched only by his fondness for splendor, luxury, female company, and exquisite food. Strangely, in him all such tastes appeared not repulsive but rather cultivated, never crude, always intelligent, never brutal, always cheerful and witty, and at no time cold-blooded and gloomy.

Piero searched for the opening through which Girolamo should enter Renaissance politics. His firm grasp of political reality led him to the Sforza of Milan. They were powerful, young, wealthy, and promising—an excellent match. Relations between that family and the papal court already were good.[48] Now Riario aspirations were helped by one of Galeazzo Maria's acts of lesser wisdom, a brazen assertion of power in Romagna.

There Taddeo Manfredi was about to lose his possession, the city of Imola.[49] He had for years been the long arm of the Sforza in Romagna. Now, at odds with the Faenza branch of the Manfredi family and threatened by dissension within his own family, Taddeo's grip on Imola was slipping.[50] The Sforza, prompted by fear of Venetian intents and by sheer expansionism, proceeded to ease Taddeo and also, for good measure, his son, out of Imola. In December, 1471, began the series of events which eventually led Taddeo into exile to Milan. He did not even get the city of Tortona, which he had been promised, in exchange, but spent the next few years as a mere pensioner of the Sforza,[51] while his son was married off to a distant Sforza relative.

The papal court watched the blatant seizure of Imola, a city within the Papal States, and remained silent. Such indulgence always carries a price in politics. Piero Riario was not slow in suggesting a payment. By mid-January, 1472, he recommended his brother Girolamo to the duke and, soon after, suggested a marital venture for Girolamo.[52] The bride chosen was neither Caterina nor Chiara but the less than exciting Costanza da Fogliano, an obscure niece of Francesco Sforza.[53] She nevertheless provided the desired link to the Sforza family. Piero could hardly ask for more, since Girolamo, although a papal nephew, was himself a mere commoner. This defect was promptly remedied. The pope arranged to buy Bosco d'Alessandria from the duke of Milan, and Girolamo acquired his first title of nobility.[54] The freshly baked count of Bosco was then bound by contract to marry Costanza da Fogliano.[55] The Sforza welcomed their new though distant relative by allowing him to carry the Visconti name and add the Visconti coat of arms to his own.[56]

In October, 1472, Girolamo, who had more recently assisted his brother in administering the papacy's political affairs, set out for the Sforza court in order to negotiate the details of the marriage contracted four months previously. The negotiations which began in November dragged on, filled with quarrels, and the prospects for success dwindled daily. Costanza's mother, Gabriella Gonzaga, drove a hard bargain. She demanded and procrastinated. Girolamo, in turn, incompletely recovered from a recent illness, displayed little patience and diplomatic polish. He became furious and shed every trace of restraint. When he demanded an opportunity to sleep with his twelve-year-old bride upon conclusion of the contract so as actually to consummate the union, the mother's "no" became final.[57] A last-minute compromise suggested by Lodovico, marquis of Mantua, failed to resolve the controversy. According to it, Girolamo and Costanza should sleep together for one night but not consummate the union ("senza altramente venire ala copula").[58] That procedure had been tried when thirteen-year-old Galeazzo

Maria had been betrothed to seven-year-old Dorotea Gonzaga in 1457.

By now Galeazzo Maria was sufficiently alarmed. A Girolamo Riario going home angry and empty-handed would certainly signal a disruption of relations between Milan and Rome at a moment when these two powers were co-operating closely in attempts to renew the *lega generale* and to bring about closer ties between Milan and Venice. The cardinal of San Sisto had just written a letter of exuberant joy over the honorable treatment of Girolamo and the latter's elevation to *cavaliere* at Christmas time.[59] The cardinal expected nothing less than a successful conclusion of Girolamo's mission. Galeazzo Maria, therefore, tried first to bring the parties to reopen the negotiations, and failed. At that point he fell back on his own resources. On January 13, 1473, Caterina, ten years old, was offered to Girolamo as the new choice of the Sforza.[60] An even longer wait for the actual consummation was in store for the eager groom. But he sensed clearly the advantages a ducal daughter presented over a distant Sforza relative. Four days later Girolamo accepted and the betrothal was arranged.[61] The dowry consisted of ten thousand ducats which Girolamo would receive when the marriage was consummated upon the coming of age of the bride.

Galeazzo Maria did not relish handing over Caterina to a mere nephew of the pope. He blamed the "strange and beastly" behavior of Gabriella Gonzaga for the impasse, but professed outwardly his devotion to the pope as the reason for the match. Galeazzo Maria also seemed to derive some comfort from the fact that "His Majesty Ferrante [King of Naples] had given in marriage two of his daughters to papal nephews."[62] All reservations were banned from the letter to Piero Riario. There Galeazzo Maria spoke of the pleasure it gave him to have Girolamo, "that ornament of virtue," as a relative.[63] The duke's letter to the pope brought forth even more florid words.[64] The tie between the papacy and Milan had been secured. Caterina had filled her first historical role and served herself well at the same time.

Before Girolamo left he proved that, although noble birth was not his, a papal nephew at least did not lack wealth. Three days after the betrothal had been arranged, a group of persons assembled in the *camera cubiculare* of the Pavia castle to witness the consignation of the groom's gifts for Caterina to the Sforza. A detailed list includes two dresses, one of gold brocade and another of green velvet, adorned with 1,538 large and 1,380 little pearls, belts adorned with silver, a purse of gold, a jewel clasp, a piece of jewelry in the shape of a peasant, three strings containing over five hundred pearls, two thimbles set with precious stones, and some smaller vestments of brocade.[65]

A few days later Girolamo departed.[66] Everybody seemed satisfied. Galeazzo Maria advised his orator in Rome of Girolamo's departure and at the same time admitted that he had even conceded to Girolamo's demand for a *pro forma* consummation. Girolamo "had once more slept with his wife and then departed content and gay." [67] In Rome the Rovere-Riario were just as pleased. Upon Galeazzo Maria's request, Sixtus IV hurriedly issued a bull which exonerated Girolamo and Caterina from all irregularities committed when a public and prior marriage contract had been broken. He guaranteed the "main culprits and their accomplices" complete immunity, since the break-up was due to the refusal of the first bride's mother "to have the marriage consummated." [68] Nor need Girolamo be satisfied with the minor position of a count of Bosco; the plans of the Riario to establish themselves in a more important manner were ripening rapidly.

Early in 1473, Piero Riario, who had long coveted the city of Imola for his brother, began his maneuvers to accomplish this purpose. The city which at that point attracted the attention of the cardinal of San Sisto gave shelter to about seven thousand to seventy-five hundred persons and was neither of striking beauty nor lucrative for its owner.[69] But location endowed it with a disproportionate importance through which it became desired by many powers. Florence had the most ardent interest in Imola. The possession of Imola would have opened another door to Romagna, established a Florentine stronghold along the Via Emilia, guarded vital roads across the mountains, and strengthened Florentine power in an area of Venetian, Milanese, Neapolitan, Bolognese, and Ferrarese maneuvering. That the area was papal territory was all too often conveniently forgotten in the power struggle. But now, with the

papal-Milanese entente strong and with a papal nephew addressed by Galeazzo Maria as "nostro conte," the papal claims
would be hard to disregard.

The disadvantages of direct Sforza rule over Imola showed
soon after Taddeo's ouster. Milan sent its officials—a governor,
a castellan, and a *podestà*. While the Imolesi did not revolt,
they showed a distinct dislike for such direct Sforza rule.[70] In
addition, Galeazzo Maria faced the predicament of owning and
defending a city to which all access routes were controlled by
other powers. He hurried the work on the fortification of Imola
and some smaller places. Yet only a few months after the acquisition of Imola, Galeazzo Maria was considering ridding himself of the city in some graceful way. A return of Imola to
Taddeo Manfredi was never contemplated, although the latter
continued to display loyalty toward the Sforza.[71] The Florentines were more than eager to acquire the city and were able to
pay for it in money[72] and in friendly behavior. They also
pledged themselves not to hand the city on to any other power.[73]
But the sale of Imola to Florence was not to be.

In May, 1473, Piero Riario introduced the Imola issue into
one of his discussions with Sagramoro, orator of Milan.[74] At the
same time the pope himself recalled to the powers of Italy the
Church's prerogatives in Imola.[75] The papal party could mar-
shal persuasive arguments: that Imola was located within the
Papal States, that Galeazzo Maria had no right to oust a vicar
appointed by the pope, and that a transfer of Imola to anybody
but the pope would be illegal and, above all, a rebuke to the
Riario-Rovere. It did not help that Galeazzo Maria protested
his faithfulness to the pope, his mere wish to protect Taddeo
Manfredi, and the reluctance with which he had in the end
taken possession of Imola.[76] Soon the duke of Milan declared
himself willing to hand Imola to the pope, that is the Riario
family, despite the severe repercussions such a course would
have for Milanese-Florentine relations.

An opportunity to seal the Imola agreement came when, in
the waning summer of 1473, Piero Riario went on a diplomatic
visit to Milan and Venice. On September 12, these two lovers of
splendor, Galeazzo Maria and Piero Riario, met, and the meeting was a memorable event.[77] In a triumphal march the duke
escorted his guest to the cathedral. Nothing was missing, nei-

ther the splendid horses, the lavishly adorned servants, the triumphal arches, the blaring trumpets, the masses of velvet and jewels, the rich tapestries on façades of houses, nor the girls with flowers, the youths declaiming orations, the ambassadors, the nobles, the college of the *juris consulti,* and the magistrates with the city keys.

Then followed days of feasting. The duke and his guest were like twin brothers in their desire to drink deeply and vigorously from the cup of life. Both loved pageantry and tournaments, cherished the arts, and shared the disregard of common standards of morality. Between entertainments, social visits with Bona, and concerts of the famous organist Jacobus Argiropulo,[78] long work sessions were held in Milan and Pavia. The chief topics were Imola and the improvement of relations between Milan and Venice as a step toward the renewal of the *lega generale*. Piero Riario soon settled the question of Imola to the satisfaction of the Riario family if not to that of the pope. Sixtus IV would buy Imola from Galeazzo Maria Sforza for forty thousand ducats—not without protest and scruples of conscience to be sure, since the pope was buying his own territory. In the end family loyalty won over papal prudence.

Before he departed, Piero Riario met the Sforza children, among them the young Caterina. He had pleasant words for all of them. Then, on September 20, a boat came to bring Piero Riario to Venice.[79]

The early October negotiations in Venice were designed to nudge the Republic of San Marco closer to Milan and the pope and to bring it to assent to a renewal of the *lega generale*. The opportunity for such a realignment was beckoning, since Naples and Venice had drifted apart over the Cyprus issue.[80] A *lega generale* could easily be formed with Milan, the pope, and Venice as the core, and with Florence and Naples joining later. On the whole question the Venetian government delayed a decision,[81] but the reassertion of papal power in Romagna seems to have been accepted.

During the cardinal's return trip, a new feature of Italian politics revealed itself. Piero Riario hurried through Florence, without stopping to pay a courtesy visit to Florentine officials or to the Medici brothers, thus betraying a newly formed gulf of distrust and dislike between the Medici and the Riario.[82] Imola was at the root of this anger and hatred. Although they refused financial assistance to the pope in the Imola affair, the Medici had to watch helplessly as a potential Florentine stronghold in Romagna escaped their grasp.[83] On October 28, by an act of cession, Galeazzo Maria sold Imola to the pope.[84] In turn, Sixtus IV, on November 5, 1473, made Girolamo Riario vicar of the Holy Church in Imola "for his many merits and by virtue of his noble blood." [85] His obligations in yearly dues were reduced from the five hundred ducats the Manfredi had been obligated to pay to a mere two hundred.[86] By December, Girolamo's plenipotentiaries were in Imola to take possession of the city.[87]

Galeazzo Maria had cemented the alliance with the papacy and assured his daughter, Caterina, of a future significant possession. But he felt uneasy about the estrangement from Florence which he shared to a degree with the Riario. He strained to proclaim his good will toward the Arno republic and to reconcile the Riario with the Medici.[88] Success was not yet in sight when the Riario fortunes suffered a severe reversal. Late in December, Piero Riario, cardinal of San Sisto, fell ill with a stomach ailment. On January 5, 1474, he died, "truly penitent," a chronicler assures us, a mere "twenty-eight years, eight months and six days old." [89] He departed, to the grief of Sixtus IV, who never again loved anybody with the same fervor, to the sorrow of Galeazzo Maria, with whom he had co-operated well, to the regret of the people, who had enjoyed his splendid pageants and scrambled for the sweetmeats he liberally threw to them on such occasions, and to the great joy of many of the cardinals, who had resented his dominance all along.

The pattern of *quattrocento* history had shifted anew. Girolamo became the heir to Piero's power and wealth. Henceforth he was to be the designer and executor of papal policies. The one-time grocer and scrivener was now the *padrone della barca vaticana* ("the captain of the Vatican ship of state"). Galeazzo Maria's reluctantly extended favor, to permit the marriage between Girolamo and Caterina, had bloomed into a full diplomatic success, with a Sforza relative emerging as the influential man at the curia. Caterina on her part, instead of traveling along a side street of history as the wife of one of numerous papal nephews, was well on her way to becoming a personage of history.

As HER FUTURE was taking on a discernible shape, Caterina experienced another more immediate change. She had outgrown the *abecedario* and simple reading and proceeded now to the revered classical and Christian texts. Her education conformed to humanist ideals—from the mechanical recitation of Latin verses to the earnest concern with *virtù*, that is, the shaping of a thoroughly educated person, adept in the art of reasoning with elegance, order, and profundity. It may be considered an omen of things to come that Caterina was never lauded for the delivery of a beautiful oration by any of the contemporary chroniclers, who otherwise were so eager to praise her smallest achievements. Virgil, Terence, Horace, Cicero, and Ovid never did strike her fancy. It remains doubtful that she ever mastered the then fashionable female accomplishment of playing the lute. Of her singing the *canzoni* we hear nothing favorable. But she listened with fascination to the tutors when they related the deeds of famous men and women of history. Here, where life, though still in an idealized form, spoke in greater immediacy, her curiosity was aroused, and her comprehension and memory were both remarkable. When the supposed lessons of history were spelled out in the great abstractions of justice, virtue, and goodness, her interest again waned. But when it came to ball-playing, horseback-riding, and dancing, she once more excelled. Caterina could only hope that life would never place her in a nunnery or in the company of scholars.

Girolamo's period of education had been short and had long since passed. He now must show his skill and judgment as the *padrone della barca vaticana*. Fortunately that position proved a light burden for him. The mid-seventies were years from which martial noise was absent. Italian diplomacy displayed its usual oscillations. In all the secret and quick changes, Girolamo steered a course quite different from that of his late brother. The papacy kept closer to Naples in its policies, particularly since Milan, Florence, and Venice had closed ranks in November, 1474.[90] The papacy and Naples found their status as allies quite agreeable to their interests. Naples with her restless expansionism found a congenial ally in a papacy which strove above all to aggrandize the Rovere and Riario families. The new political structure also fitted well with the bitter hatred between the Medici and Riario. This shift in Italian politics would eventually burn its traces into history, but for the time being it hardly disturbed Girolamo's almost effortless enjoyment of power, glory, and ceremonial tasks.

Girolamo gave little thought to Caterina. She was after all merely a child, while he could consider himself the pope's right hand man. There was furthermore no need to cultivate affections where none existed. No letters from Girolamo to Caterina remain because, most likely, they were never written. Girolamo did communicate with Roman women but in other ways. Although he lacked the imagination and the vigor of a libertine, he appreciated female company sufficiently to produce a son, Scipio.

Thus the worlds of the prospective groom and bride remained separate but resembled each other. Caterina found herself in the midst of preparing for a life designed by everybody else but herself. Girolamo savored the glories of a position which he owed least to himself. Then, a few days before the year 1476 expired, a thunderbolt struck. The two worlds met and the years of pleasant waiting ended.

On December 26 Duke Galeazzo Maria Sforza was stabbed to death by an incongruous trio of assassins: a youth who dreamed of being a second Brutus or Cassius, an impoverished opponent of the Sforza, and a Visconti outraged by the duke.[91] The inspiration for the deed and the skill with the dagger had been provided by Galeazzo Maria's former tutor, Cola Montana, whom the duke had publicly humiliated. Vengeance was taken swiftly and fiercely on the conspirators, but Galeazzo Maria was dead and the news traveled fast.

When Sixtus IV heard of it, he exclaimed in horror: "The

peace of Italy is dead." [92] It was an astute judgment, since with
Milan facing a struggle for influence between Galeazzo Maria's
brothers and his infant son, the Italian balance of power was
seriously jeopardized. What the Rovere-Riario also realized was
that their influence in Milan now was shrouded in uncertainty.
Decisive action alone could help.

The occasion for Sixtus IV to show his sympathy soon presented itself. A saddened and shattered Bona worried about the
fate of Galeazzo Maria's soul. She directed an urgent request to
Don Celso de Mafeis, *canon Regulari Sancti Augustini Congre-
gationis Lateranensis,* to put the case of her late husband, who
was killed without the benefit of sacraments, before a panel of
experts who would investigate Galeazzo Maria's life.[93] They
should recommend to the pope a posthumous absolution for
Galeazzo Maria. The list of sins which she included explains
her worry: making war justly and unjustly, sacking cities without mercy, robbing, extortion of subjects, negligence of justice,
injustice actively committed, illegal enforcement of the *gabella*
even from clerics, adultery, rape, and whoring, notorious sim-
ony, and other sins too numerous to mention. Bona promised
on her part to pray for Galeazzo Maria until his unhappy soul
should emerge from purgatory cleansed for its entrance into
heaven. The pope with his great powers from Christ could do
infinitely more. She, of course, would be willing to pay good
ducats for the defense of the faith and the endowment of pious
works in the duchy of Milan.

Sixtus IV willingly obliged her. The pope and Girolamo now
wanted to hurry the final conclusion of the marriage contract
by the performance of the actual wedding. In this case Bona
accommodated the Rovere-Riario. As early as January, 1477,
she wrote Girolamo that his bride and her dowry were at his
disposal.[94] Girolamo found it impossible to get away from
Rome for the occasion. Cardinal Legate Mellini traveled to
Milan in order to "preserve the duchy and protect the little
son" and to perform a *per procura* wedding.[95] There, in a city
where official sadness hushed all sounds of joy, Caterina and
Girolamo were irrevocably joined. Only the close relatives and
the representatives of Girolamo witnessed the wedding. Renaissance Italy could ignore it since no great dynastic interests
seemed to be at stake. But for Caterina that day signaled an

end and a beginning. For her it brought to an end the period in which her life had been shaped and her future destiny prepared by forces entirely beyond her control. The wedding on one of the fading winter days of 1477 marked the beginning of Caterina's own career. She was ready to shed the role of mere pawn in the game of politics being played by the Rovere-Riario and the Sforza and to grow into one of the players.

5

CATERINA SFORZA ENTERED Renaissance politics in a procession of triumph. Girolamo himself did not join her in it. He had advised the Milanese court that the troubled situation in Rome would not permit him to leave and meet his bride either in Milan or Imola.[96] But he sent an impressive group to Milan as escorts for her: one hundred and fourteen men with sixty-eight horses and thirty mules. Among the men were the bishop of Cesena, the governor of Imola, Domenico Gentile Ricci, eight gentlemen from Imola, and two trumpeters for ceremonial noises. Milan contributed forty men, twelve horses, and two maids for Caterina, and money to cover the complete costs of the journey.[97]

The cavalcade began its trip late in April, its first destination being Imola. Gaiety and joy were constant companions. The road traveled was the Via Emilia, hugging the northern slopes of the Apennines. Nearly straight for one hundred and sixty miles from Piacenza to Rimini, it was the main artery of Romagna and full of sombre memories of the disciplined and pounding steps of the Roman legions, the furious and chaotic surging of German tribes, and the incessant fights of medieval knights, adventurers, and citizens—a fitting beginning for a future virago, though its symbolism was not yet understood.

The Caterina of 1477 was a fourteen-year-old girl whose every step must still be carefully watched. From Modena on, she was entrusted to the supervision of a certain Gianluigi Bossi. Bona of Savoy had selected him to see that Caterina was safely delivered to Girolamo, was counseled on proper behavior, followed a sensible diet, and avoided over-exertion. He was also charged with presenting the credentials at the appropriate occasion, witnessing the repetition of the wedding ritual, and reiterating in his discussions with Pope Sixtus IV the great desire of the Sforza family for a cardinal's hat for Ascanio Sforza.[98]

As for Caterina, she was delighted by the sight of all the new places. While the *capitano de la terra* of Reggio overslept and thus made Caterina arrive unheralded, Modena sent all its dignitaries to greet her, and at Bologna the Bentivoglio welcomed, feasted, and sheltered her, and even accompanied her on her departure.[99] Such hospitality cost the city of Bologna the neat sum of one hundred and sixteen *lire bolognesi*.[100]

Caterina joyously savored the demonstrations of affection each of these cities dutifully staged for the daughter of the duke of Milan, wife of the vicar of Imola, count of Bosco, and most powerful of the papal nephews. Nothing in her education or experience had yet taught her the essential difference between genuine and official expression of affection.

Young and innocent as she was, Caterina had nevertheless absorbed the lesson that in order to dominate she must display her status. When she neared Imola, stopping for rest and food at Castel San Pietro, she put on a startling gold-brocade dress, a brown cloak, extravagant gloves and precious jewels. Thus adorned, she accepted the greetings of "her" town, Imola, which she reached on May 1 just before sunset.[101] Everybody was in the streets, shouting or just gazing. The magistrates presented her with the keys of the city, children sang and recited verses, and allegorical groups were staged along her route of entry. Finally, in front of the Riario palace, she found a great pavilion gaily decorated with flowers, draperies, banners, and the coats of arms of the pope, the Riario, and the Sforza. In it she dismounted and then entered her palace, which offered every available comfort. Her eyes feasted on the tapestries of velvet, satin, or silk which hid the walls, and her feet never needed to step off carpets. Tired but still full of enthusiasm, she participated in a sumptuous banquet late at night.

When Caterina came to rest in her chamber that evening, her heart was exuberant with joy. She had failed to notice how dreary, small, and provincial a city Imola was compared with beautiful Milan.[102] Nor did she become aware of it during the following days filled with festive masses, dances, and expressions of loyalty by her new subjects. All these celebrations tended only to solidify her image of the world as a stage on which the proud acted out history and the humble dutifully applauded: Caterina would dispense patronizing favors and words to the people; they in turn would be expected to reply with obedience and adulation.

Imola was only a foretaste. Caterina looked forward impatiently to meeting her husband and to seeing Rome. For one week and then another she waited for a word from Rome. It never came. Bona of Savoy in Milan knew the reasons through the Milanese orator in Rome. The city was ravaged by partisan strife; some men had tried to assassinate Girolamo; and a blistering heat bred a deathly fever.[103] Caterina was supposed to wait in Imola for a betterment of the Roman weather, in politics and in nature. But, unaware of these developments and burning with desire to reach Rome, Caterina showed her characteristic impatience with inaction and left Imola on May 13.

After eighteen days of traveling over mountains and on dusty roads the world of Rome reached out for Caterina.[104] Monsignore Sagramoro, bishop of Parma and orator of the duke of Milan at the papal court awaited her at Castelnuovo, and on the next day the bride finally met her groom. Girolamo Riario, clothed in sable velvet and silk and surrounded by an impressive number of attendants, greeted Caterina at a point seven miles from Rome. Both Girolamo and Caterina dismounted, shook hands, and exchanged a perfunctory kiss—no sign of great joy, just curiosity on both sides, very matter of fact. The bride could not overcome her shyness, and the groom could not hide his lack of true interest in his young bride. Both also knew that the force which had joined them was dynastic politics. Love would be only incidental.

After a short rest under a cluster of trees, the dusty road called again. But now there were pleasant interruptions to the monotony of travel. To greet Caterina at every quarter of a mile stood prelates, household members of the cardinals, and dignitaries of the city, even the city prefect himself, Giovanni della Rovere. At the Ponte Molle the papal court and the

ambassadors of Spain and Naples paid their respects. By the time
Caterina arrived at her quarters in the palace of the cardinal
of Urbino at Monte Mario, she was once more carried away
by her enthusiasm. In the evening she supped with Girolamo.
When he left, Girolamo presented his bride with a pendant
beset with jewels worth several thousand ducats.

The next day fully convinced Caterina that she indeed had
entered a most glorious and pleasant life. It was the day of
Pentecost, and Rome was in a festive mood. Even the poor had
joyous hearts. In the morning Caterina rode through the streets
to St. Peter's—old St. Peter's, which would soon be razed.
Around her were the orators of most Italian powers, cavaliers
of such noble families as the Orsini, Colonna, and Gonzaga,
and countless others, all of them luxuriously attired and on
richly decorated horses. She herself was a startling sight in a
black damask robe with gold brocade ornaments, tailored according to the newest fashion with a deep decolletage and
decked with numberless jewels.

Throughout the pontifical mass she sat with Sixtus IV and
the cardinals on a specially erected scaffold. For three long
hours she had time to study her new environment and to master
her excitement and shyness. Afterward the Milanese, papal,
and Imolese dignitaries went to a chapel in St. Peter's.[105] There
Caterina knelt and kissed the pope's feet. He in turn blessed
and praised her. Then Gianluigi Bossi, Caterina's chaperon,
added to the length of the ceremony by endlessly listing Caterina's virtues in finely chiseled Ciceronian Latin. His commission
ended when Caterina spoke once more the formula of matrimony and received a twenty-five thousand ducat necklace as a
memento of the occasion. Caterina kissed the hands of the
cardinals, among them Roderigo Borgia, the future Alexander
VI. Politely they promised to be her faithful servants. After a
final blessing Caterina was escorted to the palace of the Orsini
on the Campo di Fiori. This time the streets were heavy with
the sweet odor of perfumes, while the house façades were hung
with draperies displaying the coats of arms of the three families
involved.

The day of glory ended with a sumptuous banquet. At five in
the afternoon a little child made up as an angel came to Caterina's quarters and announced dinner. In the dining room Cate-

rina found her husband, members of the most illustrious families, and about two hundred guests. Twenty-two courses were served, and abundant sweets. After every fifth course the banquet was enlivened by such beloved entertainments as a ballet, a *danza moresca* ("a Moorish dance," often grotesque), a Florentine dance, children dressed as angels or as hunters "chasing" cooked animals restored to their original forms, classical mythological figures and groups, and Latin declamations. After five hours new thrills were needed to stimulate sluggish and sleepy minds. The tables were removed, and Caterina received her wedding presents, twelve thousand ducats worth of them. Caterina's youthful exuberance and her female longing for glittering adornment combined to give her unperturbed delight.

Once more, on the next day, she was pleasantly reminded that her marriage had placed her near the center of the Roman universe with its cardinals, nobles, ambassadors, and humanists. A tournament was staged with all the pageantry *quattrocento* Rome could master, and Caterina presided over it. She was so intoxicated by all the adulation that she even forgot to write to Bona and Chiara for a while. But they should find consolation, she assured them finally, in the triumphal entrance their relative had made into Rome.[106] For a few days she had been the central figure on one of the outstanding stages of Renaissance life—Rome. The world had made its curtsy. Soon it would stand erect and look Caterina straight in the face with eyes that revealed more than tribute to her glory.

III

WIFE
OF THE
PAPAL
FAVORITE

6

CATERINA AND GIROLAMO began their life together in Rome, a city with little of her ancient grandeur, of a fading medieval piety and none yet of Renaissance splendor. Only its importance as the headquarters of the Holy Mother Church prevented the city from slipping into utter provincialism and thus draining all support from the Roman traders, scholars, artists, tavern-keepers, water-carriers, and even prostitutes. Sun, rain, and wind gnawed away at the ancient monuments. Many of them stood sadly grandiose in areas now unpopulated and looked down on cattle, sheep, and goats roaming and grazing amongst them. It was a city filled with churches and monasteries, some the mecca of ardent pilgrims, others long neglected and beyond repair. Through the core of the city with its clutter of buildings wound a few wide streets with decent paving. From them branched off narrow side streets, dark and filled with stenches, meandering among churches, palaces, shops, again churches, and finally ending among the vermin-infested shacks of the poor, huddled together at the Tiber River, or in the vast expanse of the unbuilt area surrounding the city. As far as *quattrocento* Rome was concerned, the space enclosed by the Aurelian wall was too generous. Within this long wall there existed the Roman cosmos with the courtly life of the clerics and nobles, the rowdier joys of the taverns, and the naked misery of the many.

Girolamo, a citizen of Rome since 1477,[1] asserted his power as the spokesman for the pope over the rebellious nobles of Rome, the Colonna, Orsini, de'Conti, Santa Croce, Savelli, and della Valle, and over the proud city, with its *conservatori*, prefects, councils, *syndici*, and judges, high-sounding titles with little power to give them substance. One finds in Girolamo none of the rascality which at least at times warms the heart, but only the arbitrary and cold-blooded assertion of power, a power which was too easily won and incompletely redeemed by Girolamo's general aim to maintain and strengthen the pope's position, and with it his own. In nearly four years as the pope's main advisor, Girolamo had not markedly grown in insight and maturity.[2] He could be generous and charming, but such moments were much rarer than those in which he abandoned himself to impetuosity and vindictiveness. Even a usually cautious chronicler, after dutifully adulating Girolamo as "most benevolent, merciful and ready to do good," dared to call him "most greedy for gain and power." [3]

Caterina, the not quite fifteen-year-old bride, evoked no great praise from her contemporaries. Her beauty was still a promise. The parts of her face and beauty were not yet shaped into such unity that it would make the observer overlook their imperfections. Her too spacious forehead and overly large and slightly aquiline nose violated the Renaissance ideals of feminine beauty. On the other hand, her blue eyes, her blond hair, although still combed in a girlish fashion, her graceful swan-like neck, and her well-developed breasts already were cause for compliments. If she acted a bit forward and brash for a young lady, her contemporaries ascribed it to her youthful enthusiasm.

No records tell of the life of Girolamo and Caterina as a couple during the 1470's. The otherwise outspoken Renaissance chroniclers remain silent. There was, of course, no dynastic interest at stake to attract their attention. The marriage was probably neither worse nor better than others. Politically inspired marriages never aimed to promote the happiness of the two spouses. The true feelings of the twenty-nine-year-old Girolamo toward his girlish bride are shrouded in mystery. Outwardly he played the doting husband. He did not accept Caterina's dowry,[4] but rather invested it in her name in estates.[5] He even professed "a natural affection for my illustrious consort" and wished that "she should lack of nothing." [6]

The early Roman years were Caterina's years of apprenticeship in *quattrocento* politics. She came to know the many faces of power one by one. Until then, she had thought of power in terms of its display, with standards, trumpets, and shining swords. Now she encountered power which was asserted in the interest of greed, hate, and lust for power itself. This newly discovered world of passion, together with Girolamo's lack of warmth and his frequent and prolonged absences, made Caterina feel uneasy and a stranger in Rome. So much more eagerly did she preserve that anchorage of her life, the relationship to Milan. For three years letters went back and forth.[7] They were formal letters beginning with "Illustrissima ed excellentissima madona mia matre" and they were full of clumsy repetitions of well-wishing phrases, naïve hopes for the future, and regrets over the separation, but they still bespoke a mutual regard mother and daughter had for each other. The memories of her sister and her ladies, however, whom she had at one time showered with greetings, gradually faded.[8]

Yet despite her uneasiness during these early Roman years, Caterina had to act the lady of high station in life. Her earliest duties comprised the writing of letters of recommendation and the intercession for those who sought her help.[9] In some cases she undoubtedly did so on her husband's request.

Only a few months after the wedding, Caterina became pregnant. She hoped that the birth of a son would increase Girolamo's respect for her. Late in the spring of 1478, Caterina, then fifteen years old, gave birth to her first child, a daughter called Bianca.[10] She was disappointed, because not much was officially made of this event; a girl could not perpetuate the line and therefore Girolamo was not particularly impressed. Also, he had gone through the experience of fatherhood before when an unknown Roman mistress presented him with a son. There was, too, a first grand political scheme devised at least partially by Girolamo and with which he was already deeply preoccupied.

And what a scheme it was; no less than the doing away with the powerful and famous Medici—Lorenzo "the Magnificent" and Giuliano, his brother. The chief target was Lorenzo, who would eventually be praised in history for his statesmanship and for his eagerness to further the humanist cause, patronize the arts, worship Plato, and write both light verse and serious poetry himself. Girolamo, who was a stranger to the world of *literati,* saw Lorenzo through the eyes of an ambitious papal nephew. To him Lorenzo resembled a spider which sat in the midst of a vast cobweb centering in Florence, ever busy spinning a denser and deadlier net for his opponents. Lorenzo gave

his support to all of the despots who clung like pestering flies to
the territory of the Papal States, and who as papal vicars gave
lip service to His Holiness and then went their own ways. He
was particularly active when he worked to spoil the Riario's
plans of aggrandizement. Which Florentine statesman could
look idly on as the Riario-Rovere pieced together a domain in
the Papal States tightly enclosing Florentine territory? Giovanni della Rovere had acquired Senigallia and Mondavio and
had become the husband of the aging Federico da Montefeltro's
daughter with hopes of becoming the lord of Urbino; Girolamo
had taken possession of Imola; and the Riario-Rovere had
made every effort to tighten their hold on other cities in the
Papal States.[11] Lorenzo de'Medici and Girolamo eyed each
other at first with distrust and then with hatred.

In the spring of 1478 destiny smiled on Girolamo. Lorenzo
had made one enemy too many. The Pazzi, an old, wealthy and
respected Florentine family which had become increasingly
self-confident after having replaced the Medici as bankers of
the pope, had one of its members, Francesco Pazzi, living in
Rome. Unsteady, ambitious, and full of hatred against the
Medici, he knew his cause but not his hour and opportunity.
Another man, Francesco Salviati, named archbishop of Pisa by
Sixtus IV without previously consulting Lorenzo de'Medici,
burned with frustration and anger at being for three years
prevented by Lorenzo from taking office.[12] The hatreds were to
nurse a heady plot. Long conspiratory meetings were held.
Messages went to and fro between Rome and Florence, where
the key man was Jacopo Pazzi, a nervous man who gambled not
only his nights but also his days away. The circle of conspirators widened, but the secret was well kept.

Caterina undoubtedly had some notion of what was on foot,
but it is extremely doubtful that she was privy to the plot. Her
dealings with Lorenzo de'Medici at a later date speak against
it.

Sixtus IV remained an enigma. He knew of the undertaking
against the Medici, but the Renaissance prince that he had
become endowed conspiracy with the same respectability as an
open battle. What of the certainty of assassination? We hear
that Sixtus IV called Girolamo a brute, because in Girolamo's

vocabulary death had too prominent and too comfortable a place.[13] One could make the fine distinction that Sixtus IV was aware of the possibility of assassination but did not sanction it.

Thus, unmoved by justice or injustice, the fates spun their threads of destiny. They cut one thread on April 26, 1478. During high mass in Santa Maria del Fiore, Giuliano was felled by furious stabs of the daggers wielded by Francesco Pazzi and an associate. But one thread, unexpectedly, went unshorn, that of Lorenzo. The two priests who substituted for a *condottiere* bungled their job and Lorenzo lived.

The angry people took a mad revenge. The archbishop's men were thrown from the windows into the street below, and the archbishop himself was hanged in his splendid vestments from one of the windows. To Francesco and Jacopo Pazzi death came with equal swiftness. The two invasion forces ready to strike from Imola and Città di Castello were never able to move.

The Riario escaped unscathed. Girolamo prudently had chosen not to go to Florence, and to be a planner not a doer. However, his partial authorship of the crime was soon known to all the rulers of Italy.[14] The only Riario present in Florence was Cardinal Raffaello Riario, a boy of sixteen years and a nephew of Girolamo. The boyish cardinal had been an innocent decoy to lure the Medici brothers to all kinds of state functions, and Lorenzo mercifully protected him from the fury of the people. The frightened young cardinal of San Giorgio was compensated in many ways for his hours of danger. Among the benefactors was his fifteen-year-old aunt Caterina, who on his behalf interceded with Bona of Savoy and saw to it that he received as a sinecure the rich income from the abbey of Chiaravalle.[15] A sounder investment in gratitude Caterina never made.

The Pazzi conspiracy brought on war. The papal party was indignant that an archbishop had been unceremoniously hanged and above all, though without saying so, that Lorenzo had refused to have himself murdered. Whatever the outcome of the Pazzi war, Girolamo had earned for himself the unrelenting hatred of one of the most powerful men in Italy. Between the two men stood no longer mere questions of politics, but the murder of Giuliano. The daggers drawn would never be quite sheathed. Nearly to the day, ten years later, murder would atone murder.

The Pazzi war proceeded very much to Girolamo's satisfaction.[16] The pope and the king of Naples battled Florence, which was only weakly supported by Milan and Venice. The Neapolitan army under Alfonso, son of Ferrante and duke of Calabria, fought well and victoriously. In addition, Federico da Montefeltro, duke of Urbino and most famous of the *condottieri,* had been hired to command the papal troops. Against these the Florentine alliance had only inferior forces under Duke Ercole d'Este of Ferrara. Girolamo had no need to exert his courage, his money, or his wit. He did, however, concern himself with the protection of Imola. Even there he had found able help in the person of Count Gian Francesco Mauruzzi, best known as Tolentino.[17] The latter, a prudent man and experienced soldier, had replaced Domenico Ricci as governor of Imola.[18] Girolamo and Caterina needed all his skills to protect their territory, since Lorenzo de'Medici made good use of the now vengeful Taddeo Manfredi.[19] Tolentino strengthened the fortress system in and around Imola.[20] Above all, he won the support of the Imolesi, and the city remained in Riario hands.

When the winter came, papal policies seemed to have succeeded. The Florentines were badly beaten. For a few months Caterina had a cheerful husband.

7

BEFORE THE ANGER of war could once more demand its terrible satisfaction, the Florentines felt out the papal court on a possible peace. With the ugly events nearly a year past, almost everyone at the curia was inclined to yield. Girolamo and, through his influence, Sixtus IV saw in peace no more than a denial of goals well within easy reach.[21] By April peace talks had ended, and 1479 was to be another year of war.

Although Caterina did not suffer from the hardships of war, a weariness beset her nevertheless. The novelty of Rome and of life at the papal court had worn off, and the misery of early pregnancy had made for a long winter. By spring, full of anticipation, she was discussing a trip to Milan.[22] But the claims and dangers of war and her limited mobility due to pregnancy shattered those dreams. After the delivery, she had to tell herself. When that event finally came, Caterina added to Girolamo's good mood brought about by recent Florentine defeats. On August 31, 1479, she gave birth to the desired son. No less excited about it than Girolamo, she reported the event to Bona. "It has pleased the Almighty creator and His glorious mother to let be born on the last day of August at the 6th hour a most beautiful boy. . . ."[23] Caterina could not know that the birth notice would arrive in Milan when the duchy was shaken by the most violent tremor of the succession struggle yet.

In September, 1479, the brothers of the late Galeazzo Maria Sforza made their bid to dislodge Cecco Simonetta, the great servant of two Sforza dukes. His merits weighed less now than the fact that he stood in the way of the brothers' ambition. Cecco had only two pillars of support against the host of enemies he had acquired in faithfully serving the Sforza family: his superb political skill and the good will of Bona of Savoy, the regent and widow who tried to keep the reins of government until her son Gian Galeazzo should come of age. She had little political skill, and her willingness to listen to Cecco's council waned with the emerging influence of Antonio Tassino. Bona had become deeply infatuated with the man who had been her meat carver, a man who possessed a lithe body and knew how to make love. When Cecco reproached her for lending her ear to so unproven a counselor, the resentment of an offended woman in love was added to the hatred of the now victorious brothers, a deadly combination. Cecco was arrested in September, 1479, horribly tortured, and executed a year later.[24]

Caterina thought little of the ingratitude towards so loyal and so useful a man. She applauded the "detention of Cecco and his group."[25] For her the fall of Milan's great chancellor meant the liberation of her stepmother. Caterina fully understood and sanctioned the sensual bond between Bona and Tassino, since the demand of the senses was one of the few genuine ties which joined her to her husband. That Sixtus IV heartily agreed with Caterina about Cecco's downfall need not surprise. He viewed it as a weakening of the Florentine position in the still raging Pazzi war, even perhaps signaling a dissolution of the alliance between Milan, Florence, and Venice. Whatever other consequences the Milanese turmoil would have, Caterina's trip to Milan was quietly postponed.

Disenchantment came soon to Sixtus IV and Girolamo. Although relations between Lodovico il Moro and Lorenzo de'Medici were never cordial, Milan did not join the papal side. The Florentines stayed loyal to the Medici even under great duress. Then, in December, 1479, Lorenzo undertook a bold trip to Naples.[26] During long negotiations, Lorenzo's arguments gradually began to shift the Italian power balance. Lorenzo showed Ferrante that neither Florence nor Naples would profit from a powerful and expansionist papacy and that in a prolonged war the other side would fall back on the old trick of tempting the French with their Neapolitan heritage. On March 13, 1480, Naples and Florence made their peace.

Sixtus IV and Girolamo had lost their gamble. The Medici would stay in Florence. Girolamo wasted no time in sorrow, but did some diplomatic shifting himself. In May the world heard of the new papal–Venetian alliance, concluded a month earlier.[27] The two traditional adversaries were now outdoing each other in polite expressions of mutual support. Sixtus IV, who himself disliked Girolamo's new pro-Venetian policy, nevertheless wrote to Doge Mocenigo that the loyalty and sympathy of his nephews Giovanni della Rovere, count of Senigallia, duke of Sora, and prefect of Rome, and Girolamo Riario, vicar of Imola, would always be with the Republic.[28] In turn, Venice in the treaty of alliance promised protection for all Riario territory, present and future. This important protection clause was also included in the *condotta* which the Venetians gave Girolamo.[29] Milan, Florence, and Naples had no need to know the details of these documents in order to understand the import of the Venetian–papal alliance. On July 25, 1480, they formed their counter-alliance.[30]

By then, Italian politics was embroiled in new controversies. They were all fueled by the ambitions Girolamo harbored for himself, Caterina, and their children. No less an allurement beckoned than the acquisition of three Romagnol cities, Faenza, Forlì, and Pesaro, with all their territories. As wars of conquest have always needed justification, Girolamo made much ado about how well Galeotto Manfredi of Faenza and Costanzo Sforza of Pesaro, vassals of the pope, had served as *condottieri* against their overlord during the Pazzi war. The case of Forlì lacked that simplicity of pretext. There the career of an illustrious local dynasty, the Ordelaffi, was approaching a dramatic ending. Justification for interference would have to be found in the events of that last phase.

In the 1460's two brothers dominated Forlì. The elder Ordelaffi, Cecco, governed, and the younger, Pino, was content with soldiering. The harmony ended when they both married. Pino's wife, Barbara Manfredi of nearby Faenza, an ambitious and determined woman, envied Cecco and his wife Elisabetta, Barbara's own sister, their superior position. Cecco had pleased the Forlivesi but had added to the opposition to himself by easing his mother and her brother out of the regency over Forlì. When Pino, who had become sickish, brooding, and less attractive, yielded to his wife's nagging and ill counsel, the end came swiftly.[31] Cecco and his family were thrown into a dungeon. There Cecco lingered on, already weakened by a severe illness. Barbara, however, was in a hurry. She tried to poison Cecco, but Elisabetta prevented her from succeeding. Thereupon, on April 22, 1466, Cecco was separated from his family and slaughtered like a pig. Though after this deed the Ordelaffi kept Forlì for fourteen more years,[32] neither their rule nor their family was ever the same again.[33]

Barbara aroused the intense jealousy of her husband. At a dinner given in her honor she partook of the same kind of poison she had once prepared for Cecco. Pino ordered official mourning and bought a magnificent memorial for his wife, "most beloved, heavenly, and adorned with virtue." Pino's mother was next to die, since she had changed her mind about Pino and wanted now to give the city of Forlì to Cecco's sons. Elisabetta and her sons, still prisoners in the palace, were then served poisoned fish. Elisabetta refused the dish for her children but took, out of politeness, a little piece for herself. One year later, in 1469, she died after suffering intolerable pains. But during that year she managed to escape with her sons to friendly Faenza. It was a fateful success, affecting not so much Pino as Girolamo Riario and Caterina Sforza, who would find in one of the boys, Antonio Maria, their most troublesome opponent.[34] Pino's second wife, Zaffira Manfredi of Imola, died in 1472 of the same poison and for the same reason as Barbara.

Pino then had some leisure left for his other beloved activities: the innocent chase; the discussion for hours on end of Aristotelian propositions with Antonio Codro and his other court philosophers and *literati;* the patronizing of painters, especially Melozzo of Forlì, and distinguished architects like Matteo di Recevude and Pace di Maso del Bambone; and, of course, the pious works so dear to his heart such as the endowing of monasteries and churches. These activities, along with the Sacred Representations and tournaments which he staged, carried the fame of Forlì as far as ever. Pino was respected by Galeazzo Maria Sforza, acknowledged as the rightful ruler of Forlì by the pope, and beloved by the people of his city.

Pino's third wife, Lucrezia di Pico della Mirandola, was more successful than her predecessors.[35] She survived. But all three marriages failed in their main purpose of supplying an heir. The only chance for continuing the Ordelaffi line rested, oddly enough, in a result of one of Pino's notorious sexual excesses—a son born to a lady named Bernardina Ercolani and called Sinibaldo.[36]

The Pazzi war became Pino's destiny also. He loyally fought for the pope against Florence. When he returned, a *malattia misteriosa* plagued him, and the astrologers prophesied that he would not live to see the sun on February 13, 1480. Three days before this date he died.[37]

At this point Girolamo kept his thoroughly whetted ambitions well under control. Sixtus IV invested Sinibaldo, fourteen years old and legitimized by him, with Forlì. Lucrezia became the regent.[38] In addition, Sixtus IV contributed five hundred infantrymen, and his new friends, the Venetians, contributed three hundred more to the "security" of Forlì. All of these moves were both legally correct and cleverly designed. Sinibaldo was a sickly boy with no great hopes of living long. He would also most certainly be challenged by Antonio Maria and Francesco Ordelaffi, the sons of the unfortunate Cecco. Somewhere in these expected developments the Riario hoped to wrest the city of Forlì from the Ordelaffi.

With the three cities, Faenza, Forlì, and Pesaro, at stake, the usual Italian political chess game became even more complicated. The Riario hoped for a full success. Their Venetian allies were loath to see such an aggrandizement of one family in Romagna, but they were bound to assist it. Milan and Florence flatly opposed all Riario schemes, yet Milan was not too adamant about Forlì. King Ferrante, who as usual was the most ambiguous of allies, wanted Faenza protected, but only if Carlo Manfredi would replace his brother Galeotto. He lacked conviction on Forlì and Pesaro and busily engaged in secret diplomacy with the pope.

In the end, Girolamo and Caterina saw their dreams of a massive Romagnol territory dispelled. Milanese armed might, revocation of all of Girolamo's Milanese privileges, and fervent pleas to Caterina, together with Venice's reluctance to let even a friendly papal nephew gain Pesaro, saved Costanzo Sforza.[39] Faenza was saved by Milanese troops who "just could not find enough lodging in Bologna and Cotignola" and thus rested in that city.[40] In addition, Galeotto Manfredi received a *condotta* from Milan and Florence. That left Forlì. There events and circumstances favored the Riario. No great power, with the exception of vengeful Florence, exerted itself to help the city stay free of Riario control. Venice, true to her agreement with the papacy, even supplied armed support for the Riario.[41] Worst of all, the city itself assisted Girolamo by an ardent factionalism.

By May, Pino's last wife, Lucrezia, had retreated, together with her brother and her stepson Sinibaldo, into the fortress of Ravaldino.[42] There they sat facing an uncertain future which would be determined by the unfolding drama.[43] Among the main participants were the people of Forlì, who resented the presence of the papal and Venetian troops, who considered the nomination of Sinibaldo to the *signoria* to be an injustice to Antonio Maria and Francesco Ordelaffi,[44] and who hoped to chase the disliked Antonio Maria Pico della Mirandola from the city.[45] Two other actors were the pope and Girolamo, who watched and waited for the signal to enter the stage. Finally, there were Antonio Maria and Francesco Ordelaffi, and they acted first. On July 8, 1480, the Ordelaffi brothers rode into Forlì amid the cheers of the *popolo minuto* whose leader came from the popular Orsi family.[46] The struggle for power in Forli had begun.

The Ordelaffi fought it out with the partisans of direct Church rule. The dead and the wounded bore witness to the bitterness of the feelings. Yet the Church partisans, who at that time supported Sinibaldo, were relatively few. They lost, and their leaders, among them members of the shrewd Numai family, were exiled to Faenza, then the operating base of the Ordelaffi partisans. And the fortresses? All of them but Ravaldino surrendered, and Ravaldino soon experienced a siege.

Then, an actor interfered who had not been amongst those in the original scenario. Death removed Sinibaldo on July 18.[47] Lucrezia saw her ambitions to rule Forlì frustrated and designed her own solution. She would "conquer" Antonio Maria Ordelaffi and rule with him. Her weapons would be a charming face, an alluring body, and a sly mind.[48] One day, Antonio Maria received the beautiful armor of the late Pino III as a gift, and soon after, the city was filled with rumors about nightly visits which the young Ordelaffi paid to the fortress.[49]

Sixtus IV and Girolamo were not impressed by such idyls. With the legitimate *signore* removed, Forlì fell back to the pope, and Girolamo used his opportunity well. Immediately after Sinibaldo's death, thirty-eight squadrons and numerous infantry under the famous *condottiere* Federico da Montefeltro moved toward Forlì.[50] For good measure Roberto Malatesta, not much less well known as a *condottiere,* received orders from his employers, the Venetians, to assist Girolamo. Against that formidable force Antonio Maria tried to bring about a *fait accompli.* He sent a confidant into the fortress in order to arrange a quick wedding, but that man betrayed him and dissuaded Lucrezia. Lucrezia's brother, Antonio Maria Pico della Mirandola, went even further and took over command of the fortress and confined Lucrezia to her quarters. The last desperate hope of the Ordelaffi had failed. One month after they had come to Forlì, the brothers left it and fled to their protector and uncle, Galeotto Manfredi.[51] On the next day, August 9, Forlì became a Riario possession in fact. The official document of investiture of Girolamo Riario and his legitimate heirs with Forlì merely recognized what had happened.[52]

Lucrezia was eventually permitted to leave the fortress with all her possessions, a permission which she used to the fullest. Her baggage train carried off furniture, a one hundred and thirty thousand ducat treasury, and even the Ordelaffi correspondence.[53] She received a new papal fief, married again, and lived quietly twenty-two more years.[54]

Now that the Riario had acquired with Imola and Forlì a significant foothold in Romagna, Caterina felt relieved. Among the many risks which her husband had taken in his Romagnol venture, one had distressed her particularly. It seemed that every success of the Riario in Romagna would have to be paid for with an estrangement from her beloved Milan. How much Milan had gained by Caterina's mediating influence, exerted upon the urgent prompting by the Milanese court, nobody can say. But Costanzo Sforza kept Pesaro, and no unbreachable gulf was created between Milan and the Riario. Caterina could devote all her attention to an imminent domestic event. On August 24, 1480, occurred the birth of her second son, Cesare.[55] With two sons in the family, the Riario envisaged a long continuation of their dynasty.

GIROLAMO AND CATERINA could not for long exult over so rewarding a summer. They soon came to know the hazards of a ruling family in Forlì. Girolamo thought to secure the new possession by showing generosity. The delegation of citizens, including members of the Ercolani, Orsi, and Maldento families, who traveled to Rome to make their presentation to the overlord, returned in October with full hands.[56] Levies on dowries, on marriage contracts, on flour, and on the division of properties, and weight and gate taxes were either partially or completely remitted.[57] These concessions evoked considerable sympathy for Girolamo, since what goes under the designation

of popular approval and loyalty in politics has a deep root in
the pocket book. At this time nobody seemed to notice that the
noble gesture originated in excessive wealth rather than in a
generous heart. Nevertheless, the partisans of the Ordelaffi remained unreconciled. They were impressed neither by the subsequent amnesty for enemies of Girolamo nor by the mild, wise,
and tolerant rule of the new governor, Tolentino.[58]

The embassy had hardly returned from Rome when the first
attempt was made to overthrow the Riario regime in favor of
Antonio Maria Ordelaffi.[59] One priest and one layman tried
their hands in first befriending and then killing one of Girolamo's Ligurian cronies, then castellan of the fortress, Melchiore
Zocho da Savona.[60] They were caught by an alert *bargello*
("chief of police"). Torture and death followed. Far from
being discouraged, a month later, in November, others attempted to bring three wagons full of armed men into the city.
They took one city gate and its fortification (Schiavonia), but
when they ran through the streets shouting "Ordelaffi, Ordelaffi," people were too startled to follow them. Five leaders were
hanged from the windows of the governor's residence, and the
others were exiled. Although soon allowed to return, they only
proceeded to conspire again.

The conspiracies in Forlì were tiresome, but they posed no
serious threat to the Riario. At this point the conspirators
found no strong popular support; the Riario had the papacy's
resources at their disposal, and their military position was
being improved by work done on the fortress of Ravaldino in
Forlì. Besides, Girolamo and Caterina resided in Rome, far
from the trouble.

Caterina had become used to the duties of her prominent
position. She managed with skill the Riario household with its
scores of servants and estates, particularly the Castello Giubileo
from which most of the Riario provisions came. She was no
longer the shy and hesitantly moving young bride but a beautiful young lady. Disregarding her nearly constant state of pregnancy, she engaged in many activities the Rome of the 1480's
considered fit for a lady, and more besides. Around Caterina
collected even something of a court, including learned men and
high clerics. Cardinal Rodrigo Borgia, the future Alexander
VI, was one of the more frequent guests in the Riario palace on

the river Tiber who desired less to hear profound utterances
than to enjoy the charm of the young woman. But when the
turbulent years came, the intellectual circle broke up. Caterina
had not been genuinely fond of it. Philosophy and literature
could not fascinate her for long. Her heart was closer to the
favorite pastime of the Roman nobles, the chase. Out there in
the Roman campagna, parties hunted the evasive deer, the
proud stag, and the dangerous boar. Whenever she could, Caterina, proud owner of fine hunting dogs, joined such a party. At
the banquet concluding each chase, her beauty was enhanced
by the glow of her joy derived from the chase and the dance.[61]

Caterina's position at the papal court, although seemingly
clearly defined by her marriage, was nevertheless dependent
upon her influence at the Sforza court. Thus, the stronger
Milan was, the more valuable was Caterina's service. Both her
personal bond to Bona and the support for her position in
Rome were therefore disturbed by the news from Milan that
reached Caterina in 1480. Lodovico il Moro had once more
asserted his power. Tassino, Bona's beloved meat-carver, was
exiled, and in November Bona was detained when she set out
for her home in Savoy. Now Caterina understood the whole
scheme. Her resentment against her uncle was deep. Bona had
been the one person who had endowed Caterina's childhood
with affection, and she had been her favorite confidante of the
Roman years. But the lessons learned in Rome had had their
effect. Caterina hid her disgust and wrote most cordial letters to
Lodovico. She knew that her twelve-year-old half brother, Gian
Galeazzo, who was declared mature enough to govern, was a
duke in name only.[62] While she had lost Milan as a center for
her affections, she could by no means afford to lose Milan as a
center of support for her position. Obviously the weight of
power in Milan rested with Lodovico, who together with some
of his trusted followers was the young duke's "guardian." Caterina had learned to distinguish clearly personal and political
motives after all.

During the quiet winter months of 1480/81 Girolamo must
have revealed to Caterina his plans to travel north in early
summer. Caterina, who had been in Rome for over three years,
greeted such prospects with joy. The trip would offer her a
temporary relief from Rome and its routine. The discomforts

of early pregnancy, once more felt in March, never suggested to Caterina a withdrawal from so strenuous a journey.

Girolamo had to overcome different obstacles to the coming travel. The pope had been gripped by his old fascination with a general crusade, ever since that lazy mid-summer day in 1480 when the life of the Italian city of Otranto had been shattered by boats descending upon it. After a short siege the Turks had stormed into the city. Thousands of people were slain and twelve thousand sold into slavery. The archbishop and the governor were sawn in halves while still alive.[63] A shudder had run through Europe: the Turk was in Italy. King Ferrante, whose territory was invaded had found himself without money, soldiers, or helpful allies.[64] Now in 1481, Sixtus IV, full of new hopes for the crusade, launched a supporting force. Girolamo shied away from it. On June 30, 1481, the papal fleet was ready. Standing on the decks, Sixtus, flushed with expectations, addressed the crew; weapons were brandished; the pope's name was shouted and cannons were fired.[65] The boats sailed, the soldiers did their share, and Otranto fell in September, 1481.[66] As was later revealed, the death of Sultan Mohammed II in May, 1481, had been the real decisive event. Sixtus IV spent money, energy, and many a prayer on developing the campaign into a crusade in the grand style; [67] alas, in vain.

Girolamo never cared for such noble endeavors. Indeed, Girolamo had persuaded the pope, as the duke of Milan stated it, to forget the duties of his high office, to ally himself with those who were tribute-payers to the Turks, and to put Italy in a state of war. All of it was done "for Girolamo's ambitions, without regard for the men who are thrown to the wolves and the people who are ruined." [68] Girolamo's ambitions were still territorial and they had grown since he had acquired Forlì. Imola and Forlì were important, even very important cities, but they ranked among the second echelon of *quattrocento* powers. To Girolamo it seemed that the Riario deserved better than that, and time was running out. Under the burden of age, office, and the gout, Sixtus IV had visibly changed. Having escaped the obscurity of Savona, Girolamo could be satisfied with nothing less than a princely estate. The Venetian alliance had proved a valuable tool in 1480. Now it could be of even greater usefulness.

Faenza, on the road between Imola and Forlì, was a natural object of Girolamo's desires. In 1477 Girolamo had helped Galeotto Manfredi to take over in Faenza from the second line of that family.[69] But the events of 1480 had left bitter feelings. The relations between the Riario and the Manfredi could therefore not have been worse. Yet for the moment Girolamo thought Faenza not worth a crisis and postponed its conquest. Galeotto Manfredi was even confirmed in his vicariate.[70] Caterina added a favor by interceding on his behalf with Girolamo.[71] The latter was looking for bigger conquests.

To the south of the Papal States lay the Riario's land of opportunity, the Kingdom of Naples. Sixtus IV and Girolamo had not forgotten King Ferrante's betrayal of their cause in the Pazzi war (by making separate peace with Florence in 1480). Virginio Orsini, a close friend of Girolamo and aspiring to regain lost territories in the Neapolitan kingdom, knew well how to harness the willing Riario to his ambitions. Soon Girolamo began thinking of deposing Ferrante and of acquiring vast areas of the southern kingdom. For such an endeavor the Venetian alliance offered some powerful support, and in order to gain it Girolamo tempted Venice with rich Ferrara and its territory, of which only Lugo and Bagnacavallo would have to be added to the Romagnol possessions of the Riario. Venice could increase its land area and at the same time vent its anger at the Este family. The latter had tried in recent years to free Ferrara from a confining salt purchase agreement made with Venice (for Cervia salt) and had moved politically closer to Naples since the marriage of Duke Ercole with the daughter of the king of Naples. Such Neapolitan influence at the doorstep of Venice was less than desirable.[72]

All of this explains why the destination of the Riario family was Forlì, and, later, Venice. In the last moment, the trip was nearly cancelled because the Venetian Senate, which shared the pope's uneasiness over so long an absence of Girolamo from Rome, opposed it. "We therefore counsel that the count refrain from travel," the senators wrote.[73] But in July, 1481, the family moved north.[74] Girolamo and Caterina looked forward to days which, they thought, could hardly fail to be filled with pleasant experiences, since their possessions in Romagna had recently been in a tranquil state. Only Imola had experienced a temporary upheaval when a certain Troilo had murdered the castellan and held the fortress for a while.[75] But the incident had been due to a private vendetta without political importance. Girolamo had even earned praise from other Romagnol rulers for his prudence in dealing with the matter.[76] Thus the Riario travelled without apprehensions and in grand style.

Eight days before Girolamo and Caterina reached Forlì, caravans of mules, heavily burdened and covered with silken coats of arms, heralded their arrival. With the baggage mules came chests and trunks filled with precious household goods, accompanied by a multitude of servants, members of the household, and the children of the couple. The expectations of the city were thus profoundly heightened when the count and the countess announced their imminent arrival. The monotonous and stereotyped routine of official enthusiasm began. The city swarmed with white-clad youths waving palm branches, tapestries covered the façades of houses, and triumphal arches stood all along the way. Girolamo and Caterina stopped with their escort before the city gates. There they awaited the most auspicious hour for their entrance into the city, one which the astrologers finally fixed for early evening. Cobelli, the chronicler, poet, and amateur astrologer himself, disagreed since that period stood under the influence of bloodthirsty Mars. Nevertheless the cavalcade proceeded and the round of festivities took its course.[77]

At the Porta Cotogni waited solemn magistrates, the representatives of the guilds, and a crowd of the curious. The governor Tolentino handed over the keys of the city. Then there was music, bells rang, people shouted, the hoofs of the horses sounded their staccato on the pavement, and while the procession moved into the piazza, men and women rushed forth to kiss the hands of Caterina and Girolamo. It was a sight to fill the eyes and memories of the provincials for the rest of their years; a representative of the almighty Rome, of the pope, and of the grand politics of Italy was riding into their city. He moved amid palm twigs, candles, and solemn relics, clerics high and low, members of the guilds, and nobles with famous names. Girolamo sat on a richly adorned charger. Caterina, wearing a gold brocade dress and a French-style hat, rode proudly on a palfrey despite being five months pregnant. Ahead of and behind the couple rode and marched hundreds of armed men; ceremonial figures on that day but manifestations of power on others.[78]

At Santa Croce, Girolamo was lifted from his horse and carried to the altar. After a festive *Te Deum* the march continued to the palace. There three ladies representing Justice, Moderation, and Power sang the praises of the illustrious Riario family when the noble pair emerged. Girolamo and Caterina had hardly dismounted when a mob wrested away their horses. Caterina gave her beautiful cloak as ransom to the lucky holder of her horse. In the great hall of the palace, Dr. Guido Pepi delivered the eulogy. A man, famous for his learning, he did not hide his knowledge of Hebrew, Latin, and Greek. The words flowing beautifully suddenly transformed the rather prosaic event into a Greek mythological feast. For half an hour Minerva, Apollo, Aphrodite, and Hercules roamed Forlì, which itself became a new Athens. Girolamo answered in plain Italian with a simple message. He renewed all the concessions to the Forlivesi that he had made once before in Rome and promised to govern like a good father. The crowd heard the good news and cheered wildly. To add to their happiness, sweetmeats and pastries were thrown to them from the palace windows. Joyfully excited and pleasantly tired, they gradually disappeared. As they left the festive place, everyday life surrounded them again—dull, gray, monotonous—but for a time the Riario had filled their hearts with gratitude and pleasure.

The evening brought a ball, the joys of which Caterina drank fully. A radiant beauty of eighteen years, she wore a dress studded with jewels and a huge turban with an immensely long veil picturing a rising sun. She was easily the center of the festivity. When the deputations from all the fortresses of the state paid their homage with gifts of calves, wax, forage, sweets, and fowls, they came away deeply impressed by their new countess; of Girolamo they spoke little. Finally night fell. Within the palace, gay life continued until the early hours. The houses of the city, huddled together inside the wall, lay dark and quiet.

Some of the excitement spilled over into the next day. In the morning, coins, especially struck for the occasion and bearing for some obscure reason the image of King Philip of Macedonia, were thrown to the people from the balcony of the palace.[79] Later on a tournament captured the popular attention. A wooden castle in the form of Otranto was stormed by the martially minded nobles. The first to penetrate into the fortress, a Forlivese, earned five arms length of velvet and four ducats, but lost one eye in the fight. Then the feasting was over, the joyous shouts died down, and the hearts beat to the daily routine. Now the whispered news, formerly drowned out by the noise of the excitement, became more audible: when the couple had entered Forlì there had been a fire in the palace—a bad omen.[80]

The Riario were rulers of Forlì and Imola by virtue of legal decrees. On what basis would they establish their relationship with their subjects? Would it be naked power or a genuine affection slowly earned? How to replace the sympathies of many Forlivesi for the Ordelaffi with those for the Riario? At once the difference between Girolamo and Caterina showed. Caterina, the Sforza daughter, knew how power was linked to the ability to impress, to startle, and to assure. Realizing that a little wealth just irks the humble, while its excess awes, she used every bit of Riario wealth to inspire the proper popular respect for the new rulers of Forlì.[81] Her natural gaiety helped, and so did her marked but still inoffensive arrogance.

Girolamo on his part felt strangely lost. He missed Rome and the protective walls of ceremonial. Here the people came so close, and daily contact with them conjured up in Girolamo images of his years in Savona. The characteristic fear of the upstart of having to return to a less prominent position welled up stronger in quiet Forlì than in busy Rome. For a while Girolamo mustered enough charm to greet and meet his subjects, but it was painful to him. With relief he welcomed the opportunity to visit Imola, where Manfredi sentiment was rapidly waning and where the Riario therefore encountered little resentment.[82] But back again in Forlì, Girolamo forgot all attempts to cultivate the affection of his people and stayed in the palace. Hostile talk and rumors promptly intensified at the wells, in the taverns, and in the shops. Antonio Appiani, a Milanese agent in Romagna, best expressed the popular mood when he wrote to the duke of Milan, "the Forlivesi just do not like him, *puncto*."[83] Lorenzo de'Medici, whose agents shad-

MAPS
AND
GENEALOGICAL
TABLE

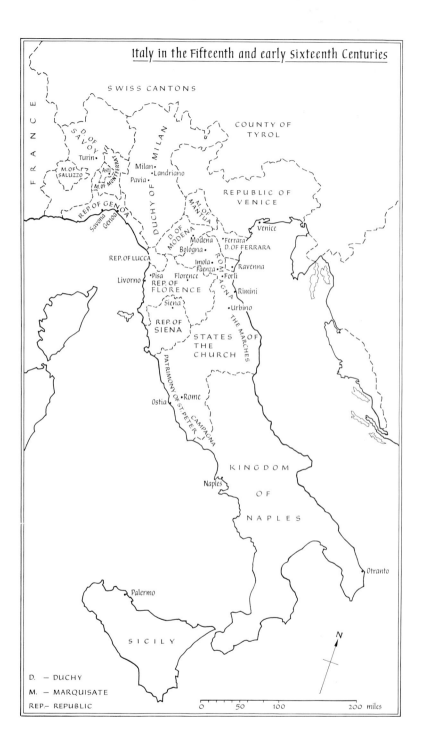

Italy in the Fifteenth and early Sixteenth Centuries

SWISS CANTONS

COUNTY OF TYROL

FRANCE

D. OF SAVOY

Turin •

M. OF SALUZZO

Asti •

M. OF MONTFERRAT

Milan •

• Landriano

Pavia •

DUCHY OF MILAN

REP. OF GENOA

Savona Genoa

REPUBLIC OF VENICE

M. OF MANTUA

D. OF MODENA

Modena •

Bologna •

• Ferrara

D. OF FERRARA

• Venice

REP. OF LUCCA

Imola •

Faenza •

ROMAGNA

Ravenna •

Livorno •

• Pisa

Florence •

• Forlì

REP. OF FLORENCE

• Rimini

Siena •

• Urbino

REP. OF SIENA

THE MARCHES

STATES OF THE CHURCH

PATRIMONY OF ST. PETER

Ostia •

• Rome

CAMPAGNA

KINGDOM

OF

NAPLES

Naples •

• Otranto

• Palermo

SICILY

N

D. — DUCHY

M. — MARQUISATE

REP.— REPUBLIC

0   50   100   200 miles

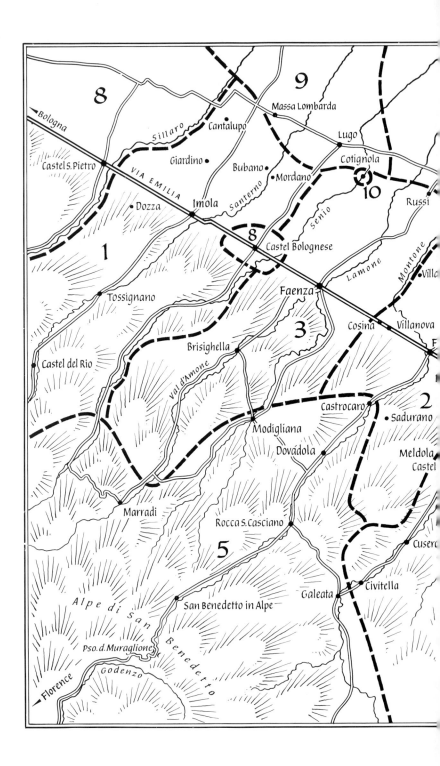

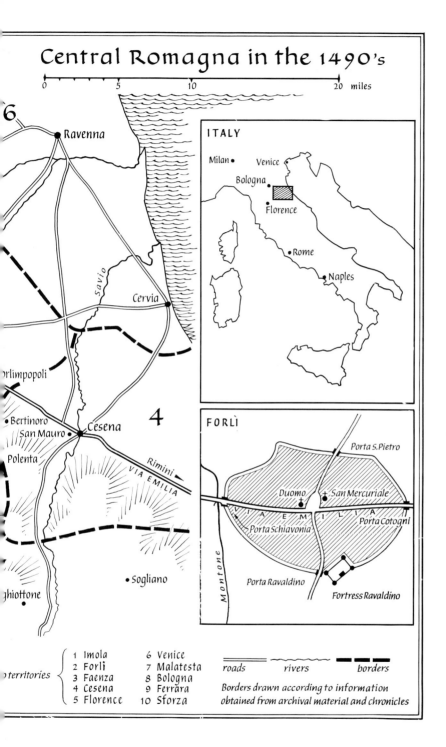

Central Romagna in the 1490's

0   5   10   20   miles

6

Ravenna

Savio

Cervia

rlimpopoli

Bertinoro
San Mauro •

Cesena

4

Polenta

VIA EMILIA

Rimini

• Sogliano

ghiottone

ITALY

Milan • Venice •
Bologna •
Florence

• Rome

• Naples

FORLÌ

Porta S.Pietro

Duomo   + San Mercuriale

V I A   E M I L I A

Porta Schiavonia

Porta Cotogni

Montone

Porta Ravaldino

Fortress Ravaldino

territories {
1 Imola   6 Venice
2 Forlì   7 Malatesta
3 Faenza   8 Bologna
4 Cesena   9 Ferrara
5 Florence   10 Sforza
}

roads   rivers   borders

Borders drawn according to information
obtained from archival material and chronicles

Genealogical Table of the Sforza and Rovere-Riario

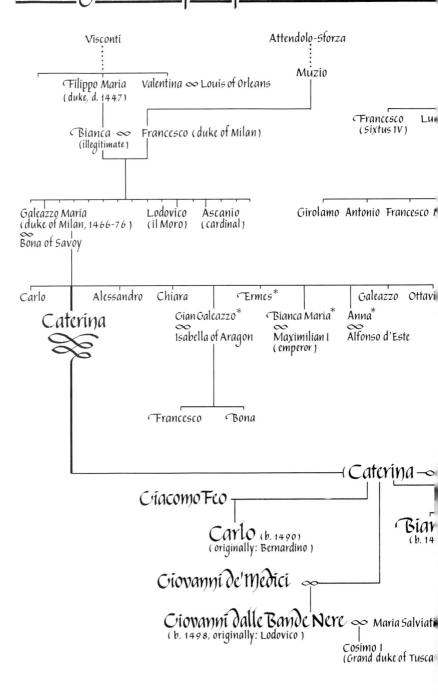

Visconti

Attendolo-Sforza

Muzio

Filippo Maria (duke, d. 1447)

Valentina ∞ Louis of Orleans

Francesco (Sixtus IV)   Lu

Bianca ∞ (illegitimate)

Francesco (duke of Milan)

Galeazzo Maria (duke of Milan, 1466-76) ∞ Bona of Savoy

Lodovico (il Moro)

Ascanio (cardinal)

Girolamo Antonio Francesco

Carlo   Alessandro   Chiara   Ermes*   Galeazzo Ottavi

Caterina

Gian Galeazzo* ∞ Isabella of Aragon

Bianca Maria* ∞ Maximilian I (emperor)

Anna* ∞ Alfonso d'Este

Francesco   Bona

Caterina ∞

Giacomo Feo

Bia (b. 14

Carlo (b. 1490) (originally: Bernardino)

Giovanni de'Medici ∞

Giovanni dalle Bande Nere ∞ Maria Salviati
(b. 1498, originally: Lodovico)

Cosimo I (Grand duke of Tusca

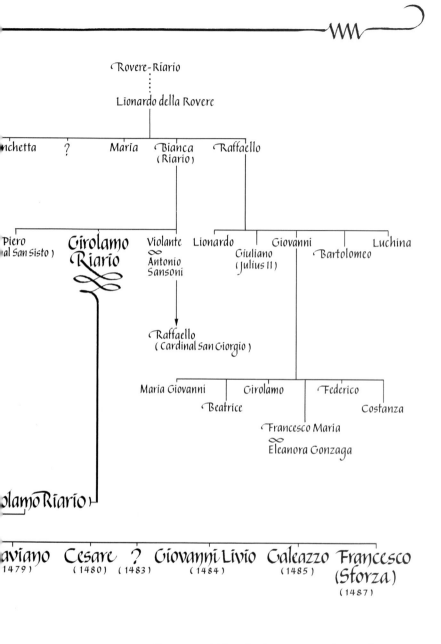

Rovere-Riario

Lionardo della Rovere

...nchetta   ?   Maria   Bianca   Raffaello
(Riario)

Piero   **Girolamo**   Violante   Lionardo   Giovanni   Luchina
al San Sisto)   **Riario**   ∞   Giuliano   Bartolomeo
                Antonio   (Julius II)
                Sansoni

Raffaello
(Cardinal San Giorgio)

Maria Giovanni   Girolamo   Federico
        Beatrice   Costanza

Francesco Maria
∞
Eleanora Gonzaga

...olamo Riario)

...aviano   Cesare   ?   Giovanni Livio   Galeazzo   Francesco
(1479)   (1480) (1483)   (1484)   (1485)   (Sforza)
                                              (1487)

* Legitimate children of Galeazzo Maria and Bona of Savoy

owed the noble pair equally closely, could thus hope for the eventual doom of one of the plotters against the Medici brothers.

Girolamo also had to carry the burden of two recent political failures. He had unsuccessfully tried to reconcile Lorenzo de'Medici [84] and to have Antonio Maria Ordelaffi assassinated.[85] Milanese diplomacy, too, made Girolamo's situation difficult even within his own family. Milan, worried about Girolamo's dealings with Venice, unabashedly used Caterina as a lever to bring about a change in Girolamo's new diplomatic position.[86] Antonio Appiani again and again tried to lure the couple to Milan for a visit.[87] Caterina was eager to go and expressed her desire clearly. But Girolamo declined all invitations, pleading that the pope would soon need him and had not even liked Girolamo to make the Romagna trip. As for the suggestion that Caterina and the childern could go to Milan alone, Girolamo protested his inability to live without them.[88] Appiani knew the real reason. It was evident when Andrea Boldù, the Venetian delegate entrusted with greeting the Riario in Romagna, had no difficulty getting an acceptance to his *pro forma* invitation for a Venetian visit.[89] All the while a disappointed Caterina entertained herself with hunts in the hills and river forests, her advanced pregnancy notwithstanding.

Both Girolamo and Caterina felt relieved when the journey was continued, although as usual their reasons differed. On September 2, 1481, the couple left Forlì for Venice. The traveling company was relatively small: Caterina and Girolamo; Lodovico Orsi, an assessor; and Matteo Menghi, archdeacon of Forlì. The declared purpose of the trip was to form an alliance against the archfoe, the Turk. Now that the fearsome Sultan Mohammed II had died, Western Christians could launch an all-out assault on the infidels. But in the negotiations that followed, the words "Este," "Ferrara," and "Naples" were mentioned much more often than the word "Turk." A third party hoped, however, to stay well informed—Lorenzo de'Medici. His source seemed reliable, since it was no other than the archdeacon Matteo Menghi himself.[90]

The Venetian Senate deliberated at length on the kind of reception which should be extended to the approaching party.[91] Ninety-eight senators prevailed in their insistence that Girolamo and Caterina were worth the best Venice had to offer; thirty-two senators disagreed; and seven sought the safety of abstention. With the decision made, Venice, most skilled in such affairs, startled the visitors and overwhelmed them with honors. At the island of San Clemente the Doge, Giovanni Mocenigo, awaited them on his bucentaur. Music, salutes, flags, and shouting blended with the gold ornaments and the beautiful carvings of the state barge to produce an awesome impression. Caterina was awaited and attended by one hundred and fifteen noble ladies. The entry into the city became a veritable procession of triumph. From then on there was no respite from the overwhelming Venetian hospitality. Visit followed visit—to the arsenal, the cradle of Venetian sea power, to palaces, and to a special session of the Grand Council. And the visits were intermingled with honors, compliments, and dances. For a few days Caterina relived the time of Milanese and Roman splendor and abandoned herself gratefully to it.

In the negotiations Girolamo, now by resolution of the Grand Council a *gentile homo di Venetia* ("an honored citizen of Venice"), achieved his goal. The plans were designed: the war against Ferrara and probably also Naples was to begin the following year. Venice would find compensation for her efforts in territories held by the Este family, and Girolamo was free to maneuver for his and his family's benefit. Matteo Menghi slipped in his assessment of the trip when he reported to Lorenzo de'Medici that the outcome was inconclusive. But Lorenzo was not deceived by such an error. The tremors of the coming war were already being felt in Italian politics.

Forlì had its own peculiar tremors. While the Riario were entertained and feasted in Venice, another conspiracy was forming in the city. Among its participants were many of the artisans of Forlì who had never forgotten their love and devotion to the Ordelaffi cause. The conspirators planned to set upon Girolamo and his family when they returned to the city and to massacre them all.[92] In this endeavor they enjoyed the hearty support of the Este of Ferrara, Lorenzo de'Medici, and Galeatto Manfredi of Faenza.[93] But the plans were betrayed and, hearing of them, Girolamo was furious. Consequently, when upon its return the traveling party rode into Forlì, the city looked grim. Gone were the gay decorations, joyous shouts, and the other paraphernalia of triumph. Girolamo and Caterina were surrounded by all the nobles and men-at-arms they had been able to gather. The *congiura degli artisani* ("conspiracy of the artisans") had failed, but the gulf separating the Riario from the Forlivesi had been openly revealed. Girolamo tried to keep it from widening by delaying punitive action until after his departure and by granting the Forlivesi new tax exemptions on the sale of food stuffs and wine. Yet little joy remained during those days in Forlì.

LATE IN OCTOBER, Girolamo's and Caterina's stay in Romagna ended. Caterina had refused to remain in Imola together with her children and the family's valuables and summer attire. Eight months pregnant, she climbed on a mule and proceeded on the seven day trip across the rugged Apennines and along the long and winding road through the Marches.[94] Toward the end of the journey she had to be carried in a complicated arrangement of baskets to favor her body.[95] Even this trip became involved in the high politics of that period. Milanese agents watched eagerly how far the Venetian orator Andrea Boldù would accompany the couple in order to gauge from it the strength of the political tie between the pope and Venice. The news was bad, Boldù went with the Riario to Rome.

A few days after the couple had arrived in Rome, Caterina gave birth to a daughter. The child died soon after.[96] The event provided a bitter ending to a promising year.

Back in Forlì, Tolentino solved the conspiracy problem in his peculiar way. He let escape whoever wanted to. Then, ten days after Girolamo's and Caterina's departure, the henchmen of the *bargello* rounded up the rest of the unsuccessful conspirators, and on November 15 those who went through the streets of Forlì noticed five bodies hanging from the palace windows.

Some well-known persons were exiled, some fined. Thus Girolamo showed his power but let his governor attract the popular
wrath. All was in vain, since the main conspirator, Antonio
Maria Ordelaffi, lived on. He enjoyed the protection of Lorenzo
de'Medici in nearby Modigliana. From there his connections
reached out to the Manfredi of Faenza and the Bentivoglio of
Bologna. Antonio Maria was now the only hope of the house of
the Ordelaffi. Earlier in the year his brother Francesco had
been murdered by two men from Perugia for reasons
unknown.[97] Antonio Maria Ordelaffi had, however, to delay his
next move. In the spirit of the papal–Venetian alliance, the
Venetian Senate had ordered both the *podestà* of Ravenna and
the captain of all troops to help Girolamo, "who now is eter-
nally our ally," maintain his state against all enemies.[98]

In the spring of 1482 the results of Girolamo's Venetian visit
showed. The great war began with the forming of the two
camps. On the pope's side were Venice and Genoa. Roberto
Malatesta, the *signore* of Rimini, was to be the military leader,
since the nominal commander of the papal forces, Girolamo,
possessed no great military genius. Ferrara received help from
Naples, Milan, Federico Gonzaga of Mantua, Florence, Bologna, the Manfredi of Faenza, and Federico da Montefeltro,
who was duke of Urbino and the captain general of this alliance.

The opening move was made in Rome.[99] The pope recalled
all of the Roman nobles who had been with King Ferrante of
Naples since the Otranto campaign. This was a test of loyalties,
since to obey the papal order meant to take sides against Naples. The Orsini obeyed, and so did the Colonna of the Pales-
trina branch. The Savelli and the Colonna of the Paliano and
Genazzano branches remained with King Ferrante. Their
hatred of Girolamo knew no bounds. Besides, Ferrante promised them considerable land gains, a promise which cost him
nothing since the land to be given away belonged entirely to
the Orsini. Girolamo did his best to stir the fighting spirit of the
Roman nobles: soon the Roman noble families were at each
others throat—the Orsini and the Santa Croce fought the Colonna and the della Valle.

Early in 1482 Naples slyly asked for passage for her troops

through papal territory in order to relieve Ferrara. The expected denial meant the beginning of the actual war.[100] With so many of the Italian powers involved, the *condottieri* and the mercenaries could breathe more easily; work was available in abundance.

The war had two theaters of action—the Roman campagna and the Po Valley around Ferrara. In the south Alfonso, duke of Calabria, swiftly moved on Rome. As his troops edged nearer and nearer, Rome took on the air of a city under siege. On June 2 a consistory was held. Girolamo and Virginio Orsini participated, and their radical counsel carried the day. By nightfall the cardinals Colonna and Savelli were under arrest for treason.[101] The Vatican itself resembled a military camp with guards standing everywhere.

But no decisive action was forthcoming, and the war dragged on. Alfonso nibbled away at the southern strongholds of the papal territory. Fortress after fortress yielded to him. Girolamo and his advisor and friend, Virginio Orsini, only infrequently left the camp of the papal army around St. John of the Lateran. There on the chests of the sacristy—some chroniclers insist it was on the altar itself—they threw dice, shuffled their cards, and played lotto.[102] Caterina saw little of Girolamo during these days.

Out in the campagna soldiers were on the rampage. The battles were brawls for hay, for seed, for flour, and for cattle. The conquests were houses with their furniture and women. An air of tragedy hovered over the area.[103] Deputations of the desperate victims and of the citizens of Rome appealed to the pope for relief. He was all graciousness and decreed restitution of all damage and loss at a future date; but even the gullible put no stock in this. The citizens sent their own guards into the fields to preserve at least the seed grain stored there. Girolamo, their protector, had it taken away and sold it to recover his losses in gambling. Grain became a scarcity in Rome; hunger was everywhere, and so were the companions of war—robbery and rape.

For the first time, the bitter side of living touched Caterina's daily life. Even a brief stay at the papal palace did not shield her from it. And in those hours she had no companionship, since Girolamo had neither the time nor the need to share his counsel with her. Whatever remnants were left in the nineteen-year-old Caterina of childish dreams of a life of undisturbed glory rapidly faded. Yet she did not feel touched by compassion for the miserable multitude since, for her, their very station in life predisposed them for such suffering. For a brief moment the tribulations even seemed to bring Caterina a personal grati-fication, when Girolamo, hedging against a possible defeat, began to cultivate Milanese sympathy. Caterina, he decided, should travel to her home city and thus emphasize the sup-posedly existing good feelings. Alas, the war soon turned for the better, such defeatist maneuvers were abandoned, and Caterina saw dispelled once more the dream of returning to her child-hood city. As for the policies of her husband, she had ample opportunity to reflect critically upon them—much more so since under the stress of Neapolitan military pressure the pope openly disagreed with the pro-Venetian policy of his nephew, calling it stupid and ill conceived.[104]

After two months of petty warfare the papal *condottiere* Roberto Malatesta arrived in Rome. The papal soldiers were readied for action. Before they left to oppose the enemy in the open field, the pope wanted to see them and bless them. One day, the whole army lined up in front of the Lateran Palace for the Holy Father. Then they marched out of Rome: at the head a detachment of heavily armed cavalry; then many crossbow-men collected from the forces of the Orsini, Mirandola, Riario, and Malatesta, followed by nine thousand infantrymen, more crossbowmen, and carriages loaded with bombards, cannons, cannonballs, and *passavolanti*.[105] After the dust had settled, Rome was frightfully quiet, especially around St. John of the Lateran. The churches showed the marks of their use as troop quarters. They overflowed with refuse, foul straw and human excrement. The nearby vineyards had been devastated, trees had been cut down for firewood, and the country houses looted.

A week later the Romans were talking excitedly about the great victory wrought from the enemy in the fever-infested swamps of the Campo Morto, an area so dreaded that even the worst criminal enjoyed automatic asylum there. At one place, the Torre di Campo Morto, Alfonso, duke of Calabria, was defeated by the superior papal force. On the battlefield, Roberto was cheered as the hero. Girolamo had kept to the safety of his tent in the papal camp, but he was quick to share the glory. The pope in his congratulatory message to Roberto Malatesta could not refrain from mentioning his "very own nephew, Girolamo." [106] In Caterina's letters, although she knew better, the hero is always "my consort" and not Roberto Malatesta.[107]

Rome welcomed back the *condottiere* with joy. The worldly-wise Romans were not easily fooled; they sensed very well with whom the real achievement rested. But fate treated Roberto Malatesta no better than the Riario had. A fews days after his triumphant return to Rome, a vicious fever gripped and killed him.

An equally bitter struggle was fought in the nothern theater of war. Venice attacked Ferrara with great vigor; yet even more soldiers died of the diseases bred by the stagnant waters of the Po Valley than died in battle. Besides, in the spring of 1482, Lorenzo de'Medici had incited the Bentivoglio, the Manfredi, and Antonio Maria Ordelaffi to a surprise attack on Forlì.[108] Girolamo had to send some of his precious forces hurrying north.[109] For once the Forlivesi remained loyal to the Riario, although they disliked the Venetian garrison and bitterly hated Girolamo's new governor Magnani, the bishop of Imola and a man of extreme sternness.[110] The anger of the Forlivesi finally boiled over when Bishop Magnani planned to execute some Ordelaffi partisans for no more than their wrongly directed sympathies. Tolentino who had been called to Rome for his great military skills, had to hurry north, taking with him a detachment of troops consisting of men-at-arms and crossbowmen on horses, and some infantry. It was Tolentino's popularity more than his military force which in the end saved Forlì for the Riario. The siege was soon lifted. Tolentino with a contingent of troops pursued Antonio Maria Ordelaffi, but the quarry escaped into Tuscany.

The war tapered off. With every passing day the dream of extending the Riario fortunes in Romagna or in the Neapolitan realm moved further from realization. In the hills south of Rome the Neapolitans still held many of the finest papal fortresses. When the anti-papal league began to speak of a council to sit in judgment on Sixtus IV, all papal fervor for warfare in alliance with the Venetians faded. In December, 1482, an apprehensive Sixtus IV made his separate peace with the King of Naples, and on January 6 of the following year entered into a "Most Holy League" with Naples, Florence, Milan, Ferrara, Mantua, and Bologna against his former ally, Venice.[111] As to the duke of Ferrara, whose "evil deeds" had been the pretext for all the martial activity, Sixtus IV magnanimously declared that he would not step so low as to agitate against one of his feudatories, that he considered it an error to let peace be replaced by the uncertainties of war, and that he would take the duke back into his grace.[112] The planner and executor of this sudden shift was Girolamo, who hoped this time to enlarge the Riario holdings at the cost of Venice. But when the new allies met in Cremona (February, 1483) to discuss the problems of common warfare, Girolamo stayed home.[113] He had no desire to meet Lorenzo de'Medici.[114] Girolamo's contributions to the exertions of the allies were as usual not martial. He favored putting the interdict on Venice and eventually succeeded in persuading Sixtus IV to do so. Although the Venetian cardinals had violently opposed him in the consistory, his influence was overpowering. The interdict did nothing except bring Venice openly to advocate a council to depose Sixtus IV.

Caterina took no particular interest in these developments. In October, 1482, she had acquired a new and unwelcome companion for her life, the quartan fever.[115] Attacks of that disease foiled one more plan to visit Milan, where she would have gone not merely for her own pleasure but also as a visible pawn of the Riario's good faith in the context of the new alliance.[116]

The population of Rome was enthusiastic about the turn of fortune. After the news of the peace arrived, parades moved through the streets day and night. The excitement spilled over into the carnival season of the year 1483, which became one of the wildest and gayest. Not that it mattered that the pope fought Venice instead of Naples and the others. But Venice was far from the fields, houses, and pastures of the Romans: their hay, seed grain, buildings, and women were safe. In addition, for a while even Girolamo could not irritate the populace. From late May to October, 1483, he and Caterina resided in their possessions in Romagna. The stay turned out not to be pleasant.[117]

At first a joyous excitement greeted the noble couple. But Caterina and Girolamo were too preoccupied with securing their territories to savor the receptions. This time the threat came not from Lorenzo de'Medici but from the Venetians, who had given a *condotta* to Antonio Maria Ordelaffi, the traditional menace of the Riario.[118] Girolamo and Caterina were thus forced to gather arms and men not only for the general war but also for the defense of their territories. Forlì and Imola supplied nearly two hundred men for the army against Venice.[119] For the first time in her life Caterina tried her hand at soldiering. She soon commanded enormous respect and was even feared by the soldiers for her insistence on iron discipline cruelly enforced. She, who had come to Forlì depressed, found feverish martial activity a tonic. Even the impossibility of accepting yet another Milanese invitation did not disturb her.[120]

Then in August the earth began to shake.[121] For a whole month tremors recurred; there were rumbles under the surface, bells rang by themselves, and buildings shook. Panic gripped the people. Girolamo and Caterina slept in a tent in the courtyard of the fortress of Ravaldino. They did not dare to enter the building. Caterina prayed with the people and showed penitence. The noble couple, the magistrate, and the whole chapter of the cathedral made a pilgrimage to the shrine of Santa Clara. They asked the saint, on whose day the quakes started, to intercede with God for the terrified city and promised an annual repetition of the pilgrimage. When the quakes eventually subsided, another conspiracy was discovered. Partisans of the Ordelaffi had again planned a massacre of Girolamo and Caterina.[122]

After such a summer Girolamo was ready to leave for Rome when Sixtus IV implored him to come.[123] The Orsini and the Colonna were feuding more than ever and the pope felt utterly helpless. The cleaning up of the conspiracy was once more left to the governor of Forlì. One morning two women, one man, and the conspiring monks were seen hanging from the palace windows. Such work was a joy to the new, one-eyed governor, Giacomo Bonarello d'Ancona, who was described as a "miserable creature, cruel and perfidious." [124]

10

As the year 1484 approached, the astrologers pronounced dire warnings since "it had pleased the omnipotent Lord to arrange for most unfortunate constellations of the celestial bodies." [125] They prophesied wars, earthquakes, floods, and the death of famous persons.

With the early stirrings of the Roman spring, the pulse of everything quickened—politics, love, and all. The war against Venice, too, breathed new life. Yet its action occurred far from Rome, leaving Girolamo to his own pursuits. He had decided to bring one competitor for power in Rome to fight another. The proud, mighty, and lawless Orsini were to help him rout the equally proud, mighty, and lawless Colonna. Reasons for such a conflict would not be hard to find. The Ferrara war had ended so abruptly that it had left a legacy of problems in its wake—counties not returned to their owners, sums of money not paid, and agreements overlapping other agreements.

What followed seemed at first to be no more than Roman routine: armed men were seen in large numbers in the streets, and there was an occasional stabbing and an air of tension. Then one day a message reached Lorenzo Colonna, a papal protonotary: "Somebody hates you and follows you." [126] The man who sent the warning was none other than the cardinal of San Giorgio, Raffaello Riario, who for one year by now had been papal chamberlain and thus a bright star in the system of the *curia*. [127] In response, the Colonna quarter of the city swarmed with armed men spoiling for a fight. Lorenzo himself stayed in his palace. When he ventured out into the streets, a swarm of young men surrounded him. Thereupon the Orsini armed their followers and just as eagerly looked for a fight.

Out in the campagna war had started already. [128] At night servants of both sides crisscrossed the area stealing cattle and horses. Each night had its murders, and in daylight everybody pleaded innocence. Girolamo watched and was pleased. The city officials, knowing the suffering of the people whenever the nobles fought each other, went to Sixtus IV with petitions for peace. Sixtus IV angrily ordered a halt to the feuding. For a brief moment war threatened to elude Girolamo. Then he got his chance.

The pope ordered Lorenzo to appear before him. No safe conduct was given, since it was supposedly not needed. Lorenzo obediently set out for the papal residence. In the streets he found his armed and angry partisans. Deeply worried for his safety, they prevented him from proceeding and took him back to his palace. "Treason," Girolamo shouted: a papal order had not been obeyed. Sixtus IV agreed, and Girolamo and Virginio Orsini heard the coveted order to arrest Lorenzo. For their troops this meant the promise of loot from the quarters of Monti, Treva, and Colonna. Hours later the Colonna palace on the Piazza della Pilotta was under heavy attack. Bombards were shot, *cerebottani* and *passavolanti* and crossbows threw their projectiles, and the dead and the wounded strewed the square. The smoke of fire and gunpowder roughened the throats of those who shouted and cursed. Finally the door of the palace was broken down, and the mob poured in. Lorenzo, wounded and sitting on a chest, surrendered himself.

Out in the Roman night, "Colonna" had become a dirty word. The soldiers of the Church and of the Orsini, and the ordinary street mob as well, took their revenge for the wrongs, real or imagined, the Colonna had done. The Colonna palace lost its silverware, gold, tapestries, carpets, dishes, and furniture. With every hour the remaining loot became more meager; latecomers enjoyed putting fire to it. There still remained other opportunities to enrich lives which were otherwise led in poverty. In the inferno of that night, even the relics and the missals of the Colonna churches were carried off.

Such a successful beginning augured well for Girolamo's plans.[129] He hopefully pursued his course during the next days and weeks. Enemies were murdered, partisans of the Colonna fined thousands of ducats, and the dungeons filled. In the Campagna baron now fought baron. But most of the damage fell on the peasants and on the fields, barns, and threshing places of the Roman citizens. Nobody dared to go out to cut the grain still standing.

Starvation and suffering aroused the forces of peace to action. The popular assembly cried out for peace, but their delegation never reached the pope. Girolamo feared whatever feelings of compassion Sixtus IV might still harbor. But Girolamo could not prevent his cousin Giuliano della Rovere, cardinal of San Pietro in Vincoli, from going to their uncle. The cardinal did not mince his words and called Girolamo a reckless adventurer who would ruin the pope and everybody else. Furious, Girolamo threatened to drive Giuliano from Rome, to loot his palace and then destroy it. Sixtus IV yielded to Girolamo, and the war continued.

To no avail the Colonna offered virtual surrender, Girolamo smelled victory and triumph. Lorenzo Colonna was wasting away in prison. Torture had cut the muscles of his arms, broken the bones of arms and fingers, cut the skin of his head, and punctured his feet. The next task must be the siege of the Colonna castles south of Rome. Artillery was needed. All workshops producing carts to transport cannons were put on a seven-day week. Soon Girolamo had enough for his bombards, *cerebottani,* and other war machines. On June 30, 1484, before the campaign against the Colonna strongholds began, Lorenzo Colonna was beheaded in one of the courtyards of the Castel Sant'Angelo. He died as only a baron knew how, with no word of reproach, asking only for a papal blessing; no outbursts of rage and abuse, only three times uttering the word "Jesus" before his head rolled from the block.[130]

July, 1484, brought Girolamo moments of martial glory. He moved his army before Cave. The carts so feverishly produced transported artillery, equipment, and ammunition (which for the bombards consisted of four hundred blocks of Travertine stone taken from a dismantled bridge), and also torches, to be used for fighting during the night.[131]

In Rome apathy, disgust, and relief at having the theater of war removed farther from the city formed the prevailing moods. Rumor and cynicism ran high. One of the targets was Sixtus IV. Rapidly aging, sick from the gout, and increasingly lonesome, the pope had lately found Caterina an enjoyable companion. Her charm and optimism enthralled him and lightened temporarily the deepening gloom around him. Of this relationship the people had their own interpretation, simpler and less subtle. Unable to stop the elusive rumors, Sixtus IV vented his anger on the first supposed offender caught. He was a little known painter, who had painted the siege of Cave with the soldiers engaged in battle and with the tents and barracks of the papal camp. This would have been a fine picture had he not sneaked into one of the corners a little scene of a Franciscan friar and a young woman in the pose of lovers, while Girolamo at the center fought bravely on. Sixtus IV had the painter thrown into the dungeon, given ten blows, and his house looted. The young artist escaped the gallows because many testified that the fellow had always been rather queer and irresponsible.[132]

Girolamo got his glory. Late in July, Cave fell to the papal forces, and so did Capranica. Flushed with victory, Girolamo moved on to Paliano. The siege began on August 3. An elaborate camp was set up, and Caterina, the children, and Virginio Orsini joined Girolamo. It soon became apparent that the siege of Paliano would be a bigger job than all the battles won up to then. Every day the Colonna men pushed their attacks deep into the papal camp. On one occasion Caterina was nearly drawn into the battle. Urgent calls went to Sixtus IV for more bombards, more oxen, more carts, for more of almost everything, especially for the troops under Jacopo de'Conti, presently in Rome. The pope's reply no longer mattered. Italian politics once more took one of its sharp turns.

Lodovico il Moro had never put his whole heart into the war with Venice. No real gains were to be expected from victory, and the losses could be severe. The operation of a Neapolitan army in the valley of the Po was against traditional Milanese policy, and the strengthening of Florence and the papal position was not worth fighting for. When Venice had engaged the duke of Lorraine as *condottiere* and tempted him with the conquest of Naples, on which his family held an old claim, Lodovico had been worried. When Venice incited the duke of Orleans to come and get his "rightful possession" Milan, Lodovico became alarmed and acted.[133] In early August, 1484, he brought about the Peace of Bagnolo. By its terms Venice received the Polesina, Florence was left to her own devices with regard to the fortress of Sarzana and the city of Lucca, and the Rovere-Riario lost out completely. Their dreams of substantial possessions in Romagna or on Neapolitan soil had been permanently dispelled. When on August 11, Sixtus IV heard the news, he cried out: "What you describe to me is a shameful and ignominious peace full of confusion, one which in time will prove to be harmful and which I can neither approve nor bless." [134] The blow of disappointment hit a body aged and weakened by the gout. The "fever," the great ravager of the weak in the summer heat of Rome, struck him. In the early morning hours of August 12, 1484, Sixtus IV died.[135] So ended the tragedy of a man who had chosen to become a Renaissance prince rather than a leader in the realm of the spirit, and had lost in that endeavor. He left behind a beautified Rome and a struggling Riario-Rovere clan.

II

THE DAY WAS very young when in one of the upper chambers of the papal apartments the body of Sixtus IV lay for the last time on his bedstead, dressed in his cassock and vestments and with his hands clasping a crucifix. The cardinals, the first to be informed of his death, had come and paid their respects. The vice-chancellor of the Church broke the seal used for all the bulls during Sixtus IV's pontificate. Then with pieces of silk dipped in balm he stopped up the mouth, nostrils, ears, and anus of the corpse. Soon Sixtus IV was naked and alone on a long table. The cardinals had left, fearing for their safety once the news of the pope's death reached the streets of Rome. The master of ceremonies must prepare the body for the lying in state. He had difficulty in finding linen. Nobody any longer cared, the world belonged to the living.

And in the world of the living the star of the Riario-Rovere was rapidly fading.[136] In the morning hours the pope's death became common knowledge, and the news provoked anger, hatred, and plain lust for loot.[137] It was an auspicious hour for such passions, since with the pope's death all law and order died in the city. A mob of armed youths hurried to the Riario palace near S. Appollinare.[138] Their frenzied cries of "Colonna! Colonna!" echoed in the streets, and their axes smashed the great gate of the palace. Behind them followed a mob from everywhere and of every intent. No Riario—neither Girolamo, Caterina, nor any of their children—could be caught, but there was still the palace to vent the passion on, with its chests full of linen, its *credenza* with silverware, majolica, glasses, and vases, its solid chairs and tables, and its rooms full of provisions. Partisan hatred combined with naked greed made an ugly picture. After the furniture and valuables had been removed, the fury and greed of the mob was manifested by doors torn from their hinges; windows, railings, and woodwork dismantled; trees and plants uprooted from the gardens; chimneys destroyed; marble statues in the fountains carted off; lead of the conduit dragged into the streets; and finally hinges and nails patiently picked from the empty ruin.

In these days no Ligurian was safe. For a week Liguria meant Riario and Rovere to the simple-minded mob. The Genoese bankers felt the effects of this hostility, and so did the papal granary at Santa Maria Nuova. Then came the turn of Castello Giubileo, which Caterina had used as the main supply depot. One hundred cows, one hundred goats, pigs, donkeys, geese, chickens, pounds of salted meat, Parmesan cheese, and heavy Greek wine all soon went to the kitchens and into the stomachs of those who were used to simpler food. The pillage was accompanied by shouts of "Colonna, Colonna—Down with the Riario." To greedy minds everything valuable and attractive became by strange magic identified with the Rovere-Riario. The loot-crazy mob plundered mercilessly. Unfortunately plain loot-seeking has an even longer life than partisan hatred. Nothing and nobody was any longer safe. Houses were barricaded, and the palaces of the cardinals turned into fortresses. Giuliano della Rovere and Rodrigo Borgia had their cannon trained on the streets. Night and day murderers and thieves roamed the streets. The great feast of evil passions was on, feared by the law-abiding and greeted with joy by those whose hearts longed for violence and easy gain.

When Sixtus IV died, Girolamo, Caterina, and their children were with the Orsini in the camp before Paliano hoping for re-enforcements and victory.[139] The death of Sixtus was also the

death of that hope and thus of the campaign against the Colonna. The foundation of Riario power had collapsed. Action
had to be taken to salvage what could be saved. The task
assigned to each of the marital partners showed their different
personalities. First, Girolamo lifted the siege of Paliano. So
hasty was the retreat that the advancing Colonna gained sixty
carts with bombards, the baggage train, and twelve hundred
head of cattle, all abandoned by the papal forces. Gone also
were the fruits of months of campaigning, the hard-fought
battles for the fortresses of Cave, Capranica, and Marino. But
the main loss was the Riario's shattered dream of a dominant
position in *quattrocento* Italy.

As Girolamo neared Rome, the cardinals moved to neutralize
his influence and ordered him to encamp his troops at the Ponte
Molle, at a safe distance from the city.[140] Girolamo obeyed, as
did Girolamo's ally Virginio Orsini and his troops. He still
spoke, however, with a powerful voice, since he commanded an
army and the Orsini supported him loyally. By staying in full
force close to Rome he could hope to sway the election of a new
pope in his favor. And then there was Caterina who had boldly
acted out her part. In that moment of supreme crisis Caterina
shook off the years of inactivity spent at the side of her powerful
husband. She now knew the importance of power and where it
rested. At Paliano she swung her body, heavy with seven months
of pregnancy, onto a horse, and, with Paolo Orsini, rode into
the city of Rome through streets bristling with hatred against
the Riario directly towards the Castel Sant'Angelo, not to take
cover but to take over.[141] Once inside she gave orders. Caterina
announced that she intended to hold the fortress until it could
legally be given to the successor of Sixtus IV. Everyone knew
what this legalistic language meant. The Riario were going to
control the course of coming events by holding a threatening
sword over Rome. The Castel Sant'Angelo was to be their main
asset, a formidable one with its thick walls and sturdy towers
sitting in the midst of the city and commanded by a lady who
had long forgotten her Latin poetry, and the other gentle arts
imbued in a young noblewoman, but who found the wielding
of power electrifying.

Caterina went into vigorous action.[142] She galloped into the
fortress shouting "Duca! Duca! Girolamo! Girolamo!" The sol-

diers stared at her in disbelief. A group of Imolesi, gathered around the vice-castellan of the fortress, whispered to each other. Caterina promptly chased them out of the fortress, including the vice-castellan Innocenzo Codronchi, a confidant of Girolamo from Imola. Then Caterina had all gates closed and barricaded. She shouted and cursed the soldiers into discipline, and they in turn considered her cruel and fierce but obeyed her grudgingly.[143] While she acted like a drill sergeant she still looked thoroughly feminine. She was of medium height with a full figure and an excellent complexion; she spoke little, wore a tan satin gown with a two-arm-length train and a huge velvet hat with long plumes, and displayed the signs of her seventh month of pregnancy. Only her belt with the curved sword and bag of gold ducats dangling from it was masculine, and perhaps her indomitable fighting spirit.

Soon some members of the *curia* received a sample of Caterina's flaring temper and stubborn defiance. Cardinal Riario, always inclined to compromise, sent a plenipotentiary to the castle with a firmly worded invitation for his aunt Caterina to come to a discussion outside the fortress. She answered from the battlements that the plenipotentiary could come into the castle accompanied by one man. But yield she would not. When he showed no interest in her offer, Caterina shouted derisively that she had just as much brains as her father and was not so stupid as to give up the fortress.

While the Castel Sant'Angelo was quiet, disciplined, and, above all, in the possession of the Riario, all order had broken down in the city. On the first day of the anarchy the *conservatori* had called for quiet and an end to pillage and murder, and had threatened to punish new excesses with the gallows. The mob ignored the order. The della Valle simply closed the gates of the Trastevere quarter, and in their area continued the murderous crusade against everything Riario, Rovere, and, in general, Ligurian. The magazine of Giovanni Battista Pallavicino (a distant relative of Girolamo) became the property of the howling mob. Among the many things which disappeared was the wax stored for the obsequies for Sixtus IV. The Genoese hospital suffered for its connection with Liguria, as did two papal galleys loaded with wine.

Slowly the exiles returned—the Savelli with two hundred

soldiers, and the freed Cardinal Colonna surrounded not by
soldiers but by a welcoming crowd. The city swarmed with
men-at-arms of all camps and families. Bitter civil war seemed
close at hand. Yet the man who held the key to outright civil
war never knew the virtue of decisive action. On August 16,
Girolamo moved himself and his troops to Isola, an Orsini
possession. He enjoyed the hospitality of the Orsini, and his
troops deployed themselves in the vineyards of the Roman
families. Girolamo thus had effectively removed himself further
from a real role in the making of a new pope.

On the next day the obsequies for Sixtus IV began with only
a few cardinals attending. The cardinals Giuliano della Rovere, Savelli, Colonna, and Cibo preferred not to venture out of
their palaces, especially not to pass the gates of Sant'Angelo on
their way to the ceremonies. Instead they spent their time
busily gathering strength, and soldiers easily found jobs. The
tension brought brawls, particularly when the Colonna venge-
fully sacked part of the Orsini quarter.

Martial activities, indiscriminate looting, lingering tension
had paralyzed the city. Shops were closed, no food was sold, no
peasants could come into the city to sell their wares, and no end
to deprivation was in sight. Hunger stalked the city. Rumors
circulated of two popes, one backed by the Orsini and the
Riario and the other by the Colonna. Haste in the selection of a
successor to the See of St. Peter was advisable if worse things
were to be avoided. The popular council met and begged the
cardinals to get all soldiers out of Rome and to meet quickly in
conclave. The petition had no immediate results. On that very
day, soldiers of the Savelli were locked in a street battle with
those of the Santa Croce. And on August 23, five hundred more
soldiers poured into the city to bolster the Colonna and Savelli
cause. Florence and Siena, in addition, offered new troops
against the threat posed by Girolamo and Caterina.

The offer was never accepted and turned out to be super-
fluous. The scale had already dipped in favor of the enemies of
the Riario when Girolamo had despaired of his case and had
moved to Isola. His final yielding came as no surprise. In an
agreement reached with the cardinals he was given four thousand ducats in back pay and indemnity for his destroyed Roman
property and was promised a renewed investiture with Imola

and Forlì by the new pope. In return, the cardinals were to be given all Church fortresses including the Castel Sant'Angelo. It was further stipulated that in order to insure a safe papal election, the Orsini would retire to Viterbo and the Colonna leave for Lazio, and that both families would stay there for the duration of one month.[144]

Girolamo was satisfied. He had rescued some bits of his former power without a fight. Caterina saw matters in a distinctly different way. She must have known of the agreement concluded on August 24, but her actions did not reveal such knowledge. During the night of August 24, one hundred and fifty more men slipped into the fortress. Caterina seemed determined not to yield either for money or to threats. Her comtempt for the quick settlement agreed to by Girolamo was clear; what others called prudence looked like a failure of nerves to her. But on the next day she too yielded.[145] The stress of standing alone against all of Rome and the Church proved to be too much. She was bothered by her pregnancy, feeling ill and alone, deadened by the heat and humid air of Rome in midsummer, trusting nobody and surrounded by soldiers-for-hire whose loyalty was given to the biggest purse. When her spirit finally broke, the cardinals lost no time in getting rid of her. A safe conduct was granted to her, and one hundred and fifty men were provided on condition that she left immediately.

She came out of the castle on her palfrey, proud, haggard, and bitter, accompanied by men of shifty allegiance but full of respect for her. This time as she rode through Rome there were no trumpets, tapestries, and nobles in velvet, yet it was her real day, a day of tragic triumph. A virago emerged from the Castel Sant'Angelo where a young gentlewoman had entered only days before.

Before joining her, Girolamo spent his last hours in Rome compiling a precise account of his money transactions with the *curia*. The balance sheet showed heavily in his favor, yet he had enough Roman experience to know that he would hardly collect a single coin.

Then the Riario, "who so far always had experienced the wind from the lucky side," [146] set out for Forlì. Each mile they traveled away from Rome was a step down the pyramid of power of *quattrocento* Italy. At the top had been Girolamo's domi-

nant position as the favorite nephew of Pope Sixtus IV; at the
bottom was the modest rank of count of Bosco, vicar of Imola
and Forlì. The rigors of travel on dusty roads in the heat of
midsummer were this time not alleviated by joyful expectations. About halfway on their journey a message telling of the
election of a new pope overtook them. He called himself Innocent VIII and was the former Cardinal Cibo [147], another Ligurian, who looked like a sturdy peasant, and, as a contemporary
put it, was not wholly illiterate. In him dwelt a strange mixture of benevolence and humaneness and a keen sense for
money and the fortunes of the Cibo family. No reformer of
morals, he was the proud father of a son and a daughter. For
the Riario the news was ambiguous. Innocent VIII had been
the candidate of Giuliano della Rovere, the cousin and competitor for power of Girolamo. As cardinal, Innocent VIII had
wasted little sympathy on the papal nephew, then so powerful,
but his hatred was not strong enough to reach Imola and Forlì.
Once the Riario had been removed from Rome, both Innocent
VIII and Cardinal della Rovere were quite content to leave
them to their fate.

III

WIFE
OF A
ROMAGNOL
LORD

12

"THE GREAT AND most noble city" of Forlì [1] received Girolamo
and Caterina without the earlier ritual of ceremonial joy. More
important, the city looked different to the Riario. Not that it
had changed since their last stay; but now they viewed Forlì as
their future permanent residence rather than a temporary stop-
over on journeys to and from Rome. In this light Forlì revealed
itself as the provincial town it was. Girolamo and Caterina
hardly shared the chronicler Cobelli's view of it as a proud
town with well-nourished and well-dressed people and of proud
dottori e cavalieri, a seat of art and learning, and a place of
virtuous life and justice. Within the city's walls lived twelve to
fifteen thousand people in solidly built houses of little grace or
beauty.[2] The city's routine was the routine of the small joys and
sufferings of the common people. One week was like another.
Whatever extraordinary excitement quickened the pulse of the
city came on the roads which cut through it. On the Via Emilia,
that artery of Northern Italy, traveled the merchants, products,
and news from Milan, Bologna, Faenza, and Rimini. Over the
winding roads from the southwest, Florence made her presence
felt, as from the north did Venice and Ferrara. These ribbons
of dust in summer and of deep mud during rainy periods were,
however, no longer routes on which the Riario could escape to
a life of splendid luxury and intoxicating power. Now they
were reminders of glorious times and of ruined hopes and
dreams.

Once more, however, the days of gay festivities were re-
enacted. On September 4, 1484, came the papal confirmation of
Girolamo's position as vicar of Imola and Forlì and ruler of a
few other minor papal possessions. Ironically, even the title of
"Captain General of the Holy Church" was renewed with the
proviso that permission to be absent from Rome and to live in
Romagna was "generously granted." [3] Forlì celebrated with

three days of merry-making, wining and dining, and dancing.

Yet, no necessary link connects legal title to actual power. Girolamo and Caterina would stay Romagnol sovereigns as long as no superior force chased them from Imola and Forlì. With Pope Sixtus IV gone, they must hold their own by means of their limited wealth, their skill in diplomacy, and the good will of their subjects. This task had to be accomplished in the peculiar circumstance that Girolamo came to Romagna after years as the late pope's right-hand man and that many people had reason either to hate him or to be grateful to him. But in power politics the past carries less weight than the present. Thus, with Girolamo's and Caterina's position radically diminished, the hatreds became less deep and the debts owed more easily forgotten.

Two traditional enemies postponed taking their vengeance. Galeotto Manfredi of Faenza, sitting squarely between Forlì and Imola, dealt with the Riario on a polite though not friendly basis. In Florence, Lorenzo de'Medici remembered vividly the Pazzi conspiracy; yet in 1484, he was not willing to provoke a new crisis by brashly working for Girolamo's ouster.[4] He preferred to support the local opponents of Girolamo and Caterina and to wait for their success. Lorenzo measured his hatred by the status of the object.

In addition, not all pillars of support for the Riario had crumbled. At the *curia*, Girolamo's nephew, Raffaello Riario, cardinal of San Giorgio, papal *camerlengo* ("chamberlain"), and holder of four bishoprics and two abbacies, had reached the peak of his influence. Equally important, he interested himself in the Riario family's fortunes, something which Caterina's uncle and another possible clerical supporter, Cardinal Ascanio Sforza, never did.[5] Accordingly when the cardinal of San Giorgio visited Girolamo and Caterina in September, 1485, he was granted a warm welcome. In turn, the cardinal, by the display of his wealth, impressed upon Caterina's and Girolamo's subjects the importance of the Riario family.[6]

The other main source of strength was supplied by Caterina's family, the Sforza of Milan. It was not that Lodovico il Moro, by now duke in all but name, geared his policy to the sentimental fact that Caterina was his relative. It was rather that Milan had always cultivated her position in Romagna, and, in this context, Caterina represented a convenient and valuable instrument. Need for support and drive for influence tied the Sforza and Riario together, and they called this bond "friendship."[7]

Fortunately for the Riario the road to Milan was unobstructed. Bologna, pro-Milan and lacking bitter memories against the Riario, was the object of early gestures of good will by Girolamo and Caterina. They extended lavish hospitality to Giovanni Bentivoglio when he passed through Imola in March, 1485,[8] and even before that they had been conciliatory in all those annoying problems which befell neighboring *signori*. In the Castelbolognese area the subjects of Bologna and of the Riario worked in adjacent fields and in hard-to-supervise forests. Friction was constant. Girolamo and his officials had always exercised proper restraint in the ensuing quarrels.[9]

To the north and further to the west the duke of Ferrara and the marquis of Mantua, too, were well disposed toward the Riario and helped to assure access to Milan.[10]

Another great traditional power in Romagna—Venice—was going through a phase of its history in which expansion on the mainland held little fascination. Venice was watchful of the Riario but not longing for the possession of Imola and Forlì.

What then of the people of Forlì and Imola? Did they constitute a hindrance or a hope to the rule of the Riario? Imola troubled the Riario little. That city had her ample share of family feuds; none of them, however, touched upon the crucial problem of governing. But Forlì, the more important of the two, proved difficult to tame. Since becoming lord of Forlì, Girolamo had restrained his tendency to outbursts of anger, and had favored the population with spectacles of splendor and with most liberal tax concessions. Caterina had done her share with a strong effort to become a popular figure. But this policy had not been conspicuously successful. Girolamo and Caterina were outsiders and only their prominence had made most Forlivesi forget that fact. Now, with their status diminished, they had come to Forlì and had brought with them the inevitable hangers-on which surround persons of influence. Most high offices were soon held by trusted Ligurians—consorts of Girolamo. The presence of these Ligurians served as a daily reminder that Girolamo and Caterina were not of true Forlivese origin. In a period which valued most highly one's ties to family and home town, such a flaw was hard to remedy. Only the patrician families felt something like loyalty to the new dynasty, while the craftsmen and the rest of the commoners looked longingly to the heir of the exiled Ordelaffi, Antonio Maria. The Ordelaffi, a local family, had grown to be a symbol of Forlì in two centuries of glory and defeat, and despite their sometimes despotic rule they were beloved by those of humble birth. But even some of the most respected families of Forlì, the Orsi, the Pansecco, the Paolucci, the Numai, the Orcioli, the Ercolani, and the Maldenti had once staunchly supported the Ordelaffi cause.[11] The last governing Ordelaffi, Pino, had in turn generously granted a measure of self-rule to the citizens of Forlì. The *Consiglio dei Quaranta Soggetti* ("Council of Forty") handled most of the internal and a few external affairs of the city.[12] A smaller group of twelve men was composed of the magistrates of the city, the *anziani*.[13] Girolamo wisely did not change such a well-functioning system, and for his forbearance he eventually commanded the loyalty of some formerly hostile families of influence. Still, the best he and Caterina could achieve with the mass of the commoners was a grudging indifference to their rule, a feeling which under strain would, however, shift much more easily and readily to hate than to affection.

None can say that the Riario did not sincerely try for a more intimate bond with their subjects. Upon their arrival in Forlì the hated governor Giacomo Bonarello d'Ancona was dismissed [14] and replaced by the just and respected Tolentino. When the harvest was disastrously small because of the dry weather in 1484, grain was imported and subsidized by the count.[15] In addition, the whole meat tax for the year 1484 was remitted.[16] Of course, this was more than a simple charitable act: both Girolamo and Caterina knew the dangerous political implications of empty stomachs. The Riario were also careful not to neglect pious works. The Corpus Christi procession, always a high light of the religious year in Forlì, became more splendid than ever; convents were made more beautiful and spacious; new churches rose and old ones were repaired. Besides showing concern of the Riario for the spiritual welfare of their subjects, these pious activities made work for those who needed it, as did the completion of the fortress of Ravaldino, the palace, the troop barracks, and the ammunition storage houses.

For nearly two years the Riario seemed to succeed and were undisturbed by conspiracies. Life in Forlì was tranquil if not always pleasant. On Mondays the peasants and fishermen crowded into the market square to offer their produce for sale. For a few hours the noise of bargaining citizens and vendors, the odors of fruit, meat, fish, and vegetables, and the rattling of carts coming and going created the bustling mood of market-day. The city stocked up on eggs, beans, wine, cheese, herbs, meat, flour, figs, olives, and fruits. In turn it gave the peasants the services of skilled craftsmen, the products of its shops, and some doubtful bargains at the pawnbroker's and the money changer's. With the evening the quiet of the week had begun. There followed days of small noises and hard work, with their odors of human sweat and ox dung. The churches provided the second high point of the week, with Sunday mass followed by general meeting, greeting, and chatting. The life of the *signore* differed little. He and his family were spared, of course, the work in the hot fields and the chores around the house. Instead they had the troubling problems of politics and the merry chase.

But while Forlì itself remained quiet, it was merely a glass house in which the Riario were living. Once they ventured outside, the rough air made them realize their isolation and diminished power. Even so insignificant a family as the Zampeschi was more than a match for them. At the end of the Pazzi war, Antonello Zampeschi had lost his three fiefs, San Mauro, Talamello, and San Giovedio.[17] From then on the Zampeschi lived near Forlimpopoli as bitter enemies of everything connected with the Rovere-Riario. The two thousand ducats they had received as compensation for their loss had brought no reconciliation. Sixtus IV had given the fiefs to Niccolò Riario, a brother of the cardinal of San Giorgio, and after Niccolò's death had added them to Girolamo's and Caterina's territory.[18] But Sixtus had hardly drawn his last breath when Antonello Zampeschi's sons, Ettore, Meleagro, and Brunoro, retook their former fiefs.[19] Girolamo, though more desirous and in need of these territories than ever, understood that he simply could not risk an armed conflict and merely protested. By 1486 the Riario had lost. The pope invested Ettore Zampeschi, who was serving him well as a *condottiere,* with San Mauro and Giovedio, while Talamello went to Ramberto Malatesta, count of Sogliano. The bitter hatred between the Riario and the Zampeschi lived on.

Another past figure of Romagnol politics did not have the luck of the Zampeschi brothers. Taddeo Manfredi, resentful and advancing toward old age, saw a last chance to recoup what he had lost in years of lesser wisdom.[20] But neither his luck nor his skill had improved. His men were caught in Imola while still spying and scouting. Mere servants, they died the death of servants. Some were hanged by their necks, some by their feet, and others were tied to the tails of horses and dragged through the city. Some "ungrateful" Imolesi shared their fate.[21]

Ever since she had shown her mettle in the occupation of the Castel Sant'Angelo, Caterina had taken a more active part in her husband's affairs. Girolamo still governed, but Caterina's advice was heard more frequently, though it often went unheeded. Outwardly, however, she continued her routine life of supervising the Riario household and bearing children. Caterina was eight months pregnant when the Riario rode into Forlì. On October 30, 1484, another son, Giovanni Livio, was born.[22] As a gesture of good will toward the city of Forlì, a prominent Forlivese, Lodovico Orsi, was included among the godfathers.[23]

On the next such occasion, never too long in coming in the Riario family during these years, the Riario did some more ambitious maneuvering. In one of those startling moves of *quattrocento* Italian politics, the nemesis of Girolamo's life, Lorenzo de'Medici, entered the Riario circle as godfather to their sixth child, a boy subsequently named Galeazzo Maria.[24] It was a desperate but vain attempt designed to show the Riario's willingness to bury the past and come to friendly relations with Lorenzo.

Late in 1484 Caterina fell seriously ill. So bad was her condition that Lodovico il Moro, who feared the loss of an important factor in his Romagna policy, sent an experienced doctor from his court to Forlì. Within a few weeks Caterina rallied and could once more share the concerns of government with her husband.[25] Their combined strength was taxed by many problems.

Of all the problems which befell them, none was more depressing, gruesome, and difficult to solve than their steadily increasing impoverishment. This new poverty of the Riario was, of course, not the poverty of the wretched with its lack of food and shelter but the poverty of the rich and mighty who, with their lives of luxury and splendor cruelly curtailed, are left with the dispiriting alternative of hiding their loss or trying to recoup. Worse yet, neither Girolamo nor Caterina had fully comprehended the implications of their diminished status. The Roman style of life they had led in their first year of residence in Forlì had steadily depleted the treasury. Gone were most of the riches they had brought from Rome when they rode into Forlì in the late summer of 1484—four hundred ducats, silverware, and jewels.[26] Every day of splendor and easy spending had made the stock of coins and silverware dwindle. Then the jewels, most of them Caterina's, had found their way to the pawnbroker's. The replenishing flow from the inexhaustible treasures of the Church had dried up. Finally, Girolamo and Caterina had to face up to the bleak reality that they were the rulers of Forlì and Imola, and no more than that. They could rely on the income from their private possessions, from taxation, and from the trade monopolies which they enjoyed as the governing family. The potential annual income derived from these sources was certainly no pittance, but the Riario were used to the standards of Milan and Rome and looked upon it with contempt.[27] They desperately sought a way out of their predicament. The nonchalant gesture of forgiving some of the most lucrative taxes when they had not needed them began to haunt them mercilessly. Conspiracies could be combatted, but the lack of funds was a much more stubborn opponent.

The constant strain combined with a sense of hopelessness finally affected even Girolamo's and Caterina's personal relationship. Caterina, tempestuous by nature and hypersensitive because of her pregnancy, could no longer bear the provincial life. Its combination of bland routine and financial worries wore her down. Girolamo, who once had envisaged himself as one of the major figures of Renaissance politics, saw his expec-

tations largely disappointed. His frustrations and Caterina's
fed fuel to the arguments the spouses had over Tolentino, the
costs of whose services offered the most likely reason for the
quarrels.[28] He was a valuable man who demanded to be paid
well and promptly. For a while Caterina thought she could find
a way out of her unpleasant marital situation by going to
Milan and surrounding herself with memories of her youth.
But Lodovico il Moro, who knew Caterina's motive through his
plenipotentiary in Forlì and Imola, Giovanni Francesco Oliva,
politely declined her request for an invitation. He spoke of the
plague which had lately claimed a few victims in Milan. Also,
Caterina and her husband should first become reconciled. An
occasion to visit Milan would present itself soon when the
marriage contract for Bianca and the son of Matthias Corvinus, king of Hungary, would be signed.[29] Caterina rejected such
reasoning.[30] The plague, she told Lodovico, did not frighten
her; she had lived with it in Rome all the time.[31] Since she was
pregnant, she would not postpone her trip for too long. As for
the suggested reconciliation, she considered it accomplished. At
one point she just announced her coming. Once in front of the
gates of the castle, who would deny her access to her childhood
home? But Lodovico, helped by the patient work of Oliva,
won. The marriage was superficially repaired. The frustrations
stayed and so did Caterina, but not Tolentino. He entered the
service of Venice.[32]

Far as the spouses were apart on most issues, they agreed on
the one necessary step to take in the financial crisis. The once-
granted tax exemptions must be revoked, and for that purpose
the representatives of Forlì must be persuaded to relinquish the
privileges granted to the city in the capitulation of 1480. Common sense and not arrogant disregard for the principle of eq-
uity dictated this solution; but the people would hardly come
to such assessment of the ruling couple's motivation, and as a
result, much of the Riario's attempt to gain a true rapport with
their subjects would be nullified.

At this point various kinds of advice came to Caterina and
Girolamo from prominent Forlivesi with whom the couple con-
sulted. The most ardent advocate of a cancellation of the tax
concessions was Niccolò Pansecco, a city notary and a supreme
opportunist who always lent his support to what he considered

the winning side.[33] He even made the tempting offer to carry the case of the Riario through the combined councils of the *anziani* and "the Forty." When Girolamo expressed reservations about the idea, Pansecco openly pronounced his contempt for the people of Forlì, "who will turn as the wind blows." [34]

There were voices of caution too. One belonged to Lodovico Orsi, the prominent Forlivese who was Giovanni Livio Riario's godfather. Another was that of Andrea Chelini, who was chairman of the Council of Forty and had been a member of that delegation which in 1480 handed Forlì over to the Church's captain, Federico da Montefeltro. He thus knew the story of the tax concessions from the beginning. Chelini also respected the people and the law more than Niccolò Pansecco did. While the latter told Girolamo that he had no respect for the Forlivesi, Chelini gave the count a long dissertation on justice and keeping one's given word.[35] A few days later Chelini died. His death came from natural causes, sinister rumors notwithstanding.[36]

Girolamo yielded to the advice of Pansecco, which held out the promise of additional revenue.

On December 27, 1485, Niccolò Pansecco, true of his promise and being one of the *anziani* himself, spoke for the Riario in the combined session of the Council of Forty and the *anziani,* a group even further enlarged on this occasion by numerous influential citizens.[37] His oratory, flowery and well designed, did not fail to impress the one hundred and fifty men present— *cavalieri, dottori e anziani* (these last being the representatives and officials of the four quarters of the city, San Biagio, Porta Schiavonia, San Mercuriale, San Pietro) . Pansecco conjured up the supposedly horrible times under the Ordelaffi, "who ate our hearts, even reached into our entrails, filled the dungeons with innocents, ruled arbitrarily and arrogantly, and persecuted us like dogs." [38] Then came, he said, Count Girolamo—"an angel sent by God, benevolent and most merciful, a gentle lamb and without evil; a deliverer from despotism and a savior from the beastly Ordelaffi." [39] And did not everybody remember the dreadful period under Pino Ordelaffi, the "Cain Nerone"? Now the angelic Girolamo and his family were in dire need. Money was lacking for the most necessary things, even for paying officials. Could those who had derived nothing but benefit from that man look callously on and do nothing? Of course not.

Thus the once curtailed or abolished taxes should be restored. Girolamo rose and expounded on the noble and lofty duties of a prince to his subjects, on how he protected them, cared for them, and provided law and order. But he, too, must live, and in addition he had duties as host and representative of the state, costly duties indeed. The tax reductions and exemptions were clearly the objects of his complaints although he carefully avoided naming them. Then he moved to leave, his face sullen and desperate. The magistrates and councilors stopped him. Pansecco, sensing his moment of triumph, called for an immediate renunciation of the granted privileges. The radical suggestion numbed the assembly. Nevertheless, when called, one man after another got to his feet and agreed to the renunciation. Cobelli, the chronicler and eyewitness, remarks: "Oh, reader! Many certainly agreed under tears and sighs; the Lord alone knows how voluntary their renunciation really was." [40] Girolamo mustered a gracious smile and word for each of them. Then the session was over. The Riario had regained for themselves the full right of taxation. On January 2, 1486, the "new" old taxes were once more enforced. The spoils of the victory of the Riario also reached the Pansecco family. Niccolò Pansecco and his son became collectors of the weight and gate taxes. [41] In their jobs they showed neither consideration nor mercy; they confiscated freely. Those who went to the scales and those who brought the firewood through the gates cursed them loudly. "Ser Pansecco, may you perish in misery." [42] Resentment and unrest mounted.

Old specters soon returned to haunt the Riario. Hatred within one family helped Girolamo to overcome the first one. On Good Friday, 1486, Girolamo was watching the bustling crowd in the square. At his side stood a citizen who suddenly advised him to seize a man just about to cross the square with a lamb on his shoulders. The arrested man was no stranger to the Riario: Antonio Butrighelli of Forlimpopoli, ex-conspirator against Girolamo, returned exile through Girolamo's mercy, and a cousin of the man who had denounced him, Bartolomeo di Giuliano Morico. [43] The denunciation evened the score in an old family grudge. Carefully tucked away in Antonio's clothing was found a letter in which Antonio Maria Ordelaffi announced to one of his friends in Forlì that he would storm the gate of

San Pietro with six hundred men on that very day. The chief victim was to be, of course, Girolamo. Conveniently all the conspirators were listed in the letter. The plot was promptly foiled, and Butrighelli was hanged.[44]

While such Ordelaffi conspiracies proved a constant threat to Girolamo and Caterina, they were still manageable as long as the patricians, a goodly number of the city dwellers, and the mass of the peasants of the *contado* ("county") did not conspire.[45] Therefore, when in the spring of 1486 signs of unrest showed among the peasants, Girolamo moved fast to find an equitable solution to the problem.[46] The quarrel centered around the protection of the peasants' fields by guards (*cavalcanti*) and the fees paid to the count for that service and for the court (*balia*) which handled damage claims. The *cavalcanti* had been arrogant, dishonest, and too expensive at that. With unaccustomed benevolence and alacrity, Girolamo settled the problem to the satisfaction of the peasants.[47] With the agreement, much of the discontent disappeared from the countryside. In this case the weather helped the Riario; after two dry years a good growing year cheered the peasants.

13

POVERTY, THE MOST bitter enemy of the Riario stayed on, however. It was worse than the plague which came to Forlì in April, 1486. During this epidemic the Forlivesi could not complain about their ruling family. Girolamo and Caterina remained in the city and went to church with the people to pray for relief from the dreaded malady. When the number of the sick and the dead failed to diminish, the couple called in a doctor, a surgeon, a special priest, and two undertakers. These men were paid good salaries by the Riario on condition that they help the poor and the rich alike and not shun contact with those disfigured by the pus-covered and evil-smelling biles of the disease.[48] Eventually the plague faded, but not the poverty.

Despite some relief from the new revenues, poverty kept a

tight grip on the Riario, paralyzed their actions, and granted not a moment of respite. Soldiers and bodyguards were no help against it, nor was there any escape. On the few occasions when the grand politics of Italy touched the life of the Riario, their poverty was trumpeted to the world.

One such occasion occurred when the last rumblings of the Barons War reached Forlì. On a September day in 1486, Alfonso of Aragon, the duke of Calabria, approached Forlì in pursuit of Roberto Sanseverino, the famous *condottiere*.[49] For a few days Roberto's forces had camped around Cantalupo while he hoped to get the right of passage through Bolognese territory. Girolamo's and Caterina's position was embarrassing, since they could not support Roberto Sanseverino, who had acted contrary to papal orders by not dissolving all of his army and swiftly leaving the Papal States. Nor, on the other hand, would it have been wise to act or speak out against him.[50] The Forlivesi gave Roberto their support because one of his captains was the beloved Tolentino. In the end the Bentivoglio refused the free passage,[51] and Roberto had to dismiss his men.

Now the Forlivesi were ready to greet Alfonso, the duke of Calabria, and he rode into the city drab from the wounds of famine and plague.[52] The palace and all life in it was gray in its mood. Girolamo lay in bed stricken by a severe sickness, which he was never afterwards quite able to shake off. The sacredness of the custom of hospitality led, nevertheless, to an invitation for Duke Alfonso to stay in the palace. He pretended to have urgent military business and declined the invitation. He spent the night with his soldiers near the Porta Schiavonia. But he did dine with Caterina in the company of such famous persons as Virginio Orsini, Gian Giacomo Trivulzio, and Antonio Pico della Mirandola. The meal had few courses, no delicate specialties, and no drummers. Afterwards the duke went to his *osteria*, startled and perplexed by a lady who in the midst of impoverishment had kept her courtly bearing. Many people of Forlì felt honored by the presence of such noble guests and accompanied them with lighted torches to the *osteria* in which they lodged. The duke's soldiers repaid these courtesies poorly: the countryside was filled with looting and cruel soldiers, who senselessly destroyed whatever struck their fancy.[53]

As the days of late fall, 1486, ran their course, poverty tightened its grip on Caterina's life. Most of her jewels were with pawnbrokers at Bologna and Genoa, and the interest had been accumulating at such a rate that the jewelry's loss was imminent. Caterina therefore tearfully declined an invitation to go to Bianca Sforza's wedding in Milan.[54] She could have afforded the trip, but without splendid dresses and glittering jewels she would not consider it. Caterina felt even more desperate about her marriage, which consisted at that time of little else but misery punctuated by violent quarrels. Whenever she reflected upon her fate she envied the dead their peace.[55] The only consolation short of death appeared to her the often postponed trip to Milan.

There were still enough occasions when the Riario had to spend the money they actually did not have. In January, 1487, Annibale Bentivoglio married Lucrezia d'Este, an illegitimate daughter of the duke of Ferrara. The Bentivoglio had been friendly to the Riario ever since the latter had come to Romagna. They were powerful and close to the Riario territory, and the friends of the Riario were so few that none was expendable. The Bentivoglio would measure the friendship of the Riario and their political status by counting the men and the horses of their delegation and by assessing the value of the gifts they would bring. Therefore the delegation dispatched to Bologna was impressive and consequently altogether too costly. Seventy horses and eighty men traveled to Bologna to bring a piece of white damask valued at one hundred and fifty ducats. And as the delegations from all over Italy piled up their gifts of wine, grain, capons, pheasants, candles, confections, pictures, rabbits, lumber, bronze, pigs, fish, money, marzipan, salt, fruits, sugar, spices, oil, baked goods, and letters of credit, the Riario cut a good figure. Their delegation was only smaller than that of Naples, Florence, and Milan, and their gift was sufficiently impressive.[56]

Girolamo and Caterina had no further interest in that marriage. Another one, closer to Forlì, was more worth watching. In 1482 Galeotto Manfredi of Faenza had married Francesca Bentivoglio because the duke of Ferrara urged him to and the Bentivoglio were powerful allies. From the beginning, trouble had beset the marriage between the forty-two-year-old Galeotto and the seventeen-year-old Francesca. The Ferrara war had interrupted the honeymoon. When Galeotto finally returned from his soldierly duties, he had all too often paid nightly visits to a certain monastery in which "Cassandra," his former mistress, lived as a nun. Not even the birth of a son, Astorre, set things straight.[57] When Francesca dared to speak out against Fra Silvestro, Galeotto's favorite counselor, her husband had slapped her face. Soon after, Francesca fled to her paternal home in Bologna, taking along the baby Astorre. Girolamo and Caterina were not interested in the marital troubles as such, but they eagerly watched the political repercussions. The enmity of Giovanni Bentivoglio weakened Galeotto's position, and the Riario felt a resurging hope that in potential turmoil in Faenza they could take possession of part or all of the Manfredi territory.

In the spring of 1487 the Riario made another of their routine shifts between their two main possessions, when they moved from Forlì to Imola.[58] So precarious did the Riario judge the situation in Forlì to be that they sent the trusted governor of Imola to Forlì. He had shown a great gift for conciliation, and the Imolesi sincerely disliked his departure.[59] Domenico Ricci did succeed in keeping Forlì tranquil.

With Forlì capably administered and with additional revenues secured, Girolamo decided to fulfil Caterina's long-cherished wish for a visit to Milan. The official reason given for Caterina's trip was that she desired to visit her half brother, the duke, and other relatives at the Sforza court.[60] But besides renewing old ties and escaping her grim routine, Caterina wanted to remind the Sforza of Milan that a member of their family co-ruled in Romagna, and that if Riario rule were ever to be threatened Milan could not look idly on.

When she finally traveled, Caterina did so in style—with a large escort of Imolese and Forlivese ladies and some gentlemen.[61] For a few weeks Caterina enjoyed life in Milan. Then a messenger abruptly ended her pleasant stay with the news of the grave illness of Girolamo.[62] Caterina hurried home, together with her escorts and her mother, Lucrezia Landriani, and her half sisters, Stella and Bianca, whom she had invited to come and live with her.

In Imola, Caterina found her husband already given up as hopelessly ill with some glandular ailment. She sent for a number of renowned physicians who came and tried all their skills. Because of, or, if one considers their remedies, despite their efforts, Girolamo's life was saved. Yet his recovery was only from the state of acute illness to one of latent infirmity. From now on Caterina ruled alone in all but name. Another turning point in her life had arrived, and she soon showed what she had learned during her long political apprenticeship.

June brought great restiveness among the people as strange lights and glaring streaks in the form of a lance appeared in the sky. Then Girolamo again fell ill. The natural course for Caterina, who once more was in a far advanced pregnancy,[63] was to refrain from any action which could disturb peace. But this would never be her style of governing, and so it was one of her moves which ended the lull.

With Girolamo's health so precarious, she felt that she had to make preparations for keeping the ruling position if he should die. By this time Caterina had learned enough about the intricacies of power to know that the key to success in this endeavor was to command the loyalty of the most important of the Riario fortresses, Ravaldino of Forlì.

The castellan of that fortress was a certain Melchiore Zocho of Savona. He was one of Girolamo's cronies, whose service propped up the Riario rule in a region in which they were strangers. Earlier Melchiore had sailed the seas: he had become castellan of Ravaldino from 1480 to 1481 and then had served as captain of the papal fleet in the Tyrrhenian Sea.[64] Returning to Forlì in 1484, Melchiore reassumed the castellan position in the *rocca* of Ravaldino. When poverty became too great a strain, Girolamo and Caterina began drawing on any accumulation of coins anywhere. Melchiore, whose ventures had earned him a goodly sum of money, generously extended loans. Girolamo never had the money to repay, and the fortress of Ravaldino had turned into a forfeited pawn. Now it was up to Caterina to test her skill on the thorny problem.

Caterina first tried surprise. In the darkness of night she rode on horseback to Forlì.[65] As usual she avoided the city of Faenza and thus was forced to use the winding and difficult roads to the south, despite her body swollen with child. At the fortress she called for the castellan and demanded admittance and the surrender of the fortress. In her hands she waived an

order from Girolamo. Zocho, standing on the wall, suspecting
that Girolamo had already died, refused to give up the fortress
to anybody but the oldest Riario son, Ottaviano, and only upon
prior payment of the outstanding debt. The latter condition
made him safe for years to come. Caterina knew it and, her
mission having failed, returned to Imola.[66]

The next move relied on treachery, and although there is no
actual proof of this, it was certainly inspired by Caterina. The
man who helped the Riario case immeasurably at this point
was the same Innocenzo Codronchi whom Caterina had ex-
pelled from the fortress of Sant'Angelo in 1484 as not trustworthy enough, and who presently was *capitano dei provvisionati*
("captain of the guard"). He had previously been castellan of
Ravaldino until ousted by the appointment of Melchiore
Zocho. Through all his rising and falling fortunes he had remained loyal to Girolamo and Caterina. He was also still
friendly with Zocho. On many occasions he drank, dined, and
diced with the castellan. It evoked no suspicion, therefore,
when on the morning of August 11 a soldier of Codronchi came
to the fortress with fresh fowl to be prepared for dinner. Nobody noticed that the soldier did not leave as usual, but stayed
on for dinner. After the meal the diners sat on at the table,
Melchiore Zocho seated between Codronchi and a Turkish
slave of the castellan who had already been bribed by the
Riario. Suddenly Zocho was stabbed by the slave, slugged over
the head by the soldier, and slashed by Codronchi, who used a
scimitar he had found in the room. Thereupon the three assassins withdrew into the main tower, raised the drawbridge, and
Ravaldino was theirs.

The city of Forlì was thrown into an uproar. Most suspected
a successful Ordelaffi coup. The presence of Antonio Maria
nearby was common knowledge.[67] The governor, Domenico
Ricci, soon found out what had actually happened and sent a
messenger to Caterina. She was close to childbirth but threw
herself on a horse and galloped to Forlì. A strange interlude
followed. Innocenzo Codronchi in the meantime had acquired
ambitions of his own and refused for a whole day to admit
Caterina. On the next day he let her, with one maid of honor,
enter for a dinner to which Caterina for safety's sake brought
her own food. During the meal the terms for surrendering

Ravaldino to the Riario were arranged, and after three days Codronchi yielded the fortress to Caterina's choice for castellan, a certain Tommaso Feo of Savona. Codronchi accompanied Caterina to Imola and disappeared without a trace. His behavior during the aftermath of Zocho's death had cost him either his life or his liberty.[68] One day after Caterina's return to Imola—a ride on horseback of many miles as she again avoided Manfredi Faenza—she gave birth to her seventh child, a son. Appropriately, he was named Francesco Sforza and nicknamed "Sforzino" after his maternal grandfather.[69]

While Caterina's determined action had put the main fortress of the Riario safely under their control, other problems defied courage and treachery. In July, 1487, Innocent VIII confirmed Ramberto Malatesta in the vicariate of Sogliano and Talamello, leaving to the Riario seemingly no hope that they would ever recover any of the former Zampeschi territory.[70] During the same summer the duke of Ferrara had also seen fit to add to the troubles of the Riario. Ercole d'Este's soldiers had conquered and burned down La Cascina, buildings which had been erected for the benefit of those of Girolamo's subjects who had pastures and fields close to Ferrarese territory at Massa Lombarda.[71] Duke Ercole maintained that the houses stood on his ground and chose this rather dramatic way of showing his rights. Four years of quarrels followed. Back of the incident lay earlier petty events.

During 1486 and 1487 Modena officials had on various occasions confiscated jewelry and materials en route to and from Caterina. Usually the incidents were settled by writing a few letters to the Ferrara court, after which the tax officials released the objects.[72] But the Cascina problem proved much harder to solve. Caterina, facing a superior force and with little of her own to exert, had few occasions to vent her anger effectively. Only when Duke Ercole demanded restitution of articles he had supposedly forgotten on a recent visit to Forlì, and which she did not have, could Caterina tell him to save his insolent words and search his own house.[73]

September, 1487, saw Caterina recovering from childbirth and Girolamo gradually shaking off the after effects of his illness. Hunger brought suffering to most families. The harvest had been pitifully small, and for two months no grain was sold in Forlì. Such an opportunity was too good to be passed up by the enemies of the Riario.

Antonio Maria Ordelaffi, now an honored guest in Venetian Ravenna, struck once more. This time he planned well and used peasants from the village of Rubano under the leadership of the Roffi brothers, Nino, Biago, and Domenico.[74] These were joined by a large number of fellow peasants and some exiles from Forlì. Antonio Maria even claimed, and probably had, the support of Faenza, Venice, and Lorenzo de'Medici. One afternoon the Roffi and a few others fought their way into the tower of the Cotogni gate, killed the castellan who lay sick in bed, and held it. For the first time since 1480, Ordelaffi partisans had gained a foothold in the city. Antonio Maria was supposed to join them with about six hundred men and then to issue a decree that the taxes would be lowered to their former level. But the co-ordination was poor, and by nightfall Giuliano Feo, the governor of Forlì, had won back the gate. After the fight five rebels were hanged and the others thrown heavily chained into the dungeon.

The fight was hardly over when Caterina rode into Forlì followed by the breathless Domenico Ricci. The rebels must have wished that their count had been well enough to deal with them. Lately he had shown an appreciation of justice and mercy in dealing with his subjects. His young wife reacted in quite a different manner. Caterina sensed the grave threat to Riario rule in Forlì posed by the Roffi conspiracy, which had involved more people than previous plots.[75] She was startled to see how shallow the support for the Riario proved to be. Her pride was wounded, and the Forlivesi learned about Caterina's way of showing such hurt. She sat as judge with full authority delegated by Girolamo. The six ringleaders were executed and their bodies quartered. Parts of them were hung all over Forlì, with their heads, stuck on lances, greeting the traveler who passed through the gates. Those other conspirators who had just run along shouting "San Marco! Church! Ordelaffi!" but had neither known what they really wanted nor expected anything in case of success were dealt with mercifully.

Once more Caterina had been the wellspring of authority and action. To such an extent, indeed, that the people began to murmur that the count had already died and that his death had been kept a secret. Girolamo, weak, pale, and ravaged by fever, had to mount a horse and ride to Forlì in order to quiet these dangerous rumors. His reappearance did quell them, but it also quickened the hatred.

In November, the routine into which Forlì again had settled was briefly interrupted by wondrous tales about the arrival and display in Florence of a gift from the "Sultan of Babylon" to Lorenzo de'Medici: lions, giraffes, exotic rams, loads of balsam, myrrh, pearls, and a tent with forty rooms, gold-plated supports, and a brilliant diamond at the top.[76] Then the excitement waned, and the Forlivesi were once more alone with themselves, their ruling family, and the discomfort of the early winter.

Girolamo's chronic sickness had a peculiar influence on his behavior. At times it increased his irritability and moodiness, while on other occasions it caused a rare mellowness. After the Roffi conspiracy he had hesitated before approving the execution of the ringleaders. Shortly afterwards he displayed a moment of true feeling for his less fortunate subjects.

Toward evening on November 18, 1487, a slim, haggard, blond, twenty-four-year-old Franciscan preacher, Giovanni Novello da Siena, entered the city. His appearance alone startled the people. He wore a white habit, a vest of lambskin, gloves of wolf's skin, a black hood, a felt cap; he was barefoot and carried a four-foot-long iron cross.[77] He took lodging in the hospital and announced two sermons to the people of Forlì. On the occasion of the first sermon the count ordered all shops closed, and people streamed into the square. There Giovanni Novello exhorted the Forlivesi to establish a *monte di pietà* ("mountain of mercy") or, as others called it, *uno bancho dala pietà*,[78] that is, a fund of money from which the needy could borrow at low interest against delivering some pawns. The Franciscans, the shock troops of the *monti di pietà,* had enemies in plenty: the usurers, those allied with vested interests for reasons of profit, and even the ever-distrustful Dominicans. But when Giovanni Novello preached, life stood still in Forlì. Girolamo and Caterina listened from a palace window. A second sermon was preached in the church of San Francesco, and Novello made an important and unexpected friend in Girolamo Riario. In a compassionate mood, Girolamo offered three hundred ducats of his own money as a contribution toward a *monte di pietà* in Forlì. He also commended Novello to the Council of Forty. There, where some professional and amateur creditors heard his plea, Novello was turned down.[79] He left to bring his message to other towns.

14

THE YEAR 1488 just could not be a good one. God had fore-warned his people through many signs, such as an especially bright new star in the northern sky, an earthquake, a comet, and three fiery streaks in the heavens, a number of collapsed buildings, and particularly, an ominous constellation of the planets.[80]

Paradoxically, the tragedy which was to befall the Riario began with no great plans for conspiracy in Forlì or outside. In the tradition of true tragedy it had its roots in the character of the hero himself. Girolamo, although he had acquired a measure of self-restraint, still suffered from spells of ill temper and a lack of true understanding for other persons. Fate carefully arranged a series of unrelated events.

The first incident involved Lodovico Orsi, who had once counseled moderation in the taxation of citizens but now, when the peasants clamored for relief,[81] told Girolamo that to listen to those stupid peasants was to listen to the devil.[82] Lodovico advised pampering the city and giving nothing but pious asser-tions to the peasants. Girolamo resented this advice and shouted his disapproval at Lodovico. He suspected Lodovico Orsi of wanting purposely to stir the discontent of the peasants in the interest of the Ordelaffi. Soon after, Cecco Orsi, Lodovi-co's brother, was called upon to deliver the rest of the meat tax which he had leased and collected for the previous year.[83] It amounted to two hundred *soldi,* and Cecco did not have the money ready. Words were not carefully weighed in the ensuing arguments, and Cecco returned to his home smarting. The next to be exposed to Girolamo's outbursts was Giacomo Ronchi, captain of a squadron. When he begged the count for his back pay in order to keep his family alive, Girolamo threatened him with the gallows. Girolamo's fury knew no bounds, since he suspected a conspiracy behind these petitions. He was wrong at the moment, but soon "the devil went to work." [84]

In a town the size of Forlì individual grudges and fears remained no secret, and the strange chemistry of conspiracy fused them in short order into a definite plan for action.[85] How much the Manfredi of Faenza and Lorenzo de'Medici contributed to that process has been disputed for many years. Judging from the events which followed, their influence, if any, was certainly small and incidental. To remove the contemplated murder from the low level of a private vendetta, the plan of the conspirators provided for lofty ideals. At a given point the words "Liberty! Liberty!" would be shouted in the streets, thus adorning the action with higher motives, attracting more followers, and soothing the conscience of the conspirators. Coming from the Orsi brothers, who had always championed the cause of the commoners in the city, such protestations of love of liberty even carried some weight.

Girolamo, Caterina, and the people of Forlì were unaware of the mounting tension when the day of judgment, April 14, 1488, arrived.[86] A nephew of Giacomo Ronchi, Gasparino, had innocently agreed to give a signal when the count had finished his supper and dismissed his equerries.[87] Gasparino assumed that his uncle merely wanted to have an undisturbed talk with the count. Actually, the conspirators were already posed for the strike. When Gasparino waved his beret, Lodovico Orsi, Agamemnon Orsi, a son of Cecco who had come to assist his father, and Giacomo Ronchi stationed themselves at the foot of the great staircase while the two would-be-assassins, Cecco Orsi and Lodovico Pansecco, raced up the steps, got the key to the Hall of the Nymphs in which the supper had been held, and opened the door. Girolamo, unsuspecting, leaned on the window sill and breathed in the good crisp air blowing from Rimini. With him were Giovanni di Casale, his chancellor, Niccolò of Cremona, his valet, and Corradino Feo, a relative from Savona. Still not grasping the purpose of the two men who, armed to the teeth, had stormed into the room, Girolamo greeted them merrily. "How are you, Cecco?" Cecco waived a piece of paper and shouted, "I have here a letter, and we shall soon be able to pay your Lordship." [88] Having thus come closer to Girolamo, he stabbed the count in the left side. Now Girolamo knew. He shouted "traitor" at Cecco and tried to flee in the direction of the Riario apartments, alas, in vain. In a last futile gesture, Girolamo dived under the table. The two conspirators seized him by his hair and dragged him back into the middle of the room. Cecco, suddenly too horrified to go on, hesitated, but the captain, used to bloodshed by profession, finished Girolamo off as one slaughters a pig. It all took just minutes; then Girolamo lay dead on the floor of the elaborately furnished Hall of Nymphs.

An attempt to overcome the assassins was made by Andrea Ricci, Corradino Feo, and others, but it failed. Agamemnon Orsi, lay dying, but the cause of the Riario was hopeless.

Niccolò of Cremona ran to Caterina's apartments. There he breathlessly described the murder to Caterina, who had already retired for the night. Under the impact of the incredible news, Caterina lost her courage for a brief span. With all hope seemingly gone, she wept. She understood better than the conspirators the necessities of politics which required the murder of herself and her children. But her despair did not last. She jumped out of bed and assumed full authority. With her servants she pushed the heaviest pieces of furniture in front of the door and ordered the servants to arm themselves. Before she barricaded herself in her apartment, Caterina had in an alert move dispatched a servant to Bologna and Milan to ask for immediate help. Corradino Feo was told to hurry to Ravaldino and order the castellan under no circumstances to surrender that fortress. So coldblooded was the thinking of this woman threatened with death by enemies who now had no need for restraint.

In the darkness, Corradino Feo, Francesco Paolucci, and Lodovico Ercolani, partisans of the Riario, hurried to the fortress of Ravaldino and sought shelter there. The castellan, Tommaso Feo, sent urgent pleas for help to the Bentivoglio of Bologna and to Milan. But these messages had consequences only in the distant future.

In the meantime the city had been aroused. At first curiosity sent many to the Riario palace. There in the square, news of

Girolamo's death spread rapidly. The cries from Caterina's windows confirmed the truth. Soon other voices were heard. Cecco Orsi shouted "Long live liberty! Long live the people!" and those in the square more and more frequently shouted back, "Liberty! Long live the Orsi!" Cecco tried hard to win support by greeting and shaking hands with those he knew. Many artisans had arrived on the scene armed with pikes and clubs. The patricians who had found Girolamo's overlordship agreeable stayed prudently away. The chanting of "Liberty! Liberty!" intoxicated the mob. Curiosity gave way to revolutionary fervor, and tension built up. Yet, though the square was filled with those who would joyfully have greeted the return of the Ordelaffi, the shouts were merely for "Liberty! Liberty!" not for the beloved family.

The first explosion came when a man ran into the square pursued by a band of artisans. He reached the bottom of the stairs to the palace, but there he collapsed under the fierce blows of pikes and spears. It was Antonio da Montecchio, the *bargello*. From her window Caterina screamed for mercy for him, but some of the mob stripped the handsome forty-year-old man of his clothes and set fire to his long black hair. The mob, still not satisfied, tore the flesh from the broken bones.

Then the revolt reached Caterina. Men stormed the barricaded doors, which gave way without great resistance. Caterina became a prisoner. Cool and collected, she kissed her children before the whole group was ushered out of the room. The mob fell strangely quiet while she walked, proud and defiant, through them. There were no catcalls or molestations. The Orsi house provided the first prison for the Riario group.

Presently the mob was deliriously shouting "Liberty! Liberty!" and "Orsi! Orsi!" while it pillaged the palace. The quick ones grabbed the silver and coins of the treasury; the slower ones contented themselves with furniture, linen, household goods, and finally with horses and mules. The guard stood idly by. After all, Cecco Orsi was their commander, and the cause of the Riario seemed irretrievably lost. In the Hall of the Nymphs three of Girolamo's favorite men-at-arms had found his corpse and thrown it down into the square. The mob dragged it by its feet across the square and then mutilated the body, some of them working with their bare teeth. Then they turned back to looting. When the last nail and hinge had been removed, the square emptied, and the palace stood a ghostly ruin. From the side streets a friar of the Black Flagellantes came and lifted what remained of Girolamo's body onto his shoulder. Quietly he proceeded to the sacristy of his order's church. The chapter of the cathedral of Forlì had refused to accept the body of the count, who had showered them with gifts during his lifetime.

The paroxysm of murder and looting was over. The Riario were either dead or prisoners. Forlì had no government. The time for constructive action had come.

The *anziani* and those of the Council of Forty who were available gathered for an emergency session.[89] The conspirators justified their deed with flowery words about freedom and tyranny and the will of God. Forgotten were the unpaid salaries and taxes and their fears of Girolamo. They even hinted vaguely and falsely that the pope had blessed their deed in advance. The Council did not rebuke them. Cecco Orsi, who spoke for the conspirators, had been careful not to touch upon the Ordelaffi cause at that point. Despite the Orsi sympathies for Antonio Maria Ordelaffi, advocating the recall of the Ordelaffi would both have weakened the image of the assassination as a revolt against tyrants and split the ranks of the Forlivesi. Niccolò Tornielli, the chairman of the Council of Forty, proposed, and everybody agreed to, an immediate delivery of the city to Monsignore Giovanni Battista Savelli, the papal governor and protonotary residing in Cesena.[90] This sudden plunge from the lofty clouds of dreams into political deliberations sobered both the Orsi and the people. Tornielli's suggestion may not have pleased everybody but it did conform to the realities of power. During the very night of the murder, messengers carried the city's act of allegiance to Cesena.

The next day Savelli's auditor arrived and took possession of the city. That is, he rode twice around the town square in view of the onlooking multitude. Savelli himself followed a few hours later and repeated the ceremony. He acted without papal sanction, and his success hinged on two possible developments: a quick renunciation by Caterina of her son's claims, and the strong active support by the pope of direct Church rule. For the time being Savelli entrusted the government of Forlì to a new

Council of Eight (*Consiglio degli Otto*).[91] Eight men could more easily meet in a hurry to consider the urgent problems so common in those days.

In a diplomatic move Savelli immediately visited Caterina. He had known the Riario from his time in Rome, where he had been at various times apostolic protonotary, canon of St. John of the Lateran, and vicar of that basilica. He had always despised Girolamo and liked Caterina. Now he was full of apologies for accepting the city under such circumstances. She should not be angered, for his presence did not mean that the pope could not again bestow Forlì on the Riario, particularly on her son Ottaviano. In the meantime she should renounce all title to Forlì and retire to Imola. That city, as far as Caterina knew, had stayed completely tranquil and remained firmly loyal to the Riario. Caterina declined. She would not give up hope of holding Forlì in exchange for the promise of a city which she had in her hands anyway. In doing so she unknowingly placed that last possession in jeopardy.

The city of Imola had indeed stayed true to the Riario; the governor of Imola had seen to it. He had "invited" four prominent citizens into the *rocca* for a renewal of their promise of loyalty. He had also selected eight patricians for the government body which would assist him in administering Imola as long as the Riario's fate was in the balance.[92] The most outstanding of these executives was Francesco Sassatelli.[93] As long as the Riario were legally vicars of the Church, Francesco would willingly co-operate with them. However, should papal policy and Riario desires part company, the traditional pro-papal (long ago, Guelphic) sympathies of the Sassatelli family would bring the influential Francesco into direct conflict with Caterina. Francesco bided his time, but Milanese agents heard him shout "Chiesa! Chiesa!" on one occasion.[94] The loyalty of Imola had shallower roots than Caterina imagined.

Savelli nevertheless gained for her one great benefit. She and her children were united and imprisoned together in the tower of the gate of San Pietro. This arrangement, however, provided no bodily comfort. The small room was crammed with her six children, one illegitimate son of Girolamo (Scipio), Lucrezia Landriani, Stella, and Bianca Landriani (Caterina's two half sisters), and the nurses. The noise was deafening and despair was contagious when the children screamed and the women cried. But gone were the guards with their grim looks and the hatred of a murderous night in their eyes. Now other artisans under the command of three sympathetic men, Francesco Denti, Bartolomeo Serughi, and Bartolomeo Capoferri, kept watch over the family. So sympathetic were they that they looked the other way when messengers came and went and plans were hatched.

Then, once more pressure bore down on Caterina, who now "was haunted like Jesus by the Jews." [95] The Orsi and Savelli were eager to possess the fortresses of the city in order to establish an irreversible *fait accompli*. The success of the revolt was uncertain and the city not firmly in papal hands as long as these strongholds continued to be grim reminders of Riario strength.

The Orsi tried threats of starving Caterina to death—an ill-conceived project, since they needed the fortresses immediately, on that very day if possible. Next they dragged her before the walls of Fort Ravaldino. She pretended to order the surrender. Feo, knowing full well her real intentions, refused. In his answer, which he shouted from the wall, he made it a point repeatedly to mention the duke of Milan. It was sure to infuse prudence into some murderous hearts. Force, then, must be tried. That night Savelli personally supervised feverish preparations for an attack.

The following day witnessed a repetition of the comedy of Caterina's ordering a surrender. This time the objective was the smaller fortress of Schiavonia. The castellan, Pezino da Genoa, proved even less pliable. He ordered everybody to get away from his fortress or he would open fire.

The morning of April 16 saw Caterina back once more in front of the walls of Ravaldino. Again she told Feo to yield; again he refused. Yet finally there seemed to be a break. Tommaso Feo sent a messenger, Lodovico Ercolani, to Savelli to offer a surrender on condition that he, Tommaso Feo, could first have an interview with Caterina and get his pay and certificate of loyalty which would assure him a good name for further employment somewhere else.[96] The interview, of course, must be conducted within the fortress for reasons of security.

Thereupon a bitter dispute rent the city. The Orsi smelled

treachery and violently objected. Savelli and the Council wanted to trust Caterina. After all they still held her children, her mother, and two half sisters. What woman could ignore a threat to such loved ones? After a long argument Savelli gave Caterina permission to enter for three hours.

The drawbridge was lowered, Caterina and some citizens of Forlì walked across, and it was raised again.[97] Before she disappeared, Caterina turned around and hurled profanity at her captors.[98] Then the wait began, and it was to be a long one.

The drama of the hour gripped the participants as it has the imagination of the historians who have related the subsequent events. There are various versions of what happened next. One of them is highly picturesque—not at all out of character with Caterina Sforza—but less likely to be true. It tells how immediately after her entrance into the fortress Caterina mounted the battlements and shouted insults to the Orsi standing below. Thereupon they threatened to kill her children. But Caterina, unimpressed, lifted her skirt and exclaimed defiantly, "Don't you think, you fools, that I have the stuff to make others?" [99]

The actual events do not yield such a colorful story, although they do not at all lack excitement and suspense. Caterina entered the fortress and took command of it. Once inside the fortress, the escort of citizens soon found that Caterina entertained no thought of surrender, either for herself or for her fortress. Their protests left her unmoved. When they hinted that such a betrayal would lead to the murder of her children, Caterina shouted at them the lie that a new infant was just now growing in her body and the obvious truth that she could always remarry and produce others.[100] The castellan on his part added that after a murder of the children he would level the town with artillery bombardments and that the duke of Milan would seek some vengeance of his own. Then Caterina celebrated her escape with a festive dinner. After it, the desire for sleep became too strong, and she retired to a room on the opposite side of the drawbridge.

When the gates of the fortress stayed closed even after three hours had passed, and the treachery became known, the Orsi began to maneuver in order to get their prize prisoner back. They and some of their partisans shouted pleas and threats up the thick walls. The noise swelled when others joined them in

protesting against the treachery. Lucrezia Landriani, Stella, Bianca, the children, and the nurses were dragged to the moat.
The crying, wailing, shouting, and cursing was shattering. Tommaso Feo decided to act on his own. The cannon fired a few
shots over the heads of the crowd. When the smoke lifted, the
people were seen scurrying home.[101] When Caterina, awakened
by the noise, arrived in the front tower, she found the area in
front of the fortress empty. "Now," as a chronicler shrewdly
observed, "prayers will no longer suffice to get Ravaldino." [102]

15

LIFE HAS NEVER been merciful to those who make great plans
but execute them half-heartedly. The Orsi had envisaged the
complete doom of the Riario. For the sake of that great plan
they had murdered; but then they began to maneuver. Their
ruthlessness was the ruthlessness of drunken frenzy, of angry
hearts, and of excited fears, not that of cold blood.

When they left the fortress of Ravaldino that day to return to
their houses, they knew that their case was lost. This unadmit-
ted knowledge oppressed them. Old Andrea Orsi, the father,
bluntly prophesied their downfall. One either kills all of one's
enemies or none, he told them. Now it was too late; and he
cursed himself for having such stupid sons.[103]

There were those who wanted the season of lawlessness prolonged just to satisfy their greed. A mob stormed the pawnshops
of two Jews. One disappointment awaited them: Simone di
Pontremoli had fled in time into Ravaldino and had taken
along his most precious articles. And when the mob poured
into the second shop, owned by a man named Abraham, Savelli
came and stopped the pillage halfway. The time for treachery
and pillage was over. Now naked power counted. From the
fortress of Ravaldino, Caterina had holes shot into the houses
of her most prominent enemies with well placed cannon.

Savelli dispatched messengers to Cesena to summon all papal
soldiers from there to Forlì, with all available siege machinery,

bombards, a *spingarde,* and ammunition. With them eventually came Ettore Zampeschi, who was glad to assist in what promised to be the ruin of the Riario family. Actually the events in Forlì became more and more an indecisive sideshow of history. Their only importance lay in the stalemate they produced within the city. As the hours passed, intervention from outside moved ever closer, as all of the participants were soon aware; and Savelli and the Orsi looked anxiously to the south and the southwest.

Florence was one source of hope.[104] After all, Lorenzo de'Medici had hated Girolamo ever since that bloody Sunday of April, 1478. The Orsi dispatched a letter to him.[105] It overlooked no possibility of stirring the emotions of the great Florentine to lure him into action. Had not the accursed Girolamo spilled the blood of the Medici? Had he not disregarded God and the saints, drunk the blood of the poor, broken his word, and governed like Nero? What a glorious deed it had been to free the city from such a tyrant. The Orsi had succeeded though Girolamo had been heavily guarded, and they had committed the deed for the sole purpose of doing away with a despot for the good of the people and in the name of God the Almighty. The fortresses should not worry Lorenzo, for they would be in Orsi hands in a few days. They, the brothers, however, needed Lorenzo's advice on how to preserve the freedom won. Without his wise counsel—they meant, of course, support—they saw no way to success. Giovanni Corbizzi, who on behalf of Lorenzo de'Medici established the first contact with the assassins, heard the same views expressed.

Lorenzo hesitated. He decided to learn about the situation in Forlì for himself [106] and advised Stefano Castrocaro, a man in his service, to speak with the Orsi brothers. Stefano heard the same complaints about Girolamo, the same optimistic assertions concerning the fortresses, and the same denunciations of tyrants in general. He also received dark hints that the Riario children were where they never would be seen again. All of this he reported faithfully to Lorenzo.[107] Stefano omitted all the brave declarations in favor of the pope and Florence and all the virulent denunciations of the "evil Girolamo." Stereotyped words too often repeated and too lengthy to be reported he called them. More to the point, he added some doubts of his own about the imminent fall of Ravaldino, a fortress with provisions which Stefano Castrocaro estimated to be sufficient for years. He also noted that the Church was slow to support Forlì and that Caterina's artillery had done some good work.

The temptation to push Florentine power and influence deeper into Romagna by taking over Forlì, or at least having it as a protectorate, was strong. To "protect" Forlì, however, would mean a sharp clash with the Sforza and thus endanger whatever little remained of the alliance between Naples, Florence, and Milan. The pope, on his part, would hardly rejoice over Forlì becoming a Florentine satellite. Lorenzo's policy of tying Innocent VIII to him had just reached the culmination of success in the marriage contract between the pope's son Franceschetto and Lorenzo's daughter Maddalena. Forlì was not worth giving up the fruits of such a success. The road from Florence remained empty. No soldiers, no money appeared, not even messengers with the cheerful but empty promises so abundant in Florentine foreign policy.

Even worse, Lorenzo's decision not to intervene did more than deprive the Forlivesi of direct help; it also influenced those who always prudently inquired first about Florentine policy before they made their own decisions. In this case Giovanni Bentivoglio, the ruler of Bologna, took Lorenzo's attitude as permission to join Milan in her endeavor to support Caterina.[108]

There still remained Rome. The pope clearly was Forlì's overlord. His protonotary Savelli had taken possession of the town. Surely help must come from there. During the early days of the rebellion the Council of Eight had dispatched four prominent citizens to Rome [109] to assure the pontiff of the undying loyalty of the Forlivesi, to bring him the document of capitulation, and to ask for troops to protect them. Innocent VIII savored the urgent declarations of love for the *libertà ecclesiastica*, but his preference for the status quo remained stronger. His first concern was for the safety of Caterina and her children in order to "avoid a scandal involving a person beloved in all of Italy." [110] Only if it were possible without offending Milan and Florence would he assume direct control over Forlì and thus oust Caterina and her children. As a small step in that direction, Innocent VIII slyly proposed to remove Caterina and her children to Cesena "for their own good" and reminded all powers gently that Forlì was under the overlordship of the "patre Universale." [111] He had not yet heard that Caterina had found a solution to the problem of her safety. And so the roads from Rome also remained empty, with no soldiers marching north, no money arriving, and again not even messengers with a promise.

As for Venice, the Republic of San Marco favored any solution which would not disturb the political situation in Romagna too much. Given such a detached attitude, nobody tried to gain Venetian support, and the Republic exerted no influence on its own.[112]

At last soldiers approached Forlì, but they came from the northwest, from Milan and Bologna. The Bentivoglio contributed eight hundred men-at-arms and a thousand foot soldiers, and Lodovico il Moro had dispatched some of his best captains, Galeazzo Sanseverino, Count Pietro della Valle, nicknamed "Bergamino," and Rodolfo Gonzaga, with three thousand men-at-arms and an even larger infantry contingent. Giovanni Bentivoglio had asked the Manfredi for permission to cross through Faenza with his troops. The answer of Galeatto Manfredi, a bitter foe of the Riario, was an emphatic and expected "No." [113] It did not matter, since there were plenty of other approaches to Forlì. Ahead of the main force rode the routine messengers and heralds.

On April 18 a herald of the Bentivoglio rode into the city to demand the reinstatement of the Riario and a guarantee for the safety of the children. He subtly underlined his demands with reminders of the power of the duke of Milan. Despite these veiled threats Forlì was not yet ready to submit. Savelli quietly and firmly asserted the papal claims and demanded the surrender of Ravaldino and the retreat of the Riario to Imola. The Orsi, anxious to leave the rift between the Forlivesi and the army as deep as possible, shouted insults at the herald.

The people, however, had a keener sense of changes yet in the making. Why, for example, should Savelli, if he were really sure of his success, send such prisoners as Lucrezia Landriani, Stella (one of Caterina's half sisters) , and her new husband Andrea Ricci (Savelli himself had performed the ceremony) to Cesena? Some of the artisans promptly deserted and went to work for Caterina in the fortress. Their wives were brought to the moat to call back their husbands; the Orsi threatened to kill the wives and their children if the deserters did not respond. The gesture was futile.

Where was Antonio Maria Ordelaffi in these days of high promise for his cause? He limited himself to an unusual action. On April 20, he went from Ravenna to the environs of Forlì.[114] Growing dissatisfaction with papal policies strengthened the pro-Ordelaffi sentiment in that city; [115] but since no faction in town was willing openly to support him, Antonio Maria fell back on a scheme tried once before in 1480. One day two letters were brought to Caterina, shot into Ravaldino attached to two arrows. They both told the same message: Caterina should marry Antonio Maria Ordelaffi and thus secure her and her children's position in Forlì. In a letter to Duke Ercole of Ferrara, Antonio Maria admitted to being the author of these letters.[116] Few persons heard of the incident, but Caterina remembered it well. The Florentines, however, knew about it and shared Antonio Maria's disappointment when no answer came.[117] They would have welcomed the renewal of the Ordelaffi *signoria* under the circumstances of such a wedding, since Antonio Maria and his new wife Caterina could only have gone to Florence for assistance.

Letters came from Giovanni Bentivoglio to Savelli demanding that he leave the city which belonged to the Riario. The threat of an invasion could actually be felt now. The people became insecure and restive. Just in time, two papal breve arrived to assure the Forlivesi of forthcoming papal support. At least the Forlivesi thought the letters to be papal breve and Savelli left them their pleasant illusions. Actually the letters had been written by a relative of the governor, Cardinal Savelli, and had no official character.[118]

On April 21 another envoy arrived, accompanied by a trumpeter, this time from the duke of Milan. He never got to see the Council of Eight that day. Both men were taken by a mob to the Orsi, who shouted at them, threatened them with death, and finally detained them in an inn. Yet the power of Milan was already close. The night had hardly waned when an orator from Milan appeared to protest the detention of the envoy and his companion. He received both an apology from the embarrassed Council of Eight and the return of the envoy and trumpeter, but no other concessions. Some of the spirit of the rebellion was still alive, as two agents from Bologna found when they tried to smuggle a letter for Caterina into Ravaldino. They were swiftly hanged.

Savelli went about his duties unperturbed. The pope had commended him for his actions and promised all possible support. Savelli now made preparations to take Fort Schiavonia.[119] For that purpose he stationed his artillery—one bombard, one *serpentina,* and one *spingarde*—in the gardens of the houses on the northwest side of the town. The Orsi had the cannon shoot at Ravaldino with much noise and little effect, but Savelli reaped his first success. The fortress of Schiavonia surrendered. Pezino da Genoa, the castellan, another of the Ligurians so trusted by the Riario, though able to withstand cannon fire, succumbed to the lure of twelve hundred ducats.[120] A few days later came a second limited success. On April 28 another Ligurian, Battista di Savona, surrendered the fortress of Forlimpopoli in return for the payment of four thousand *soldi*.[121] Some say that he was unaware of the army which approached Forlì from the northwest, others that he was short on food. This success called forth more cheers of "Chiesa! Chiesa!" Significantly the name of the Orsi was no longer attached to them. Such spells of enthusiasm were precious now, and few.

The moment of decision was approaching. The Council of Eight assembled and dispatched two respected citizens to Rome with urgent pleas for succor. There the pope had issued a breve on April 24, which asserted papal jurisdiction over Forlì without giving a resolute promise of support to the *communità Forlivese*.[122] Innocent VIII cleverly tried to use the cardinal of San Giorgio in order to block Caterina and Milan from regaining influence in Forlì. The cardinal was to name a castellan and a governor for Forlì and to convey a *procura* for the Riario sons. The question of who would govern until the oldest son came of age remained unanswered and purposely so.[123] But the time for such ruses had long passed.

On behalf of the Council of Eight, the Orsi brothers once more pleaded with Lorenzo de'Medici for his active support.[124] He was the last hope of a brave city before Caterina and Milan would again have their way. Savelli wrote, too.[125] They all learned now about the light weight of noble sentiments and lofty words when balanced against the interests of states and soldiers.[126] While all kinds of high ideals were at stake, Lorenzo simply had the small castle of Piancaldoli in the county of Imola occupied and annexed to Florence.[127]

Then the great news came, spreading immediate gloom: the Milanese and Bolognese forces had reached Villanova and Cosina, both points close to Forlì.[128] There they were, thousands of soldiers, adventurers of all kinds, women camp followers, and plain rabble, all of them lusting for pillage and greedy for easy gain. The chances were good. No enemy army was in sight to contest the violent dreams. The city was waiting like a sacrificial lamb to be offered on the altar of righteous punishment for its crimes. On the popular level, such lofty explanations for governmental action became good excuses for satisfying greed. Mercifully, according to the rules of the *quattrocento,* negotiation must precede any slaughter.

The diplomatic wrangling was opened by the illustrious noble who headed the pillage-greedy army, Galeazzo Sanseverino, count of Caiazzo, a trusted general of Lodovico il Moro and later his son-in-law. The messenger chosen to convey his terms to the Council of Eight was the Milanese Giovanni Landriani.[129] He argued with the city officials in simple terms: Sixtus IV had invested Girolamo Riario and his heirs as lords of Forlì; therefore Milan and Bologna and their allies, Naples and Ferrara, asked for nothing but the restoration of the legitimate and legal Riario rule.

The city spoke with three voices. Savelli gave the legalistic answer, that the Riario never had paid their dues and therefore had forfeited their claims. The second voice, the Council of Eight, meekly seconded this, though in their hearts they were already trembling for their lives. The third voice belonged to Cecco Orsi, who thundered threats, told of the Orsini coming with a papal army, and cursed his opponents. When all three factions had declined a last conciliatory move to name two temporary administrators, one for each side, and to wait for a decision by the pope, the die seemed cast.

In the strange ways of politics, the joy of pure and senseless defiance overcomes faintheartedness. Although terrified, the people still shouted "Chiesa! Chiesa!" Rumors bolstered this

sham confidence. They spoke of a huge papal army under
Virginio Orsini which supposedly had reached the environs of
Forlì. Landriani had to return emptyhanded to the camp of the
invaders.

When the rumored army appeared at Forlì, it turned out to
be a mere fifty horsemen. Precious few indeed; and to the
consternation of the Forlivesi they disappeared into Ravaldino,
a gift of Cardinal Raffaello Riario to his aunt.

One of those moments when the turning of the tide of events
can be acutely sensed was close at hand. The revolutionary
current had run its course; the counter current could not yet be
felt. For a historical second a strange lull, an indecisiveness,
replaced fluid developments. Rome remained silent; Florence
did not stir. The fountains of hope, real and illusory, had dried
up. Those who misjudged the realities of power in the hours of
murder and pillage were left to curse their leaders.

At Cosina the soldiers knew that victory would be theirs and
planned for their version of judgment on Forlì. The army
prepared for the march on the city; tents were folded, dishes
and provisions were packed, arms were made ready and tried,
and the bags which would hold the loot were lovingly stored
away. Nothing stood between the greedy military with their
accompanying mob and the city. The Forlivesi braced themselves for the oncoming storm. Some went to the camp to be-
friend a soldier in the hope of protection, but most were busy
hiding their small treasures, even the utensils of daily life. Just
as anticipation of the terror to come was gripping the city,
however, Caterina, planning ahead, intervened and vetoed the
pillage. Her action was prompted by neither love nor compassion for her subjects. On the contrary, she was bitter, vengeful,
and contemptuous. But she saw clearly that a conquest and
sacking of the city was not in her interest. The hour of Caterina's victory would also be the time when her interests and
Milan's would no longer be entirely the same. Lodovico il
Moro had regretted the murder of Girolamo as one regrets any
disturbance of a favorable situation. But he was not too much
grieved by the murder itself, since as he saw it, "we shall govern
as long as the children are small." [130] At this point Lodovico il
Moro did not feel much respect for Caterina's governing ability. He saw in Forlì a future clientele city and in Caterina a

pliable puppet. A looted Forlì, filled with hunger, misery, and hatred against Caterina would serve as an excellent pretext for a long occupation of the city by Milanese troops.[131] Unwittingly the city co-operated with Caterina in its own salvation. The guarding of the gates of the fortress was haphazard, and the messenger who carried the order for the troops to postpone temporarily their conquest of the city slipped through.

She was furthermore helped by the mood in Forlì. "And on that day the people started to murmur and to fear and to wonder that the envoys sent to the pope had returned no word and no succor." [132] Thereupon the cannons of Ravaldino shot into the city spiked bombs carrying placards saying: "My people, people of Forlì! I tell you to punish and kill all enemies. For it I will consider you my good brothers for evermore. Do not hesitate to act, and fear nothing, because the deed will benefit you and your children. And if you fail to act you will regret it in a few days." [133] The Forlivesi, who had been plunged in deepest gloom, sensed a way out. The first mutterings against the conspirators were openly voiced.[134] The Orsi and their supporters learned a belated lesson about the fragility and shiftiness of popular support. They decided on a desperate gamble.

In the dark of the night, with all houses securely locked and dark for fear of the approaching army, the conspirators and fifty men hurried to the gate of San Pietro in order either to seize the children of Caterina or to kill them outright. As hostages they could be used for bargaining; as corpses they would stimulate desires for vengeance and erect an unscalable wall of hatred between Caterina and her subjects. But the guards who watched over the family refused the demands to deliver the children into the "protection" and "custody" of the conspirators. Perhaps they did so out of loyalty, perhaps only out of a keen sense of the true situation. The "no" was followed by stones thrown from the tower and the threat to ring the alarm bell.

A short time later riders left Forlì in an easterly direction. Their bags and pockets were stuffed with jewelry and silver plates taken from the Riario palace. Lodovico Orsi, Cecco Orsi, the Ronchi, the Pansecci, and some of their male kinsmen rode into bitter exile.[135] The moment of hesitation was over. The opposing current had risen, and the realities of power had over-whelmed revolutionary dreams.

The people filled the streets, shouting themselves hoarse: "Duca! Duca! Ottaviano!" The great bell of the city rang to wake those who were sleeping through the anxious wait for the army. While the people milled in the streets displaying their new brand of partisanship, the first articles removed from the Riario palace were stealthily returned to it.

The eighty-five-year-old Andrea Orsi and the wives and children of the conspirators who had fled scurried into hiding. Andrea found shelter in an empty tomb, and the women sought refuge in San Domenico. Savelli and his officers were arrested. Ettore Zampeschi escaped at the last minute.[136]

The sounds of joy and celebration also reached the army. There they spelled an end to dreams of new and easy riches, of gallons of wine from broken kegs, and of women at the mercy of their violators. They foretold coming days of unbroken routine filled with vague hopes. The rabble from all over Romagna who had joined the army in expectation of loot went home with their sacks for carrying plunder sadly empty.

IV

LADY
OF
FORLÌ
AND IMOLA

16

AT DAWN ON April 30, 1488, the days of Caterina's deliverance and triumph began. The Council of Forty and the *anziani*, as constituted before Girolamo's murder, called on her to express their unswerving loyalty. Caterina awaited them in the fortress of Ravaldino. She held her fury in check long enough to thank the men graciously. But that act of submission was the last thing the officials did for a while. Deeply wounded by the experience of the revolt and disdainful of her subjects for their turning with the political winds, Caterina suspended all agencies of self-government in Forlì. She wanted to be the governing lady without limits.

To the persons close to Caterina it still appeared, however, that she felt merely grateful for having escaped from dangers and that she harbored not bitterness. Her men went out to bring Ottaviano, her oldest son, from the gate of San Pietro. Before he met his mother he circled the square three times amidst a cheering population. After that tears flowed generously in Forlì: Caterina cried when she saw her children again, the children wept, and so did the people, who were touched by the scene. The popular hatred of a few days ago inexplicably yielded to joy, childlike and ephemeral.

As a pleasant continuation, a shower of rewards fell on those who had helped Caterina—the guards at San Pietro, especially the Capoferri, Serughi, and Denti, and the army whose mere presence had toppled the Orsi. But at the same time there appeared frightening forebodings of the vengeance to come. With official encouragement, the same mob which only days ago had been wildly enthusiastic about the conspirators now gathered around the houses of the Orsi, Ronchi, Galassi, and Pansecci to celebrate victory with a thorough pillage. Through the city moved hunting parties to flush out conspirators and their families. A cavalcade of men hurried east to Forlimpopoli to catch all traitors there. Hour by hour the dungeons filled with prisoners, wretched figures in chains, frightened, hungry, and miserable.

Sounds of joy nevertheless drowned out the moans and shouts of suffering. Caterina made her triumphal entry into the city while soldiers lined the streets.[1] The procession moved through the Cotogni gate into Forlì. At its center rode Caterina, surrounded by the *condottieri* in shining armor and nobles in splendid attire. The people shouted their approval. Their relief over having escaped so lightly from a grim menace was apparent. Mass was celebrated in San Mercuriale, where Caterina entered through a passageway formed by pikes and lowered standards. Afterwards, Ottaviano once more circled the town square three times. At the age of twenty-five, Caterina had wrested from destiny a moment of supreme triumph.

Then everybody moved to the fortress of Schiavonia which still had a castellan appointed by Savelli. He held out for a few concessions, especially for all his possessions at Cesena and an official release from Savelli so as not to be labeled a coward and an easy turncoat. Then Schiavonia, too, was Caterina's.[2] Forlì was now firmly in her hands. Two squadrons of troops remained in the city and the rest stayed in the suburb of Ravaldino. As a concession to the duke of Milan, she had to appoint the Milanese captain "Bergamino" as governor of Forlì.[3] His task was not burdensome. The Forlivesi had all but forgotten their revolt of a few days ago. Cowed by the military around them and deserted by their leaders and by the pope, they gave themselves up to that by-product of political upheaval, the naked gain of looting.

The same night, the first fruits of Caterina's deliberations showed in the decrees which she ordered "cried out" to the people. Those exiled enemies of the Riario who had returned after Girolamo's assassination would have to leave within three hours or they would hang on the gallows. All institutions of mercy which commonly sheltered refugees must now deliver them to Caterina's agent.[4]

While the crier made his announcements the mutilated body of Girolamo, buried in unconsecrated ground near a column of the cathedral, was exhumed. For three days it lay in the church of San Francesco. Girolamo found his final resting place in the cathedral of Imola.[5] The cathedral of Forlì and its chapter, on the other hand, were treated by Caterina with scorn for having refused to accept Girolamo's body on the night of the murder. A callous act it had been, since he had lavished money and privileges on them and had faithfully kept brothels and slaughterhouses at a safe distance from the house of worship.

The dinner concluding the day of victory was given in the house of Luffo Numai. The Numai family, whose members had a keen sense for the changing of political tides, was one of the most respected in Forlì. The Numai had held high positions under Pino Ordelaffi. Upon his death they had assessed the situation and decided to back Girolamo Riario against Antonio Maria Ordelaffi. During the revolt of the Orsi, Luffo Numai had wavered ever so slightly, but had soon judged rightly where the real strength rested. Indeed, he had initiated the turn of the tide after the Orsi had fled. Now he spared no cost to be a generous host. The table talk did not avoid the problems of the day. The captains insistently urged Caterina to permit a partial sack of the city. Later, soldiers came with the captured Battista di Savona and his followers, who had surrendered the fortress of Forlimpopoli to Savelli. Caterina's disposition of this case was easy and predictable: to the dungeons they went. Then a large delegation from Imola arrived. With them came Francesco Sassatelli, the well-known patrician of Imola, whose faithfulness had been in doubt for a brief period. All of them assured Caterina of the unbroken loyalty of that city. Finally there was, all through the dinner, Luffo Numai, who wanted a pleasant word, an assurance of renewed grace. Afterward, Caterina returned to the fortress of Ravaldino in which she preferred to live during the coming months.[6]

Some in Italy shared Caterina's exuberant joy. In Milan, the illumination of buildings and special processions were ordered.[7] In Rome, the mood was considerably less buoyant. An ill concealed anger over the swift Milanese success prevailed at the *curia*. But those who had not acted when the opportunity beckoned could now do little but choke their anger.

As the sounds of triumph receded in Forlì, the dissonances of brutal vengeance began to dominate everything. On May 1, Caterina sent for Matteo Babone of Castel Bolognese, her instrument for the vendetta. He was a frightful looking man, tall, fat, and sly, who moved a contemporary to cry out: "Oh, Madonna! How horrible to look at him. He cannot be a Christian; he must be one of the dreadful Turks." [8] We are assured, however, that Babone had the necessary skills to be a *bargello*—one "with that special skill and experience." [9]

One of those periods was close at hand in which Caterina ignored her courtly manners and brushed aside all the proper restraints so patiently acquired in the Sforza castle and at the Roman court. She yielded to her always strong desire for action. This time it was fueled by the raw anger Caterina felt over the audacity of the Forlivesi who by assassinating Girolamo and looting the Riario palace had made a mockery of Caterina's image of the human cosmos. Power and its violent assertion was the prerogative of the elite. Caterina, shocked and outraged, was about to stage a spectacle of brutality as a lesson to the mob on the duties of subjects.

The chase was on in earnest. [10] The old Orsi was soon betrayed, dragged out of his hiding place with a rope around his neck, and set upon by his captors who kicked, insulted, and spat upon him. He joined the dozens of others in the dungeons who wailed and despaired. There Gian Griffone, Savelli's captain of the guard, had been secretly strangled. Other executions became public spectacles. Marco Scossacarri, fifty-five years old and healthy looking, paid for having thrown Girolamo's body out of a palace window. From the same window he was dropped into the square with a rope around his neck. When he reached the ground soldiers dismembered his body and proudly and jocosely carried its parts on lances. In the same manner died the young Pagliarmo, a Ronchi and Ordelaffi partisan, and Piero Albanese (Cobelli calls him Niccolò Maccto), who unwisely had made insulting remarks about Caterina across the moat of Ravaldino. Soon the piazza was littered with human limbs and pieces of flesh, and covered with blood. During the following night the merciful friars came and buried whatever remained.

Trembling, the people obeyed a new edict to restore all stolen property to the Riario. A few hours later everything was accounted for except what the Orsi had taken, and that was not the least valuable.

On the next morning the drummers woke the people and summoned them to gather in front of the Orsi house. [11] There they found old Andrea Orsi, dressed only in a vest, a shirt, and one sock, with his hands tied behind his back. Yet somehow he still conducted himself proudly. Babone forced him to watch as hundreds of peasants, artisans, and soldiers swarmed over the Orsi house to demolish it. After the walls had fallen, bundles of wood were ignited to burn whatever remained except stone, mortar, and dust. Then Andrea had a chance for a few last words. He cursed his sons, implored the people to be wiser than he had been, and recited the Lord's Prayer for his own soul. For the moment the people were stunned into silence. Then the lust for blood won out. They cheered Babone when he put the Orsi on a board with his head hanging over and tied the board to a horse's tail. Three times, in mockery of the custom of taking possession, the horse galloped around the square. Then the soldiers cut the body to pieces, one carving out the heart and biting into it, others throwing the fragments to the people. Half a day later the friars were allowed to proceed with their work of mercy. Sobered by a few hours distance from the bloodshed, the people fell into a desperate sullenness. Caterina herself seemed to tire of the vengeance, since during the same day she set all arrested women free. But during the night more houses of opponents were demolished and enemies executed.

Compared with the preceding days the third day of May was mild. The city lay quiet. In Ravaldino, Caterina dined with the four commanders of the army, Galeazzo di Sanseverino, count of Caiazzo, Count Gian Pietro della Valle ("Bergamino" or "Brambilla"), Rodolfo Gonzaga, a brother of the marquis of Mantua, and Giovanni Bentivoglio, *signore* of Bologna. She paid her respects to these men whose coming had saved her, and thanked them in gracious words.

After dinner she staged still another spectacle designed to emphasize her triumph and to give her a firmer rule over Forlì.[12] Caterina had gained power over Forlì by means of arms, but at that point she had no legal right to govern the city. A pledge of loyalty by all prominent Forlivesi was to bridge the legal gap until the hoped-for papal confirmation would arrive. With her sense of pomp and circumstance Caterina made the loyalty pledge a memorable occasion. The men of Forlì had been ordered to gather in the fortress of Ravaldino. Now they were led in groups of twenty-five into a large, dimly lit room for a face to face encounter with Caterina. Seated behind a large table, she lectured them on their duties, told them of the advantages of obeying, and of the dangers of conspiring. After the lecture each group took an oath of loyalty to Ottaviano as their new lord and to Caterina as their temporary regent. The notary Francesco da Palladino, standing at Caterina's side, and a missal, prominently displayed, were to impress upon the Forlivesi that they should not take their pledge lightly.

In order to smother all sparks of revolt which might still have been aglimmer she did two more things. First, edicts were "cried" and affixed in the town square. A fine of ten lire and three strikes with a whip were the penalty for those who carried arms to which they were not entitled. The streets must be cleared after the great bell was rung. Then, on the next day, she added some more pomp and circumstance—a solemn procession, a thanksgiving mass, and a renewed taking possession of the city by Ottaviano. The masses must understand that the Riario were again lords of Forlì.

Gradually the city returned to normalcy. Caterina released Savelli, who never had much to fear, in return for the hostages he had sent to Cesena.[13] When he left he had to part with his artillery. Caterina considered it bounty of war.[14]

Yet there were still unresolved matters of vengeance. A premium of a thousand ducats was put on the head of each of the conspirators at large. Five hundred ducats would be paid for an assassination of one of them.[15] In addition their slayer or captor would receive a landed estate and a pension for life. The premium was attractively high but remained an unsuccessful incentive. The conspirators had scattered all over the peninsula. First they had tried to remain in Cervia, a town located safely in Venetian territory and close enough to Forlì in case the Orsi fortunes should rise again. The podestà of Ravenna thought differently and ordered them to leave. From there they went their own ways. The Orsi brothers fled south, where they eventually found an employer in the signore of Camerino.

A thorny problem was the Council of Eight which had governed the city during the Orsi and Savelli dominance. One after another of the Eight was led to a furious Caterina, who gave them a stern lecture.[16] For four of them that was all of the punishment because of the benevolent intercession of the

Serughi and Capoferri. The other four were saved from being executed by intercession of the Numai family and exiled to Milan.

Simone Fiorini's confrontation with Caterina was the most dramatic. The tall, strongly built man approached Caterina on his knees. With the rope dangling around his neck he muttered the perennial excuse of the unsuccessful rebel: "Oh, glorious Madonna. Be merciful with a miserable sinner. I went to the square out of mere curiosity since I had heard that the *bargello* had been killed. There I saw the dead Count and, carried away by the uproar around me, I shouted 'Traitor.' But that is all, and soon I knew better." [17] Caterina, hardly in a mood to appreciate such excuses, shouted: "Let vengeance rule, not pity. I shall let the dogs tear you to pieces." [18] In the end, however, it was exile to Milan for Fiorini too. The estates of all four exiles enriched those who had supported Caterina. Of these four two would reappear in Caterina's life, Niccolò Pansecco and Simone Fiorini. Pansecco, once a trusted advisor of Girolamo, did not accept his exile lightly. One day he fled Milan to go to his home in Cotignola. Caterina's *bargello* Babone and his men caught and killed him. Fiorini was luckier. He also fled, but escaped Caterina's men. For ten more years, however, she tried to get her vengeance.

The Milanese army departed, except for "Brambilla" and a sizable contingent of men-at-arms.[19] With the army went Ottaviano, but only as far as Imola where he was acclaimed *signore*. A number of Forlivesi went all the way to Milan. Some, among them Bartolomeo Serughi and Lodovico Ercolani, went to express Caterina's gratitude; others, four members of the revolutionary Council of Eight, were forced to go along as exiles.

Outwardly the rule of law was re-established. For the sake of appearance, the killings prompted by vengeance were duly legalized by retroactive acts of the *podestà* of Forlì, Count Pietro da Cantagallo.[20] He also ordered still other executions. All along, the Nanni family had hated the Riario. The father, Giovanni Nanni, had lost his life in the conspiracy of the Cotogni gate in 1487 (the Roffi conspiracy). The sons, Paolo, Stefano, Andrea, and Scaramuccia, had therefore needed no urging to join the Orsi after the assassination. Bursting with hatred, the Nanni brothers had proclaimed loudly that their greatest joy would be to kill Caterina.[21] Now they were arrested and doomed.

During the late spring of 1488 some lustre was returned to embittered Forlì by Cardinal Raffaello Riario.[22] The young frightened cardinal who had innocently furthered the Pazzi conspiracy had long since become a powerful man in Rome. Affluent and influential as papal *camerlengo,* he was just then building his startlingly beautiful palace in Rome. The money came from the cardinal's benefices and his luck at the friendly gaming table. Now the cardinal of San Giorgio approached Forlì in style. He had with him three bishops, numerous protonotaries, a hundred and fifty retainers, and a hundred horses. His presence in Forlì did many things. It showed the belated papal approval of Caterina's conduct in the face of the bitterness of those who had sincerely trusted the good will of the pope; it enabled Caterina to exhibit the influence she wielded at the papal court, fickle as this influence would many times prove to be; it brought some gaiety back to Forlì, as could be expected from a person who could see no merit in denying himself and others the pleasures of this world.

The cardinal had hurried to Forlì in order to offer his counsel to Caterina, whom he did not trust to govern prudently.[23] Caterina's merciless vengeance had left the cardinal and many others in Italy aghast. He wanted to be present when the stage was being set for the future government of his young relative Ottaviano. Raffaello Riario was also the main author of that conciliatory measure in the important field of taxation which was supposed to shore up the rather shaky loyalty of the Forlivesi. Caterina had an edict "cried" which considerably lowered taxes: the grain tax dropped to one *soldo* per hundred *libbre* [24] from the previous one *soldo* five *quattrini;* the salt tax was reduced from fifteen to ten *soldi* per *quartarolo;* [25] and the military tax was reduced by one third.[26] Her display of power and fury was thus followed by a show of magnanimity.

The cardinal's policies of moderation were supported by Milan, which also had sent an advisor to Caterina.[27] Branda Castiglione, a Milanese diplomat and lawyer, had come to Forlì in the middle of May. Through him Lodovico il Moro expected to govern as much as was possible without arousing Caterina's ire, for which Lodovico had fast developed considerable respect. The tenets of the suggested policy for Caterina were prudence in Forlì, sweetness in dealing with the neighboring *signori,* and consultation with Lodovico il Moro.[28] In return, Milan would provide protection and work for a swift investiture of Ottaviano with Forlì and Imola.

This occasion was not long in coming, since Milan and the cardinal of San Giorgio exerted themselves strenuously for it and the pope could do nothing else. Later in the summer, ceremonies were staged with great pomp in Forlì to celebrate the publication of the bull of investiture.[29] It gave the vicariates of Forlì and Imola to Ottaviano and, should he die, to his brothers. Caterina became *tutrice e curatrice* of and for her sons; in short, she received the legal title to govern during Ottaviano's minority.

In the meantime another storm had gathered and vented its fury. This time its center was Faenza, that city which so inconveniently sat midway between Imola and Forlì. There the Manfredi family had more and more come to resemble a powder keg ready to explode as soon as the fuse of hatred should be lighted. Francesca, the wife of Galeotto Manfredi, had returned from her self-imposed exile in Bologna with her father Giovanni Bentivoglio. As the price for her return her husband had, in the summer of 1487, dismissed his favorite counselor, Fra Silvestro, who had always been a thorn in the flesh of the Bentivoglio. He had also guaranteed respectful treatment of his wife upon her return and accepted as guarantors the pope, Lodovico il Moro, Lorenzo de'Medici, and Ercole d'Este. In addition Galeotto, after prolonged resistance, granted Francesca the privilege of bringing with her one lady-in-waiting from Bologna and of visiting her father once or twice a year. Francesca's partisans were delirious with joy.

Thus the summer of 1488 found Francesca back in Faenza with their son Astorre, one lady-in-waiting from Bologna, and a servant named Rigo. No cordial marital relationship existed, however, nor were relations friendly between the courts of Faenza and Bologna. On the last day of May, 1488, the whole tragicomedy ended.[30] Francesca lay in her semi-darkened room, supposedly ill, and watched over by her Bolognese lady. She sent for her husband to come to her with a physician. He obeyed, bringing with him a Jewish doctor, Lazarus. Francesca's servant, Rigo, engaged the latter in a discussion outside the chamber. Galeotto entered it alone and was immediately set upon by three assassins, who held him and tried to strangle him with a long piece of cloth. But Galeotto, who was strong and quick, freed himself. Alas, in vain; he was felled from behind by Francesca who had hidden a dagger in her bed for just such an emergency.

With the murder the passion was spent. Now Faenza became the object of fervent political maneuvering. Milanese, Florentine, Bolognese, Venetian, and Forlivese influences vied for dominance in that city which was subject to the legal overlordship of the pope and populated by people with a fierce spirit of independence. Milan was delighted by the development. Galeotto Manfredi had been Florence's man in Romagna. Now Lodovico il Moro sensed a chance to increase his influence in Faenza. He advised Caterina to support Francesca with all her might in the interest of both the Manfredi and the Bentivoglio cause. Caterina had little reason to ignore the advice of her powerful uncle. The Bentivoglio had always been friendly to the Riario. Nor could she act contrary to Lodovico's wishes as long as his soldiers were busily upholding her rights in Forlì. Besides, with either a grateful Francesca or the young Astorre governing Faenza, that city would cease for quite some time to be a threat to Caterina. The pope acted slowly in this political game, willing to let the people of Faenza settle their problem of succession and to invest their choice with the city. Giovanni Bentivoglio on his part had hoped all along to become the real ruler of Faenza, either directly or as tutor of the boy Astorre. Francesca and Astorre themselves were secure for the time being in the fortress at the Porta Imolese. Giovanni Bentivoglio, quietly supported by Lodovico il Moro, moved first with the aim of establishing himself as the "protector" of Francesca and Astorre. Early in June he arrived in Faenza with a few soldiers. "Brambilla" had come from Forlì with a sizable detachment. On June 4 the people were even in a festive mood, shouting "Duca! Duca!" for the Sforza and "Sega! Sega!" for Bentivoglio.

Then Florence, which stood to lose one of its footholds in Romagna, fought back. Ridolfi, the Florentine representative, went to work. He aroused a number of Faenza citizens against the Bentivoglio, the "murderers of Galeotto," and saw to it that the *valligiani* ("Valley dwellers") of the Val d'Amone flocked into Faenza.[31] The mood of the people rapidly changed. By three o'clock in the afternoon the populace was shouting "Death to all the traitors." A few minutes later the "Bergamino," Caterina's contribution to the cause of the Bentivoglio, lay dead, and Giovanni Bentivoglio had to escape through a rear window of the palace. Shortly afterward he found himself temporarily in the "protective custody" of Florence.[32]

Caterina could not ignore this alarming turn of events, especially since Antonio Maria Ordelaffi suddenly had appeared in Faenza. But Florence had no desire to let things get out of hand. After Ridolfi had skilfully brought about unrest, Lorenzo de'Medici "graciously" offered his services as mediator. The pope invested Astorre with Faenza under the tutelage of a group of citizens of Faenza and the Val d'Amone.[33] Francesca left for Bologna. The assassins were tried and executed. Milan and the Bentivoglio could not hide their disappointment, but Caterina soon reconciled herself to the solution, which had failed to establish a threatening power between Imola and Forlì.

One young man who just then entered the world of Romagna and of Caterina learned about the pitfalls of being the instrument of a great power. The sixteen-year-old Ottaviano Manfredi, to whom traditional Manfredi family usage would have given the position of *signore,* had had his hour of promise.[34] The Florentines had found him a useful instrument in the early stages of the Faenza crisis. But the better his protectors did, the worse Ottaviano fared.[35] Eventually, only the support of the *valligiani* of the Val d'Amone was left to him. Under the leadership of the Naldi family they had proclaimed Ottaviano *signore* on June 4, 1488.[36] All of that was to no avail. A pensioner of the Florentines in Arezzo and, later, in Pisa, Ottaviano was nourished on six hundred ducats and great hopes.[37]

In Imola and Forlì, the cardinal of San Giorgio meanwhile had continued his generous sponsorship of all that makes life lighter and more pleasant.[38] Before he left for Rome on October 19 he once more counseled Caterina to be benevolent. The advice found Caterina in a receptive mood. Her bloody vengeance had not expressed a wounded woman's fury, but the anger of a lady of station who found it abhorrent that subjects should forget their place in life and proceed to murder, loot, and depose rulers. She was satisfied that they had learned their lesson.

The prophets of gloom who had spoken of 1488 as a black year for rulers could take comfort. In the fall, a serious conspiracy against the Bentivoglio was discovered in Bologna. Then in December, tragedy struck once more closer to home. Francesco Sassatelli, the powerful Imolese, was returning from Forlì to his home town after intricate negotiations with Caterina. Two miles west of Forlì, masked men set upon him and killed him with fourteen dagger blows. The assassins were never found.[39] Was their reason one of the quarrels with the Vaini, archenemies of the Sassatelli, or had his wavering in April cost him his life? The only indication of what might have happened was the distrust which after the murder persisted between the Sassatelli family and Caterina.

17

FOR THE FORLIVESI, half the year passed in daily routine without violence or unusual excitement. The dark and narrow streets of Forlì were filled with slow traffic, the noise of working artisans, and the smells of cooking, livestock, and man. Occasional processions and the erection of buildings cheered the masses, and so did a number of unconfirmed but nevertheless revered miracles. Later in the year the minds of people were concentrated on the price of barley and beans which climbed steadily because of an extraordinarily bad harvest.

Such relative tranquility was also reflected in Caterina's letters of that time. Some of them asked other rulers to permit the export of certain goods, for example, a request to the Gonzaga of Mantua for the purchase of a large quantity of down.[40] Others conveyed gracious words about exchanged gifts, as the customary one hundred salted eels from the duke of Ferrara [41] in return for Caterina's fine rose apples and *maroni confecti*

("candied chestnuts"). Still others replied to Francesco Gonzaga, a horse fancier, who wanted one of the fine horses she was
fond of breeding; and others apologized to Virginio Orsini
because she could not let him have a sparrow hawk for which
he had asked.[42] There were problems, but they were manageable. One such was the quarreling over appointments to the
chapter of the cathedral of Imola.[43] The canons there did not
always accept Caterina's candidates. Additional worries were
provided by the duke of Ferrara, whose soldiers still stirred up
frequent trouble in the area where the two jurisdictions met.

Future problems appeared disguised as joys. At that point a
ceremony staged in Milan would hardly have been grouped
among the problems. It seemed pleasant to send envoys to the
wedding of her half-brother Gian Galeazzo, titular duke of
Milan, to Isabella of Aragon, daughter of the Neapolitan
King.[44] While Caterina's position appeared strengthened by
such close ties between Milan and Naples, the splendid festivities actually were the overture to events which would be tragic
for everybody concerned.

Tranquillity deceives easily because it pleases. But Caterina
knew that her hold on Forlì was tenuous and she recognized the
need for additional strength. She courted neighboring Bologna
now by arresting a man wanted in Bologna, now by holding her
temper when one of her subjects became the victim of a bride
kidnapping.[45] To the Imolesi and to God she offered money,
time, and interest for the benefit of the sanctuary of Santa
Maria del Piratello.[46] Fortunately she did not need to concern
herself much with her relations to the great powers. At that
time Italian politics did not challenge her ingenuity.

Caterina's next problem was not the city or revolt or intrigue. At the time of Girolamo's death she was twenty-five
years old and, as all contemporaries agreed, a most beautiful
woman. The years of marriage to Girolamo had awakened her
passionate sensuality but denied her the full experience of love.
How troublesome it would be for a ruling lady if the desires of
her body and her emotions should clash with political necessities. It surprises only that the first incident came so soon.

It all began with those two arrows shot into the courtyard of
the fortress of Ravaldino while Caterina was still besieged by
the Savelli and the Orsi forces. The arrows had brought to

Caterina the most interesting anonymous advice: for her to marry Antonio Maria Ordelaffi, because his support alone could make her completely secure in Forlì. Antonio Maria, who had shot the two arrows himself, had to wait a long time for his answer. Yet when it came it was startlingly friendly. During the summer of 1489 the handsome and ardent twenty-nine-year-old heir of the Ordelaffi received an invitation to visit Caterina, which he bravely—or should one say recklessly—accepted. Soon he and Caterina were almost invisible for weeks.[47] Caterina, madly in love, kept the young man exclusively to herself in her idyllic country house close to Giardino, four miles from Imola.[48] The summer days spent in that country house were filled with continuous delight for the senses. There were pleasant walks, picnics, ball-playing and, above all, fervent love-making. For the first time in Caterina's life, however, sensual pleasures were ennobled by a love which pervaded her whole personality. She cared little that the people began gossiping about the lovers. Nor did the news strike the people as unpleasant.

Forlì, especially, was filled with joyous expectations, since the Ordelaffi still had plenty of partisans. Rumors began to spread of a forthcoming wedding between the beautiful and intelligent pair. People even designed a new coat of arms by joining the Riario and the Ordelaffi insignia. The over-anxious readied their good clothing and their flags for the festive occasion. Bets were made, and for weeks there was no dearth of what to talk about in the taverns. Then came a sudden chill. In Rome, distrustful of Caterina's government since the days of the bloody vendetta in May, 1488, the cardinal of San Giorgio was shocked by the news of the love idyl.[49] What perturbed the cardinal was not the Caterina found her pleasure in the arms of a handsome young man but that she blinded herself to the possible damage such behavior could do to the future of Ottaviano and her other sons. There were many other young men to serve her passions besides the Ordelaffi claimant to Forlì. In long discussions with Giovanni Lanfredini, the Florentine orator in Rome, Raffaello Riario revealed his fears.[50] Caterina might marry Antonio Maria Ordelaffi and then give Forlì to Lodovico il Moro in exchange for a more secure position in Milanese territory. Or she might just marry and hope for a Sforza-Ordelaffi dynasty in Forlì. In either case Girolamo's sons would inherit little more than frustrated hopes and Imola.[51] Even the pope entered the scene for a brief period. "Because of Caterina's disorderly life" he considered giving Forlì to Franceschetto Cibo, who, though hardly less dissolute, was however the pope's son.[52] This prospect and rumors that Caterina would marry shortly infused urgency into the cardinal's actions. What he did, he did in secrecy. He could rely on a position of strength. Tommaso Feo, castellan of Ravaldino in Forlì, was his relative, and Giovanni Andrea de'Gerardi of Savona, castellan in Imola, was his partisan. All over Italy persons of consequence were willing to help a man who as papal chamberlain had influence to offer and exert. Consequently, by early fall, Antonio Maria Ordelaffi had returned to Venetian territory and once more received a generous *condotta* from the Republic of San Marco.[53]

The Ordelaffi heir, simultaneously deprived of the joys of love and the hope of power, left in bitter disappointment and full of plans for revenge. Citizens who had been openly confident in expressing their joy were fined, whipped, or thrown into the dungeon. For having prepared Riario-Ordelaffi coats of arms, the chronicler Leone Cobelli was jailed until Tommaso Feo, the castellan of Ravaldino came to his rescue.[54]

Caterina once more faced a dreary fall. Her people shared her black mood since the harvest made food dear. The rural people of Massa Lombarda suffered more than was usual from the inroads by Ferrarese soldiers. Hardly reconciled to the abrupt end of her love idyl, Caterina was coping with these and other problems when a vicious attack of quartan fever kept her confined to bed for weeks.[55] Only in October did she regain the strength to govern.

But one cannot rule with the keys to power in other hands. Caterina was again reminded of that truism when she traveled to Imola. Her children had preceded her and had taken up lodging in the fortress. At first the castellan of the fortress bluntly refused to admit her.[56] Later, she was allowed to enter with four innocuous ladies-in-waiting. Giovanni Andrea de'Gerardi, castellan and another of the cronies of Girolamo from Savona, declared himself ready to surrender the fortress for five thousand ducats (four thousand ducats as repayment of loans and one thousand ducats for services) which must be

securely deposited outside of Caterina's territory.[57] Caterina
had neither the money to buy him off nor the power to throw
him out. It was also to no avail that Caterina called on Raffaello Riario. The cardinal hurried north from Rome without
his usual numerous coterie.[58] He established Caterina's nominal authority over the fortress of Imola, but he left the castellan
in office. Giovanni Andrea's cause was just, and in addition he
was useful to the cardinal.

Caterina with her anger glowing at white heat vowed to win
full control over her states. The opening round of that battle
turned out to be a wedding. Caterina honored the castellan of
Ravaldino in Forlì by giving him her half sister, Bianca Landriani, as his wife. In addition, Tommaso received fifteen hundred ducats, not in cash, since Caterina did not possess such a
large sum of money, but in form of the small territory of Bosco
d'Alessandria.[59] Such generosity was equally motivated by Caterina's gratitude for the loyal services Tommaso Feo had rendered in the crisis of 1488 and by her hope for better control
over him and the fortress.

The Feo family, which had established a firm foothold in
Forlì, had followed Girolamo Riario from Savona to Rome and
from there to Forlì, and Imola, eager to prove their loyalty and
to reap the benefits of it.[60] While Tommaso had been the first to
succeed, he was soon eclipsed. Late in 1489 Caterina fell recklessly in love with Tommaso's brother, Giacomo Feo, who was
about nineteen years old, virgorous, handsome, and vain.
Though we do not know the circumstances under which the
first fateful glances were exchanged, we do know the nature of
the love which bound Caterina and Giacomo to each other.
Distant and chaste adoration was the ideal of neither Giacomo
nor Caterina. Her joy over a newly found love was intensified
by her conviction that this time no political necessities would
force upon her another painful sacrifice. For weeks the love
affair remained a well-kept secret and the routine of Forlì went
on as usual.

Forlì bore the hardships of the winter 1489/90 with apathy.
One condition, however, had become nearly intolerable. Ever
since the turmoil of 1488, with its attempted and partially successful looting of pawnshops, Jews had avoided politically rest-

less Forlì.[61] Credit had dried up, and money had become hard to get. In February, 1490, the council humbly asked Caterina to admit some Jews to the city. When with her permission a wealthy Jew from Bologna came to live in Forlì [62] the normal flow of money was restored.[63] The Forlivesi no longer needed to travel to other cities in order to obtain loans.[64] The commune had, however, to give the money-lender securities against financial loss during possible new turmoil in Forlì.

Caterina had full understanding for the financial plight of her subjects. She herself fought desperately to rescue the best of her jewels from the eager grasp of pawnbrokers in Genoa. Presently she stood to lose twenty-five thousand ducats for a four to five thousand ducat cash payment. Of course she could be easily relieved of such troubles if her uncle Lodovico il Moro were to send some subsidies to his niece and her sons.[65] For a man who governed the duchy of Milan in all but name, the sums involved were small. He must have helped her since Caterina kept her jewels.

The joys of love and spring combined to fill Caterina with energy to the brim. When a short political storm raged in Imola, she acted decisively. The feud originated in an old and by now meaningless antagonism. The Tartagni faction (including the Tartagni, Vaini, Codronchi, and Pighini families) espoused the Ghibelline cause, and the Mercati faction (the Mercati, Sassatelli, and Calderini) claimed Guelphic sympathies. The governor, Giovanni Altodesco, was forced to call for help, and Caterina sent an armed detachment to restore peace. The Mercati family was punished with perpetual exile for too quick and too treacherous use of the dagger.[66]

Caterina's next move occurred in August, 1490, and aimed at her becoming the ruling lady of Forlì without limitation. Years of apprenticeship in treachery and cunning helped produce a masterpiece of intrigue. The victim-to-be was the loyal Tommaso Feo, her castellan of Ravaldino and her brother-in-law. As much as she liked Tommaso, Caterina desired a castellan to whom she owed nothing except his pay. Tommaso Feo derived too much independence from his past services to his lady. Foolishly, he had lately displayed a useful weakness. Caterina had at times noted a distinct glimmer in Tommaso Feo's eyes when they rested on her body, which belied the matter-of-fact attitude Tommaso showed her as her official. On this observation she built her plan.[67]

The thirtieth of August was a pleasant but hot day in Forlì. In the morning Caterina entered the fortress with Giacomo Feo and her son Ottaviano. After the noon meal she invited Tommaso to view the new gardens she had laid out. Tommaso demurred with good reason; the gardens were well outside of the walled area he was determined not to leave. Caterina showed no trace of anger over his refusal. The conversation drifted on aimlessly but pleasantly. The burning sun sent both of them to seek refuge in the shade of a large fig tree, where they sat nibbling on fresh figs, talking and jesting. With foresight, Caterina had worn light clothing which in her every movement showed the fascinating beauty of her body. Excitement rose in Tommaso, and when Caterina offered him her arm and invited him to accompany her to her chamber he eagerly obeyed. But after a few steps he stopped. Cold reason had warned his demanded senses that Caterina's chamber was outside the fortress walls. Caterina walked on, turning around from time to time and whispering seductive words. Tommaso Feo followed and stopped and followed. In that manner they crossed the garden, entered Caterina's residence, and went up the winding stairs to Caterina's apartment. Tommaso, now willing to gamble his position for the favors of his alluring sister-in-law, entered the anteroom. There hands fell on his shoulders from behind, and a voice shattered his dreams of erotic pleasure: "You are the prisoner of our Madonna the Countess. You will suffer no harm." [68] Tommaso delivered his sword to his captor, Giovanni Ghetti, captain of the main tower at the gate. Then he fled. He swam across the moat only to find that the gates of the fortress had already been locked. Tommaso was at Caterina's mercy after all. Unwittingly he had even supplied a "just complaint" for her cause. She wrote to the duke of Ferrara that "today at the fourteenth hour it was necessary to proceed with all firmness at my disposal against Tommaso Feo who had been my castellan in said fortress (Ravaldino) and who during all of today has shown an indecent behavior toward me; thus I had to take him prisoner." [69]

Another farce followed the first. Caterina "revealed" to Giacomo Feo what could hardly have surprised him, namely that he had been chosen to succeed his brother as castellan. He declined with a show of modesty; Caterina persuaded him, and finally an agreement was reached. Giacomo would forget his "shame" at being a member of the "disloyal" Feo family and in all modesty accept the offered position. In return Tommaso would be freed and could leave for Savona, bitter and bent on revenge although he was given a forty man honor guard as far as Bologna. Giacomo Feo, who had hired Ghetti, helped unknowingly bring Tommaso's revenge one step closer when he did not pay Ghetti the agreed-upon reward for his part in the treachery. Giovanni Ghetti was wise enough not to protest loudly. Giacomo Feo had become too powerful for that, and Caterina had showered gracious words and gifts on Giovanni's wife, Rosaria Ghetti. She was Caterina's favorite lady-in-waiting and had been given a house in Imola. Thus, on the surface everything had been satisfactorily solved. Caterina on her part was in possession of Ravaldino and—one could say—of Giacomo Feo, too, for at this point she was still mistress of the love affair.

Caterina, flushed by victory, prepared for another attack, this to be waged against that stubborn castellan of the fortress in Imola. She knew how little a daring decolletage would avail her there and hatched a complicated plot. After a proper measure of bargaining Caterina agreed to pay Giovanni Andrea de'Gerardi four thousand ducats. She would deposit three thousand ducats in cash and one thousand ducats-worth in silverware as security with a brother of Giovanni Andrea in Modena. When the castellan, who had generously been given a safe-conduct, reached Modena, all he found was an instrument of payment and a letter of credit.[70] On paper he had been paid; in fact, he had given up the fortress in return for nothing. Deeply chagrined, Giovanni Andrea traveled to Milan in order to protest at the ducal court there the shabbiness of such behavior by a Sforza.[71] In the meantime Caterina strengthened her rule by giving positions of trust to persons who were utterly dependent on her. She established her stepbrother Pietro in the fortress of Forlimpopoli and her stepfather in that of Imola.[72] Both of them apparently had come to Forlì with the expeditionary force in 1488. With the fortress of Ravaldino in Forlì under her lover's command, the keys to power were hers, and Caterina felt reasonably secure.[73]

CATERINA HAD GAINED control of her territory, but now she was gradually conquered herself. Her love for Giacomo Feo turned into a consuming passion. All the world could see it, and the pretense of secrecy became absurd. Lodovico il Moro who worried about his influence in Forlì and Imola began once more to shown concern. Late in 1490 he sent another of his special envoys, Battista Sfondrati, to Forlì as a visible sign of Milanese influence and interest.[74] Lodovico il Moro was not the only one who wondered whether complete abandonment to passion and the duties of governing could be combined without conjuring up grave consequences.

Caterina, happier than at any previous time, neither experienced such anxieties nor knew about them. For the moment all that meant most to her—power, love, health, and beauty of body—were hers. No war and no serious threats interferred. Giacomo partook of her vigorous enjoyment of life. One of the few things which he did not share with Caterina was her interest in collecting and experimenting with cosmetics and medicines. From it came a voluminous book of prescriptions.[75] While her recurrent attacks of quartan fever and her sheer insatiable craving for a beautiful body combined to arouse in Caterina these pharmacological interests, it was her position as the lady of Forlì and Imola which made the collecting and experimenting financially possible.

Letters asking for prescriptions went to *scienzati* and *alchimisti* and anyone who claimed to have knowledge of drugs and magic formulae. Because Caterina was willing to pay good florins or ducats, the prescriptions came in abundance. The Forlivese apothecary, Lodovico Albertini, her special confidant in these affairs, bought both the ingredients and the pre-mixed drugs for her. And although he was eventually left to absorb a debt of five hundred and eighty-seven florins, his dealings with Caterina were on the whole profitable.[76] He had good reason to call her *mia dolce patrona* ("my sweet patroness"). Caterina's thirst for such practical knowledge and drugs caused her on one occasion even to free a prisoner. Lorenzo de Mantechitis had played a prank on Caterina's auditor and for it was serving a prison term. He went free on the condition that he put his supposedly rich knowledge of alchemy at Caterina's service. It proved to be a poor bargain, since Lorenzo had little to contribute.[77]

Caterina's book of prescriptions carefully preserved the results of her enthusiastic collecting and clearly shows her overpowering concern for beauty. It abounds with means of preserving the smoothness of face and hands, untarnished by sunburn, freckles, and warts. Blond hair, another aspect of the Renaissance ideal of feminine beauty, received plenty of attention in a large number of solutions offered for hair dyeing. Some prescriptions dealt with female problems of less routine character, such as ridding oneself of unwanted pregnancies. The preservation of health was another powerful concern. Prescriptions against asthma, toothaches, headaches, sciatica, and other common ailments are not surprising. More fanciful are those against deafness, muteness, all forms of the plague, leprosy, and for the exorcising of devils and demons, as well as an oil to improve one's memory. A third group of prescriptions interested Caterina in her position as a *quattrocento* ruler. These showed how to alter the metallic content of the florin without qualms of conscience, how to make silver from tin, how to mix together an invisible ink, and how to prepare an efficient deadly posion. One of these, the formula for making eighteen carat gold from base matter, fascinated Caterina as late as 1504 when she was gradually losing interest in her collection.

A number of prescriptions resulted from Caterina's own experimenting. In her garden she had areas reserved for growing the necessary herbs.[78] Most of the experiments aimed, however, at modifying known prescriptions, particularly to substitute cheaper ingredients for exotic and expensive ones.

The ingredients called for in the prescriptions were a mixture of the outright absurd and of traditional folk medicine. They included time-proven herbs and materials, such as ginger and saffran against stomach ailments, poppy seeds and opium for sleeping potions, cinnamon for digestive problems, and opium as an early anaesthetic. Other ingredients were of a more sordid nature as in the case of a certain beauty compound which contained pulverized sediments scraped from urinals or the "lute of wisdom" prepared from dry horse excrement.

While in some cases the connection between the drugs and the hoped-for relief seemed to depend on empirical knowledge, that connection eludes explanation in other cases. Roasted mouse or lion meat were the main ingredients of a remedy against frenzy; a miracle water with some thirty odd ingredients could cure all ills; medical oil concocted of olive oil, a skinned white snake, and lard supplied the curing power of many a salve; and a memory water produced from a multitude of herbs was supposed to help the struggling student. There was also the element of the pseudo-connections. Thus it was thought that *finocchio* ("fennel") must be good for diseases of the eye, since the word contained *occhio* ("eye") ; that pulverized coral was good for the heart, since *corallo* resembles *cuore;* that the oil of scorpions must cure plague, since the constellation of celestial bodies called Scorpion was often blamed for the epidemics; that the pulverized tusks of the wild boar would help against *puntura* ("insect bite") since they themselves could puncture things; that talcum found at Cyprus had special powers, since that island was the seat of Venus, the goddess of beauty; and that old olive oil would help old people while fresh oil would better serve the young. In the administration of drugs, number magic played an important role, and three and its multiples were the preferred numbers.

How well did Caterina fare in the battle for a healthy and beautiful body? The quartan fever returned despite Caterina's defense with potions of the Pentafilon herb and strong wine or with a rabbit heart tied in a white cloth and fastened to her chest. But the beauty of her body was another matter. Her natural blond hair gleamed in the sun after being rinsed with any of the lotions of nettle seed or of ivy leaves or of saffron, cinnabar, and sulphur. Her skin was a flawless white, with unwanted hair removed, protected from the sun and with chapped spots healed by the application of a salve made of oils, wax, chickenfat, and mastic. The teeth stood straight in two lines, whitened by daily cleaning with a piece of cloth on which charcoaled rosemary stems or pulverized marble, coral cuttlebone, or mastic were spread. The mouth was then rinsed with a mouthful of good wine. Caterina's blue eyes took on a special sparkle after a washing with rosewater. Her prominent breasts were smoothed to satin texture by massages with a cream of which one ingredient was lard from a male pig. Because, or it may be despite all of this, men celebrated Caterina as an extraordinary beauty. In addition, Caterina knew how to enhance the beauty of her body by dressing well. She lavished much money and effort on her wardrobe.[79] Giacomo Feo could not be blamed for being infatuated.

While her love for Giacomo transported Caterina into "the heaven of Venus and Mars," [80] life in Forlì went its usual course. Her euphoria colored even some of her political actions. Early in 1491 Forlì received two benefits. The instruments of self-government, the *Consiglio dei Quaranta* and *Consiglio degli Anziani* had been suspended since 1488. A city which revolted against and then murdered its overlord did not deserve them. Now Caterina restored the councils.[81] In one of its early meetings the Council of Forty was delighted by a message from Caterina. In line with her new attempt to win popular support she declared her readiness to rid her people in Forlì of two major nuisances: the annual tax for the quartering of troops, and the soldiers who roamed the city streets, smashing things, molesting people and being a continuous danger for the ladies.[82] She would, so the Council heard, erect between the fortress Ravaldino and the Porta Cotogni special military quarters, consisting of forty wooden houses, surrounded by a moat. A drawbridge to be raised every evening would be the only means of access. The soldiers would thus effectively be confined and could no longer bother the citizens. Naturally, the city would have to help pay for the costs of the project by a tax on grain, by carrying lumber, and by excavating for the foundations. A new assessment of everyone's ability to pay quieted some of the murmurs of discontent.

As for Caterina and Giacomo, they were officially just people who understood each other well and no more. Giacomo was referred to merely as Caterina's equerry. Such hypocrisy augmented the rumors of a secret marriage between the two. Also, what should the people think of her pregnancy and the son Bernardino born afterward?[83] Then, everybody knew the truth; some spoke too frankly and openly about it. One old man was brought before Caterina and for his audacity in repeating the rumors was whipped to death.[84] It did not help. Neither was it enough that Giacomo Feo handed the position of castellan of Ravaldino over to his uncle Cesare Feo. The Forlivesi saw Giacomo at Caterina's side when she attended to state business, when she went to church, and when she rested or strolled in her gardens. Early in the year Giacomo was knighted by the duke of Milan on Caterina's urging.[85] He also was the commander-in-chief of her troops and gradually also of all her emotions and actions—a situation which a chronicler bewails, saying, "all this did our Madonna we all know as virtuous, wise, and prudent." [86]

Vague notions of safeguarding Ottaviano's rights and plain envy of Giacomo's sudden fortune soon bred the first conspiracy. In September, 1491, Caterina and Giacomo went to Imola and were saved from serious harm only by a trick of destiny. A carefully planned conspiracy had been hatched in the fortress of Tossignano, close to Imola. It had lately been strengthened by additional construction and the couple wanted to inspect the work done.[87] The Tartagni and the Vaini families, who had neither been enthusiastic about the Riario rule nor shown any gratitude for Caterina's impartiality in the past Mercati-Tartagni quarrels, planned together with the castellan, a Bolognese, to take Caterina and Giacomo prisoners as soon as they entered the fortress. But two Imolesi discovered the plot and the visit was called off. The four main culprits were arrested, interrogated (Cobelli remarks dryly "one can imagine how they were interrogated"), tried, and sentenced to death.[88] Instead of being executed they remained for years in the dungeon of Ravaldino. All through their trial they had insisted on their ardent desire to uphold the rights of Ottaviano against the intruder Giacomo, who alone had been destined to die. Executing the conspirators would, therefore, have looked too much like the vengeance of an overprotective lover. From that time on, some members of the Vaini family, particularly its head, Enea, spent their years in exile, prison, or uneasy liberty.

The Tossignano affair had been like a thunderstorm, frightening but quickly passing. Other problems hung on and on. Relations with the Este became chilly during 1491. Duke Ercole, as Caterina put it, killed her subjects in the area of Massa Lombarda for bundles of firewood in a renewal of the border incidents.[89] He also gave shelter to one of Caterina's worst enemies, Enea Vaini of Imola, implicated in the Tossignano conspiracy.[90] Caterina could do no more than spitefully deny every favor to persons recommended by the Ferrara court and appeal to her uncle Lodovico il Moro for his mediation.

The old specter of low revenues also refused to fade away. Earlier in the year, before the renewal of the quarrel with the Este family, Caterina had had to admit that she could not loan silverware and tapestries to that family since most had been pawned.[91] The occasion had been the wedding of Caterina's half sister Anna to Alfonso, the eventual successor to Duke Ercole.[92] Forced by the circumstances, Caterina had tightened the taxation rules in Forlì, although she knew that antagonism sprouted in Forlì as quickly as mushrooms after a rain. But a dangerous leak of revenues must be stopped. The city dwellers had always felt contempt for the peasants who came into the city on market days to peddle their wares. The two classes co-operated readily, however, in welshing on taxes. Sturdily built, clothed in grey cloaks, and with their hair cropped short, the peasants looked unimpressive, but, as an old Florentine saying went, "the peasant's shoes are rough but his mind is subtle." For a while Caterina had reason to know their subtle ways. Some peasants had found an easy way to escape the payment of the land tax. They had conspired with city dwellers to exploit the tax advantage enjoyed by the latter. Fictitious land sales had proved profitable to both groups. On September 17, 1491, a decree put a stop to this constant draining away of revenue: [93] from now on, the personal permission of Caterina was required for any sale of land, and when that did not help matters, she ordered a year later that the tax was still to be levied on the land even after the sale. Her subjects would have to find other means of cheating.

But 1491 had all in all been a pleasant year, and it ended appropriately: several of Caterina's bitter enemies destroyed each other. Ettore Zampeschi was murdered by his brothers,[94] whereupon Pope Innocent VIII declared their fiefs, San Mauro and Giovedio, forfeit. The day after the murder Caterina dispatched an urgent plea for Milan's help in regaining San Mauro.[95] An old Riario wish moved closer to fulfilment.

19

THE INDIAN SUMMER of the Italian state system continued. Republics, *signori,* the king of Naples, and the pope—all of them basked in it. For Caterina it meant the yearly recurrence of similar joys, problems, and routines.

In January, 1492, Antonio Maria Ordelaffi was heard from once more.[96] He had tempted a certain Giovanni di Piero Solombrino of Villanova and his associate Giovanni di Montanari of Forlì much in the manner "the devil did when he made Eve eat the apple." [97] Solombrino knew the family of the castellan of the fortress of Schiavonia and hoped to use that friendship to gain the fortress. He was soon hanging from the gallows at the fortress and his friend Montanari barely escaped the same fate.[98]

Enea Vaini, too, reappeared in Caterina's life, but this time he lost. His own fault it was. Why did he trust Caterina's safe-conduct pass and commend himself on his knees to her not-so-ample mercy? [99] He had time to ponder that question "in a chamber of the fortress of Forlì." [100] Revenge was one pleasure Caterina could never get enough of. Before she had caught Enea himself, she had harassed the Vaini family by depriving some of their young brides of their dowries. That their father, Cosma Gentile de'Pallavicini, protested from Genoa to Lodovico il Moro availed little. Lodovico's appeals for mercy went unheard, and in December, 1492, she defied all protests and drove the young ladies from Imola.[101] Vaini relatives deserved no mercy.

Caterina put a better foot forward in her dealings with her neighbors. It was not easy, since she had devised new schemes to raise revenues. Checkpoints had been established, and those passing had to pay fees.[102] These new *pedaggi* ("tolls") irked especially the Bolognesi since their merchants and pilgrims used Caterina's roads regularly.[103] In the end, good relations outweighed Caterina's desire for additional revenues and the checkpoints were removed. Caterina knew she could ill afford to create new antagonisms. How unsure she was of her hold on Forlì showed when another attack of quartan fever befell her. Only when the fever and the severe headaches had left her was the population given the news. Even then the household officials did not admit that she had been seriously sick.[104]

The new and ostentatious prudence did not affect her relations with Milan as had been shown in the Vaini case. Relations with Lodovico il Moro became cool and eventually unfriendly. Lodovico just could not find the right approach to Caterina. When he scolded her for the harsh treatment of the Vaini family, she told him angrily that it was she who proceeded correctly and those condemning her who were blinded by passion.[105] She met with outbursts of fury his attempt to withhold supporting funds from her. How could he be so callous as to abandon his loyal relative and servant when she was exhausted and bankrupt? If he were either not able or not willing to assist her, he should at least give her some recommendation to other lords in order to help her obtain loans.[106] Caterina's protest, in turn, had little impact, since despite all her angry words she could not really break with Milan. The special envoy Battista Sfondrati, however, left Forlì either as an official sign of displeasure or because he was convinced of the futility of any attempt to influence Caterina.

With Lodovico il Moro frowning, Caterina at least knew the measure of support she could expect from Milan. On other occasions it had been less easily discerned. Early in 1490, she had fancied herself to have the support of Lodovico for the slowly evolving plans for a marriage between Bianca Riario, Caterina's daughter, and Astorre Manfredi, the young lord of Faenza. On the surface the Bentivoglio, the Sforza, and the Riario worked together for a success. Giovanni Bentivoglio, grandfather of Astorre, had already in 1489 sounded out Lorenzo de'Medici on such a dynastic connection.[107] Caterina had been less subservient and had simply announced to Lorenzo the plans for such a union.[108] Actually, Lodovico il Moro was less enthusiastic about the marriage project than he pretended to be. He advised his main representative in Romagna, Filippo Visconti, neither to encourage nor to discourage the match.[109] Visconti promptly advised Giovanni Bentivoglio of Lodovico's wish and the Bentivoglio, too, began to delay.[110] Lodovico played one of the wait-and-see games which appealed to his inclination for procrastinating, and Caterina, too, had to wait.

Caterina in the meanwhile partook of the joys of life. The hunts, the parties, and the dances, though not elaborate were filled with *joie de vivre*. Love can glorify even the most humble event. In these years of Caterina's life Giacomo Feo was the source of all her happiness and contentment. The dangerous sides of the affair were not yet visible. People whispered about the "jolly widow" to each other secretly. The arrogance and vanity of Giacomo were not yet unbearable, and Ottaviano was not yet old enough to serve as the center for either contrived or genuine conspiracy. The turbulent forces were still sleeping in Forlì.

As far as the whole of Italy was concerned, the stillness of the year 1492 was deceptive. Although the surface was tranquil, undercurrents were already moving below it—currents that would eventually sweep away the protective dikes which had first made possible a self-contained Italian state system. Ever since Lodovico il Moro had muscled his way into the *de facto* leadership of the duchy of Milan, Italian politics had been filled with ominous rumblings. Lodovico had brutally pushed into the role of figurehead the rightful heir, his nephew, the young Gian Galeazzo. The boy's wife, Isabella of Aragon, daughter of the king of Naples, resented such treatment much more bitterly than did her husband, who adored his uncle and otherwise lived in a world of dreams.[111] Thus the hostility of the court of Naples grew with every increase in the power of Lodovico il Moro.

Fearful of the power of Naples, Lodovico il Moro fell back on an old trick of *quattrocento* Italian politics and sought French support. It had worked well for all of the Italian powers who had used it before. The hint of French aid was a powerful threat, though the possibility of an actual French invasion was remote. France in the 1460's and 1470's, and even in the 1480's, had been restoring the strength so badly weakened by the Hundred Years War. Should Lodovico "whose cunning surpassed all rulers on both sides of the mountains" [112] have known that this time the French king, Charles VIII—twenty-one years old and not very intelligent—would greet the invitation eagerly and take it seriously? Charles VIII did not need to be tempted by Lodovico to covet Naples, which once had belonged to the Anjou, his relatives. The French court had become the refuge for many disgruntled Italian exiles, each of whom was only too ready to strengthen Charles VIII in his determination to realize his grandiose dreams of conquest. When, in January, 1492, Lodovico il Moro began to depend on France for support against Naples, these dreams came a step closer to realization.[113] Caterina, who relied on Milanese support for her rule despite all her disagreements with Lodovico, would not be left out of the events to come.

Italy was not yet alarmed. The old *lega generale* languished, and its core, the alliance between Milan, Florence, and Naples, had all but disintegrated. For a historical moment no meaningful alignment of Italian powers existed. Each of the great powers was isolated from the others by personal or political resentment or by plain indifference for the other's fate. Then, the man whose skills, personal friendships, and high reputation had been instrumental in maintaining the status quo, left the Italian stage. Lorenzo de'Medici died on April 8, 1492. He had followed a policy of keeping the Italian states in equilibrium because Florentine self-interest required it.[114] While peace in Italy had resulted from many factors, Lorenzo's work was at least as important as others. Caterina sent condolences to the Florentine government and to Piero de'Medici.[115] She, who considered Florentine support a valuable assurance for her position, was sincere in her regrets. The role which Lorenzo had played as opponent in Girolamo's life had long been forgotten.

The readjustment of Romagnol politics which followed Lorenzo's death did benefit Caterina, however. Faenza was trying to maintain traditional ties with its protector, Florence. The regents governing for the seven-year-old Astorre Manfredi conceived a scheme which would have given Faenza ironclad assurance of Florentine protection: Astorre should marry a daughter of Piero de'Medici.[116] But Caterina need not have worried about losing a prospective son-in-law. Piero de'Medici had no intention of having a Medici become the wife of a mere *signore* of Faenza.[117] But he offered a *condotta* for Astorre, thus reaffirming Faenza's status as one of Florence's clientele states.[118] The solution also left Caterina content since the projected marriage between Astorre and her daughter Bianca Riario remained feasible.

In addition to Lorenzo de'Medici's death, the change of pontiffs in 1492 was in the end detrimental to the prospects for Italian peace. Innocent VIII died in July. For Caterina he had been a tolerable overlord, though not always reliable in his support. The man who emerged victorious from a scandal-ridden conclave as Pope Alexander VI seemed at first likely to improve Caterina's cause.[119] Cardinal Rodrigo Borgia, as he had called himself, had admired Caterina during her Roman years as a connoisseur of ladies would be expected to do when confronted with a beautiful one. As godfather, he had also held her oldest son, Ottaviano, over the baptismal font. Caterina, of course, sent the obligatory envoys and messages to the coronation. They were most graciously received and showered with compliments for their *madonna*. Eventually all of that would mean little when overbalanced by Alexander's love for intrigue, material gain, and his son Cesare. But at this point it was reassuring. Things appeared even more promising when Ascanio Sforza, cardinal, and Caterina's uncle, became vice-chancellor of the Church in return for his decisive support of Rodrigo Borgia in the conclave.[120] The good news gave assurance to the Riario for the undisturbed possession of their territories. It reached Forlì in August and was welcome tonic for Caterina, who was just fighting off a particularly severe onslaught of quartan fever.

While the danger for Italy from the northwest loomed larger and larger, little note was taken of it. Life in Forlì still ran its normal course. In December, 1492, a ceremony marked the dedication of one Riario to the clerical career. The tonsure was given to Caterina's second-born son, Cesare.[121] With his relatives Ascanio Sforza and Raffaello Riario in high Church positions, Cesare's chances of obtaining a prominent and lucrative ecclesiastical office were splendid.

Giacomo Feo continued to do well for himself. He rose higher and higher. He collected revenues and spent them. He rode through the city streets dressed in a red satin coat and short cloak of cloth-of-gold, accompanied by cavaliers and rowdy companions, sometimes as many as a dozen of them.[122] His arrogance reached heights equaled only by his actual power.[123] Caterina adored the dashing young man and paid no attention to the envy and hatred he created. She either did not recognize or did not want to recognize her duty to restrain his overbearing behavior. It might well be that she found those who opposed Giacomo unworthy of consideration. Nothing impressed upon her clearly enough the potential dangers inherent in her love affair. She was so filled with love for Giacomo that as one observer said: "She would rather bury her sons, her relatives, and her possessions, abandon her soul to the devil and her state to the Turk than give up Giacomo." [124] There was still time for the exuberance of love.

Outside of Forlì, however, the French specter had finally shaken some complacencies. Lodovico il Moro regretted his close association with the French and tried hurriedly to rebuild his system of support. On April 27, 1493, Caterina received a letter from the duke of Milan which told her of the formation of a new league between Milan, the pope, and Venice.[125] It was clearly a desperate attempt by Lodovico to cope with the Neapolitan threat without French help. Caterina immediately recognized the difficulties which arose for her from this shift in great power relations. She would have to steer her course between alignment with the new league and friendly relations with Florence, which in turn had allied itself with Naples. The latter camp would exert an even stronger attraction when, soon after, Caterina's overlord, Alexander VI, deserted the new alliance and joined the Florentines and Neapolitans.

Lodovico il Moro continued to maneuver. Seldom have two allies beneath the surface of friendliness disagreed so fundamentally as did the French and the Milanese in 1493. Lodovico sent his wife Beatrice to Venice in order to tie Venice securely to his side.[126] This move, which would have saved Italy much grief, failed because of the curiously detached attitude the

Venetians chose to assume. A major motive for their inaction
was their distrust of Lodovico and his shifty policies. Then
Lodovico went to Ferrara to meet the rulers of Romagna: the
Este, Bentivoglio, Malatesta, Sforza of Pesaro, and an outsider,
the duke of Urbino. The obvious reason for his trip was to line
up support for the new alliance. Although at times he was only
a few miles from Forlì he did not visit Caterina. She and her
subjects greeted his restraint with relief, since he would have
been too powerful a guest for their taste. Signs of his power
were already clearly visible in the bands of armed men from
Milan who roamed through Romagna, seemingly without spe-
cific purpose.[127] Even so professional an observer as Puccio
Pucci, the Florentine commissioner in Faenza, warned Piero
de'Medici that Forlì was in danger.[128] Actually Lodovico il
Moro tried only to pressure Caterina to join the league and, if
possible, to dismiss Giacomo Feo. Lodovico distrusted Giacomo, whom he suspected of having Florentine sympathies.
Lodovico also tried to impress upon Caterina how unreliable
Florentine support was now that Lorenzo de'Medici had
died—"nature would not so soon produce another man of
equal stature." [129] Caterina did not listen. On the contrary, she
established most cordial relations with the new Florentine commissioner, Puccio Pucci.[130] Soon the two exchanged intelligence
on a frank basis. All the while tension mounted in Romagna.

Under such stress two hopes of Caterina proved to be illusions. Her attempt to keep her political actions separate from
her love affairs had failed. Lodovico il Moro's dislike of Giacomo Feo eroded her relations with Milan. After entrance to
Forlì was denied to the troops of the ducal captain, Francesco
Casate, Caterina had to write off Milanese support for a
while.[131] With the cardinal of San Giorgio already resenting
Giacomo Feo as a rival for power to Caterina's oldest son,
Ottaviano, Caterina was driven to link her fate to Florentine
interests and good will.[132] In doing so she had chosen sides in
the arena of Italian politics and destroyed her second hope, that
she could stay unaligned until a clearly superior camp emerged.
It did not matter that formally she remained unattached to
either group.[133] Deeds are better indicators.

In accomplishing her immediate tasks an anxious Caterina
was equal to the occasion. For a while by her orders the city of

Forlì admitted nobody but its own residents. The fortresses of the Riario were alerted, and Caterina herself supervised the preparations for a possible war. Later in the summer she did not leave the fortress of Ravaldino at all. Giacomo as her plenipotentiary conducted inspections and gave commands and in doing so provoked new resentments.

The tension in Romagna faded as quickly as it had mounted, but unfortunately the respite, just like the league between Milan, Venice, and the pope, was to prove short-lived. By this time France stood poised to invade Italy. In May, while Caterina worried about the soldiers crisscrossing over her territory, Emperor Maximilian I and Charles VIII of France made their peace at Senlis. All the French strength which up to then had been poured into the struggle with the Habsburgs could now be devoted to the Italian venture.[134] In Italy the French envoy, Peron de Baschi, went from court to court to gather support.[135] Venice indicated neutrality,[136] and Lodovico il Moro willy-nilly had to pretend to be enthusiastic about the French plans. Thus the trail was blazed.

Still, the news from Milan was good. Bianca Maria Sforza, Caterina's half sister, was to become the wife of Maximilian I, emperor and king of the Romans, in return for a good dowry and, although not known openly, Lodovico's investiture as duke.[137] Caterina cannot be blamed for being too optimistic about the support which she might get as a result of that marriage. She lacked insight into the character of the groom, filled, as he was, with good intentions, high purposes, and lofty dreams, and into the immense difficulties which prevented him from acting decisively. Nor could she know that the beautiful but irresponsible Bianca would have little influence over Emperor Maximilian once the enormous dowry of three hundred thousand ducats had been paid.

Even as late as fall, 1493, Italy was tranquil. The French seemed to encounter troubles in gathering money and soldiers in Lyons, their staging base for the prospective Italian invasion. But then events began to move mercilessly and with great rapidity. In January, Naples crowned a new king, Alfonso II. While his father, Ferrante, had disliked Lodovico, Alfonso hated him and was willing to follow up his obsession with definite political and military actions.[138] Lodovico il Moro knew that only too well. He also saw clearly that his new Italian so-called allies, Pope Alexander VI and Venice, could not be trusted. The pope showed definite sympathies for the Neapolitan cause, and Venice would not overexert itself for the Sforza. Since the pact of Senlis, Charles VIII had become the master of the Milanese-French relationship, and the shrewd Lodovico had momentarily lost his sure political touch.

The French for their part needed no urging. Early in 1494 they dismissed the Neapolitan ambassadors. Despite all difficulties, the French had brought together a powerful army. Its core consisted of six thousand Swiss mercenaries, about fifteen thousand French and Italian horsemen, and a brilliant artillery corps; and it was supported by French infantry of doubtful value and a numerous navy.[139] When these soldiers fought, they disdained the elegant maneuvering of the Italian *quattrocento* style in favor of brutal power. Caterina's world was in grave danger.

V

ROMAGNOL
LADY
AND FIGURE OF
GRAND
POLITICS

THE EXPERIENCED FLORENTINE statesman Giovanni Lanfredini once expressed well in a letter to Lorenzo de'Medici what
the Italian powers now feared, namely that "the strength of the
Most Christian King must be considered and that once he has
entered Italy he will subjugate the land step by step." [1] Maneuvers to strengthen one or the other group of powers were feverishly executed, but they lacked the quality of statesmanship.
Each power tried to save merely itself and thus became either a
helper in the destruction of others or a victim itself.

Caterina could only pray that God would save her the necessity of making grave decisions. While God might have done so,
geography did not. Romagna soon figured in the strategic plans
of the papal-Neapolitan camp. A swift move of forces into
Romagna would threaten Milan's southeastern frontiers, while
naval operations around Genoa and along the Ligurian coast
would stab at Milan's southern flank. [2] The Neapolitans soon
decided to follow such a course of action.

In the meantime the diplomats visited Caterina. Late in the
summer Cardinal Riario arrived as the voice of the pope, who
had aligned himself with Naples after all. Not wishing to mar
the image of her neutrality, Caterina received her illustrious
relative with great honors and pomp in Forlimpopoli rather
than in Forlì. [3] The cardinal was not successful; Caterina remained neutral. His failure was surprising since the pope had
only a few months ago invested Caterina's sons with San
Mauro, [4] thus helping the Riario to recover a territory they had
longed for since losing it to the Zampeschi family in 1484.

Caterina returned from Forlimpopoli raging with anger.
Representatives of two powerful Forlì families, the Marcobelli
and Orcioli, had hurried to see Cardinal Riario minutes after
his arrival and complained of Feo's influence and arrogance.
Knowing the cardinal's thought on the matter they professed to

be concerned about Ottaviano's future. The Marcobelli and
Orcioli did not talk about the disappointment they had experienced when after those days of glory and great influence with
Caterina in 1488 they had seen their prominent position taken
up by the upstart Giacomo. To Caterina their motives for
going to Forlimpopoli did not matter; she was determined to
make them pay for what they had said. Caterina imprisoned
these men who in 1488 had helped her in her gravest predicament.[5] But she soon released them, partly in recognition of their
past loyal services, partly because they were just too mighty to
antagonize in her present situation.

Why must some years be so unpleasant? At that time Caterina could easily have believed that those demons against which
she had long tried to find home remedies bedeviled her life.[6] In
February her supposed good friends, the Florentines, molested
her subjects when they passed through Castrocaro or its environs.[7] A little later, Cesena erupted with factional strife in
which her partisans, the Tiberti family, were threatened.[8] Now
the two hostile Italian camps pressured her for a decision in
their favor while as yet no clear superiority of either one could
be discerned. She decided to wait until the Bolognesi had made
their choice.[9] But armies were already moving, and they would
not pause for Caterina's benefit.

Lodovico il Moro sent Francesco Tranchedini, his top diplomat in Bologna, to persuade Caterina to join him and the
French.[10] He promised her protection against the Neapolitans.[11]
As the time grew shorter he became impatient and bluntly
reminded Caterina of his past services for her. As an additional
lure, Lodovico added the promise of a *condotta* for Ottaviano
and a new friendliness towards Giacomo Feo.[12] A few days later
Caterina was coldly advised that Galeazzo Sanseverino had set
out to occupy her states.[13] She still hesitated to declare herself
for Milan and against her overlord the pope and the Florentines, friends both of herself and Giacomo.

In September the duke of Calabria approached her states
from the southeast.[14] He too needed her territory but preferred
to gain her support without bloodshed, since Caterina's states
bristled with well-provisioned fortresses.[15] In order to garrison
them adequately, her banker, Marcantonio Zuntini, had hired
infantrymen for eight lire each.[16] Caterina's people had been

warned of the imminent danger of an invasion. They had hidden their valuables, and many had taken themselves and their possessions into the security of the fortresses. Finally, after the Neapolitan army had already proceeded past Forlì and was encamped around Imola, Caterina declared her preference for the Neapolitan cause.[17] On September 23, she dined with the duke of Calabria in an open field near Bagnara, since to have received him in Forlì would have destroyed the frail neutrality she still maintained.[18] But two weeks later Caterina officially joined Naples and the pope. To improve her defenses, especially in Imola, Tossignano, and Mordano, she was promised sixteen thousand ducats. She never did receive all of the money, principally because Alexander VI insisted he should pay only a fourth of the sum and not a third as originally agreed upon.[19]

The population, which had lived in great fear, felt somewhat relieved and fraternized with the Neapolitan troops. Caterina showed her good will by having some roads improved, by having her citizens bake bread for the soldiers, and by letting products be sold without taxes to the allies from the south. But the Neapolitan protection was worth little. The Florentines did not provide their share of the funds needed to pay the soldiers, and the duke did not press his initial advantage hard enough.[20]

From the north a large contingent of the French army approached under the command of brilliant captains.[21] As Giovanni Bentivoglio had permitted them to pass through his territory, they appeared at the gates of Caterina's territory with greater speed than expected. Early in October, thousands of Italian, Breton, Swiss, and Gascon mercenaries camped close by.[22] Not being engaged in military activities they spilled all over the area around Cantalupo like a swarm of hungry locusts. Caterina remained confident, that is until the French and Milanese troops showed their mettle. Since Caterina had seen to it that the fortresses of the northern approach received the best equipment, soldiers, and provisions, the French avoided an attack on Imola and relied rather on the conquest of a smaller fortress to make their point.

By the middle of October the garrison and people of Mordano were confronted by a siege army of about two thousand men.[23] Before the city was completely encircled, the governor had prudently sent away many young and attractive women.

With them went messengers to Caterina carrying a fervent plea for help. She turned for assistance to the duke of Calabria, who to her disappointment ordered his troops to stay away from Mordano.

On October 18, 1494, Gaspare Sanseverino, commonly called Fracasso, accompanied by a trumpeter, went into Mordano to offer the defenders an honorable surrender. Count Calderini and Monsignore Gianfrancesco Borelli, the two responsible officials, refused. They told Fracasso that they would rather die for Ottaviano and Caterina. Fracasso returned to his camp after uttering dire warnings of things to come.

The attack on Mordano began slowly. The ravelin was defended bravely by two hundred men, and for a while the French made little progress. Then a cannonshot changed everything. When the French saw some of their men fall and die they became furious. Their artillery shot a breach into the wall; through this and over scaling ladders the enemy swarmed into Mordano. The French mercilessly killed everybody in sight and set fire to the buildings they took. Only the town hall and the local church, in which all remaining women knelt and prayed, were saved. Fracasso hurried his Italian soldiers into the unfortunate city. The people surrendered to them in droves, counting on the mercy of compatriots. But the French resented being denied their vengeance. They shouted for blood, loot, and women. To appease them a certain Giovanni, a German responsible for the Mordano artillery, was publicly and while still alive hacked to pieces. The castellan and the governor were imprisoned, and the loot-hungry French eventually received eight hundred ducats ramsom for the two.

The Mordano incident inflamed the latent hatred against the French in Romagna. Caterina was wise not to be governed by this feeling. She was furious at seeing the French ruin her possessions and torment her subjects; but she also saw the unwillingness of the duke of Calabria to help her, and henceforth cool considerations of the realities of power guided her. Three days after the sack of Mordano her agent held secret meetings with the count of Caiazzo, one of the top captains of the enemy army. The tone of the discussions was friendly. Even as an opponent Caterina had shown her fondness of Milan. Giovanni Taverna, who had sought to reach and implore her on behalf of Lodovico il Moro, had been captured by the Neapolitans. A letter fastened to his clothing told much, and examination under torture would tell more. Caterina had saved the envoy from that ordeal.[24] By October 24, she was once more Milan's ally, which meant at that point the ally of France as well. Somewhat embarrassed by her quick change of fronts, she justified it with the suffering of her subjects and the smoldering ruins of Mordano. In this case the given reason was no pretext.

With impressive fairness she facilitated to the utmost the passage of the duke of Calabria through her territory in his retreat. The Neapolitan soldiers reciprocated by venting their anger and brutality on Caterina's peasants. In senseless rage they burned houses, cut fruit trees, stole and spoiled grain, and dragged men and women along to satisfy their whims. These soldiers had hardly disappeared in the direction of Cesena when the French came. They sacked what remained and stole even the vital seed grain. Wherever they stayed, they stripped the area to the absolutely unmovable. The people were secure only in the fortresses which were closed to outsiders.

Forlì, filled with refugees and hoarded property, was the goal of the soldiers' desires.[25] Tommaso Feo, since November, 1493, back in favor as governor of Imola and now in charge of Forlì, had his hands full thwarting the constant attempts of the French soldiers to scale the walls and penetrate into the city. Only one gate, the best fortified one at Ravaldino, was opened during the day. The Forlivesi became even more apprehensive when they heard that the French had sacked Meldola, Cusercoli, and Castelvecchio and now were roaming the *montagna* ("the valley regions") in search of booty.[26] Caterina, forced into the French alliance by the sheer weight of circumstances, was deeply embarrassed by the behavior of her new allies. She expressed her regrets to the Council of *Anziani* and her hope that the beasts would soon have to leave.[27] All attempts to better relations with the "allies" failed. The French captains refused to pay taxes on any purchase, claiming that a royal decree prevented them from acting otherwise. A market established outside the city for soldiers was promptly looted by the French. Tommaso Feo barely escaped with his life. Even the French commanders found that incident a bit excessive and with the threat of the gallows ordered all soldiers to leave the mills and seed grain untouched. After all, how could the French army provision itself in a country stripped bare of all essentials?

The French stayed longer than expected. Charles VIII, who had crossed the Alps in September, was stricken in the same month by small-pox. The illness forced him to interrupt his march in Lombardy. In the castle of Pavia where he lodged during his recovery, Isabella of Aragon visited him on behalf of her husband, the Duke Gian Galeazzo, who had never had a chance to be the actual ruler, and of her brother, King Alfonso of Naples, who would not much longer be king. Not long afterwards complete tragedy overtook Isabella. On October 20, Gian Galeazzo suddenly died. He had always been frail; recently his "bad stomach" had plagued him more than usual and had responded neither to the rhubarb pills prescribed by the doctors nor to the fresh fish hauled in baskets all the way from the Ligurian Sea on the order of Isabella. Thereupon, this half brother of Caterina was "like a little lamb without reason withdrawn from the number of the living." [28] There were, of course, the inevitable rumors of poisoning, of which the historian can neither prove nor disprove the credibility. All that is known is that Isabella and her four children were henceforth confined to the castle of Pavia and that Lodovico was later proclaimed duke of Milan.

Caterina was still shocked by the sacking of Mordano when a letter arrived from Lodovico saying that "this noon under the jubilation and with the acclamation of all our citizens we took possession of the city and were greeted as *Signore.*" [29] Bells were rung in Forlì and Imola, windows were illuminated, and there was much officially decreed joy. As to her thoughts, Caterina kept her own counsel. Lodovico il Moro was *de facto* duke of Milan, and she would again need his support.[30]

Finally, late in October, Charles VIII moved against Tuscany and ordered the troops in the Forlì and Imola area to join him in his new campaign. On the evening before their departure Caterina entertained in splendor the French commander, Beraud Stuart, *seigneur* d'Aubigny et Ligny, the Italian *condottieri*, Galeazzo and Gaspare Sanseverino, and other Italian nobles.[31] The atrocities of Mordano, the miseries of the people, and the latent hatred against the foreigners were forgotten. Caterina was praised and courted by these men, and she enjoyed it. Giacomo Feo found the affair unobjectionable, since he had been named a baron of France by Charles VIII.

The next day the army departed. Behind them the soldiers left a destitute people whose curses were now shouted, not whispered; also left behind were the French artillery pieces, since the lateness of the season discouraged an attempt to pull these weapons over the steep passes of the Apennines. Before them lay new and ever more victories. The French won with such ease that their very victories became their undoing; the frightened Italian rulers began to scheme against the French army.

Forlì had survived another war and returned to its stolid winter routine. The city's governing lady too resumed her "normal" activities. Francesco Quartieri, Milan's new special envoy, shadowed her closely and devoted his special efforts to watching her relations with Giacomo Feo.[32] Well he might, because storm after storm disturbed that once splendid love affair. Ever since May, idyllic and violent periods had followed each other in the Riario household. But Caterina still granted her audiences while Giacomo sat on the windowsill, splendidly attired and arrogantly interfering in her business.[33] After all, it was he who determined what should be done anyhow. While her complete dependence existed more in Giacomo's fancy than in reality, Caterina's passion for the young man had forced upon her a degree of servitude painful to her pride.[34] She was not allowed to enter her fortresses unaccompanied by Giacomo, to pay her officials, or to remove any of her possessions from her castles.[35] A few attempts by Caterina to assert her independence in such matters led to furious fights, after which she inevitably humbled herself.[36] Caterina had been able to rescue her foreign policy from Giacomo's spell, though that was for the most part easy since they basically agreed in that field. In leaving the papal-Neapolitan camp after the Mordano debacle, however, she had disregarded Giacomo's preferences. In most other regards she had become content with the position of a chattel of her lover. All that mattered was that Giacomo satisfied her longing for love and passionate pastimes. By December, Francesco Quartieri, who in the interest of Milan had hoped for Giacomo's fall from grace, had to write regretfully to Lodovico il Moro that "about the countess there is little to report because she has no other desire in this world than to see Giacomo Feo beloved by your Excellency [Lodovico il Moro]. . . ." [37]

ON A SUNDAY early in February, 1495, Caterina's auditor announced to the crowd which had gathered in the square before mass the good news of a marriage match between Bianca Riario, Caterina's oldest daughter, and Astorre Manfredi, the heir of Faenza.[38] The union had long been talked about, but now that the old protectors of the Manfredi, the Medici, had been swept from power in the course of the French invasion, Faenza was suddenly eager for the match. So was Lodovico il Moro, who so far had skilfully temporized. He saw an opportunity to assert, through Caterina, Milanese influence in unattached Faenza.[39] The people, longing for some kind of cheer, partook joyfully of the festivals staged on the occasion. Nobles of both sides visited each other, and in June, Astorre himself came to Forlì. The actual wedding had to wait. Astorre was only ten years old and Bianca sixteen. The celebrations in the spring of 1495 left only one trace, a number of medals struck for the occasion by Caterina. One side showed a poorly executed portrait of Bianca and the other the three graces. The inscription read: *in te D (omi) ne speravi no (n) co (n) fundar in etern (um)* Psalm 70 (71) .[40]

Spring continued its pleasant ways. The annual Lenten gift of salted eels arrived from Ferrara, and Caterina reciprocated with candied chestnuts. The letters to and from Milan were full of sweetness, with Caterina complimenting Lodovico il Moro profusely on the occasion of his investiture as duke of Milan.[41] Even Cesena, that turbulent city, tasted of peace. But the storms which raged in other areas of Italy soon spread their clouds over Romagna.

A number of powers had begun to listen to the counsel of Lodovico il Moro, who was now thoroughly disillusioned and frightened by the quick and easy success of the French against Naples. After all Charles VIII had an equally good claim to Milan; and his cousin Louis, duke of Orleans, who possessed an even better claim, was already urging Charles to attack the duchy. The league of March 31, 1495, attested to the many other self-interests which the overwhelming French victory threatened. In the league's declaration, Aragon, the Empire, the pope, Venice, and Milan voiced their concern for peace, the welfare of Christianity, the dignity of the papal office, and the preservation of imperial rights in Italy. It all meant that Charles must be driven from Italian soil. Caterina would have to make a choice between Florence, which stayed allied with the French, and Milan, now the leader against France. But for the moment Lodovico il Moro did not force the issue.

The legacy of the French invasion fueled still other unrest. Turmoil involving Caterina again occurred in Cesena. The Martinelli plotted to massacre Polidoro Tiberti and his nephew Achille. The plan was discovered, and the Tiberti took the offensive. They stormed into the crowded church of San Francesco and massacred ten Martinelli and many of their partisans. All through the summer the two factions fought for the control of Cesena.[42]

Caterina unabashedly interfered in these quarrels. Polidoro Tiberti was a long-time friend of the Riario. Moreover her hopes of gaining advantages from the feud increased when Count Guido "Guerra" of Giaggiolo became involved in the struggle.[43] After initially supporting the Tiberti he turned against them, and, by consequence, against Caterina. During the upheaval of the French invasion of 1494, when everybody was busily engaged in his own affairs, Count Guido had helped himself to possessions of Caterina and of the archbishop of Ravenna. Now she hoped that the bitter fight in Cesena would enable her to recover her own and the Ordelaffi's former possessions, and some more. But her ambitions had to be tempered by patience. Late in August a setback in the Cesena fighting brought Achille Tiberti in temporary exile to Forlì. He did not reside long in the house of Francesco degli Orcioli, his relative. After a few days a messenger of the commune of Cesena invited Achille to return, since Count Guido "Guerra" had left the city. Caterina gave him a strong escort of crossbowmen and infantry soldiers. The Tiberti won out over their foes, the Martinelli and the count of Bagno. Caterina, however, could not benefit from their success since at this point Forlì experienced its own upheaval.

At its center stood Giacomo Feo. While Caterina unsuspectingly danced, hunted, dined, and officiated with her beloved consort at her side, the fine webs of intrigue were spun. Caterina's love for Giacomo had sufficiently cooled to make room for reflection on the demands made by her position. On occasion Caterina tried to tone down Giacomo's overbearing manner and to show that it was still she who was the regent of Imola and Forlì. But Giacomo was not ready to change the ways which had brought him so far. He continued unwittingly to feed the anger and resentment directed against him. Giacomo's enemies cursed him, but they also rejoiced, since they knew that every act of overbearing behavior brought closer the hour of vengeance. The Orcioli and Marcobelli waited patiently for Giacomo's fall from Caterina's grace. They were joined by Ghetti, who resented not having been paid for his arrest of Tommaso Feo in 1490, and who fancied himself that with Giacomo out of the way he could become a close associate of Caterina. A noble motive for trying to ruin Giacomo was readily available: Ottaviano's rights must be safeguarded. Such a motive found approval with a powerful man, the cardinal of San Giorgio.

Antonio Maria Ordelaffi also felt tempted to use the increasing opposition to Giacomo Feo for his own purpose of regaining Forlì. One of the Ordelaffi exiles approached members of the Tornielli and Marcobelli families and promised high positions to those who would conspire against the Riario. All along it was assumed that the death of Giacomo Feo was a necessary condition for the success of such a plot. But a letter that found its way into the hands of Caterina brought torture to Giacomo Tornielli and disgrace to some Marcobelli.[44]

Finally Gian Ghetti decided to do what had so far been merely an idea tossed around in secrecy. He had to rid Forlì of Giacomo Feo. The Marcobelli and Orcioli, old foes of Giacomo, had either too little courage or too many scruples to assist him. Ghetti had to proceed on his own. Some men, however, were willing to help: Domenico Ghetti, a relative; a servant who knew how to wield a knife whether to slaughter a pig or a man; and two priests, Domenico da Bagnacavallo and Don Antonio di Valdinosa (Don Pavagliotta), who loved women and money and hoped to gain favor in Cardinal Riario's eyes by the assassination. These men were in a hurry and set August 27, 1495, as the day of the murder.[45]

On that day toward vesper time a cavalcade approached Forlì from the west. In it were Caterina, Giacomo Feo, Ottaviano, Bianca, equerries, servants, and guests. They all sang gaily after a day in the outdoors filled with chasing game, playing ball, and dining on the green. The spoil was displayed on the carriages and on sticks carried by the servants. At the bridge close to the gate of Schiavonia, men waited in hiding until the carriage with Caterina and some of her children had passed. When Giacomo Feo came, they jumped out from under the bridge. Giacomo recognized Gian Ghetti and as usual asked, "How do you do? Where are you going?" Ghetti smiled and answered, "Well! Very well!" [46] while the servant, who had been standing beside Ghetti, speared Giacomo through and through. Then everything happened fast. Caterina turned, saw what was happening, and fled into the fortress of Ravaldino. In the ensuing confusion Ottaviano and Cesare, who had been riding behind Caterina's carriage, sought refuge in the house of the Denti family, fearful of their mother's wrath and her suspicion of their complicity. Giacomo, meanwhile, was further attacked by Gian Ghetti and by the two priests, who stabbed him furiously. Then, terribly mutilated, with his head split open and his throat cut, Giacomo was dragged to a pit and kicked into it. The chronicler and eyewitness Cobelli wept at the terrifying sight.[47]

Utter confusion followed. Gian Ghetti and his fellow conspirators shouted to the world that they had acted for and on the orders of *Madonna* and Ottaviano. Therefore even Giacomo's armed companions gave up all attempts to rescue their lord or to arrest the assassins. The people poured into the square and were met by the two priests in their blood-soaked clothing. The mob took up the chant of the conspirators: "Ottaviano! Caterina!" Caterina's auditor, Giovanni Dipintore of Imola, came to inquire about the cause of the uproar.[48] He listened to the story and to the protestations of loyalty, and, half-believing, sent a man to Caterina for further instructions. When the man returned accompanied by two of Caterina's men, Forlì stood once more on the threshold of a bloody vendetta.[49]

Caterina ordered immediate action against all conspirators. The auditor, who had always disliked Gian Ghetti for personal reasons, now tried to arrest him. The square became filled with turmoil; people shouted, shrieked, and scuffled; the principals of each side attacked each other, and still others tried to flee. Gian Ghetti finally succeeded in freeing himself, but being wounded, was too slow in his dash through the loggia of the cathedral. Armed men caught up with him, split his head, and then vented their wrath on his body. His attempt to escape had, however, distracted attention from the other conspirators, and they slipped away. Don Domenico ran to the house of a good friend, where he jumped into a big chest which in better times had held the dowry of the daughter of the family. The other conspirators scaled the city wall, slid down a rope procured by a certain Pietro Bocchi, and escaped. But they left behind their families and possessions, and this time Caterina's fury knew no limits. When her first husband had been murdered in 1488, she had taken it as an insult to the lofty position of the Riario family. Her brief rule of terror had been a political instrument, and her anger had been directed against the disobedience and neglect of due respect shown by the conspirators and the mob.

Now in 1495, her intense love for Giacomo turned into equally intense hatred for those who had murdered him. She felt utterly alone. Her life-fulfilling love had been brutally destroyed. Treachery seemed complete when even her two oldest sons, by fleeing into the Denti house, cast a shadow on their innocence. In the early days after the assassination, Caterina's loneliness was transformed into a burning desire to avenge, to hit back, to hurt those who had brought misery to her, and to annihilate purely for the sake of destruction. The passions of a woman obliterated all restraints of prudent government.[50]

On the evening of the same day, the house of Gian Ghetti had been given to the mob to vent its lust for loot and for the excitement of destruction. Gian Ghetti's wife Rosaria, the one-time friend of Caterina, and two of her sons were seized, thrown down a spiked well, and left there to die. All Ghetti relatives, however remote, were sent to the dungeons. Days later, one of Caterina's men found the five-year-old son of Gian Ghetti, who had been in the care of another woman, and slit his throat.

Very few in Forlì slept that night. There was too much to be pillaged from houses and too much to hear and talk about. One who permitted himself no rest at all was Tommaso Feo. For him this was the time of perfect vengeance. Ever since the day in 1490 when he had felt Ghetti's hand on his shoulder in the anteroom of Caterina's apartment, he had smarted under the treachery of that act. As governor of Imola, Tommaso had already arrested a Ghetti relative there and quartered him alive. Now, summoned to Forlì by Caterina immediately after the deed,[51] he did not tire of rounding up all the Ghetti and sending them to their deaths or to the dread anguish of the dungeon. They were joined by many others, among them Pietro Bocchi, who had supplied the rope which helped the conspirators to escape. For a short time he had hidden in a canal until Caterina's manhunters had spotted him.

The terror continued. The warehouses of the Marcobelli, so filled with beautiful stuff that it took days to clean them out, were the center of attraction for the mob, together with the houses of some of the Bosi, Olivieri, and dalle Selle. While thus a few got rich the easy way, the women of the doomed families were either hanged or driven from the city with no possessions but the clothing on their backs. Then Caterina's henchmen found the Marcobelli men and threw them into the dungeon, where they died.

The arms of vengeance were long. Don Pavagliotta, who had scaled the wall and then slid down to freedom, eventually reached the safe city of Ravenna. But he did not escape Caterina's fury.[52] In Ravenna he met a man from Forlì who cursed Caterina and persuaded Pavagliotta to go to Ferrara, where he would be even further removed from danger. This friend even offered to accompany the refugee, and the offer was gratefully accepted. They set out and were promptly intercepted by Caterina's soldiers. The "friend" had done a good job for Caterina, whom he loyally served as an agent. Don Pavagliotta found himself in the dungeon of Ravaldino. His mistress, a beautiful peasant girl, had days ago been imprisoned there, and their three children had been brutally slaughtered by Caterina's men.

The somber note in those frenzied days was struck by the funeral for Giacomo Feo. The city streets through which the cortège passed were lit by torches. Every person of rank marched in the procession. Only the sons of Caterina by Girolamo, who were still in the shelter of the Denti house, were absent. But Bernardino, the five-year-old son of Caterina and Giacomo Feo, accompanied his father to his last resting place in the church of San Girolamo. There Giacomo was buried in the Cappella Feo, which he himself had had decorated.

The time of reckoning had also come for Domenico da Bagnacavallo, the second of the priests.[53] Somebody whispered information to the soldiers. They searched the house of Giorgio Gobbi and found the strange dowry in the chest. Taken to the fortress, Don Domenico underwent merciless torturing to squeeze the last fragment of information from him. In his agony he told how he had wanted to do Caterina and the cardinal of San Giorgio a favor, and mentioned the names of the Marcobelli, the Orcioli, and others. Afterwards he received the last sacraments. At dawn the next day he was dragged to the square. There he was beaten to death by brutes while he dedicated his soul to God. For the soldiers his body provided lurid entertainment: they dismembered it and carried the pieces on their weapons as souvenirs.

Days later Don Pavagliotta was the center of still another bloody spectacle.[54] On a Monday, when the piazza was filled with peasants for the weekly market, he was brought out like an animal to the slaughter. While he prayed and invoked Jesus, the curious crowd closed in. Mercifully he was beheaded with one stroke. This time the parts of the body were officially displayed at conspicuous places in the city as a warning to the peasants who passed them that the price of conspiracy was high.

Caterina, who now took a jaundiced view of man's trustworthiness, suspected the older sons to have been accomplices in the crime and let two full days go by before she decided to bring her two sons back from the Denti house. When her soldiers came to fetch them, a hostile crowd surrounded them on the way back as if wanting to protect the children. But after the group had arrived in front of Ravaldino, a few cannon shots took the courage out of the mob. The soldiers carried their charges off into the fortress amidst the curses of the populace. Ottaviano received only temporary house arrest. But Scipio, the illegitimate son of Girolamo Riario, who had stayed with Caterina all along, was put in the dungeon for criticizing Caterina's furious vengeance. After eighteen months he was set free.[55] Paradoxically, however, he was to come back to help her in her blackest hour.

Slowly the bloodshed and pillage waned. The dungeons were still full, and their dampness and stench broke the health of many. In the great hall 'of Ravaldino the cross-examinations went on and on, now legally conducted by the *podestà* of Forlì, Conte Pietro da Cantagallo, in the presence of two notaries. The torture machines were kept busy, and the cries of the victims could easily be heard in Caterina's apartment. But people also began to be released from the dungeons, the exiles became fewer, and wholesale pillage stopped. The first urge for vengeance, aroused in Caterina by violated passion, lost its strength. Already too many had died, among them twenty children. She returned to the realities of her position and her life and found that the horror of the past days and nights had left a permanent mark on her face and mind. As for her subjects, they looked at Caterina with a mixture of hateful disgust and fearful respect.

In the normal ironies of life, the days of horror for many had brought joy and reward for others. The soldiers were thankful for a break in their dull routine. Those who had been quick in pillage and those who had won additional property through legal actions looked with satisfaction upon their gains. The possessions of the conspirators had found their way mainly into the hands of Caterina's favorites and into the houses of various religious bodies. One man was especially well satisfied. Tommaso Feo had been made governor of Forlì as a reward for his loyalty. Another man, the chronicler Leone Cobelli, expressed disgust over the brutality and greed of his fellow citizens. But despite the nightmarish events of the past days, his belief in the beautiful harmony of the world finally prevailed.

THE WOUNDS INFLICTED by the assassination and by her furious vengeance were still raw when Caterina attempted to heal them by dedicating herself to works enhancing the beauty of Forlì and her own comfort. She had the old *palazzo pubblico,* in which Girolamo had been murdered, torn down.[56] The material salvaged from it was used for extensive building projects, among them a new flight of apartments for Caterina (later called "il paradiso") in the southwest ravelin of the fortress of Ravaldino. She also spent much time and money on adorning her new park, which she had laid out towards Busecchio. In this endeavor she imitated many of her contemporaries, who cherished parks for their beauty and the opportunity they offered for entertainment. The park at Forlì was slightly more utilitarian, since mere beauty and amusement were beyond Caterina's means. It contained gardens, orchards, woods, buildings, and opportunities for hunting and for pasture. Where it came close to the city wall, the park was also a military nuisance, if not a hazard.[57]

But the remainder of the 1495, after the cruel days in August, was not only filled with the sponsorship of local projects, religious or secular. Caterina, whose energy was once more abundant, became "desirous to augment and extend her state." [58] In November, 1495, she started her campaign in the area southeast of Forlì; it aimed mainly at Cusercoli and Castelnuovo.[59] Both strongholds, located south of Forlimpopoli, had years ago been Ordelaffi possessions. Castelnuovo had lately been in the possession of the archbishop of Ravenna ("protected" by Venice) and during the French invasion had been pocketed by Count Guido "Guerra." Caterina planned to take the fortress and settlement from him for her own benefit.[60] In Cusercoli she wanted to re-establish the friendly count of Cusercoli, who had been betrayed by his brother in favor of Count Guido "Guerra."

For her venture Caterina mustered a formidable force: Forlivesi under Achille Tiberti, Paolo Bezzi, and Cicognano da Castrocaro, and soldiers from Faenza, and *valligiani* of the Val d'Amone under Vincenzo Naldi. All in all it comprised four hundred men and the artillery the French had left behind. Success came rapidly. Cusercoli fell, and so did Castelnuovo. In addition, Count Guido "Guerra" was decapitated in Rimini,[61] not so much for his numerous misdeeds as for siding with the Milanese and French in 1494 and for profiting from it at the cost of Rimini and Venice. Caterina even had the satisfaction of ordering the destruction of one of the castles of the count of Sogliano, an old foe. Then her expeditionary force returned.

Cusercoli was given back to the count, while Castelnuovo was once more for a few days a Forlivese possession.

Caterina could take castles and win skirmishes, but in the field of politics she learned once more a lesson about the limits of her capability. Every military success brought her a step closer to the interests of the great power to the northeast, Venice. The Republic of San Marco "protected" the interests of the archbishop of Ravenna and of the Malatesta of Rimini. It made no difference that Count Guido "Guerra" was no longer a competitor. Now, Venice threatened with word and deed. Late in November, 1495, Caterina had told the peasants of her county to come, if possible, to Forlì with their beasts and possessions, because in Ravenna a force of *stradioti* [62] and infantry was gathering.[63] In a fast move, that detachment went to Meldola and from there to Castelnuovo. The Venetian *provveditore* gave Caterina's garrison three hours to surrender.[64] This they did. Now, not even the ardently sought papal investiture, if it ever came, could help her. At the end of 1495 Caterina possessed no more territory than at the beginning. Military defeat had one advantage: it removed the pressure exerted by Milan toward stopping her expansionist venture.[65] On the debit side, Venice would remember her impetuous action and be less benevolently tolerant of Caterina.

The Tiberti were more fortunate. In April, 1496, the Martinelli made their expected gamble to return to Cesena.[66] They captured a fortress together with Polidoro Tiberti, women, children, and good provisions. But later in the month, twenty-four of the Martinelli were hanged from the battlements of the wall of Cesena, sentenced to die by the commune. The Tiberti were safe *in perpetuum* and Caterina rejoiced.[67]

Such joys were few in 1496, which did not surprise those who watched the omens. Those for the year 1496 had been none too good. In the midst of winter it had thundered, and then to the consternation of everybody, stones had fallen out of a clear sky. Astorre Manfredi gave his future mother-in-law, Caterina, one of the five stones he had collected. It weighed one and one-half pounds and was shown to everyone in her household.[68] Later in the year lightning struck the fortress of Bertinoro, ignited the gunpowder, ruined the fortress, and killed a few persons. Awed by such occurrences a chronicler cried out: "Oh reader, you can be sure that this calamity is a frightful warning by God." [69] Events confirmed the trust the Forlivesi put in such prophesies. The winter was severe. The weather stayed exceedingly wet all through the growing season and ruined large parts of the harvest. In some months Caterina had to supply five hundred pounds of flour for her subjects at a reasonable price. In February a disease appeared in Forlì, never before seen and puzzling to the doctors. It was called the "French disease," and at that point seemed to the Forlivesi preferable to many other illnesses since it caused only rashes which healed slowly. Thus the great ravager syphilis entered Forlì, with the people unaware of its fatal impact.[70] Another disease killed Bianca Landriani, Caterina's half sister and Tommaso Feo's wife.[71] The summer brought restiveness to the countryside over the tax burden.[72] Both the town and the rural areas were plagued by a serious salt shortage, since the rains prevented the open-air salt flats of Cervia from drying out.[73]

Caterina shared those anxieties and sorrows, but others troubled her more. They derived from the assassination of Giacomo Feo, from a new expansionist policy of Venice, and from the unresolved tension between the pro- and anti-French powers of Italy. These problems, all interconnected, spun a tight web around Caterina which forced her into a desperate struggle for a measure of security and freedom of action. When she rode through the streets of her cities, the people saw a proud and beautiful lady whose appearance commanded respect. Fear was not absent from the hearts of her subjects after those two periods of terrible vengeance which "had the whole Romagna shout to heaven." [74] Caterina's subjects did not know about her brief spells of despair, when governing and being a lady of station became a burden. Would they ever have suspected their fierce *madonna* of writing that if Lodovico il Moro deserted her she would feel like drowning herself? [75]

First there were the dark shadows which fell on the vitally important connection between Caterina and the cardinal of San Giorgio. Under torture some of the conspirators against Giacomo Feo had blurted out incriminating statements against the cardinal. Caterina's secretary, Antonio Baldraccani, traveled to Milan in order to put the matter before Lodovico il Moro.[76] Soon recriminations went back and forth. The pope,

Lodovico, and Ascanio Sforza defended Raffaello Riario's conduct.[77] The matter stayed unresolved. Relations between the cardinal of San Giorgio and the Lady of Forlì and Imola were cool. But when the cardinal fell seriously ill, Caterina unabashedly asked Lodovico il Moro to make sure that her son Cesare would be given two abbacies in Raffaello Riario's will.[78]

The tortured conspirators had in their agonies also uttered the name of the Bentivoglio. Suspicions thus aroused in the mind of Caterina seemed confirmed when Giovanni Bentivoglio gave asylum to a certain Giovanni Battista Brocho of Imola. Caterina thought him to be a confidant of the cardinal of San Giorgio and demanded his extradition. Giovanni Bentivoglio saw no reason for obliging her, and a bitter quarrel ensued. Reconciliation was hardly Caterina's aim when she sent a handful of men to kidnap or assassinate Brocho. She showed no understanding of Giovanni Bentivoglio's and Lodovico il Moro's shock when the plot was discovered.[79] Could they not understand her right to defend herself? Far from being contrite, she threatened to give refuge to the bitter enemies of the Bentivoglio, the Malvezzi.[80]

Such acrimony destroyed the contemplated marriage match between Caterina's oldest son, Ottaviano, and Isotta, a daughter of Giovanni Bentivoglio.[81] In June, 1496, the girl decided on a conventual life and went into seclusion. The Bentivoglio wholeheartedly approved of her decision. Ottaviano, the future lord of Imola and Forlì, now seventeen years old, was too busily engaged in his first love affair to notice. The lady of his heart came from a lowly carpenter's family. In June, 1497, a daughter was born to them,[82] the first and only child of the affair [83] which ended in 1499 when Ottaviano lost much more than this lady.

A rude shock came from Faenza, the city located between Forlì and Imola. Early in 1495 the prospects for an eventual cordial relationship had looked bright. Bianca, Caterina's daughter, as the future wife of Astorre of Faenza, was to be a friendly link between the two families. Accordingly, Caterina strongly supported Astorre when his position became endangered in December, 1495.

In 1488 the Florentines had used Astorre's cousin, Ottaviano Manfredi, as a pawn in their gamble for Faenza, and when they no longer needed him had held him for seven years under

virtual arrest. The French had changed that. Ottaviano Manfredi had been freed and was bent on returning to Faenza.
Astorre refused an offered reconciliation and barred his cousin
from the city.[84] In December, 1495, Ottaviano gathered a force
from among his supporters in the Val d'Amone under Dionigi
Naldi of Brisighella.[85] The attempt was in vain because of the
prompt help Astorre received from his grandfather, Giovanni
Bentivoglio, his intended mother-in-law, Caterina, and his future all-too-powerful "protector" Venice, which now actively
entered Romagnol politics.[86] Ottaviano gave up, but Faenza
soon found itself smothered by the support of Venice. At first
the new treaty signed between Venice and Astorre Manfredi
implied merely the protection of Faenza by the Republic of San
Marco.[87] The instrument was a *condotta* for Astorre, according
to which he would receive eight thousand ducats each year in
return for providing one hundred men-at-arms and twenty
crossbowmen on horses.[88] But already in the early part of 1496
the representative of Venice in Faenza,[89] Domenigo da Treviso,
acted as if the city were a Venetian province and tried to
separate Astorre, *il signorino* ("the little signore") , from the
strong man in Faenza, Niccolò Castagnino (castellan of the
main fortress) .[90] Florence and Ferrara took alarm. Caterina
became greatly disturbed and complained bitterly to her uncle,
the duke of Milan.[91] Lodovico had assented to the "protection"
of Faenza by Venice simply to spite the hostile Florentines and
to please the Venetians whose good will he still courted at that
time.[92] Caterina, whose ardor for supporting Astorre had
cooled, could not take the issue so lightly. Her relations with
Faenza became more strained with every assertion of Venetian
power in that city. It was unbearable to see Venice controlling
the link between Imola and Forlì. The tension eased temporarily when Venice advised her *provveditore* to be more careful.

Plagued by such problems, Caterina welcomed any type of
good news. There were a few encouraging developments. The
Este family of Ferrara settled its long-standing quarrels over the
Massa Lombarda incidents with Caterina. No less pleasant was
the news of the death of both Orsi brothers. Cecco Orsi met
his end in faraway Madeconia as an officer of the *signore* of
Camerino (September, 1496) . A few months afterwards Lodo-

vico Orsi, *podestà* of Camerino, was wiped out, along with his son and many others, by a fierce epidemic.[93]

The summer of 1496 also brought the proud moment when Caterina ordered coins struck. To support her right to do so she cited a document in which the Emperor Frederick II had granted that privilege to the people of Forlì, and also the bull of Sixtus IV which had invested the Riario with Forlì and renewed the right of coinage. The Riario had used the privilege only once before, in 1481, when they triumphantly entered the city and thrown coins to the people as souvenirs. Now Caterina needed coins for more commonplace purposes and appreciated the enhancement of her status which came from coins showing variously the cathedral of Forlì, the fortress of Ravaldino, the name of Forlì, and her initial, C. S.[94]

The gravest and potentially the most dangerous predicament remained; its roots reached deep in the general Italian political situation. There the aftermath of the French invasion could still be felt in the presence of French troops in the south, in bitter memories, and in feverish diplomatic activities. In addition, another storm from the northwest could not be ruled out.[95] Forlì and Imola felt the repercussion, inasmuch as the Holy League, including the pope, Venice, Milan, Emperor Maximilian I, and some minor states, and the French party, namely France and Florence, were both working feverishly to sway Caterina to their respective sides. The League had powerful levers. The pope was Forlì's overlord, and in May, 1496, he had hinted strongly to Cardinal Ascanio Sforza that Caterina should declare for the League, and the sooner the better.[96]

Lodovico il Moro remained the most potent weapon of the League in forcing the hand of Caterina. Although Lodovico, in 1495, had made his separate peace with France,[97] he knew by now only too well the importance to Milanese security of a well-functioning Italian League; hence his fervent advocacy of the League. In nearly every letter from Milan came an invitation to join the League, complete with arguments in favor of such a move and warnings against allying herself with the Florentines.[98] Caterina procrastinated and maintained neutrality.[99] She flattered Lodovico by telling him again and again how much she depended on his wise counsel. Yet when it was given

she did not in most cases accept it. In June she started bargaining in order to gain time: if Lodovico il Moro wanted her
support, he should "think about" the future of the seventeen-
year-old Ottaviano.[100] One bit of counsel resulting from such
hints Caterina refused to welcome: she rejected a suggested
marriage of Ottaviano with a daughter of the late Gianfrancesco
Gonzaga.[101] In her opinion Ottaviano was too young, the situation in Italy too unsettled, and although she did not say so, the
bride too unimportant. Also, Ottaviano would have first to become a famous *condottiere*. Such correspondence consumed
time, and Caterina was glad of it.

Her anxious clinging to a neutrality which clearly favored
France and Florence puzzled the duke of Milan. It stood to lose
her the support of Milan for little apparent gain. Lodovico
could have found his answer in Caterina's fear of Venice, which
had suddenly become fiercely expansionistic in Romagna. Caterina had visions of Venice first taking over Faenza and then
spreading her influence to engulf Forlì, Imola, and Cesena, in
order to extend the Venetian border to the watershed of the
Apennines.[102] Because Lodovico did not at that time share her
apprehensions he looked for more sinister motives to explain
Caterina's behavior. He thought to have found it when
Tranchedini, his orator in Bologna, reported in October that
for a few days Giovanni di Pierfrancesco de'Medici had stayed
in the fortress of Ravaldino. Already Tranchedini had heard
talk of a new love affair, which Caterina would supposedly
carry as far as marriage "in order to satisfy her passion." [103]
Florence, it seemed, had wormed her way into the most intimate councils of Caterina.

GIOVANNI DE'MEDICI, born five years after Caterina, belonged
to the less fortunate branch of the Medici who saw their close
relatives dominate Florence for generations, while they themselves were excluded from power, wealth, and influence.[104] In-

termittent attempts to reconcile the two branches had failed, and Giovanni himself had tasted both confinement and exile. The French changed all that. Giovanni rode into Florence with the French army and received position, honor, and wealth. In deference to the newly established republic of Florence, he and his relatives became known as the *Popolano,* thus avoiding the name Medici.

When Giovanni came to Forlì, many assumed that he did so as a Florentine official with a diplomatic purpose.[105] Yet, far from working for the Florentine republic, Giovanni wanted to put a long distance between himself and the democratic regime he disliked. The *Popolano* branch agreed in one important aspect with the rest of the Medici family, namely in their preference for the oligarchic form of government. Giovanni, in a later discussion with the Milanese diplomat Tranchedini, even admitted to his strong dislike of the republican government of Florence and of the strong pro-French sympathies of the populace. He gave these feelings and a weariness with the troubled Florentine political scene as the very reasons for coming to Romagna.[106] But Milanese officials considered such assurances to be merely nice phrases to fill their ears.

Actually, what had made Giovanni de'Medici travel to Romagna and visit Caterina had been not so much questions of high politics as of grain, money, and trade. Giovanni and his brother Lorenzo, both of them shrewd businessmen, had come into contact with Caterina soon after their return to Florence, though they had never met her personally. At one point Caterina had extended a loan to the Medici brothers.[107] Then early in 1496 Giovanni arrived in Romagna to pursue several matters which included the hiring of troops for Caterina.[108] Later that year, news having arrived about the catastrophically poor harvest in Tuscany, Giovanni sensed possibilities for advantageous grain deals. Speculators and Florentine officials were already hard at work scraping together every bit of grain available in the Florentine possessions.[109] Giovanni well understood that Romagna would soon receive much attention from Florence because of its grain surplus and its proximity. In August, 1496, Florentine officials frightened by the specter of unruly hungry masses began shopping for grain in Romagna.[110]

When Giovanni first rode into Forlì he was about thirty

years old, extremely handsome, intelligent, and a charmer of ladies. Because of his family's prominence he was assigned an elaborately furnished room in the fortress of Forlì. Soon not even that seemed good enough, and he was given still more elaborate quarters which in addition were adjacent to Caterina's.[111] This quick metamorphosis of formal relations into the personal ones of love had already been rumored. Bernardi wrote, "the people wondered much but they knew nothing exactly and, like me, they find the affairs of the great hard to understand." [112] And while the Forlivesi whispered sarcastically to each other how afraid Caterina was of a *freddo letto* ("cold bed"), most of them agreed nevertheless with Cobelli's strange moral sense which condoned the new affair since Giovanni was after all a rich and noble gentleman while Giacomo Feo had been objectionable because of his lowly origin.[113]

Giovanni found himself in an enviable situation. He had entered into a love affair with a beautiful, sensual, and politically powerful woman. Inevitably, Giovanni's business interests became the beneficiaries of the romance. The officials in charge of the Florentine food supply, noting his privileged position in Romagna, soon turned to him and, in fact, made him the main agent for the contemplated vast grain imports from that region. In doing so, the officials appealed to Giovanni's sympathies for his native Florence (notwithstanding the political antagonism) and to his well-known desire for good profits.

The relationship between Giovanni and Caterina assumed a new dimension when love was intertwined with business and, later, with politics. Insiders knew that Giovanni had loaned Caterina ten thousand florins. With this money she could redeem some of the silverware and jewels which over the last ten years had been pawned in Modena and with Domenico Ricci. Caterina consigned six thousand *corbe* of grain, as security.[114] Giovanni himself continued to live in high style, surrounding himself with sixteen retainers and a number of counselors, and handing out lavish gifts to Caterina's children.

But the loan, the security, and the gifts were small matters compared to the big grain deal which was arranged between Caterina and Florence, with Giovanni as the intermediary. From December, 1496, to late spring, 1497, 64,944¾ *staia* of grain (approximately 129,888 bushels) were transported from

Caterina's territories to Florence.[115] Under the watchful eyes of Florentine officials, convoy after convoy moved from Florentine Castrocaro, near Forlì, to Firenzuola, and from there across the Apennines to Florence.[116] Caterina had hesitated before taking the risk inherent in such large exports. The harvests in her territories had not been the best and food prices had remained high all through 1496.[117] A bad harvest in 1497 and depleted local reserves could spell political trouble for her. But Caterina's restraint never lasted too long when it stood in the way of gaining the love of a man or of accumulating money—or, as in this case, of both.[118]

The powers of Italy viewed Caterina's latest love affair from still another angle. For them Giovanni de'Medici, whatever his political sympathies, was a representative of Florence, and Caterina by her business deal had helped the Florentine republic weather a severe crisis. As rumors and diplomatic correspondence carried the report of her new infatuation to Milan, Venice, and Rome, Caterina had to walk another tightrope. The position of Venice showed the essence of the great powers' concern. Venetian officials pretended to be shocked by her seemingly boundless sensual appetite. The Doge granted that such behavior, natural to her sex, could be understood, but insisted that because of her political situation such errors in judgment could not be tolerated. In short, while moral lapses could be overlooked, mistaken political sympathies could not; or, even shorter: Florence mattered, Giovanni did not.[119]

Rome remained silent. The pope was too preoccupied with the grand matters of European politics and the furthering of the Borgia fortunes to take note of the private affairs of the Lady of Forlì. His anti-French and anti-Florentine fervor had lessened, and Caterina's re-enforced attachment to Florence held no interest for him. The cardinal of San Giorgio was unconcerned, too. Giovanni de'Medici just did not constitute the same threat to Caterina's sons that Giacomo Feo had posed. Giacomo, a nobody, could be suspected of trying to make a fortune at the cost of the Riario boys. No worry of that kind beset the cardinal when he heard that Caterina had fallen under Giovanni's spell.

Caterina welcomed Rome's indifference the more since Lodovico il Moro behaved as though Florence and France had invaded Forlì and Imola when Giovanni de'Medici entered Caterina's bedroom. Early in October, Lodovico received the first of many reports about Caterina's new love affair.[120] He wanted clarity and certainty. Had Caterina and Giovanni married already? Was Giovanni an agent of Florence or even of France? On Lodovico's behalf Tranchedini sent an agent to Forlì with the mission of looking and listening.[121] After the agent had brought back inconclusive reports, Tranchedini himself went to Forlì and had discussions with Giovanni and Caterina.[122] He too returned to Bologna not much wiser. Caterina knew how to talk, seeming to clarify, while actually hiding her intentions in a haze.

Caterina's official position remained that Giovanni was just an honorable gentleman whom she knew as a good friend. She kept her people keenly aware of the danger of talking too forwardly and too much. Giovanni dalle Selle, a jurist, traveled to Milan in order to persuade Lodovico il Moro that the relationship between Caterina and Giovanni was innocuous.[123] In her letters she assured Lodovico of her continued obedience, loyalty, and dedication to Milan. She promised that Ottaviano would always be available to Milan first for a *condotta,* and begged Lodovico to regard all those who told him otherwise as mischief-makers and rascals.[124] As for the rumors that she negotiated with the king of France for permission to marry Giovanni, Caterina asked sensibly why she should seek such a sanction. Assurances of that kind became fewer and fewer after February, 1497, in direct proportion to Lodovico's decreasing nervousness over the affair. Caterina still denied a marriage to Giovanni in August, 1497, when pregnancy forbade her to speak of him as merely a welcome guest.[125] In September, Giovanni de'Medici secretly married the beautiful, lively, and pregnant Lady of Forlì and Imola.[126] Coming after months of incessant denials, the marriage must have recalled to Lodovico il Moro what Tranchedini had once written him: "Cursed are those who trust a man, even more so, however, those who trust a woman." [127]

The task left to Lodovico il Moro was to prevent the relationship between Caterina and Florence from growing too intimate. He did not mind letters of the kind which Caterina had sent to Florence in the summer of 1497. At that time a troubled Caterina had written to the most famous spiritual counselor of

those years, the friar Hieronymus de Ferrara, better known as
Girolamo Savonarola. He had advised her to practice justice, to
redeem herself through pious works, and to trust in God, counsels which could not save Savonarola from execution the very
next year and which gave Caterina little immediate assistance.[128] The duke of Milan's concern derived from other possible dealings and must have been shared by many Forlivesi.
Cobelli called the pro-Florentine policy ruinous to Forlì.[129]

All these matters overshadowed lesser events which in other
years would have been sufficient to fill Caterina's life with joy
and grief alike. She poured much energy into pushing the work
on the fortress of Bubano to a conclusion.[130] In 1497 both Imola
and Forlì gained additional protection by that fortress, which
shielded Caterina's territories more effectively from any danger
brewing in the northwest. Stamina, not energy, helped her to
overcome the shock of the death of her son Giovanni Livio,
sometime in 1496 or 1497,[131] and that of her half sister Anna in
November, 1497.[132] This second loss deprived her of hoped-for
support in Ferrara when Anna's husband would have become
duke of Ferrara.

Early in 1498 the mood in Forlì was once more gay, and the
carnival of that year overflowed with boisterous festivities. For
the moment Caterina and her subjects delighted in life despite
the cold and damp weather, strange and frightening cloud
formations, and the high cost of food. Nobody in Forlì worried
too much about some bloody incidents which occurred around
San Mauro concerning traditional lumbering rights. Caterina
restrained herself and reacted merely with protests.[133] The second party to the dispute, the Malatesta of Rimini, suspected a
grander design behind the incidents. Then in January, 1498,
another effort was made to oust young Pandolfo Malatesta
from Rimini, and the Lady of Forlì and Imola figured prominently in the rumors about the plot. Caterina pleaded her
innocence with sincerity and vigor. Her concern centered less
on offending the Malatesta than on angering their protectors,
the Venetians, whose increasing influence in Romagna Caterina saw with misgivings.

Caterina had another reason not to want a major controversy
in early 1498. She was in the late stages of her pregnancy, and
while in former years such a condition had not prevented her
from galloping around on horseback, she now preferred to

spend these months quietly with Giovanni. April brought her to a peak of happiness when a child was born to her and Giovanni de'Medici. Eventually, as Giovanni dalle Bande Nere, he would be hailed by the Italians as their hero.[134] Yet even so joyous an event was muffled by Caterina's situation: she did not want to admit to a supposedly illegitimate child, and she could not reveal her marriage to Giovanni. Marriage, the birth of a son, and her joy had to be wrapped in secrecy lest Pope Alexander VI, whose family looked for comfortable establishments, should be provided with a good excuse for expelling the Riario family from Forlì and Imola.

The pope tested soon enough Caterina's determination to maintain her position as Lady of Forlì and Imola. Late in May the bishop of Volterra arrived in Forlì with an astounding proposal. Ottaviano should marry Lucrezia Borgia, daughter of Pope Alexander VI and former wife of Giovanni Sforza, lord of Pesaro.[135] The bishop subtly indicated that acceptance of such a marriage tie would bring the favor of the Church and vast amounts of wealth to Caterina and her family. Of course, she would have to relinquish Forlì and Imola in favor of Ottaviano. Yet the pope would most graciously bestow new territories upon her, the names of which would be revealed after the marriage contract was signed. Caterina, wise in the ways of Renaissance politics, recognized at once that whatever answer she gave, the implications would be serious for her cause. It is true that the Borgia had not yet established themselves as the ruthless family of later notoriety, nor had they any grand design of which the suggested marriage would have been a part. Cesare was still a cardinal, although chafing under the restraints of that office and filled with other ambitions. But Alexander VI was Caterina's overlord and, in addition, was concerned with the political fortune of his children. Enough of the Borgia shrewdness had already been displayed for Caterina to know that to accept the proposal meant first giving up control of Forlì and Imola in return for some lofty and meaningless promises, and then seeing her son put at the mercy of the Borgia. The unhappy experience of Caterina's relative, Giovanni Sforza, in his marriage to Lucrezia was another warning. Caterina realized that her "no" to the papal suggestion could only produce an uneasy relation with the Borgia family, but she decided to risk that consequence rather than get entangled in the present Borgia schemes. She gave as the reason for her rejection that Ottaviano was going to be a man of war and that his marriage would have to wait. Caterina could truthfully point out to the bishop that she had used the same argument when in January, 1498, she once more had declined a proposed marriage of Ottaviano to the daughter of the late Gianfrancesco Gonzaga.[136] Ottaviano's marriage would have to wait. For the rest she kept her own counsel. Even so good a friend of the bishop as Giovanni de'Medici, on whose influence the Borgia had counted, could not have swayed her determination to reject the Borgia tie.

Unfortunately no amount of prudence and slyness on Caterina's part could stave off the threats brought forth by the larger context of Italian politics. There issues were hardly ever completely settled, and whenever the spring sun warmed the soil, the unresolved conflicts sprouted anew; 1498 would be an especially favorable year for one of them, the Pisan war.[137]

The French invasion of 1494 had shaken the traditional Italian state system. When ties were destroyed and new ones established, Pisa had succeeded in freeing itself from Florentine dominance. Predictably, the Florentines tried their best to subjugate Pisa once more. At first the war was one of those numerous local struggles normal to Renaissance Italy. In 1496, its scope was widened when Venice sent *stradioti* and Milan dispatched light horsemen to help the Pisans against Florence, the last major French ally in Italy. Even Emperor Maximilian I was invited to take part in the defense of Pisa. He did so although his status never transcended that of a high-level *condottiere*.[138] After his departure in the fall of 1496 the Pisan war died down. Florentine internal instability reduced the threat to Pisa in 1497. Late that year Milanese and Venetian cooperation ended; Milan no longer intended to rescue Pisa from Florentine attacks;[139] Venice must find new ways to help the city. The Venetian motive for such eagerness to assist Pisa was eventually disputed, but for Caterina this policy of continued assistance had only one meaning: the Venetians would soon probe all possibilities Romagna offered for attacking Florence if not for reaching Pisa itself. Caterina would have to accommodate or oppose Venice.

24

On MAY 16, 1498, Caterina expressed for the first time her gnawing fear of Venice in a letter to Lodovico il Moro.[140] On the next day, Giovanni, now a *commissario fiorentino* in Romagna, took over command of the key Florentine fortress of Castrocaro in order to secure it.[141] For a while politics interfered with Giovanni's business ventures, such as his attempt to corner the grain market in the Mugello.[142] Additional signs of trouble ahead were not missing. Recruiters crisscrossed Romagna and neighboring areas searching for willing young men. Choice of employment was wide. Vincenzo Naldi,[143] Guidobaldo da Montefeltro, and Bartolomeo d'Alviano would need their services for Venice. Dionigi Naldi, Ranuccio da Marciano, and Ottaviano Riario would offer employment on the side of Caterina and the Florentines. The Arno Republic had finally pleased Caterina by acknowledging her son Ottaviano as a military leader. For seventeen thousand florins the Florentines received the services of Ottaviano, one hundred men-at-arms, one hundred crossbowmen, and the good will of a grateful mother.[144]

Every day the war moved closer. The Venetians gathered their troops around Ravenna. With them were two exiles, Antonio Maria Ordelaffi and a son of Taddeo Manfredi.[145] Like any great power, Venice knew how to make use of exiles, these frustrated and angry men who could provide some support in their home territories. Against the threat from the north Caterina put her grim determination, some ill-equipped troops, and some well-provisioned fortresses. Tranchedini assessed the situation well when he told Lodovico il Moro that Caterina would soon need Milanese help.[146]

Caterina did not panic easily. At the moment she was much more occupied with her son's transformation into a soldier. The proud mother refused to see him as he was, a fat, apathetic, lazy, and completely uninterested young man who sat on his

Bona of Savoy, duchess of Milan, by Bernardino Luini. In the Uffizi Gallery, Florence. Courtesy Alinari.

Galeazzo Maria Sforza, duke of Milan, by Antonio Pollaiuolo. In the Uffizi Gallery, Florence. Courtesy Alinari.

Pope Sixtus IV, his nephews, and Platina, by Melozzo da Forlì. From left to right: Giovanni della Rovere, Girolamo Riario, Platina (kneeling), Giuliano della Rovere (cardinal of San Pietro in Vincoli, later Pope Julius II), Raffaello Riario (cardinal of San Giorgio) or Piero Riario (cardinal of San Sisto), Pope Sixtus IV. Courtesy Pinacoteca Vaticana.

Raffaello Riario, cardinal of San Giorgio, detail from *La Messa di Bolsena,* by Raphael. In the Vatican Palace, Rome. Courtesy Alinari.

Medal, Raffaello Riario, by Lysippus the Younger. Courtesy Staatliche Museen zu Berlin, Muenzkabinett. Verso, St. George and the dragon.

Lodovico il Moro, by Maestro della Pala Sforzesca, detail from the Pala Sforzesca, in the Pinacoteca Brera, Milan. Courtesy Alinari.

Medal, Bianca Riario (daughter of Caterina
Sforza), *ca.* 1495, by Niccolò Fiorentino.
Courtesy Trustees of the British Museum.

Medal, Ottaviano Riario (oldest son of Caterina Sforza), *ca.* 1498, by
Niccolò Fiorentino (or Domenico Cennini). Etching from Guidantonio
Zanetti, *Delle monete forlivesi.* Bologna, 1778. Table in Appendix, illus-
tration VII. Recto: profile portrait; verso: as *condottiere.*

Medals of Caterina Sforza

(Left) *ca.* 1480—Lysippus the Younger (or D. Cennini). Courtesy Victoria and Albert Museum, London.
(Center) shortly after 1488—Niccolò Fiorentino. Staatliche Museen zu Berlin, Muenzkabinett.
(Right) ?—Niccolò Fiorentino (or D. Cennini). No known location. Reproduction from A. Gottschewski, *Ueber die Portraets der Caterina Sforza.* Strassbourg, 1908. Table II.

Giovanni di Pierfrancesco de'Medici, by Filippino Lippi. (Giovanni is in the foreground being crowned.) Detail from *Adorazione dei Magi*. In the Uffizi Gallery, Florence. Courtesy Alinari.

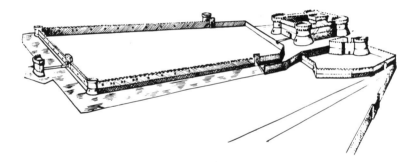

(Above) Fortress of Imola, *ca.* 1499.

(Below) Fortress of Ravaldino in Forlì, *ca.* 1499.

Both drawings according to L. Marinelli, Italian military historian. Re-printed from F. Mancini and W. Vichi, *Castelli, rocche, e torri di Romagna.* Bologna, 1959. Plates 26 and 96. Courtesy of Cassa dei Risparmi, Forlì, publisher of the work.

horse like a sack of meal. For her he already was a hero of future battles. Before he left with his men two reviews were held, largely because Caterina loved them.[147] Medals were struck which showed Ottaviano in a flattering light. Wisely, even after the departure of Ottaviano, his soldiers were commanded as much by experienced captains as by him, just to make sure everything would be right.

Then Venice made her first move, and it aimed right across Faenza, Brisighella, and Marradi at the mountain pass which leads from the Val d'Amone to the Mugello. There Venetian troops would be a mere forty-odd miles from Florence. At the same time Caterina began to pay the price of opposing Venice. Venetian mercenaries roamed freely over her territory.[148] Caterina begged the duke of Milan to send the captain Gaspare Sanseverino, named Fracasso, together with sufficient troops.[149] Until their arrival she tried to stall off further raids by talking to the Venetians. Caterina, officially at peace with the Republic, feigned surprise about the raids and dispatched an orator to find out why Venice would do such things. She reminded the Venetians that the Florentine *condotta* for Ottaviano was a personal contract and not a formal alliance between the two states of Florence and Forlì. She pleaded official neutrality.[150] Venice knew better and paid no heed. The raids continued.

Caterina's situation while not encouraging was not yet serious. Although the Florentines sent no money or soldiers, they lifted Caterina's spirits by awarding her the citizenship of Florence.[151] Lodovico's gesture of support was more immediately useful: Fracasso arrived on August 2, 1498.[152] A council of war was held, and Fracasso acquainted himself with the fiercely independent spirit of Caterina. In the same meeting she must have told him about a fascinating scheme which would ruin the Venetian strategy. Ever since the middle of July Caterina had secretly negotiated with the castellan of Faenza. The latter disliked the Venetians, supported the Florentines, and defended the rights of his *signore*, Astorre,[153] because his own influence depended on Faenza's independence. Caterina hoped that upon the coming expiration of the Venetian *condotta* the castellan would help her persuade those who governed Faenza to accept Milanese protection as a better choice. She pleaded with Lodovico il Moro to offer a *condotta* to Faenza. If the Venetians could be ousted from Faenza by such a coup [154] their plan to secure the Val d'Amone as their main route for reaching Florence and Pisa would be wrecked and at the lowest possible cost.[155]

Until such clever plans could be carried out, Caterina must go through anxious days. The area north of Forlì was the playground for the Venetian captain Manfroni's soldiers, who feasted on the peasants's cattle, raped the women, and carried off the valuables. Antonio Maria Ordelaffi's aspirations gilded the pillage with a layer of noble purpose.[156] The pine forests around Ravenna, where the raiders had their base, swarmed with many more soldiers and captains. By the middle of August the duke of Urbino joined them.[157] Fracasso and Caterina interpreted this move as a direct threat to Forlì and Imola. They were happy to hear Lodovico's promise of additional troops, one hundred men-at-arms, and one hundred light horsemen.[158]

The hot days of late August bred sicknesses. One of the recurrent summer epidemics attacked Bianca, Caterina's daughter, and other members of the Riario household. Giovanni de'Medici, who only recently had been in Ottaviano's camp, also felt weak from an attack of the traditional Medici sickness, the gout. The doctors advised him to seek the relief granted by the waters of the Bagno di Romagna area.[159] At least his sickness appeared not to be dangerous. Letters came from San Piero in Bagno telling of the routine in a spa. Caterina, distressed and alone, shared her feelings with the duke of Milan. "War," she wrote, "is not for ladies and children like mine." [160] Then after reflecting on her timidity she told the duke apologetically, "If I might be more fearful than desirable, Your Excellency must ascribe that to my being a lady . . . and thus by nature fearful." [161]

The Venetians did not experience much of Caterina's fearfulness. They knew only the Lady of Forlì who pushed her captains into more aggressive campaigning and who slyly intrigued against them in Faenza. They might have suspected her dealings with the Castellan which drove the price of holding on to Faenza ever higher. Astorre Manfredi's *condotta* once more was up for renewal, and Venice offered a mere six thousand ducats for the young lord's services. Caterina made the most of the Venetian niggardliness. When the Venetian negotiator, Vernier, left empty-handed, Caterina was greatly relieved.[162] But only three days later Vernier yielded and raised the offer. Venice needed Faenza too badly for the attempt to break through into Tuscany.

Fracasso, too, would have been surprised by Caterina's well-turned phrases about her timidity. Ever since his arrival she and Fracasso had crisscrossed over her territories inspecting, correcting, and planning. Unfortunately the two were very unlike. Fracasso was a rough and unpolished Renaissance soldier. His speech was that of the military camp, crude and well larded with curses. The soldiers obeyed his curt orders with reluctance and complained to Caterina. When these complaints increased, Caterina bitingly asked Fracasso why there should be so much discontent. Thereupon Fracasso cursed the Holy Virgin, damned Saint Peter, and blamed his patroness for calling him stupid. He would leave at once and she should not try to keep him with those feminine tears which come so easily and mean nothing. In the end he stayed. Caterina on her part followed Lodovico's advice to be patient with the old and coarse soldier.[163]

Also, where was the supposedly timid Caterina when, in the midst of an exhausting military campaign, she must master another severe blow. The letters from San Piero in Bagno had been filled with political matters, business deals (especially the grain business), and news about mutual friends. Giovanni de'Medici never complained, but his continued bodily discomfort was evident when he appealed to Caterina for berets, warm clothing, and some hemp to wear under his beret.[164] On September 15, Fracasso had to hurry to Forlì. He must take over the governing while Caterina was galloping southeast; she had received distressing news from San Piero. Giovanni de'Medici was dead when she arrived.[165] This time she could not bury her sorrow in fury, have houses sacked, and enemies executed. For a short while she kept to herself. Then Caterina again wrote letters, commanded, and acted.[166] She did not even complain. It was as if she had locked Giovanni's memory tightly into herself. On the outside she kept a mysterious silence.

Caterina's iron constitution saved her ally Florence much embarrassment. Instead of being paralyzed by shock, Caterina took her part in the now unfolding decisive phase of the fight for the Val d'Amone. The Venetians had the odds heavily in their favor, possessing the base of Faenza and fielding an expeditionary force of one thousand men. Their captain, Vincenzo Naldi, could utilize his prominence in the valley. Caterina and the Florentines decided to make their stand at Marradi. There the fortress of Castiglione was commanded by Simone Ridolfi, a Florentine commissioner,[167] and Dionigi Naldi, an experienced captain. From their camp at Brisighella the Venetians sent a strong detachment to Marradi. It took the village but not the fortress.[168] Since not enough forces had been brought into the fortress in time, the small band of defenders looked forward to dire days. Caterina did not hide her opinion on such defense planning. She had long warned of such a Venetian attempt, but as usual "nobody believes me . . . being just a lady and timid, too." [169]

How long would Marradi hold out? The prospects were gloomy. One problem was water. The besieged had lacked water ever since the enemy had dug into the springs which supplied the fortress. The thirsty soldiers vowed to build a toy castle from pure silver for the Holy Virgin in exchange for water. Rain came promptly, we are assured, and dumped about fifty tons of water into the cisterns.[170] Such stories make good legends but poor military history. While rains might have relieved the water shortage, the Venetians just did not lift their siege because of a weather change. The Venetian flanks were under attack, by Galeazzo Sanseverino from Riolo,[171] and by Fracasso from the direction of Modigliana.[172] The aim of both attacks was Brisighella, the fall of which would destroy Venetian power in the Val d'Amone.

The calculations proved correct. The Venetian *provveditore,* Giacomo Vernier, made one more valiant effort to conquer the fortress of Marradi (called Castiglione).[173] His force did not succeed, and retreat began by October 12. The battle for the Val d'Amone had ended. Florence, which had contributed no money, two captains,[174] a few soldiers, and many good wishes, could consider her northern flank secure. The Lady of Forlì and Imola "fighting like a tiger" against the Venetians [175] had served the Florentines well.

The main body of the Venetian force had already begun to

shift, first to Villafranca and then further to the east.[176] Caterina warned the Florentines to guard their mountain defenses, but she could do little at the moment to help Florence. The Venetian soldiers on their march to the east often camped only a few miles from Forlì. They acted as they had sworn they would, namely "to give back to the Madonna in kind" what she had done to them.[177] The countryside showed the scars of their ravages. One October morning a priest, posted as guard on the high bell tower of Forlì, saw Venetian soldiers approaching. The great bell of the commune rang out, six cannon shots were fired, and the citizens swarmed to the gate of Schiavonia. There, Caterina, calm as usual, directed the disposition of her men. But the Venetians had no heart for a fight. With their sudden raid foiled, they turned their backs on Forlì and disappeared.[178]

While the Forlivesi bid good riddance to the Venetians, Florence could only have wished that the Venetians had stayed in Caterina's territories. The Venetians had quietly surveyed the mountain passes and found a gaping hole in the Florentine defense and also an old foe of Caterina, Ramberto Malatesta of Sogliano,[179] who was willing to lend one of his castles to the Venetians as a base. In the dark of night, Venetian soldiers under Bartolomeo d'Alviano proceeded from Villafranca to Galeata and Camaldoli and from there to the key position of Bibbiena. Dressed like Florentines they took the city and fortress by surprise. They received valuable support from the Dovizi family, respected citizens of Bibbiena, foes of the Florentine republic, and supporters of the ousted Medici. With one bold strike the Venetians had acquired a dangerous foothold in the Casentino, the upper valley of the Arno.[180]

In Bibbiena, Piero and Giuliano de'Medici gathered their partisans for a decisive blow at the hated Florentine republic. They had no difficulty in strengthening their forces, since Bibbiena was a traditional Medici stronghold, and since the duke of Urbino and Annibale Bentivoglio had also joined the Venetian forces under their command to those of Bartolomeo d'Alviano. Now the Florentines urged Caterina to take immediate action. Caterina could not help but tell Florence that her advice on warfare, if taken, could have prevented Florence's predicament. "It just is not my nature to needle anybody, yet the interest of my states and the common welfare compels me to speak out and appear contrary when I cannot help but regret that I was not believed." [181]

But loyal ally that she was, Caterina called her captains together for a war council. She suggested a counterattack on all Venetian troops still remaining in central Romagna. Later she urged an all-out attack on Brisighella.[182] The Venetians must be pushed back into the pine forests around Ravenna where they had come from.[183] The captains listened to her, muttered something about too late, too bold, and maybe next year. They clearly did not feel like fighting so late in the season.

Indifference to the war was strengthened in many ways. Galeazzo Sanseverino fell ill and took no further part in the martial activities. Spending his days in the fortress of Ravaldino of Forlì, he came to know Bianca Riario and got it in his mind to marry her.[184] Since by now, Astorre Manfredi had become an improbable son-in-law, and Galeazzo was a famous Milanese noble, Caterina could have assented. Yet she hesitated. Faenza was still worth a try. She told Galeazzo to wait until Bianca was a little older; and nothing came of the project.[185]

Money, the *nervus belli,* was an even greater problem. The Florentines had relied greatly on Caterina to help block the Venetian thrust into Tuscany and to hire soldiers for them. Unfortunately they felt not always the same urgency when payments were due. Caterina who dealt with Florence through the Florentine commissioner in Romagna, Andrea de'Pazzi, and her brother-in-law Lorenze di Pierfrancesco de'Medici (il Popolano) , complained often and bitterly about tardy payments to her. For all her efforts she eventually received seven thousand florins.[186] But actually that sum was payment for past services; little new activities could be financed with it.

Caterina's people were tired of a war which they never had favored or understood. Caterina learned a lesson about her subjects' feelings when at one time she tried to levy some soldiers for her own defense and to satisfy a Florentine plea for more men. One September dawn Caterina ordered all ablebodied men to appear in the evening in the fortress for selection for the contingent "under the penalty of displeasure of her Highness, the Madonna." Nobody came. Once more she tried, now "under the penalty of the gallows." [187] One man came, and she gave up. Some peasants and soldiers from other castles were then pressed into defensive service around Forlì.

Little cheered her in those waning days of the campaign except some raids on the territory of Faenza. For the rest she had the difficult task of persuading her captains to guard all the strongpoints well. After days filled with tiresome discussions, with frantic juggling of accounts in order to find money for the war, and with laboring over a correspondence containing little good news, she cherished her evenings. But Fracasso managed to irritate her even then. He had no interests beyond eating, drinking, sleeping, and soldier talk. Caterina, regardless of personal tragedy, political problems, and despair, never lost her joy in life. After gloomy and joyful days alike she would return to her quarters to dine in style. Following the meal the tables were cleared away, the fifers and tambours played, and she and her companions danced. Fracasso just sat there bored. Asked on one occasion to dance with Caterina, he gruffly declined. Caterina then suggested that he listen to some music or have a pleasant talk. Fracasso told her bluntly that neither of these matters was his business. War alone interested him. Caterina, both angered and amused by his answer, advised Fracasso that as long as he was not at war and had no need to fight, he might better have himself well greased along with all his arms and stored away so as not to get more rusty than he already was.[188]

VI

REBEL AGAINST THE BORGIA

IN THE MERCIFUL ways of Renaissance warfare one avoided, if possible, combining the hardships of winter with those of war. After hesitating for some time, even the Venetians disbanded a part of their forces.[1] Caterina had lost most of her troops long before. The Sanseverino brothers had left in November, and with them went many of the Milanese soldiers. The scarcity of money prevented her from keeping those remaining. For weeks Caterina had worried whenever she looked in the direction of the Venetian encampment in Ravenna. At last, relief came when the Venetians partially disarmed.

Despite her anxiety Caterina faithfully considered helping her ally Florence. As if her own forces were fighting in the Casentino, she did not tire of discussing that campaign with her brother-in-law Lorenzo de'Medici.[2] Partly as an act of good will toward Florence she initiated a small campaign of her own.[3] But Caterina also needed vengeance to still her fury over the behavior of Ramberto Malatesta of Sogliano. The count had taken possession of some Riario land and had helped the Venetians in many ways. In December she sent a detachment of forty men against Gulfarello, one of Ramberto's villages. Her soldiers returned with sixty head of cattle and even more small animals.[4] Other raids destroyed some strongholds before lack of money choked off this little war which had gratified Caterina deeply.[5] The Florentines had shown no interest in it since by that time they had converted the spectacular Venetian advance to Bibbiena into a terrible ordeal for the Venetian troops.[6] These men had hardly enough food left to keep alive, could not flee across the snowbound Apennines, and were all too often deserted by their officers. The Florentine troops pressed forward slowly but steadily. In February, Guidobaldo da Montefeltro, duke of Urbino and commander of the Venetian troops, fell ill and was permitted free exodus from the valley. In the following spring a peace treaty ended the Venetian-Florentine struggle, but not the Florentine-Pisan antagonism.[7]

The pressures of the war months had not allowed Caterina to devote herself to her children. Now, as she turned her attention to them, she realized the necessity of providing stations in life for them. She worried least about her oldest son. Forlì had hardly returned to its relaxed and dull routine when Caterina welcomed home Ottaviano, the reluctant soldier. His employers had not been enthusiastic about him, and Ottaviano had disliked the relatively low pay and its delayed payment. Back home he found little to do; his mother governed and made no effort to initiate him in the affairs of politics. He spent much time with his beloved horses and in waiting. Caterina, her eyes blind to evidence and her mind open to imagination, still planned for his future as a *condottiere*.

Eighteen-year-old Cesare, whom Caterina loved dearly for his pleasantness and wit, provided his mother with good news. In November one of Caterina's counselors, Polidoro Tiberti, traveled to Rome. He found the pope most graciously disposed toward Cesare, the young man "full of modesty and virtue" who had dedicated himself to the priestly career according to his mother's order.[8] With the cardinal of San Giorgio ready to shed one of his numerous offices, that of archbishop of Pisa, in favor of his relative, Alexander VI gave every assurance that Cesare would soon join the higher clergy. Caterina was elated. In order to give him a bit of sophisticated fun, she sent Cesare away from provincial Forlì to Milan for some carnival pleasures.[9]

Little was left to Galeazzo Riario but that perennial way of life of the third- and fourth-born noble sons, soldiering. The duke of Milan held out some hope for employment, eventually.[10]

Another relative contributed only anger to Caterina's life. Domenico Ricci, the faithful and gentle companion of many years, finally shed the restraints imposed by loyalty. By process of law he acquired some Riario possessions around Savona to cover the long-standing debts for which Caterina's pawns offered only partial security. Such "disloyalty" outraged Caterina, and she stormed at Lodovico il Moro to interfere on her behalf.[11] He did not, because he saw the justice of Ricci's claims.

The men of Forlì who huddled in the taverns during the idle winter hours were hard put for topics of conversation. When everything else failed to generate discussion, the question of their Lady's latest male conquest never did. Surrounded by male advisors, the beautiful and sensuous Caterina could easily be suspected of love affairs with any or all of her associates. Thus at one time or another Achille Tiberti,[12] Polidoro Tiberti, and the ever more prominent priest, Francesco Fortunati, were included in the rumors. Of the three, only Achille Tiberti, who shared Caterina's unbounded love of life and power and had been a close associate for years, may at times have stepped across the line delineating mere friendship. The rumor mongers were certainly wrong in suggesting an amorous link between Francesco Fortunati, the priest of Cascina, canon of San Lorenzo in Florence, and apostolic protonotary *non-partecipante* (on a fee basis), and Caterina. Fortunati, who had made his career as the confidant of the Popolano branch of the Medici family, had increasingly become Caterina's right-hand man in her dealings with Florence—be it business [13] or politics. The jovial, soft-spoken and energetic priest possessed all the characteristics desired in an *agente generale:* loyalty, an agile mind, discretion, courage, and a shrewd business sense. Yet a lover he was not. Curiously enough the name of the young man, Ottaviano Manfredi, who actually was the new lover, escaped the gossipers. He was cast exactly to Caterina's taste. He had good manners, a quick mind, refined tastes, and a most attractive appearance. In politics, too, he was an asset, since he could be used against his cousin Astorre Manfredi, whose betrothal to Bianca was by now hypothetical to say the least, and also against the Venetians, who maintained their hold on Faenza in the face of the castellan's and foreign opposition.[14] Caterina herself never made any attempt to conceal her intense interest in the handsome young man. Beset by all her problems, Caterina found in Ottaviano both emotional lift and sensual release.

Caterina and the Romagnol people were anxious to see the snow, which had fallen in generous amounts during that winter, melt. Unfortunately, not only nature prepared great changes for the coming spring. France had been Italy's destiny in 1494, and since then life on the peninsula had not been the same. The eventual French defeat had taught the French not a lesson of prudence but one of vengeance. The French aspirations had been infused with new life in April, 1498, when Charles VIII died suddenly.[15] His successor, Louis XII, leader of the House of Orleans, left no doubt about his plans when he accepted the titles of King of France, King of the Two Sicilies, and Duke of Milan. Louis had a flimsy legal claim to Milan through his ancestors and was clever enough to see that any penetration into Italy which would leave Milan in the hands of Lodovico il Moro was sheer suicide. The next French army to descend into the Po River valley would therefore aim directly at Milan and the destruction of the Sforza rule. Military common sense, ancestral rights, and the burning wish for revenge on Lodovico Sforza, whose intrigues had forced Charles VIII out of Italy, would all be satisfied by such a procedure. Needed were some allies whose self-interests would keep them at least temporarily loyal, and Louis XII proved himself a formidable diplomat in acquiring them.

In August, 1498, when Caterina had been fully occupied with the campaign in the Val d'Amone, Venetian and French diplomats had begun to meet in Blois.[16] At stake was the peace of Italy, since a hostile Venice would impede a French invasion as much as a neutral or friendly Venice would assist it. All through the winter they negotiated.

French progress had been much faster elsewhere. The French king had dire need for the favor of the Borgia. Anne of Brittany, widow of Charles VIII and heiress of Brittany, once more must be bound to the French throne. Brittany was too precious a territory to lose. There was, however, a difficulty to overcome before Louis XII could marry Anne. He already had a wife— one who was "horrible to look at," [17] who could not help to tie Brittany to France, and who offered no promise of delivering the desired heir. Alexander VI granted the necessary annulment. The incentive for such prompt consideration of the royal French wishes arose from the slowly emerging plans of the Borgia for the establishment of effective papal control over the Papal States.

The man to fulfil this lofty aspiration was Cesare Borgia, the twenty-four-year-old son of Pope Alexander VI. Cesare had never appreciated his father's thoughtfulness in making him a cardinal. In the summer of 1498 he finally received his release from the burden of being a prince of the Church and accepted with relish the task of making himself into a prince of the world.[18] Cesare's brilliant mind and boundless energy served him well, especially since neither of the two acknowledged any limitation by law, morality, or just plain decency. Cesare would be a potent weapon of the French as long as they succeeded in tying his interests to theirs.

In October, 1498, while Caterina still worried about how to defend the mountain passes, how to incite her captains to act, and how to pay her soldiers, Cesare Borgia traveled to France. He left Rome secretly and without pomp as it befitted the simple layman he now was.[19] But soon the papal willingness to accede to the royal French wishes paid handsomely. Cesare Borgia became duke of the Valentinois (Valence), husband of a princess of the House of Navarre, Charlotte d'Albret,[20] and an ally of the French king in the conquest of Italy. Charlotte d'Albret was really less important than the political bargain between the French and the pope: Louis XII would help Cesare Borgia drive out some of the ruling families from the papal possessions in Romagna, Umbria, and the Marches. The outlines of such a policy were thus fully known to Pope Alexander VI when he received the delegation from Forlì, promised to invest Cesare Riario with Pisa, and praised Caterina. But then, perfect treachery is a work of art.

EVEN THOSE NOT fond of reading the omens could only wonder what kind of year had just begun. To the north the Venetians increased their troops in numbers too large to go unnoticed. Caterina was deeply concerned. Then, early in February, 1499, Corbizzo Corbizzi of Castrocaro, returning home after long consultations with Caterina, was set upon and killed. The matters discussed are not known although they could easily have had reference to her relations with Florence, since Corbizzi came from an old and respected Florentine family. A well-liked and trusted counselor, Corbizzi had made the trip from Castrocaro to Forlì and back a number of times. On this occasion when he came to a little wooded area he met four men. One of them, Bernardino Macarone of Faenza, embraced him and, in doing so, pushed him from his horse. Corbizzi was promptly killed by Macarone's three companions.[21] This murder was grist for the already busy mills of gossip. Venice added her share. Venetian partisans diligently spread the news that the assassination had been the handiwork of Caterina. Of this there is no proof and little likelihood. The Riario had never quarrelled with the Corbizzi, but the Naldi family of Brisighella had, and Bernardino Macarone was a relative of the Naldi. While, as the chronicler Cobelli frequently put it, only the eternal God knows everything, all indications point to the Naldi family as the originators of the bloodshed. Caterina knew the customary laws which Romagnol families followed in such cases, and she had an edict "cried" which forbade the taking up of arms for the purpose of vengeance.[22] It was clearly addressed to the Naldi and Corbizzi families.

Soon the Manfredi of Faenza reminded Caterina that Girolamo Riario had made a mistake when as the right hand of Pope Sixtus IV he had not driven them from their city. Upon Venetian request, the Manfredi forbade Caterina to transport provisions and to send troops through Faenza. That left Imola and Forlì for the purposes of defense connected only by winding side roads.[23] Worse yet, the Venetians stationed a large troop contingent in Faenza.[24]

But not every aspect of the relationship between the Manfredi and Caterina mirrored the tension showing on the surface. Astorre, or better, those who spoke for him, suddenly displayed renewed interest in the marriage contract which, although by now nearly forgotten, still tied Astorre to Bianca Riario.[25] Such an attitude had three advantages: it improved the bargaining position of Faenza in coming re-negotiations of Astorre's *condotta;* it diminished the threat from Ottaviano Manfredi since Caterina could hardly support him with any conviction against her prospective son-in-law; and it might even help to get Milanese support if at some time it were needed. Despite her love for Ottaviano Manfredi, Caterina, too, was not averse to keeping the marriage project alive, since she knew how quickly changes in the political situation in Romagna occurred.

Despite such problems occupying her mind, Caterina fully grasped the import of the news reaching her from Cesena. There the people had wildly celebrated the conclusion of a league between the pope, France, and Venice.[26] Although not quite accurate (the pact referred to was the Treaty of Blois between Venice and France, February 9, 1499), the news was a shattering blow to Caterina.[27] At once she must have looked through the flimsy curtain woven of such well-worn phrases as "defense against the Turks" and glimpsed the truth. In turn, for territorial expansion in the Po River plain, Venice opened the gates of Italy to a French invasion and abandoned Pisa. Caterina's mainstay, the Sforza of Milan, were to be among the main victims of the French onslaught.

Fate did not wait long to reveal to Caterina that she too was to be one of the victims. On March 9, 1499, a papal bull was issued, signed by seventeen cardinals, investing Cesare Borgia with Imola, Forlì, and all other papal territories held by the Riario family.[28] Caterina, that "daughter of iniquity" as the bull called her, and her sons had for three successive years failed in their obligation to pay annually to the papal *camera* one thousand florins for Forlì, two hundred florins for Imola, and two silver cups of six ounces each for San Mauro.[29] In doing so they had not given true recognition to the Holy See. Equally serious, Ottaviano had accepted a *condotta* without the permission of the pope, his overlord. Caterina, knowing full well that all the reasons given, while legally correct, were not the real ones for ousting her and her family,[30] decided to test papal sincerity. She sent the renowned Forlivese jurist Dr. Giovanni dalle Selle to Rome in order to settle the financial question.[31] He took along three thousand florins and also the compilation of accounts Girolamo Riario had made before he had left Rome permanently in 1484. The latter showed sixty thousand ducats balance in favor of the Riario,[32] indicating that the Church had no reason to complain about the non-payment of fees as long as the papal *camera* was really in debt to the Riario. To nobody's surprise such arguments were of no avail, and dalle Selle was never received by any high Church official.

Caterina saw clearly that the defense of the Riario could be neither financial nor legal; it had become a question of naked power. In the spring of 1499 a contest with the Borgia looked far from hopeless for Caterina. Her strongest pillar of support, Lodovico il Moro, still held the duchy of Milan, although he was gravely threatened by the oncoming invasion, and personal tragedy had made Lodovico a lonely man. In 1496 his beloved illegitimate daughter Bianca had suddenly died, and soon afterward his equally beloved wife, Beatrice d'Este, the center of gaiety and glamour at the Sforza court, had failed to recover from a stillbirth. Supporters became rare as Lodovico began to understand the old saying "he whom fortune deserts has no friends." Other friends left Lodovico, but not Caterina, who had no choice. Even the fiction of Milanese support was better than nothing.

Faced by dire emergencies Caterina and Lodovico il Moro stood solidly together as never before. The duke of Milan sent a new envoy, Alessandro Orpheo, to Forlì and Imola.[33] His instructions were to shadow Caterina closely, to please her whenever possible, and to see to it that the ties to Milan were maintained.[34] In the tradition of his predecessors, Orpheo busied himself ferreting out Caterina's private secrets. Soon he thought to have spotted her present intimates, Antonio Baldraccani, her first secretary,[35] and Achille Tiberti, an unofficial counselor.[36] Orpheo liked neither of the two men, although he admitted that both were most favorably disposed toward Milan. The longer he watched, the less Orpheo liked Baldraccani. Toward Francesco Fortunati, the third of Caterina's advisors, he kept a benevolent neutrality, although this priest whom Orpheo characterized as "a creature of Lorenzo de'Medici" preferred Florence over Milan.[37]

All during the spring Caterina displayed a cocky self-confidence which, when viewed in the context of the grave threats facing her, appeared paradoxical. But there still existed sound reasons for her attitude. Venice had given up her attempts to gain Pisa, and the Venetian attacks in Romagna ceased. After all, the solidarity of the Romagnol rulers might be needed when the expected assault came. Milan and Florence were still strong and cordial toward Caterina. Even the pope seemed not too eager to harm the Riario. In May, the cardinal of San Giorgio resigned the archbishopric of Pisa, and Cesare Riario was invested with it.[38] Dispensation for the age deficiency was granted, and Cesare was allowed to begin administering his archdiocese, although full right of title had to wait until the now nineteen-year-old lad had reached the proper age.[39]

Caterina felt so secure that in late spring she even considered a trip to Milan to see the city and Lodovico il Moro and to re-affirm the Forlì-Milan bond. Eventually Lodovico and events convinced her that such trips were not opportune in 1499. The first military activities had started in the western half of the Po Valley; Lodovico, hesitantly to be sure, planned his actions. And Caterina in those April days of 1499 had another personal tragedy to cope with.

She had sheltered, supported, and loved Ottaviano Manfredi. Her sensuality had been satisfied by Ottaviano's beauty and his youthful love. His claims on Faenza also made him a welcome ally. The liaison even had the blessing of her oldest son, Ottaviano; the two young men were close friends. All worked out well until the young Manfredi wanted to get some feeling of independence by collecting money due him from the Florentine government. Early in April he set out for Florence. Caterina begged him to accept some soldiers as guards, but for reasons of his own he declined. On his approach to a pass in the Apennines he stayed one night at an inn at San Benedetto. Going on the next day he met thirty armed men under a certain Galeotto de'Bosi. They had overtaken him during the night to prepare an ambush. There was no escape. When the men were through with their gruesome job, Ottaviano's corpse had little resemblance to a human body.[40]

Ottaviano's remains were carted to Forlì by the ever-merciful Black Flagellantes and buried there in the church of San Girolamo.[41] A hundred masses were said for the peace of his soul. In the meantime Caterina arranged for earthly justice. Her spies, sent out in all directions, soon brought her the name of Galeotto de'Bosi of Faenza. From then on Caterina's henchmen hunted him relentlessly. Early in the summer of 1499 his right hand was given to Caterina as a sign that the chase was over.[42]

Sadness and bitterness filled a few quiet weeks following the murder of Ottaviano. That mood contributed to Caterina's harsh treatment of a prominent Imolese: Enea Vaini ended on the gallows.[43] Ever since the abortive Tossignano plot against Caterina and Giacomo Feo in 1491 the Vaini had experienced Caterina's displeasure. Enea had succeeded in escaping. Then he had made a major mistake: he trusted Caterina's safe-conduct for his return to Imola.

The political quiet continued despite the ominous insight that the second invasion of Italy, better prepared for and launched with greater fury, could no longer be prevented. In March all of Italy learned that it was imminent. Contingents of soldiers were gathering in northern Italy to secure the crossing of the Alps by the French army.

But Milan was strong, and in the early summer of 1499 Lodovico il Moro's troops achieved a number of limited successes. The duke of Milan had finally shaken off his lethargy and had collected troops and money. His success or failure against the awesome French was still in the balance.

Caterina did all she could on her part to earn Milanese support. Sometime in late May or early June her staff of close assistants was completely changed. Baldraccani lost his pre-eminent position and Achille Tiberti left for Cesena. Risorboli, who had done a good deal of her accounting, paid for losing an account book. The new rising star in Caterina's firmament originated in Milan. On May 12, Caterina had requested that Lodovico il Moro send Giovanni di Casale to Forlì.[44] Giovanni, whom Caterina characterized as most loyal to the duke of Milan and most beloved by her, should make his way to Forlì in utmost secrecy. His presence in Forlì was merely to be temporary, yet he soon replaced Antonio Baldraccani as first secretary and the late Ottaviano Manfredi as love companion.[45] No wonder then that Lodovico il Moro had easy access to the recruiting grounds of Romagna. In July and August detachments of crossbowmen, men-at-arms, and light horsemen marched towards Milan, hired by Lodovico il Moro.[46] Even Dionigi Naldi entered Milanese services.

But what about the unthinkable possibility that Sforza Milan's power would be crushed? Caterina faced up to that eventuality, while not with pleasure, still without hesitancy. In such a case her security would rest with Florence. With the support of the Arno republic she could withstand any onslaught. In the coming months one question would be crucial: how could Florence be persuaded to venture forth in defense of the Riario? Florentine foreign policy had never been prompted by emotional ties or charitable feelings. Florence furthermore was presently bound by the French alliance. The obvious fact that Cesare Borgia had the support of Louis XII pushed Florentine help for Caterina further and further into the area of wishful thinking. Caterina nevertheless decided to try to draw the Florentines to her side. She sent to the Arno city appeals which were well devised by Giovanni di Casale but coolly received by the Florentine *Signoria*. Recriminations followed for leaving her alone in her worst hour, she who all her life had been such a faithful ally of Florence. Pleasant words came back from across the Apennines, but nothing else.

Now Caterina tried pressure. She would consent to a renewal of Ottaviano's *condotta* only if Florence assented at the same time to an alliance. But in diplomatic bargaining gold coins are hardly ever exchanged for ordinary stones. Caterina must herself have known that Florence did not value Ottaviano's services to the extent of risking the wrath of the French and the Borgia. A *condotta* for the young man was possible, while an alliance was not.[47] Yet no other course was left to Caterina than to plead, sulk, beg, threaten, and persuade. Her counselor Francesco Fortunati carried her case to the Florentine authorities, particularly through her brother-in-law Lorenzo di Pierfrancesco de'Medici.[48]

It may have sounded like a good omen to Caterina when she heard that Florence was sending her a special envoy to settle all outstanding questions. For a moment the flash of hope was blinding. The name of the envoy was Niccolò Machiavelli and his instructions were clear enough: to keep Caterina friendly to Florence at the least possible expense. As for Ottaviano Riario, he could have a *condotta* for one more year with the pay reduced from fifteen thousand to ten thousand ducats. An alliance to protect Caterina was out of the question.[49]

On July 16, 1499, Niccolò Machiavelli, yet unknown and a beginner in the art of diplomacy, arrived in Forlì to test his wits on his first major diplomatic mission. The initial audience was granted him by Caterina's counselor and present lover, Giovanni di Casale. Pleasant words were spoken about old friendship and sympathy for each other. The following day Machiavelli met his real opponent. Caterina received him in the *paradiso*, an especially high bulwark in the wall facing toward the mountains. Here were the new apartments of the Lady of Forlì, beautifully adorned and with a splendid view of the mountains. Caterina played the hard-to-get ally. She tried the device of using her allegiance to Milan and the threat of a possible alliance with Milan as a weapon of diplomacy. She talked with enthusiasm about the *condotta* offered Ottaviano Riario by Lodovico Sforza, with high pay and honors.[50] However, Caterina graciously accommodated Machiavelli on the question of supplies and recruitment. After such a kind yielding to Florentine wishes Machiavelli sent a favorable report to Florence. He suggested full payment of all the money owed to Caterina for past services and also, to please her maternal pride, raising the reward for Ottaviano in a new *condotta* to twelve thousand ducats. At this point Machiavelli had indeed not quite seen through Caterina's tactics.[51]

On July 22, Machiavelli noticed that Caterina ostentatiously sent five hundred crossbowmen under Dionigi Naldi on their way to Milan.[52] A day later she was ready for her decisive play for a Florentine alliance. That day Machiavelli was startled by her abruptness; their discussion lasted only a few minutes. After having thus confused Machiavelli as to her political motives, Caterina apologized and gave as the reason for her behavior her worry over the severe illness of Lodovico (later known as Giovanni dalle Bande Nere), her one-year-old son by Giovanni de'Medici (Popolano). Then she immediately brought up the discussion of an alliance with Florence. Was Florence going to defend her when Cesare Borgia attacked? Machiavelli correctly pleaded that his instructions did not permit him even to discuss such matters. Caterina saw no difficulty there; he should get new directives. She did not, however, give much time to do so.[53] On July 24 she put it clearly to Machiavelli that there must be an alliance or no formal agreement on anything could be concluded. Machiavelli had no choice but to leave.[54] The realities of the situation excluded an alliance. Caterina felt no great distress over the shattered negotiations. The French had not yet shown the full extent of their power, and Milan remained a more than respectable support. Besides, she could still try to sway the Florentines.

27

NEITHER A TROUBLED diplomacy nor the violent events which had commenced in the northwestern corner of Italy did away with the quietude of the Romagnol summer. Caterina savored the pleasures of the chase, of eating on warm summer evenings in her garden, and of living in an area brimming with nature's abundance. Her vigor and strength were augmented by such moments of sheer joy.

Caterina also devoted herself for days to her private business. Beside her plenipotentiary, Francesco Fortunati, Leonardo Strozzi was the most active partner in her far-flung business deals. Among them were the usual grain deals which Caterina could conclude with much profit in good harvest years because her states were blessed with fertile soil.[55]

Time consuming and eventually even trouble making was the disentanglement of the late Giovanni de'Medici's estate. His silverware had been sent to Lorenzo by December, 1498.[56] But Lorenzo longed for more of his late brother's possessions.[57] Knowing also that Caterina sometimes could not and often would not repay obligations promptly, Lorenzo pressed for a quick settlement. Giovanni's accounts of his grain trade must be sorted out and his personal belongings inventoried.[58] In addition, Lorenzo had borrowed money from and loaned some to Caterina and Ottaviano, and things were somewhat confused.[59] The correspondence between Caterina and Lorenzo became filled with words such as credits, debts, accounts, and estates together with talk of alliances, soldiers, and subsidies. Misunderstandings occurred, or so they were called. They really came to be hostilities. By the time Caterina and Lorenzo exchanged views on the tutelage for Giovanni (dalle Bande Nere) they were angry with each other.[60]

For the time being Caterina kept all her children under her own tutelage. In the case of her youngest son, Giovanni, she had to deposit two hundred and fifty thousand florins as security in Florence for the right to do so.[61] The other sons presented no such problems. They even voluntarily gave Caterina the right to speak and act on their behalf.[62]

It was not meant for Caterina merely to settle her private affairs and enjoy the Romagnol summer. The Florentines prepared themselves for a period in which they would have to watch their so-called friends, the French and the Borgia, with the same measure of distrust otherwise reserved for enemies. For them, Caterina and her trouble with the Borgia remained a thorny problem. Early in August she had sent Giovanni di Casale to the Arno city on the heels of the returning Niccolò Machiavelli.[63] He brought explanations for the failure of Machiavelli's mission and renewed the request for an alliance between Florence and Caterina Sforza. Florence, motivated by sound self-interest, refused.[64]

On August 27, 1499, Lodovico il Moro expressed his shock over Florence's callousness to Caterina.[65] But although he reaffirmed his love for his niece, the Lady of Forlì and Imola, he regretted that he could do nothing at that moment for her. Understandably, since Lodovico fled from Milan four days later. He had with him his brother Ascanio, his sons, a bulging treasury, and burning hopes for a triumphant return to Milan.[66] Milan became French except for the Castello Sforzesco. Soon that fortress fell too when the French bought off the commander and the garrison. By then, Lodovico had taken refuge with his relative Maximilian I, and Caterina's strongest pillar of support had collapsed.

Caterina stood amid the ruins of two hopes, Milan and Florence. Wherever she looked she now found only those who sympathized with her but dared not support her and those who bitterly hated her. The intentions of the latter group became clearer by the day. Everything seemed to co-operate to help them achieve their goals.

Only hope, stubbornness, and determination to keep her sovereign position were left to Caterina. But she felt as she had once written to Lodovico: "Should I have to perish I want to perish like a man." [67] In a new mood of stark realism she dropped all pretext of bargaining with Florence and accepted a *condotta* for Ottaviano on Florentine conditions, that is, without protection for her states.[68] Caterina furthermore humbled herself and approached the Venetians on the possibility that they would protect her.[69] She found that door closed.

By then, a new and merciless enemy had to be coped with. On a hot August day an artisan returned home from work.[70] He found his wife feeling unwell and complaining about an assortment of aches. It was thought to be just one of the recurrent summer sicknesses until the dreaded signs of the plague showed on the poor woman's body. A few days later the whole family fell ill, then their neighbors, and their neighbors' neighbors. In terror people isolated themselves in their houses, bathed in aromatic waters, prayed, burned incense, and prayed some more. The deathly sick were placed before the housedoor where the priest dispensed solacing words and the last sacrament. The stench became thick and the threat of death ever-present. Caterina, preoccupied with saving her state, negotiating, buying supplies, and drilling her soldiers suddenly saw the strength of her main city severely imperiled. In a conference with Forlì's governor, Ridolfi, and her chief magistrate, Tornielli, she ordered sound measures which, however, required drastic action. No one was to flee; the city was to be temporarily reorganized to battle the disease. Ridolfi lost his courage and subsequently his position.[71] Caterina and Tornielli divided the city into small districts to facilitate the supervising of the sanitary and other health arrangements. Brave priests assisted the dying. Doctors were hired at a salary of twenty-five lire a month, their assistants were called into the city, and two extra undertakers were taken under contract. For a good wage they had to promise to cart the sick to the hospitals and to bury the dead. The city gates were closed for the duration of the disease and free food was distributed. Forlì lost only one hundred and seventy-six persons. This relatively small toll proved the effectiveness of the measures and bore witness to the courage of those who had carried them out.

Meanwhile history ran its course toward the fulfilment of French aims. In October, 1499, Louis XII of France moved into

Milan. He had power and success, and consequently the representatives of the Italian powers flocked to Milan to greet him. Florentine orators also arrived, but found their objectives hard to attain. Pisa proved to be the main obstacle. That city, ardently pro-French and defending itself valiantly, was finally betrayed by Louis XII in return for a contingent of Florentine troops. Ironically, even the foes of Lodovico il Moro suffered. Isabella of Aragon, who once had aspired to become the duchess of Milan in reality rather than stand in the shadow of Lodovico and his wife Beatrice d'Este, saw the complete doom of her family approaching. Her nine-year-old son Francesco was handed over to Louis XII for "protection." Most conveniently for the French he "discovered" a longing for a clerical career and lived to become abbot of an obscure French monastery. Isabella's relatives in Naples were also at the edge of a political abyss. The French were within reach of their aim to be masters of Italy. And now their faithful allies reached out for the promised rewards.

Cesare Borgia longed for his chance to sweep the Papal States clear of the ruling families and to build his own state. The road was open. A generous and shrewd attempt by Florence to save Caterina by having her states inserted as Florentine allies or adherents in the Florentine-French alliance had failed.[72] Louis XII pleaded that he could not interfere in the jurisdiction of the pope. This clever move which would have prevented Cesare's campaign against Caterina had been designed by her and loyally carried out by the Florentines. Just as futile was a Florentine attempt to persuade other states such as Bologna, Siena, Piombino, and Ferrara to band together with Caterina Sforza for mutual defense. These states refused to risk their existence for the sake of the Lady of Forlì and Imola. Some of them were hopeful, and others knew that they would not be objects of Cesare's present campaign.[73] In Romagna itself, Bertoja Filicaja, the Florentine commissioner, kept a strict neutrality in matters concerning Caterina. Florence was willing to help Caterina secretly and quietly, but not openly. The road to Forlì and Imola was open for Cesare Borgia and he entered it without hesitation.

Late in October, 1499, a brave individual made an attempt to help Caterina. Vincenzo Calmeta, poet and writer, had worked in former years for the Sforza family. The experience had been a happy one and Calmeta felt a true sense of loyalty to the Sforza. His attitude did not change when he joined the entourage of the rising star, Cesare Borgia. Now, in the fading days of October, 1499, Caterina became the beneficiary of Calmeta's loyalty, which in turn may very well have been strengthened by Florentine prompting. Calmeta approached the French king in order to dissuade him from supporting Cesare's Romagnol campaign. He failed because considerations of higher politics (and not, as Louis XII pleaded, respect for the jurisdiction of the pope over Forlì and Imola) obligated the French king to aid Cesare. Thus two days after sending an encouraging message to Caterina,[74] Calmeta had to notify her that she now had no important allies left, that her friends at the curia had deserted her, and that the French king would supply troops and artillery against her, while the pope would willingly pay for everything.[75] Cesare had already begun to hand out money to his soldiers in order to bolster their spirits for the coming fights.[76]

For a while, one feeble hope for active help had remained in the person of Raffaello Riario, cardinal of San Giorgio. The year 1499, however, was not a good time for him either. In August his daughter Faustina had suddenly died in Forlì, where she had stayed with Caterina.[77] The formerly powerful cardinal now carried little weight in the councils of the church, and whatever was left of it he did not exert in favor of Caterina but only of her sons. Giuliano della Rovere, the second remaining Rovere-Riario cardinal, had never liked his relatives and, besides, he could not even dream of influencing the policies of the Borgia, a family whom he thoroughly hated and who in turn despised him.

The most sensible course of action for Caterina would have been "temporarily" to abandon her states and seek refuge in the safety of Florence. After all, she was a Florentine citizen, and young enough to wait a few years. Alexander VI could not live forever, and his successor might well reinstate her. Such a procedure was safe, not unusual, and dictated by political common sense. But Caterina decided on another way, which was resistance to the last. It was a course running counter to the realities of power and fraught with nearly certain disaster. But it also was the stuff which the glory of history's heroes and heroines is made of, all too often senseless, but enthralling.

Caterina was about to add another chapter to her legend and a respectable chapter to the history of the Sforza. Lodovico Sforza had fled before the French onslaught, and Giovanni Sforza, lord of Pesaro, would soon do the same before that of Cesare Borgia. Caterina was the only Sforza to face her enemy without yielding. The fame and dread which surrounded her adversary did not deter her. True, Cesare Borgia had not yet shown his military and administrative skills. But everyone knew his utter ruthlessness which recognized no restraints of mercy but only those of political expediency.

Work crews prepared the environs of the city of Forlì for the coming siege. All potential cover for the enemy was destroyed, be it whole suburbs or the beautiful trees and bushes of her elaborately planned park. The evicted people clamored for consideration and were promised compensation in future years. Much good such promises would do them in case Caterina lost, murmured the discontented. Their lady had no such doubts, or at least showed none of them in public. She had some areas around the city flooded, the walls and gates strengthened, and provisions stocked in the city and in the fortress of Ravaldino. The armorers of Forlì and Imola worked feverishly. Other arms and armor were bought abroad and shipped into the two cities. Soldiers were hired with a reckless abandon which speedily drained away Caterina's slender funds.

Cesare Borgia had gathered his troops, fifteen thousand in all.[78] Their fighting quality was uneven, with the reliable core formed by three hundred *lanze francesi* (about eighteen hundred armed men) [79] at horse and four thousand Swiss soldiers. The French were captained by Yves d'Allegre and paid by the French king. The Swiss, commanded by Antoine de Bassey, the *bailli* of Dijon, were kept in the field by French and papal money. Finally there were the papal troops, who had supported Louis XII in his campaign. It was indeed a formidable instrument which could easily inspire hope in Cesare for the complete conquest of all of the territories in Romagna, especially since no assistance for the various ruling families was forthcoming. Only Venice extended her protective hands over Rimini and Faenza. That did not matter, for the Malatesta and Manfredi families could be destroyed later.

Another hope failed Caterina. For years she had studied with passionate interest the medical and cosmetic knowledge of her time. Her book of prescriptions contained both the fanciful and the sensible. Her beauty had been the first incentive for the voluminous collection. Now she would use it to save herself from Cesare. She knew the basis of Cesare's stature and power only too well. If Alexander VI should die, the Borgia influence would wane rapidly. So on a dreary November day a small group of men set out for Rome carrying a cylindrical container, in which, wrapped in a scarlet red cloth, were letters for the pope. In them were pleas to Alexander VI for a compromise, but also something which Caterina hoped would cause his health to deteriorate rapidly.[80] Some claimed that the letters had been placed for a while on the chests of plague victims and others that they had been treated with a special kind of poison.

Yet the leader of the assassination contingent, Battista da Meldola, bungled his job. A few days after the men's arrival in Rome the darkness of the dungeons of Sant'Angelo surrounded him and his helpers. For a while they had little to fear since the Borgia preserved them as a potent weapon against Caterina. Cesare, already involved in his campaign against Caterina, hurried in a forced march from Modena to Rome in order to express his joy over the failure of the plot.[81] On November 24, a special celebration of thanksgiving to God for saving Alexander VI from such a threat was held in the church of Santa Maria della Pace in Rome. The pontiff used the incident to warn the government of Florence that any support of Caterina would now be doubly dangerous. The "daughter of perdition" had attempted to poison the pontiff.[82]

Although he had had nothing whatever to with Caterina's plot, the cardinal of San Giorgio felt thoroughly ill at ease in Rome. Dressed in plain clothes he left his palace. Officially the cardinal and papal *camerlengo* had gone out for the chase. It took a few days for everybody to find out that he had no intention of returning to Rome for a while.[83]

As for Caterina, she remained defiant. She never defended herself or denied the deed. Had she spoken, she might have chosen her own words of another occasion: "One cannot defend a state with mere words." [84]

THE WHEEL OF DESTINY had turned. Cesare's army, papal and French, was on the march to Imola and Forlì.[85] The only possible serious obstacle to its progress had been removed when Bologna came to terms with the French king. The Bentivoglio, lords of that city in all but name, had been among the very few who had favored the Milanese cause to its very expiration. Fifty archers and a detachment of infantry had left Bologna for Milan as late as the day of the general French assault. Still, in September, 1499, Bologna succeeded in soothing the French wrath, and Cesare, who eyed Bologna as covetously as all other cities in the Papal States, decided to remain jovial and pleasant. He wanted first to subdue his weaker opponents before attacking such a powerful city as Bologna. Consequently, instead of a dreadful clash of arms, Bologna experienced a great feast with roasted calves, capons, and pheasants, and mountains of sweets. Cesare's army passed through Bolognese territory not without incidents but without conquest. Once on Caterina's soil the soldiers showed their bias by atrocities and devastation.

Caterina's strongholds would, however, not be such easy prey. Forlì was taking on a grim look. No building had been left standing within a quarter of a mile from the wall, and within a mile circuit all trees and shrubs had been cut down.[86] Caterina went further. She wanted a clear declaration of loyalty from her Forlivese subjects. A gathering of the *Consiglio Aperto e Generale* ("General Council") was called and its members heard Ottaviano plead the Riario case.[87] He and Caterina's auditor besought "the most beloved people of Forlì" to see the injustice of the papal bull voiding the rights of the Riario. Ottaviano also told of the unsuccessful mission of Dr. Giovanni dalle Selle. The auditor, more aware of how to influence the citizens' mind, ignored legalistic subtleties and told of the terrible barbarian hordes marching toward them from the northwest. They were Swiss, Germans, French, and Spaniards, foreigners with no Italian blood in their veins and no sympathy or mercy for those who surrendered. Furthermore to side with Cesare would be to build on shifting sand. Whenever his father, Pope Alexander VI, died, Cesare would disappear into obscurity. Yet Caterina would remain to reward her friends and punish her enemies. As a first reward she was reducing the grain and meat tax. Cheers of "Ottaviano, Ottaviano" followed such oratory. Full of optimism, Tornielli, head of the council, assured the Riario of the city's support.

The very next day this spirit of resistance was put to work. The people helped strengthen the defenses of the city. The four quarters of the city became military districts each with a commander. Among them was Luffo Numai, still staunchly loyal to Caterina. The three others came from the Capoferri, Moratini, and Bezzi families. The soldier-poet Marullo Tarchionata would be chief of the city's defense.[88]

Early in November Caterina sent her son Ottaviano to Imola to achieve a state of preparedness there.[89] He found a city which, with the exception of a few families, had always been easy for the Riario to govern. Ottaviano needed, therefore, little power of persuasion to convince the citizens of the justice of his cause. In addition he granted to the Imolesi important concessions in taxes. When the city council asked also for the return of all exiles, Ottaviano consented.

The fortress, the core of the military strength of Imola, was given a new commander. That office had been bestowed as a plum on Caterina's stepfather, Giampietro Landriani. Old and with no experience in soldiering, he welcomed relief from what promised to become a critical position. Dionigi Naldi of Brisighella took his place.[90] Dionigi had a unique reason for loyalty to Caterina. The Florentines had tried to apprehend him as a prime suspect in the murder of Corbizzo Corbizzi, a Florentine citizen. So outraged had the Florentines been by the murder that Machiavelli on his way to Forlì had made a special point of stopping in Brisighella to do some detective work on his own and to seek clues to the truth. Caterina had protected Dionigi. Now, one hundred and eighty soldiers moved with Dionigi Naldi into the fortress of Imola, and in the city itself a new unit, recruited from among the *contadini* who had fled their homes, was drilled for battle by Giovanni Sassatelli.[91] It was indeed a strange and fateful act by the Imolesi to make one of Caterina's worst enemies captain of the improvised militia.

On November 13, Ottaviano left for Forlì. The Imolesi thereupon walled themselves in by completely closing the city gates with stones and mortar.

In the meantime Caterina had made a determined effort to gain the allegiance of the Forlivesi. The people, unused to such a display of concerned affection for them, sensed a weakness in the position of their lady and exploited it. They rejected the ten *capitoli* which Caterina had drawn up concerning the tax structure in Forlì.[92] After pleading that she could not reduce taxes any further since the twenty-two thousand *lire bolognesi* revenue from Forlì permitted neither her nor her sons to live in the proper style of *signori*,[93] Caterina dropped plans to impose any surtaxes (with a minor exception) and reduced some taxes. Such a buying of loyalty was a reckless gamble. In the midst of a costly military campaign she really could not afford to be generous with her revenues. But she hoped that self-interest would spur the Forlivesi to greater efforts on her behalf in the coming fight. When the city celebrated the agreement with her and when the councils and some other prominent citizens pledged their unwavering loyalty to her she could be content. For those who entertained thoughts of conspiring against her she had a gallows erected on a conspicuous place in the town square.[94]

The Forlivesi resumed their preparations for the coming siege.[95] The peasants of the surrounding area were notified by twenty strokes of the big bell to come to the city and bring their families, their valuables, and all their food stuffs. It was hoped that provisions for four months could be secured for every family in Forlì. The burghers of the city closed their shops and worked on the walls. Even nuns and priests pushed wheelbarrows filled with stones and sand, as did Ottaviano himself, who for once showed a remarkable outburst of energy. Much of the work was done on the wall between the gates of Schiavonia and San Pietro where the fortifications had been allowed to deteriorate. In the fortress of Ravaldino the battlements were provided with new wooden covers and the walls of the main tower were repaired. A census of all arms in the city was taken. When it showed a lack of preparedness on the side of the Forlivesi, Caterina generously supplied cuirasses and arms.[96]

Caterina's determination to hold her possessions knew no relaxation. Soldiers were hired wherever they could be found. Fond as she was of strict discipline and order, Caterina was reduced to picking up even such rabble as a band of four hundred Gascons and Germans under the leadership of a French adventurer called Gianotto.[97] Five days later three burghers lay dead and many others wounded in the main square of Forlì where the soldiers and the Forlivesi had fought a pitched battle. There is no telling what went on in the monasteries in which the soldiers were lodging. Suffice it to say that the monks called the soldiers demons and that the brawls could be heard throughout the city. Caterina regretted and abhorred the incidents but went right on gathering more soldiers and drilling them for the coming battle. To make sure that no grave obstacle to a firm resistance to Cesare Borgia should arise, she demanded and took hostages from prominent and hostile families. For a few months they would live in the *rocca* of Ravaldino, Caterina's headquarters.[98]

In such an atmosphere of apprehension Caterina showed once more her unbelievable composure. While the noise of the drums of war could be heard not too far away, she penned a letter asking for some glass implements for use in certain experiments.[99] A few days later she sent two of her fine horses to Mantua to fill a request of the marquis.[100]

Doubts of Caterina's success were scarcely uttered. Those careless with their words and sympathies slowly filled the dungeons. Yet many indications point to the realism with which Caterina evaluated her position. While Ottaviano had talked bravely in Imola, Caterina's jewels—or whatever was left of them—costly furniture and clothing, and her other children already had begun their trip to safety in Tuscany. In Florence they could await the turn of events in the tranquility of Santa Maria delle Murate, a convent for nuns which Caterina had always favored with gifts.[101] Shrewdly she had at first approached the Venetians concerning safe refuge for her children, a sly maneuver to draw her old adversary ever so slightly toward her. The Republic of San Marco had politely refused. "After all the Venetians were extremely ill disposed toward her who had been so arrogant a ruler." [102] While such a simple explanation sufficed for a chronicler, Venetian foreign policy had little to do with emotions, past or present. Although it was against Venetian principles to let the pope establish himself firmly in Romagna, the Venetians, threatened in the east by a new Turkish offensive and tied to the French by an alliance, could at that point only "let happen whatever destiny had in store." [103]

Cesare's army had moved closer to Imola and encamped at Cantalupo. From there a detachment of five hundred horsemen under Achille Tiberti rode to Imola. In the past Caterina had valiantly upheld the Tiberti case whenever it had been threatened in Cesena. Achille Tiberti refused, however, to recognize any obligation stemming from past benefits or love and chose his stand in accordance with the power constellation of the hour.[104] Now it clearly favored Cesare. Achille served his new patron well.

At the Spavuglia gate of Imola, Achille Tiberti asked for a discussion with the constable in order to demand the surrender of the city to its overlord, the pope. Fatefully, Achille's partner in the discussion turned out to be Giovanni Sassatelli, who like all of his clan, traditionally pro-papal and bitter about the murder of Francesco Sassatelli in 1488, harbored every feeling toward Caterina but sympathy. Sassatelli, with the consent of the General Council, offered the unconditional surrender of Imola [105] and had the gate reopened. Achille Tiberti received more than he had dared to dream when he had set out on what was to be an exploratory mission. He and his soldiers were given quarters, food, and forage. Later, on Tiberti's insistence, he was even given the keys to the city.

Cesare granted the city favorable terms of capitulation: he would provide justice, benevolent rule, peace, and defense of the city; nobody would be persecuted for having opposed Cesare in the past; and only Imolesi could hold the positions of *podestà* and castellan.[106]

Cesare had taken the city of Imola in a matter of minutes. The fortress was a different matter. Grim and threatening, it had to be conquered before Cesare could proceed to Forlì. His fifteen thousand soldiers swarmed into Imola like hungry locusts. Until the artillery had softened up the defense of the fortress they had nothing to do but indulge in their own ventures and conquests in the kitchens and bedrooms.[107]

The ritual of the siege began.[108] Cesare placed his artillery to the west of the fortress and had it fire at the top of the walls. The barrage hardly dented the fortifications. Persuasion came next. A trumpeter signaled Cesare's wish to talk with the castellan. Cesare's message was simple: give up and depart in safety and honor; or go on defending and be hacked to pieces if you are an ordinary soldier, or be hanged with your family if you are Dionigi Naldi. Yet the castellan had courage and a sense of honor. He would, he answered, only regret being hanged for treason. Death itself did not frighten him, since he had partaken of the sacrament. When Cesare brought another member of the Naldi family to the wall to plead with Dionigi that he had already done his duty, the latter pointed out his oath of loyalty and might justly also have mentioned that his wife and two of his children were being held as hostages by Caterina. Cesare realized that he had failed.

Force was the only answer, a not particularly promising one when he reckoned with the strong walls, the plentiful provisions, and the excellent spirit of the garrison. All the while Dionigi Naldi battered the disloyal city with his cannon.

Cesare's success came finally by way of treachery. A man from Imola approached him with a plan.[109] He had worked on the defenses of the fortress as a carpenter and knew every inch of the walls. If the artillery were to be concentrated at the weak spots which he pointed out, the walls would collapse and leave a breach for the infantry to pour into the fortress. From that moment on the fortress had no chance.

Cesare had sent Achille Tiberti to Cesena for more money from the papal treasury. It was used to double the pay of all soldiers in order to generate in them sufficient fighting spirit, if only by the way of induced drunkenness. One night long and through the next morning the Imolesi heard the booming of Cesare's cannon. By midday the wall had a gaping hole near the main gate of the *rocca*. Infantry poured through it but soon wavered, startled by the fierce resistance of the garrison. Another wave was sent forward, then another, and still another. Cesare's supply of troops seemed inexhaustible. By sunset the fortress was without hope. A trumpet blast came from one of the towers. Naldi asked for a three-day truce during which he could send messengers to Caterina. They would ask for a relief attack by Caterina's troops and inform her that otherwise the end of her fortress in Imola had come. Cesare granted the request. He was on safe ground. Caterina was in no position to send a relief contingent; and the inevitable and peaceful surrender of the fortress would save him further casualties.

Cesare's calculations proved correct. On December 11, Naldi yielded the fortress. He was allowed to leave unmolested with all his men and their property. Cesare even consented to a march of the defeated garrison out of Imola with full military honors. Only now did it become known that Dionigi Naldi had suffered a serious head injury in the fighting. According to the rules of *quattrocento* soldiering he had behaved spotlessly.[110] He had given Caterina fair warning of the impending fall of his fortress, and thus she did not blame him. The ideal of fighting to the last in a hopeless situation was alien to the Renaissance soldier, call it cowardice or common sense.

The fall of Imola turned out to be as disastrous for the morale of Caterina's camp as it was harmful militarily. One immediate consequence was the fall of the small fortresses defending the northwestern approach to her territories. Their conquest cleared the way for Cesare to march on Forlì. Yet he was in no hurry. His soldiers longed for a rest and the army needed reorganizing.

Cesare proceeded slowly in a southeasterly direction. In Faenza he behaved with the utmost tact and graciousness toward Astorre Manfredi. Cesare planned to rid the Papal States step by step of unwanted families. At present, Faenza, like Rimini, was under Venetian protection,[111] recognized as such by King Louis XII of France, and Astorre Manfredi's neutrality was helpful.

EVEN WHILE THE FORTRESS of Imola still resisted bravely, the Forlivesi began to waver in their determination to defend themselves. Popular support for Caterina, never uniformly strong, crumbled at its edges. Ominous economic storm signals appeared. People hoarded their valuables despite an edict which ordered that all gold and silver be desposited with her banker, Zuntini. The Forlivesi also refused to accept recently struck coins because it was obvious that their silver content was below expectations.[112] Edicts threatening with the dungeon those not conforming to Caterina's wishes could not remedy the loss of faith revealed in these actions.

In her main fortress, Ravaldino of Forlì, Caterina held on defiantly. She was surrounded by a motley crowd whose members came from everywhere: [113] three Sforza who had fled Milan, Alessandro, "Francesco" (?), and Galeazzo Sforza; some Riario and Sanseverino relatives; her lover and chancellor Giovanni di Casale; her advisor Antonio Baldraccani; numerous *condottieri* from all parts of Italy, among them the castellan Bernardino da Cremona and Marullo, the soldier-poet; finally and surprisingly, Scipio, the illegitimate son of Girolamo Riario.[114] At Caterina's command were about nine hundred men. Blown together in a haphazard manner, these soldiers knew how to fight for a day's wage, but only that. Their equipment was good. Caterina had sacrificed all her money and more to buy them cuirasses, lances, and ammunition. While they waited for the enemy, they loitered, caroused, molested, and quarreled without aim or limits.[115]

Imola was on the verge of surrender when Caterina renewed her official inquiries as to what the city of Forlì would contribute to the defense in case of a siege. Alessandro Sforza, her stepbrother and emissary, spoke with the chief magistrate Tornielli.[116] The latter reflected the increasing anxiety in Forlì when he assured Alessandro that all Forlivesi felt the deepest loyalty and devotion to Caterina but also pointed out that Caterina should understand that even greater rulers had fled on occasion both in order to save themselves and to keep war from their people. Politics had its ups and downs. Pope Alexander VI could not live too much longer, and who could keep Caterina from returning after his death? The citizens would gratefully greet her upon her return if she now showed concern for the fate of her subjects. These, however, were only his own thoughts, and since Caterina wanted an official expression of sentiment, Tornielli promised to gather the *Consiglio Aperto e Generale,* the members of which came from city and *contado* alike.[117] Before it could meet, the defense of Imola collapsed.

The impact of Imola's fall made loyalty to Caterina and naked fear fight a pitched battle in the *Consiglio*. By nightfall of December 12 no decision had been reached. Tornielli still kept assuring Caterina that all men of Forlì would fight for her, to a reasonable extent that is, should she decide to stay. Such words failed to impress the realistic and furious Caterina. She sent her stepfather Landriani into the city to call the Forlivesi cowards and rabbits who should do whatever they pleased. As for her, she would "show the Borgia that a woman, too, can handle artillery." [118] She may have hoped that such strong words would rouse the town's pride and swing opinion in the *Consiglio* in her favor. But she also knew that she had better gird for a lonely fight. A fascinating duel it would be. Both opponents were pleasing to the Renaissance ideal of beauty: Cesare slim, vigorous, with a handsome face framed by a reddish beard, and of elegant composure, and Caterina with her delicate skin, expressive face, supple body, and steely blue eyes. Both were also ideal representatives of Renaissance politics, shrewd and cold-blooded.

Ottaviano, accompanied by the auditor Dipintore, was ordered to join her other children in safe Tuscany. [119] Caterina did not want worry about anyone dear to her to interfere with her determination to give Cesare a good fight. Meanwhile all bridges had been destroyed in the surroundings of Forlì, more provisions had been crammed into the fortress of Ravaldino, and the pawnshops in the city had been ordered to return all pawned articles to their owners upon proper payment or other arrangement. Empty pawnshops would attract no looters and would free the city from all legal obligations. Then Caterina rode to Forlimpopoli to oversee the last preparations there.

With every mile that Cesare's army moved closer to Forlì, support for Caterina dwindled in the city. At that moment the Numai family, rich and respected, lived up to its long-standing pro-papal policies, particularly since Cesare showed the greater strength. Luffo Numai had supported the Ordelaffi family until 1480, when their cause began to falter. With a keen sense of reality he had nimbly stepped into the camp of the Church, represented by the Riario. When Girolamo and Caterina had entered Forlì for the first time, the most conspicuous figure in their triumphal greeting had been Luffo Numai. After the assassination of Girolamo, Luffo had wavered slightly, but had soon realized the impossibility of the Orsi cause. It was he who had shouted "Duca! Ottaviano!" during that fateful night when the tide had turned in Caterina's favor. As a gesture of appreciation Caterina had accepted his hospitality for temporary lodging and for the victory banquet. Now as the political weather changed once more, after careful analysis of the situation, Luffo Numai decided to stake his life and fortune on Cesare. Caterina learned of his change of heart and ordered him arrested.[120] She knew only too well the powerful impact this man could have on her position in Forlì. But her search for him failed.

When the General Council finally reconvened, Luffo Numai came to be the main speaker.[121] His arguments justified all of Caterina's apprehensions: that the Riario had lost all legal right to the city, that the Forlivesi should not play judge between Caterina and the pope, and that Caterina, who had arrested, tortured, exiled, and executed people at will, was not worth a sack of the city. These words were well chosen, and Luffo Numai had a most convincing ally in the creeping fear which now infected everybody. At this point any advice on how to escape the terror of war was more than welcome, especially when the arguments attached to the advice made surrender seem a reasonable action prompted by law and logic.[122]

Before Cesare's troops could yet see the wall of Forlì, the city was ready to yield. After the council meeting the commanders of those gates beyond the reach of Caterina's cannon were replaced. A new governmental authority, the Council of Twenty (five representatives from each quarter) was invested with all power. In it, Luffo Numai and Niccolò Tornielli were leading figures.[123] The people, delirious with joy at having saved themselves from the horrors of a sacking, joined the monks and priests of San Mercuriale in their thanksgiving procession. No time was lost in notifying Cesare of the city's change of heart.

Caterina, grimly waiting in Ravaldino, took the news calmly. It was brought to her by two of the town's most respected citizens, Niccolò Tornielli and Lodovico Ercolani. They assured her of the continuing and undiminished love of her subjects and promised that none of her personal possessions would be touched. When the two men returned to the city, it was hard to believe their report that Caterina understood and forgave. Especially so since a little later the cannon of Ravaldino hurled stone balls into the city, killing and wounding some and spreading terror. It was apparent what Caterina's tolerance really meant—she had written off the Forlivesi, whose desire for safety she considered to be mere cowardice.

The transfer of power to Cesare was yet to be engineered, and the new council began to work out the conditions for the surrender. In the meantime the city remained quiet and orderly. The pawnshops were empty and the Riario property was protected by city decree.[124] There were, however, still those who did not like the course of events. The patricians working on the capitulation thought it hardly worthwhile to write into it provisions for the *contadini* and the other "voiceless." Thereupon resentful *contadini* poured into the streets of Forlì, shouting in an ugly mood.[125] The rule of law was gravely threatened after all. Now the patricians suddenly discovered warm feelings for social justice and prudently reworked the document of capitulation so as to provide equal tax provisions for the city and the county.

Caterina was completely surrounded by enemies. At that point Florence, motivated less by sympathy for Caterina than by her own interests, tried to slow Cesare's progress. No supplies reached the Borgia from Florence, and Pope Alexander VI complained bitterly to the *Signoria* of Florence.[126] Then in another desperate move to prevent the establishment of Cesare Borgia in Romagna, the Florentines once more tried to persuade the French king to take Caterina under his protection, but to no avail. As for Caterina, she seemed almost cold-bloodedly to ignore the events around her.[127]

Only a few yards from the moat of Ravaldino, however, was the world which had turned against her. On December 17, Dr. Giovanni dalle Selle and Monsignore dell'Aste left for Imola to take to the new *signore,* Cesare Borgia, the document concerning the capitulation of Forlì.[128] The negotiations were swiftly concluded, and Cesare moved closer to Forlì. By now his soldiers were impatient to enter the city. All through the night they tried to get into Forlì by any means possible. The alert citizens pushed them back. On the next day, December 18, 1499, the capitulation was signed and Forlì became legally and factually Cesare's, except for the fortresses of Ravaldino and Schiavonia, and the area which was within the reach of their cannon. Catrina promptly made her presence felt by firing merrily into the city. She singled out the houses of the Numai and the others who had betrayed her. Some members of those families were just then on their way to Rome to deliver the declaration of allegiance of the city of Forlì to the pope.

Cesare issued his first decrees: each peasant must carry two bundles of green wood into the city for use in the coming siege of Ravaldino and some lumber for repairs on the church of San Mercuriale.[129] The merchants must sacrifice by not raising prices for bread, wine, wheat, and beans.[130] Cesare's imminent arrival with such a strong army gave force to his orders, and for the time being there was no resistance to them. This awesome force also demoralized the contingent of Caterina's troops which guarded the Schiavonia gate. They meekly surrendered.

After noon on December 19, the twenty-four-year-old Cesare made his entry into his new city.[131] The people saw a sizeable detachment of Cesare's army pass before he himself appeared mounted on a palfrey, with a plumed beret on his head, a silk coat over a suit of armor, his spear pointed downward, a sign of his conquest of Forlì. Just as Caterina had been a beautiful Lady of Forlì, Cesare was an attractive master. His entry was impressive, but it lacked spontaneous cheer. A pouring rain mixed with ice chilled the onlookers, and not all of the magistrates had turned out to receive him. Cesare, therefore, proceeded straight to the house of Luffo Numai. The rain which continued throughout the night unfortunately did not dampen the spirit of Cesare's soldiers, who were elated by the easy conquest.[132] The citizens hurried home and securely locked their houses. But the night was soon filled with the noises of war and its ravages.

The soldiers knew what they wanted and where to get it. They talked their way into houses here and battered the doors into splinters there. A few hours after the entrance of the army the homes of the citizens overflowed with cursing, blaspheming soldiers who took food, furniture, and all valuables which had not been prudently hidden or buried. Women and girls paid the price of the city's surrender. The warehouses of the merchants stood empty after the first waves of soldiers had finished their work. The town hall became a tavern dispensing free wine taken from the citizens, with crying and abused women doing the serving. In the streets the French soldiers amused themselves by dragging statues from the churches through the mud. Others broke down the wall surrounding a nunnery. The nuns were to share the fate of other Forlivese women. But in this case Cesare sent some courageous officers and crack infantry to drive the soldiers off. As the hours of the night went by, the Forlivesi were given a preview of hell. Caterina felt no pity. Like the Venetian chronicler Sanuto, she considered such happenings as "just punishment for a city which had surrendered like a whore." [133]

It is no wonder that on the next day delegation after delegation of frightened and outraged citizens approached Cesare. They all made the same demand: restrain your troops. Cesare promised remedies, redistributed his troops, issued orders at least to leave the nuns alone, originated inquiries, threatened his soldiers with stiff penalties, and spoke of restitutions. It did not help; the soldiers did what they pleased. They could not understand Cesare's admonitions. The city was theirs, after not much fighting to be sure, but still by conquest.

Fear paralyzed the city. The political sympathies of the Forlivesi shifted away from Cesare. Now they were either pro-Ordelaffi or pro-Caterina. Caterina could only welcome such encouraging developments. Not that she was depressed, or showed any sign of discouragement, although by that time some doubts about her ultimate success must have troubled her. Yet her hopes for success were far from absurd. Caterina's half sister was still the wife of the Emperor Maximilian. More promising even was the expected return of Lodovico il Moro to Italy. If he came, the French king would have to recall his troops from Romagna for his own use. Caterina could cope with Cesare and the papal troops. Thus resistance made sense, and the longer the siege lasted, the better her chances would be. In addition, Cesare's troops were ill fitted for a long siege. These soldiers became easily demoralized by stubborn walls and men who did not yield. Those were Caterina's real hopes, although she told her soldiers that she and they were fighting for a just cause and that God would see to it that such a cause won. There also was the slim chance that the Forlivesi might one day rise against their tormentors. The population already had displayed some acts of defiance. The French and the Forlivesi became so distrustful of each other that the army began to be suspicious of the death of any soldiers. One had died in the house of Giorgio Folfi under mysterious circumstances. Giorgio had his right hand cut off, and then was bound to a cart by his feet and dragged to death.[134]

Christmas was quiet and dreary. Cesare gave a banquet for his relative and papal legate, Cardinal Giovanni Borgia, who deserved all of Cesare's gratitude.[135] Ever since September, 1499, he had worked tirelessly in the diplomatic field to prepare Cesare's success in Romagna. A short time after he left Forlì, the cardinal died suddenly. Rumors of poisoning persisted, but nobody could prove them or give any good reason for such a murder.

On Christmas morning Cesare received a shock. From the main tower of Ravaldino flew a flag with a lion on red ground. Had Caterina found a protector in Venice? Cesare remembered hearing from obscure sources that Venice was drifting away from the Holy League. He called on Meleagro Zampeschi, the Venetian liaison man in his camp. Zampeschi assured Cesare that there must be some mistake since Venice had no intention of deserting the League. He was right, and the flag turned out to be not a Venetian flag after all, but a Bolognese standard similar to that of Venice.[136] One of Caterina's constables, a certain Francesco Roverse from Bologna, had acted on his own.

Perhaps Cesare hoped that Caterina would be mellowed by the spirit of Christmas. He chose the holidays of the nativity for making the usual moves of conciliation before the assault. Dressed in black and white, Cesare and one of his trumpeters rode to the edge of the moat of Ravaldino. Trumpet blasts brought some of Caterina's men-at-arms to the battlements. A few minutes later Caterina herself appeared. A courteous greeting on both sides opened the battle of wits. Cesare marshaled examples from history to show how honorable and how safe a surrender would be compared to the risks of battle. As for her and her sons specifically, she could count on a new state or could even live on a comfortable pension in Rome. Caterina remained unimpressed. If history teaches anything, it is only that the brave are favored and that cowards live to rot in obscurity. As a daughter of a Sforza she knew no fear. Cesare's kind words were appreciated, but who in his right mind would really put any stock in the word of a Borgia? Caterina did not even bother to wait for an answer; she turned around and disappeared. Cesare returned to his quarters not sure what to do next.

He decided to go back for another talk on the following day. This time he offered Caterina guarantees for her safety. D'Allegre, Antoine de Bassey, the *bailli* of Dijon, and other illustrious Frenchmen would protect her. Caterina only wondered cynically why she should trust Cesare's satellites when he, the main figure, was not trustworthy. Then she left once more. The siege would have to proceed.

Cesare was furious. Caterina had said things to him that others had dared merely to think. And a woman, of all persons, had refused to take the easy way out and surrender. He would show her. Caterina remained calm although slightly disappointed. She had hoped to lure Cesare close enough to kidnap him. Cesare, however, had properly been wary of the "bellicosa signora di Imola e Forlì." [137]

Pope Alexander VI tried his hand at negotiations. He gave the cardinal of San Giorgio, who still kept a safe distance from Rome, permission to send an envoy into Ravaldino to Caterina. She scornfully refused to admit him or even talk to the man. Alessandro Sforza negotiated with him from the battlements. Through the envoy, Alexander VI offered assurances for Caterina, her sons, and their possessions, and a yearly pension of four thousand ducats.[138] Caterina ordered Alessandro to reply that the fortress was well provisioned, that she had always followed the cardinal's suggestions with little spirit and even less trust, and now that he had made himself a partner in a dishonest enterprise she was even less likely to follow his suggestions, and finally that she would hold on to the fortress at least until the grain ripened again.[139]

30

THE FORTRESS OF RAVALDINO was a proud monument to *trecento* and *quattrocento* building.[140] In shape it was square, thereby giving a maximum of space and a minimum of wall length. Ravaldino's towers, one at each corner and a main tower, were orthodox in pattern. Wider on the bottom, they had extra strength against all instruments of destruction, the battering ram and the mines. When artillery became part of a fortress's equipment, cylindrical channels had been broken through the walls in such a way that always three cannon could fire through one outside opening. In addition, some of the artillery pieces were stationed on the platform behind the battlements. The main tower, much stronger, wider, and higher than the other four, was a fortress in itself. It guarded the principal gate and the *sportello* (a little gate for pedestrians). In order to further strengthen her fortifications Caterina had added to Ravaldino a number of ravelins.

Attached to the *rocca* (the fortress proper) was the *cittadella,* a spacious walled area in which troops could be lodged, service shops maintained, and exercises held. A drawbridge connected the two defense systems.

The French and Italian artillery had readied their emplacements. Cesare had seven heavy guns and ten lighter ones (falconets).[141] The biggest gun, called *Tiverina* ("the gun from the Tiber area"), was nine feet long and could throw projectiles with the diameter of nine inches. Cesare positioned his artillery around the three ravelins, particularly around the one called the *paradiso.* On December 28, 1499, his cannon fired against Ravaldino in earnest.

Caterina's guns answered, and with one of their shots were lucky enough to kill Cesare's artillery expert.[142] The incident renewed Cesare's fury, and unfortunately, it diminished neither the rapidity nor the effectiveness of the siege artillery. More and more often Caterina's garrison spent their nights repairing the gaps and holes made in the fortress during the day. Caterina herself had to leave the *paradiso* and take lodging in the main tower.

For a few days the droning of artillery fire went on. Nevertheless Ravaldino was still in good shape. As for Caterina's hopes, Maximilian I had not come to Italy to help her; but every day brought closer the return of Lodovico il Moro. It was no secret that the French protégé Trivulzio who governed Milan had become thoroughly hated by the populace.[143] In addition, the Swiss cantons had offered to let Lodovico il Moro, not Louis XII, recruit their men. Early in January, 1500, Lodovico's army would be ready to march. Once they began to pour out of the Alpine valleys, the army besieging Forlì would dwindle with the French abandoning Cesare. Even the ever-cautious Florentines took heart [144] and in deepest secrecy promised four hundred infantry men to Caterina. One day forty pilgrims, chanting hymns and prayers, marched by the main gate of Ravaldino. Suddenly the drawbridge was lowered, the pilgrims turned and disappeared into the fortress.[145] Caterina had a fresh supply of soldiers, artillery experts, and stone masons. Never disheartened, Caterina in these days was even jollier than usual. The siege army could hear the fifers and drummers playing deep into the night as Caterina and her lover Giovanni di Casale danced surrounded by their cheerful companions.[146] The fortress appeared a comfortable place to the French and papal soldiers who manned the siege guns. These men had to shiver in the cold to keep up the bombardment of Ravaldino's walls.

Cesare became impatient and moody. Persuasion had failed, and the artillery fire was doing less than well. Nobody had delivered Caterina dead or alive although Cesare had promised ten thousand ducats for her.[147] This just showed that he was richer than Caterina, who could promise only five thousand ducats for a dead Cesare and ten thousand ducats for Cesare alive. Her prolonged defense of Ravaldino was a nuisance for the jubilee year; the pilgrims streaming through Romagna toward Rome dreaded the thousands of soldiers whose cruelty and greed knew no bounds. The Forlivesi could bear witness to that. Few houses had much furniture left, few women had escaped the violators, and few Forlivesi still had enough food to save them from the pains of hunger. The hatred became so intense that it finally troubled the army. Cesare, for his part, feared popular unrest because of the long duration of the siege. He tightened his reins on Forlì. The edicts ordered all citizens to deliver whatever arms they possessed to his army or to hang from the gallows which had been erected at the Porta Schiavonia. What good were those weapons anyhow? Anybody who vented his anger on the soldiers found no mercy.

On Epiphany the French celebrated their high holiday. Food and drink were plentiful and, like women, cost nothing. Even the officers smashed the furniture and dishes of their gracious hosts—just an old custom, they explained. Through the streets moved groups of drunken soldiers, with army tambours and fifers spreading riotous noise, laughing and singing. Those women who willingly participated in the festivities were, so the chronicler tells us, *donne di mala vita* ("prostitutes") .[148]

Finally, with all the celebrating over, Cesare decided to gamble on an assault.[149] The artillery fire was resumed, intensified, and again aimed at the southern part of the fortress system. The cannon protected by parapets of wood and earth were moved closer to the fortress. The gunners dug protective trenches for themselves in the slightly frozen ground. Quite against all rules of fighting, the guns continued their barrage even during the night.

The defenders ignored the artillery fire and rolled barrels filled with sand to wherever the projectiles had shattered the wall. Their own guns aimed at Cesare's batteries but failed to destroy them.

By January 11 pieces of the wall on the side toward the mountains had fallen into the fifty-two-foot-wide moat. Hour after hour the gap widened. Worse, the fallen debris was slowly building a bridge across the water. Caterina shouted at and tried to drive her soldiers to erect a new wall from the sand-filled barrels she had at hand. But none of her mercenaries wanted to step directly into Cesare's artillery fire. His falconets, small artillery pieces about three or four feet long, showered the defenders of the open space with one-pound iron balls. The gap stayed open.

Cesare was ready. Days before, he had required all peasants to supply five bundles of wood each and to pile them up at that side of Ravaldino where later on the breach in the wall occurred. Two boats, brought overland from Ravenna, were also at his disposal. Now new bundles of wood were lugged to the moat. At noon on Sunday, January 12, Cesare bet three hundred ducats with his officers that by Tuesday Caterina would be at his mercy.

Caterina knew that the breach in the wall had to be barricaded and strengthened by additional forces if she were to preserve her chances, her states, and her honor. Bravely, some of her men emplaced guns in the courtyard in such a way as to make any attempt to cross over the by now half-filled moat a risky enterprise. Sand-filled barrels and strong wooden barriers protected the gunners who manned these free-standing guns. Pleased with their work, the defenders shouted insults at their opponents, calling them cowards and worse.

Their courage could only be admired, since at that moment everyone was aware of the imminent general assault. Cesare had once more paid his soldiers extra money to stimulate their fighting spirit. For just one moment it had seemed as if Giovanni Sforza, *signore* of Pesaro, could help Caterina. He almost intercepted the money transport for the extra pay of Cesare's soldiers.[150]

Noon passed and the assault began. It concentrated on the stretch of broken wall. Cesare's men had fabricated rafts from the bundles of fresh wood supplied by the peasants. On them the soldiers set out on the short trip across the remaining moat, which no longer presented a great obstacle. Yet, if Caterina's guns had fired at the approaching soldiers, a bloodbath would have followed. Mysteriously the barrage never came; the guns were loaded and their mouths stared at the attackers. Someone forgot to order them to fire. Afterwards, the captains accused each other and called each other "traitor" and "coward." Nobody knows the real reason for the fatal mistake. What mattered on that day in January of 1500 was that Cesare's soldiers were permitted to cross the most critical area unmolested. Once the attacking soldiers had reached the breach in the wall and begun to pour through it, the battle of Ravaldino became a mere proving ground for desperate courage. Its duration was in question, but no longer its outcome.

Soon another mistake in the defense became evident. The defending soldiers had all been neatly distributed along the walls of the fortress and at its strongpoints. Nobody had provided for a mobile reserve to be thrown into critical spots. Cesare's troops crawled, jumped, and dashed into the fortress.

Caterina's standard came down from the tower towards the Cotogni gate. A Swiss mercenary had scaled its walls and taken the valuable symbol. The attackers saw the event as a sign of victory being near and redoubled their efforts. Caterina shouted at her captains to resist to the utmost. The castellan, Bernardino da Cremona, gathered all his courage and set a trap for the enemy. He waited until quite a number of German and Swiss soldiers had made their way into one of the towers, then he shut the gate and set fire to the ammunition in the tower. The whole group of trapped soldiers perished. The fire and smoke from the explosion stung everybody's eyes, and unfortunately the defenders yielded in order to get fresh air. Thus, Cesare's troops found another gaping hole.

The enemy now sat squarely inside the fortress.[151] Caterina's men remained entrenched around the main tower which she still held. Her soldiers, working for a daily wage, were ready to give up, but in her presence none dared to do it. When she gave orders to counterattack there was some hesitation. Yet they followed her, lowly soldier and respected commander alike, cursing the enemy as much as their stubborn lady. Caterina protected by her cuirass and by her own furious fighting stood in the midst of her mercenaries for an hour. Then the men wavered and retreated. She refused to yield and barked commands at her companions to stand fast. After another hour the onslaught overwhelmed them all. Caterina ordered fire set to great heaps of wood and retreated behind the wall of fire and smoke. A little later, when the fire had burned down, Cesare's troops saw groups of soldiers storm through the biting smoke rising from the ashes. Amidst them came Caterina. The clash of arms was heard again, an outpouring of desperate anger, no more. White flags were hoisted everywhere. While Caterina made her valiant last stand, one soldier after another laid down his arms. Giovanni di Casale, the Sforza brothers, the castellan, and the other captains were taken prisoner. Caterina fought her way back into the strong main tower. The gate had hardly closed behind her when she directed the first orders to the soldiers in the tower. She prepared for another siege, this time holding only a tower.

Cesare rode on horseback close to this, her last stronghold. The trumpet sounded, and the third meeting between the two began. Cesare, with the confidence of the victor, implored Caterina to stop the defense. He pointed out the unnecessary bloodshed which otherwise would still have to come—not too convincing an argument from a man who did not usually value human life so highly. Caterina had no chance for a long argument. She appealed to Cesare for mercy for her soldiers and her subjects. Then she felt a hand placed on her shoulders and heard the words: "Madam, you are the prisoner of my Lord, the *bailli* of Dijon." [152] With it Caterina's freedom of action ended, taken away by a French captain who somehow had made his way into the tower. Exhausted, dispirited, and deeply unhappy, she did not care who her captor was. But strangely enough, the sheer accidental fact that the Frenchman had reached her first was to become of the utmost importance for her future. French law made it impossible to take women as prisoners of war, and thus Caterina was, for whatever it was worth, not really a prisoner but under the protection of the French king.[153]

At the time such niceties did not matter. She was led out of the main tower into one of the smaller buildings. There she met Cesare, who made her give the necessary orders for the complete surrender of the fortress, an order which had no real significance. The Germans, Swiss, and French had made nearly all parts of Ravaldino their own. Remembering the dreadful cries of their fellow soldiers trapped in the burning and exploding tower, full of frustration over the prolonged siege, and driven by the lust for blood and loot, these soldiers slashed their way into every corner of Ravaldino. For thirty-six hours to be one of Caterina's soldiers or subjects caught in the fortress meant to be a victim of the cruelest torture. Soldiers fought among themselves over the loot, prisoners, food, clothing, furniture, money, and women. Pleas for mercy went unheard; the drunken shouts of triumph dominated. Even the dead found no peace. Their bellies were slit open to discover whatever jewels might have been swallowed for safekeeping.[154]

Cesare soon ran into his first obstacle. Caterina's captor claimed his reward; otherwise he would not deliver her to Cesare. His stubborn insistence was supported by his overlord, the *bailli* of Dijon. The words became harsh, the voices louder, and an armed scuffle threatened.

French commanders intervened. D'Allegre, enthusiastic over Caterina's combination of beauty and courage, initiated a temporary solution. Caterina would be handed over to Cesare but would remain legally under the protection of the French king. At two o'clock in the morning, in darkness scantily lit by a few torches, Caterina, one lady in waiting, a few of her maids of honor, Cesare, and a large group of soldiers set out for Caterina's new quarters. They stumbled across the courtyard littered with the dead, where the wounded shouted for help and the drunken soldiers mumbled about victory, wine, and women. The biting smell of smoke and the nauseatingly sweet smell of dead bodies irritated the throat and turned the stomach. The moat was full of mud and slippery, and the water chilling.

Cold, miserable, but still proud, Caterina arrived at the house of Luffo Numai. There she suffered the final consequences of defeat. She had lost her state, her fortress, her men, and her possessions. In those hours of the night her body also was violated. Cesare, the fancier of ladies, rejoiced that military and political victory had also delivered a beautiful thirty-seven-year-old woman into his hands. In abusing and degrading Caterina, Cesare triumphed fully. Cynically he shouted to his officers in the morning that Caterina had defended her fortress better than her virtue.[155]

Then came Caterina's turn for a small triumph. Hour after hour Cesare's soldiers searched every corner of Ravaldino. Her children could not be found. Cesare had caught the regent, but the important heirs had escaped. The Borgia was furious. During the following night he vented his rage on the helpless body of his prize prisoner.

The battle of Forlì was over. The soldiers had to leave the fortress. Before closing it nearly seven hundred dead were removed and buried in the anonymity of mass graves. The drawbridge was raised and entering the fortress prohibited. Offenders were to be hanged.

CESARE HAD ACCOMPLISHED his objectives in Forlì. He had eliminated a dangerous foe and launched his career as a brilliant general of the Church. But Romagna was not yet under firm papal control, and new campaigns were ahead. The next ruler to be ousted was another Sforza, Giovanni Sforza, *signore* of Pesaro. One obstacle remained to the march eastward against Giovanni—Caterina. Her detention in Luffo Numai's house was merely a temporary solution. The issue of whose prisoner she was and who would be awarded permanent custody of her was unresolved. If Cesare were to attain his goal of delivering Romagna as a truly papal territory to the Holy See, and also, of course, of becoming himself the eventual duke of Romagna, he had to keep Caterina under his control. A dead Caterina would be the best solution and a Caterina kept in the obscurity of a life in prison the next best. In the latter case she would sometime become willing to sign away her rights in return for freedom. Although the pope had the right to oust Caterina from her position, only her voluntary resignation could insure real papal control over Forlì and Imola. The *bailli* of Dijon and Caterina's captor, a certain Captain Bernardo, had simpler motives; they both counted on a reward for taking her prisoner. The French custom which forbade taking women prisoners of war was for them a good bargaining point since it could be used to threaten Cesare with Caterina's release. Another Frenchman, d'Allegre, had tried to conduct himself according to the code of chivalry. He admired Caterina and held exalted ideas of how the honor of France was involved in her case. Obviously he would be the mediator when the political consideration of the Borgia, the greed of the two French officers, and the honor of France had somehow to be reconciled.

That time soon came. The army had been readied for the
march to Pesaro. Cesare, still in possession of Caterina, prepared to take her with him. At a street corner he was confronted by the *bailli* of Dijon and three hundred of his soldiers.
The *bailli* mumbled something about the honor of France and
his rights to the prisoner. Cesare, outwitted and outmanned,
released Caterina. The French took her to the house of the
Paolucci family.[156] For the moment she had escaped the wrath
and brutality of Cesare Borgia. Suddenly Pesaro became unimportant for Cesare. He had to gather his wits to get Caterina
back.

By torchlight Cesare discussed the affair with d'Allegre, who
had hurriedly been summoned from Forlimpopoli. An agreement to meet again was all that resulted from the dramatic talk
in the city square of Forlì.

The next meeting at noon on January 22, 1500, made the
Forlivesi tremble.[157] From the main square came furious shouts.
Cesare called the French mere aides whose claims were unfounded. The offended French likewise spared no words. They
pointed out that the French king always referred to Cesare as
his *luogotenente* ("representative").[158] The *bailli* of Dijon sent
for the Swiss. With their pikes and standards they posted themselves grimly around the palace. The onlookers scattered in all
directions. Barricades went up in the houses, and the Forlivesi
prayed to San Mercuriale, the patron of the city. A fight between
the French and the papal sides would leave them little but
ruins and utter deprivation. But the two sides were still allies,
and Caterina was not a weighty enough problem to drive either
to extreme measures. D'Allegre designed a *modus vivendi:* Cesare would receive the right to keep Caterina and take her to
Rome. Since she was under the protection of the French king,
her treatment could not and should not be that accorded a
prisoner. As for the *bailli* of Dijon, he and his troops got fifty
percent more pay than they would have otherwise. It was a
solution, temporary yet permanent, gentle yet harsh, depending
on whether one looked at the letter or the fact. For Caterina it
meant above all that the *bailli*'s soldiers called for her at the
Paolucci home, accompanied her through the streets, and returned her to the Numai house. For once she lost her composure.[159] Shrieking, her arms flailing wildly, kicking and writh-

ing, she fought the soldiers. Only the desperate awareness that nothing could help her made her cease her resistance, certainly not the soothing words of the *bailli* of Dijon, who told her how much better off she was to be now that she was protected by the honor of the French. She knew only too well the lonely hours of the night when Forlì was quiet, the French king far away, and Cesare's lust and brutality at a peak.[160]

Next morning the sound of trumpets filled the air and soldiers hurried to their units. Some, who had become used to their quarters had to be flushed out of their lodgings by detachments of fellow soldiers. "Criers" informed those who most stubbornly delayed joining their units that the gallows were being prepared for them. Gradually the army gathered, its soldiers fully equipped and burdened with spoils. Orders were shouted, and the soldiers moved out through the Cotogni gate.

The officers attended mass with Cesare. Afterward, the representatives of the four quarters—a Lambertelli, a Todelli, a Moratini, and the ubiquitous Luffo Numai—rendered a loyalty oath to Cesare as the ruler for the Holy See. Then the commanders, too, left Forlì. In their midst Caterina, bitter, proud, and miserable, rode quietly. The people looked sullenly on. The events of the past weeks had changed the popular mood. Those who formerly had hated her showed a benevolent indifference; those who had been indifferent to her felt stirrings of sympathy; and those who had loved her wept. For better or for worse, there were many who would have agreed with the Venetian chronicler Priuli when he praised her as "without doubt at that time the outstanding lady of Italy." [161]

Forlì licked its terrible wounds. The inhabitants gazed at homes void of everything of value, littered with shattered possessions, and nauseatingly dirty. Families took up their lives, suffering from the wounds of body and spirit. Early in the year the well-known and beloved chronicler Leone Cobelli died.[162] In his last written lines he cursed the French, "those barbarians and people without law" [163] whom Julius Caesar had once defeated, for bringing misery to Italians. The gray, dull, and uninspiring routine which curiously heals so many afflictions was resumed.

The Borgia ruled firmly. The city had repeated its promise of loyalty to the pope through four ambassadors to Rome. They had knelt at the feet of Pope Alexander VI and pledged the city's undying devotion to the Holy See. In return, Forlì kept its Council of Forty which had been the instrument of self-government under Pino Ordelaffi and the Riario.[164] But the relations between the city and Cesare's representatives grew frostier by the day. The era of the Ligurians had ended with the ouster of the Riario. The era of the Spaniards began when the Borgia, who were of Spanish origin, paid off political debts to their supporters from their home country. Ramiro de Lorqua became governor of Forlì and Imola; Gonsalvo de Mirafonte was given command of whatever was left of Ravaldino; and a certain Magnares was made governor of Forlimpopoli.[165] The days of Cardinal Albornoz and his Spanish governors in the 1300's seemed to have returned. The Forlivesi in true Romagnol tradition despised the foreigners, but their exhaustion prevented any hostile action. Even when Lorqua and his officers tortured the population with wholesale murder, rape of women and girls, and extortion, no revolt ensued. It was Cesare himself who eventually dismissed and executed his former friend and trusted governor, but it was for Ramiro's doubtful loyalty rather than for his harshness and corruption.

Caterina traveled eastward, well escorted by Cesare, the French captains, and their soldiers. In Forlimpopoli she had to witness the ceremony which bestowed the loyalty of yet another of her former possessions on the Holy See, in actuality on Cesare.[166] Among the dignitaries who pledged the city's devotion to Cesare was a member of the Butrighelli clan, a family which had received its ample share of exiles and executions from the Riario. The next station, Cesena, brought new humiliations. Her body suffered through one more night when Cesare indulged his insatiable desire for women. The following morning brought hope, however. Since he could not very well take Caterina along to the siege of Pesaro, he left her in the safe-keeping of d'Allegre. A period of honorable detention seemed ahead until history played a cruel joke on Caterina.

As Cesare left Forlì and made his way toward Cesena,[167] the star of the Sforza was again rising swiftly in the constellation of political power. The Milanesi had long been disenchanted with their deliverers from the Sforza rule. A series of mistakes in government and the general distrust of foreigners turned the

eyes of most Milanesi longingly northeastward. There Lodovico il Moro was ready to march with about twenty-five thousand men of excellent fighting caliber. Late in January, 1500,
the Sforza was at the doors of Milan, and a few days later his
standard flew over the city, except for the *castello*. The French
needed all of their troops. Messengers galloped to Romagna to
order all soldiers under French command to Lombardy. Had
that happened a month earlier the fortress of Ravaldino would
have flown the flag of victory. Now the return of the Sforza
destroyed even the temporary respite Caterina enjoyed in
French captivity. D'Allegre and his troops hurriedly marched
northwest, and Caterina was returned to Cesare.[168] Only Pesaro
profited from Lodovico il Moro's last dash into history. The
siege of that city was postponed; Cesare, left without French
support, decided to postpone further endeavors in Romagna.
As a sign of his overlordship he left nine hundred soldiers in
Forlì and two hundred in Forlimpopoli under Cardona, a
Spanish captain, and Ercole Bentivoglio of Bologna, an Italian
from a family which would have given a fortune to see Cesare
dead, but at that time shrewdly co-operated with him.

   Late in February, 1500, Cesare made his entry into Rome in
a manner worthy of a Roman emperor.[169] Alexander VI "interrupted his audience and cried and laughed alternately." [170] At
the church of Santa Maria del Popolo waited the ambassadors,
conservatori of the city and the Church, the scholars, the
scribes, and many more. Burchard never saw such extravagance, not to speak of the license and disorder which the event
brought into an already exuberant carnival. Caterina was
spared the humiliation of being led through the streets of the
city as chief evidence of Cesare's triumph. The Borgia were
aware that the Romans, like many other Italians, admired the
lady who had defied Cesare Borgia while others did not even
dare to match their wits with him. Caterina might very well
have detracted from Cesare's glory in such a procession. Instead
she was hurriedly lodged in the Belvedere Palace, a pleasant
prison indeed, from which she could view the gardens around
the Vatican.[171]

   At that point the battle between Caterina and the Borgia
came to a standstill. She had no choice in the matter. She could
only wait for the next move by her opponents. In the meantime

she "was still full of the devil and strong willed" [172] and firmly refused to sign away her rights to Forlì and Imola. Although she and her family had legally been deposed, the Borgia could not feel really safe until she had made such a declaration of renunciation. For the moment Pope Alexander VI and his son Cesare did not press her for it. They hoped that imprisonment and future political developments would bring Caterina to surrender. The Sforza case no longer had any strength. Lodovico il Moro, having lost the decisive battle after initial successes, was a prisoner in France; Cardinal Ascanio was held in Venice (later also by the French); Caterina was confined in Rome; and Giovanni Sforza of Pesaro would soon hide out in Venice. Why then hold on to rights which had no chance of realization?

For Caterina there was also the pertinent question, "for whom." She had thousands of admirers but few friends. Of the Romagnol days of power, love, and glory, only the priest Fortunati remained with her.[173] From her children, whose future welfare was one of her major reasons for holding out, came little encouragement. Ottaviano and Cesare, the two sons old enough to act on Caterina's behalf, soon showed themselves more inclined toward an accommodation with the Borgia than toward a contest of will. In Ottaviano's case such a conciliatory spirit had its roots in his openly displayed longing for "questo cappello" (the headgear of the higher clergy).[174]

Her former subjects had not forgotten her, but they hardly appreciated her stubborn refusal to admit defeat. They had made their peace with the pope and were just then bargaining with the papal *locotenente* ("local representative" of the pope) over an old problem, the level of taxation. The Imolesi were granted the generous conditions they had asked for when they offered their city to Cesare in November, 1499. The Forlivesi, too, were in no mood to revolt; nor were they greatly receptive to Caterina's return—the less so since Cesare named a capable and just man to be *procuratore generale* for Imola, Forlì, and Forlimpopoli (Giovanni Olivieri, bishop of Isernia), and the articles of capitulation were favorable.[175] Caterina's insistence on keeping her rights in Romagna for the benefit of her sons offers one valid explanation for her refusal to yield. Another concerned herself. The rights to Forlì and Imola made the difference between the admission on the one hand of total defeat by the Borgia and with it failure in Renaissance politics, and on the other a vestige of status and the flicker of hope of regaining what seemed lost; in short, between Caterina as a public figure and Caterina as a private personage. For her the choice, which to the historian seems totally illusory, was real, and her whole past life, personal pride, and ambition revolted against retirement into obscurity.

Her sad situation contrasted starkly with Cesare's, who now was named *Gonfaloniere e Capitano Generale della Chiesa Romana*.[176] Caterina's trials, on the other hand, grew even more severe as a result of one of her own reckless schemes, an abortive escape plot. One of her confidant's, Fra Lauro Bossi, an honest and devoted but rather muddled friend, had persuaded a guard to help in Caterina's escape. But then a letter to that man had fallen into wrong hands, the plot had been exposed, her partisans arrested, and the bribed guard drowned.[177] Instead of having escaped, Caterina found herself on May 26 in a prison cell of Sant'Angelo.[178]

While the city of Rome was gradually filling with the pilgrims of the jubilee year who piously went from church to church, from monastery to monastery, and climbed Pilate's stairs on their knees, Caterina accustomed herself to the darkness around her. The thick damp walls muffled all noise from the outside, and only the swishing of the ubiquitous rats interrupted the terrible silence. Food was scarce and foul. The air stank from human sweat and excrement. The world outside reached her only in the person of the jailer, who came infrequently, and through the letters from her sons. These were far from encouraging.

As they saw it, Caterina's stubbornness was senseless and presented a serious obstacle for Ottaviano in his attempt to gain high church office. At one point the sons even scolded their mother for her stand, which in their view reduced her children to absolute beggary. Could she not exchange the now worthless rights for lucrative benefits for her sons? Pope Alexander VI, *giustissimo e clementissimo* ("most just and merciful") they called him, would be eager to come to good terms.[179] It is not surprising that the Borgia made no attempt to interfere with such a correspondence. Fortunati, who voluntarily shared Caterina's imprisonment, answered the sons in bitter terms. Had the devil deprived them of all feeling and memory? [180] The sons were not impressed. In the spirit of realism they continued to see in a conciliation with the pope the only hope for Caterina's release and for salvaging some benefits from the Riario's past prominence. All through these exchanges Caterina maintained a quiet and restraint. The Mantuan ambassador to Rome was of the opinion that she suffered from *passion de cuore* ("Weltschmerz"). [181] It may have been true, since her personality in the years following indicates that the weeks and months spent in the dungeon were a decisive turning point in her life. What had once been strongest in her, her lust for life, her preference for action over contemplation, and her unconquerable spirit and vigor gradually weakened. In the long nights when the stillness surrounding her became unbearable, and when every sudden noise might signal the approach of Cesare's murderous henchmen, Caterina learned to know the corrosion of fear. During the day every mealtime was another nerve-racking experience. When would the Borgia decide that she was not withering away fast enough? A sudden diarrhea from specially treated prison food would kill quickly. The accusation of another poisoning would hardly perturb the already notorious Borgia. Still, she had enough stamina to face these fears. Others were more destructive. Lorenzo di Pierfrancesco de'Medici (il Popolano), Giovanni's brother, always hostile to Caterina as an intruder into the family's fortunes, succeeded in a law suit. [182] At his insistence the Florentines decided that Caterina's captivity was sufficient reason for wresting from her the custody of her little son Giovanni. Ever since his birth she had cherished the boy more than her other children. The loss of guardianship over him was therefore a disturbing thought.

All through these weeks and months the pressures on Caterina to yield Forlì and Imola to the pope added to her trials. Her sons usually sided against her, quite willing to exchange their rights to the territories for a high church office for Ottaviano, small benefices for his brothers, and a dowry and good husband for Bianca, their sister. Their anger over Caterina's stubborn refusal was less violent but just as strong as that of the Borgia. Alexander VI and Cesare were at a loss as to what to do next. An ecclesiastical trial would have been appropriate for a lady who had at one point attempted to poison the pope. The men whom she had sent to Rome for that purpose had been carefully kept in another part of the Castel Sant'Angelo. But such a trial would have given Caterina an opportunity to speak her mind and tell of her treatment by Cesare in those horrible days and nights early in 1500. The Borgia preferred to let life in the dungeon do its destructive work. The two would-be assassins were hanged since they were no longer useful. Caterina stayed in the dungeon without hope and with the Borgia still at a loss as to what to do. What saved her at that point was the strange accident that a Frenchman had reached her first on that grim day in Ravaldino. The Borgia were less impressed by the legal nicety of Caterina's right to French royal protection than by the continued threat of a French army returning to Rome. If that happened, some of the French captains would be sure to remember Caterina Sforza, and her death could have unfortunate consequences. Thus the months dragged on indecisively.

Caterina missed no great political chances by virtue of her imprisonment. Cesare Borgia continued his successful campaign to make the pope and himself supreme in Romagna. Caterina's two former allies were now valuable instruments of Cesare. At one point Achille and Polidoro Tiberti and their men had murdered twenty opponents during Sunday mass. Alexander VI absolved them in return for one hundred ducats and the promise to deliver Cesena to Cesare. The Tiberti did so by force.[183] Faenza, Rimini, and Pesaro became Cesare's next objectives.[184] In August, 1500, when it mattered most, Venice reluctantly withdrew its protection of Faenza and Rimini. The former city defended itself so well that Cesare had to suspend siege operations for the winter of 1500/1501. The presence of a considerable army in and around Forlì and Imola waiting for the resumption of the siege seemed a golden opportunity for the Riario to recoup some sympathies. Cesare staged veritable orgies of wine, women, and extravagance. There were feasts, contests, bullfights, dances, and chases.[185] Some people lost their lives in the brawls and rowdy entertainments; many lost considerable property. Nor were Cesare and his officers particular about how they secured female company. Still, the people did not hate or blame Cesare, since on the whole his administration was just, orderly, and strict.[186] There was no nostalgic longing for Caterina or her sons. In the spring of 1501, Faenza, too, fell.[187] Although Astorre Manfredi had been promised a safe conduct, he ended up, not surprisingly, as a prisoner of Cesare. Caterina was unaware of his presence in Sant'Angelo. A year later (June, 1502) Cesare's henchmen dragged the young man out of his cell, strangled him, and threw him into the Tiber River.[188] In Astorre's case they need not worry about the French, only about the moral conscience of the world, which has not yet saved too many lives.

Cesare, "Borgia de Francea, Duca de Valencea, Conte de Diena, Signore de Cesena, de Forli et Imola, Bertenori et Isodunio, Gonfaloniero della romana Eclesia et Capitanio generale," [189] was not resented by his subjects. That he ordered all the fortresses in his new territories restored to their full strength was more the result of his concern about the aging of his father than for any defense against popular unrest. Pope Alexander VI was clearly in the last phase of his life, and Cesare knew that only tangible power would eventually determine whether he continued in the limelight of Renaissance politics or disappeared into obscurity or worse. He could sense everywhere the hatred of those whose rights or honor he had infringed, and there were many such.

Caterina's destiny was finally altered by the same people who had initiated and helped to bring about her doom. In the spring of 1501 the French army once more moved against Naples. By then, Ottaviano Riario had skilfully worked on the French sense of honor. He had approached King Louis XII of France, the cardinal of Rouen, and Captain d'Allegre.[190] The Borgia began to receive inquiries about Caterina and her imprisonment. But the ways of diplomacy are slow and abound with possibilities for deliberate delays. Such methods did not satisfy d'Allegre. He well remembered the lady whose courage he had admired during the siege and capture of Ravaldino. D'Allegre had on various occasions fought beside Cesare and had been assured that Caterina was in the honorable safekeeping of the pope. When he learned of her imprisonment in the dungeon, his sense of chivalry was revolted. Now he and three other officers took time out from their command duties to make a detour to Rome and present themselves to Pope Alexander

VI.[191] D'Allegre demanded that Caterina be immediately released or the French army would act to preserve the honor of the French king, who according to French law had Caterina under his protection. The Borgia knew their predicament. The liberation of Caterina could undermine the very foundations of Cesare's power in some of his territories. Cesare, who had hurriedly and secretly returned to Rome,[192] had a sound respect for Caterina's fighting spirit and courage, but he overrated the number of her partisans. In any case she could be a definite nuisance for him once he himself lacked papal support. With the utmost fervor Cesare pleaded with the French and with his father for Caterina's continued detention.[193] His persuasive talent did not suffice. D'Allegre insisted on freedom for Caterina.

The Borgia thereupon put the burden of decision on Caterina. She would be set free if she abandoned her claims to Forlì and Imola. Since Caterina had for so long resisted all threats, all promises, and all deprivations of the dungeon to keep at least a shadow of influence in her former territories, both Alexander VI and Cesare assumed that she would once more refuse to yield. Such a decision, they hoped, would end French interest in Caterina's fate and thus doom her. But although she had become emaciated, hollow-eyed, and ashy pale, and had been worn out by severe attacks of quartan fever, Caterina had lost none of her sagacity. With the French guaranteeing her freedom upon her renunciation, she finally yielded. Who had actually won, only the events of the coming years would show. Caterina hoped for a collapse of Borgia power after the death of Alexander VI, and Cesare was looking for some way finally to get rid of her. In this he was helped by a provision in the surrender agreement which obligated Caterina not to leave Rome without papal permission.

On June 30, 1501, Caterina emerged from the dungeon.[194] The horrors and sufferings of the months spent in the darkness of her cell had taken their toll. Of her beauty and her bold affirmation of life only traces remained. To the ceremony of publicly signing away her rights she was led by Troccio, the Borgia secretary and assistant in the elimination of foes. Caterina dutifully made her renunciation and promised to stay in Rome under papal supervision until the pope relented and a sum of two thousand ducats was posted on her behalf with the papal *camera*.[195] In the latter case she would be free to go where she pleased. The Borgia felt secure, since nobody seemed inclined to pay such a sum for Caterina. After the notarizing, Caterina thanked d'Allegre for his gracious help and then took up lodging in the palace of the cardinal of San Giorgio. D'Allegre hurried away to catch up with the army which had left Rome two days earlier.[196]

Caterina could not complain of neglect. Visitors flocked to her in an unending procession. Cardinals, archbishops, bishops, nobles, and lesser figures were eager to present themselves. The talk concerned mostly the years from 1477 to 1484 when Caterina had been the first lady of Roman society. The Orsini were particularly anxious to show their sympathy for her. As the days passed, spent in pleasant company, Caterina's thoughts constantly strayed far from Rome. She knew the precariousness of her position in the center of Borgia power; she longed for her children, and wanted to move to a place from which her reentry into Renaissance politics would be at least feasible.[197] At last Pope Alexander VI agreed to let her go. On July 13, 1501, he wrote to the Florentine *Signoria* that they should treat benevolently "that delectable daughter in Christ, the most noble lady Caterina Sforza whom we had to detain for certain reasons and for some time . . . and whom We now graciously set free. . . ."[198] Florence assured Caterina of a friendly reception, not because Alexander VI had asked for it, but because the old sympathy for her was still alive there. Yet neither the Florentines nor the Romans were quite sure that Caterina would ever reach that city. Many spoke openly of the dangers that awaited her on the roads leading to Florence. Cesare Borgia was totally unreconciled to Caterina's freedom. There was little likelihood that he would let Caterina, one of his prize prisoners, go unmolested to Florence.

Caterina knew the dangers but appeared unperturbed. Then one evening in July, she boarded a river boat on the Tiber and went on it to Ostia.[199] A few days of sailing brought her to Livorno (Leghorn).[200] From there she rode to Florence through a peaceful Tuscan landscape and in perfect safety. Near the city she met her children, with the exception of the beloved Giovanni (who was still a ward of others) and Bianca. After long months at the brink of total disaster, Caterina had again found firm footing. Florence was quick to permit her to stay in the city. This action only increased the disappointment and bitterness of Cesare, who in this case had been prevented from following his maxim that only a dead enemy is harmless.

EPILOGUE

FOR THE TIME being Caterina was not involved in the grand matters of Renaissance politics. Such a period of inactivity had its benefits: her body needed rest and recuperation; the effects of her previous strain and suffering were visible. But now the animosity of Lorenzo de'Medici (Popolano) reasserted itself. The intrusion of a sister-in-law, Caterina, had destroyed his dream of possessing all of the Popolano property. When she was confined in the dungeon of Sant'Angelo his dream had seemed close to realization, especially when he received control over the little Giovanni. Such a position gave Lorenzo and his son Pierfrancesco full access to the Popolano wealth, and they took advantage of it. When Caterina was released Lorenzo was no less disappointed than Cesare Borgia. Now Caterina was forced to regain what was rightfully hers by the slow processes of Florentine law.[1]

As her strength returned, Caterina felt a resurgence of her craving for power, influence, and a life of action. Gianbattista Tornadello, a patrician of Imola, became her main link to her former possessions.[2] His letters created the impression that a goodly number of partisans were waiting with great impatience for Caterina's return.[3] In a florid style he described how these men were supposedly meeting every day to pray for her coming. Other news from Romagna seemed to support Tornadello's assertions of the existence of widespread dissatisfaction with Cesare's rule. Cesare's captains, Spaniards and Italians alike, revelled in extravagant pleasure for which the Imolesi and the Forlivesi had to pay, whether with good ducats, with the products of their labor, or with the honor of their wives and daughters. A costly affair occurred when in January of 1502 Cesare's sister, Lucrezia Borgia, passed through Forlì on her way to Ferrara.[4] Her entourage was commensurate with her status as a papal daughter and a future duchess of Ferrara. With her came

718 men, among them clerical and secular dignitaries, relatives, household officials complete with housekeeper, doctor, court jester, and cooks, and 393 horses and 234 mules loaded with her possessions. Her bridegroom, Alfonso d'Este, brought a similar number of people, horses, and mules. The Forlivesi gave them a fine reception with white-clad ladies singing the praises of the noble pair, a lavish parade, expensive gifts, and good lodging. When the guests had departed, some of the Forlivesi were left with pleasant memories but fewer coins.

Caterina still expected to return to her states. But she must have become aware that her dream exceeded reality when she looked around for allies. Only one hope remained—her brother-in-law, the Emperor Maximilian I. History records, however, not so much as a hint of imperial support for Caterina.[5] Maximilian had lost all of his former enthusiasm for Italian ventures and also for his Italian wife, Caterina's half sister Bianca Sforza.

In this period of alternating hopes and disillusionments, the long expected happened. Pope Alexander VI died in August, 1503, and the Borgia family, particularly Cesare, now had to show that they would not be ruined by the loss of papal support as the Riario had been by the death of Sixtus IV in 1484. Caterina was more than eager to contribute to Cesare's doom. Forlì and Imola beckoned, and the developments were auspicious. Post-papal anarchy paralyzed Rome; political maneuvers riddled the College of Cardinals; the French and Spaniards moved closer to Rome to control the forthcoming papal election; and Cesare was helpless. A sudden and severe sickness brought him to the verge of death. He had to watch while much of his work collapsed with the actual or attempted return of the Montefeltro to Urbino, the Malatesta to Rimini, the Baglioni to Perugia, the Varani to Camerino, and Giovanni Sforza to Pesaro.[6] This was to be the hour for Caterina and her sons. Tornadello pleaded for action.[7] Yet even in his most fervent appeals for action a shadow of doubt can be detected. He advised Caterina to send Ottaviano with some soldiers to Imola and Forlì and not to go herself. Tornadello must have agreed at that moment with the assessment of the Florentine commissioner in Romagna, Giovanni Battista Ridolfi: Ottaviano might be acceptable to the Imolesi and Forlivesi, but not Caterina.[8] She was resented, feared, and even deeply hated. The sons exchanged ideas and unknowingly agreed with Ridolfi's judgment. Nothing could erase past mistakes now, they wrote, certainly not a few pleasant words.[9] But try the Riario brothers must.

Caterina set some trusted people to work in Rome, hoping to obtain legal sanction for her return to power. But what she heard from these men gave her little encouragement. Aloisio Ciocha, who had been one of Caterina's agents for years, sent her the most enlightening and also the most discouraging reports. The cardinal of San Giorgio took no interest in her cause, showed no co-operation, and did not even bother to talk at length with Ciocha.[10] Ascanio Sforza was well disposed toward Caterina, but as usual he proved to be of no help. When Ciocha pressed for a campaign in order to reinstate Caterina in her territories, Ascanio, and everybody else, changed the topic of conversation. Another of Caterina's emissaries, Giovanni Francesco de'Cichi, agreed with Ciocha's assessment. He too found Ascanio Sforza friendly, the cardinal of San Giorgio disinterested, and most others full of ill will toward Caterina.[11]

These were futile maneuvers for yet another reason: Rome did not at that point command enough influence in Romagna. The Venetians were momentarily more important after having decided in September, 1503, that they would take over as much papal territory as possible.[12] Venetian actions soon provoked Florence to increase her meddling in Romagnol politics. Therein lay the hope of the Riario, who did not have enough money for a campaign of their own.[13] They had tried to go it alone in regaining Imola. Ottaviano, who with the benevolent support of the Bentivoglio could operate from Bologna, sent a letter to the city fathers of Imola extolling the virtues of renewed Riario rule. The Imolesi refrained from hanging the man who had brought the letter only out of respect for the Bentivoglio.[14]

Florentine support would radically have changed the Riario's situation; but the Florentines decided on the Ordelaffi as a better choice for building a strong bulwark against the Venetians in Forlì. On October 22, Antonio Maria Ordelaffi entered Forlì with a contingent of Florentine troops.[15] He did not, however, gain the fortress of Ravaldino. It remained under the control of Cesare's castellan, Gonsalvo de Mirafonte. Caterina certainly must have agreed with Tornadello, who upon hearing of the Ordelaffi's return called the Florentines thieves whom God would punish severely for their wrongdoings.[16] Desperate for support, Caterina turned to Venice. On her behalf Antonio Giovanetti of Bologna tried to persuade the Venetian officials. But when they heard that Caterina stood alone, that is, without the support of the cardinal of San Giorgio, they lost interest.[17]

All of these plans were a credit to Caterina's ambition and political astuteness, but they did not solve her basic difficulty. In her former territories she was widely unwelcome because of her past actions. Ottaviano shared none of her liabilities, but unfortunately also none of her skills and courage. The key man for all Riario hopes, he was fat, lazy, and constantly striving for a position in life which would require only his presence, not ardor or daring. While his mother maneuvered and suffered under the strain of inaction, Ottaviano wavered between two courses in which to channel his dreams, not his energies. At one point he hoped for a cardinal's hat, an archbishopric, or just any high clerical office to which he thought the mere fact of being a Riario entitled him; and at other times he eyed the possibilities of marrying a rich young lady who would bring him wealth and comfort. At times Ottaviano still talked bravely of collecting support in order to regain his states and of never resigning them; [18] but actually, he found his mother bothersome with her constant pushing him away from Rome in the direction of Imola and Forlì. Consequently, he stayed in Rome to maneuver, beg, or just hang around for companionship and wining. He hoped the fact that Ascanio Sforza had been restored to an honored position and that Giuliano della Rovere had returned to Rome would eventually help to get him the desired clerical plum. His hopes soared even higher when his relative Giuliano della Rovere became Pope Julius II.

In Rome the ambitions and plans of the Riario were tossed around aimlessly and listlessly. Alessandro Sarti was still going from office to office on behalf of Caterina. He fancied himself successful: the cardinal of San Giorgio, while he had never come out in favor of Caterina's restoration, had given the distinct impression of supporting her sons. But Julius II was plainly biding his time. Words of sympathy for Caterina and her sons were mixed with assertions that all final dispositions would have to wait. Julius II was preoccupied with destroying whatever was left of Cesare's power. Until that had been accomplished he was unwilling to reveal the fact that although he hated Cesare Borgia he cherished the latter's work in reestablishing papal control over the States of the Church. Such an achievement could not be sacrificed even for the benefit of his own relatives, the Riario.

The winter months of 1503/4 brought the steady decline of the once powerful Cesare. By the spring of 1504 he had agreed to surrender the fortresses which his officers still held in Romagna, especially Forlì, Forlimpopoli, and Bertinoro. Thereupon Cesare was left to his fate, which he hoped would be favorable once he joined the Spaniards. But May, 1504, saw him a captive of the Spanish monarch and on the verge of an obscure life in prison and an even more obscure death in the faraway Pyrenees. Caterina observed the course of events and knew that it was now or never, since Julius II would soon have to make his final disposition.

As Caterina watched the unfolding of events her despair must have increased from day to day. The cardinal of San Giorgio agitated for Ottaviano and for himself, since he had his eye on the papal throne, but not for Caterina. Ottaviano's situation grew steadily worse. Immensely fat and apathetic, no doubt because of some glandular disorder, he was not taken seriously. Being the son of Caterina militated against him, and there was little to speak in his favor. The mothers of eligible daughters did not want him for a son-in-law, and the only possible career left for him was to become a *uomo di chiesa* ("a clergyman"). There also, things were far from promising. At that time Julius II was unusually restrained in handing out offices as favors, and he saw no reason to make an exception for the Riario.

In Romagna it became apparent that although the days of the Borgia had ended, those of the *signori* were not about to return. Julius II evinced more and more his determination not to let secular lords again get a grip on papal territory, even under the euphemism of "vicars." In January, 1504, the pope graciously greeted an Imolese delegation which swore obedience directly to him.[19] On that occasion he still spoke vaguely of the possibility of a vicar, but it soon became evident that he had not been serious about it.

Forlì offered no better prospects for Caterina or her son. In

October, 1503, Antonio Maria Ordelaffi had returned to Forlì
and been greeted jubilantly. He had also succeeded in taking
Forlimpopoli after a two-month siege. But all did not go well.
Quartan fever put him in the sickbed. In addition, he lacked
the military strength to conquer the fortress of Ravaldino. In
November, 1503, a delegation of Forlivese citizens asked the
pope to reinstate the Ordelaffi as vicars.[20] Julius II gave an
evasive answer since he did not want to grant the request and at
that time he lacked sufficient strength for an outright denial.
Antonio Maria's illness proved to be a powerful papal ally, for
on February 6, 1504, the last legitimate Ordelaffi claimant
died.[21] From then on the pope moved swiftly. Ordelaffi partisans had one more month of glory during which they chose
Lodovico Ordelaffi, an illegitimate son of Cecco and half
brother of Antonio Maria, as their *signore*.[22] But in March of
the same year a papal force marched on Forlì with orders to
take the city and its fortress Ravaldino by force, by money, or
any other way. Lodovico declared his allegiance to Venice. This
did not help him, since the Republic of San Marco had too
many other commitments and could not spare any soldiers.
Lodovico ended as a pensioner of the pope for the rest of his
life.[23] The arrangement proved inexpensive for the *curia* since
Lodovico Ordelaffi died very suddenly in May, 1504. A few
months later Gonsalvo de Mirafonte surrendered the fortress of
Ravaldino. The city of Forlì, like Imola, came under direct
papal rule.[24]

By the summer of 1504 Caterina was forced to realize that
her career in Renaissance politics had actually ended when
Cesare's soldiers swarmed into Ravaldino. The opportunity for
a return to power had not come and, in light of the pope's
policy regarding the Papal States, would never come. Nothing
was left for her but a life in retirement, slightly dull, slightly
bitter, slightly futile. Only a few years before, such a prospect
would have been unbearable to Caterina. Now she accepted it
without protest. The time of suffering and fear spent in Borgia
captivity had not only destroyed her beauty, they had also
speeded her maturity and strangely mellowed her. It had been
a gradual process. Caterina had emerged from Sant'Angelo
with no profound philosophy of life or new enthusiasm for
things intellectual; she had simply learned to accept life even
when she was only the pawn, not the player.

During the years that followed she coped quietly and patiently with problems which were neither pleasant nor politically important. Her hands, which had firmly gripped swords, were now embroidering shirts; and her mind, once given to keen analysis of the problems of state, was directed toward her garden, her horses, and her household. Memories of the past years of prominence intruded by way of letters from and to relatives and former associates. Her stepfather, Giampietro Landriani, wrote of his life in renewed obscurity.[25] The melancholy Lauro Bossi, a fumbling conspirator on Caterina's behalf in 1500, now told of the adverse turns of fate he had experienced, indicated his need for money, and dispensed wise counsels of how patience and trust in God heals everything.[26] Caterina's narrowed world, of nostalgia, of routine daily life, and of the sicknesses of aging was shared by Antonio Baldraccani,[27] her former secretary, and Lodovico Albertini, her *speziale*.[28]

Another former companion, the lack of money, had remained with Caterina. During those early Florentine years many of her jewels were, as usual, pawned as permanent securities for equally permanent loans.[29] Ottaviano, still in Rome and still maneuvering, begging and demanding a clerical office, always wanted money, whether for proper clothing, for influencing people, or just for enjoyment. Finally, in 1507, he became bishop of Viterbo and Volterra,[30] a position considerably lower than the "red hat" or archbishopric he had been clamoring for all along; nevertheless, it suited Ottaviano—so well, indeed, that history heard no more of him. Caterina was not so fortunate. Ottaviano now asked for more money so that he could be as well outfitted as the rest of the prelates. Galeazzo, too, made his peace with the world as the husband of Maria della Rovere, a respectable lady with an equally respectable dowry. Bianca became the wife not, as had been planned, of the *signore* of Faenza, but of Troylus de'Rubeis, count of Sancto Secundo.[31] With Cesare Riario ensconced as archbishop of Pisa, Caterina was left to care for the little Giovanni, her son by Giovanni de'Medici.

After years of suit and countersuit the Florentine court had awarded her Giovanni and the villa, Castello.[32] Lorenzo de'Medici, deprived of the prospects of quick and easy wealth and despised by many, died soon after. Just before his death he had so alarmed Caterina about Giovanni's safety that she had hidden him in the girls' school of the monastery of Annalena. With Lorenzo de'Medici dead, Giovanni could shed his girl's clothing and return to his mother in the Castello. Possibly that educational experience had permanently spoiled his taste for book learning. Caterina hired tutors,[33] and Giovanni wore them out. Some of them stayed a few weeks, others only ten days. It did not matter. Caterina rejoiced in the lad who was ten years old in 1507, and taught him whatever she could herself. But Giovanni liked best the things which were not taught by books—a rigorous swim in cool waters, a ride on a good horse, a fencing match, and endless talk of war. He had the steely eyes of the Sforza, and his manners were brusque. From the moment Giovanni showed such preferences Caterina was a most happy woman. Her other interests, her horticultural experiments, her horse-breeding, and even her collection of prescriptions, all faded in comparison with Giovanni. There were no more requests for prescriptions which would guarantee a pretty face or show how to make eighteen-carat gold from base metal. Only Giovanni and the shaping of his personality counted. Then in the spring of 1508 her health began to fail. In the short intervals of recovery Caterina resumed her work on Giovanni, who more and more revealed the potential of a fine soldier. But after May, 1509, Giovanni had to fend for himself. In that month Caterina Sforza, forty-six years old, died of what some contemporaries called a *male de costa* ("rib sickness").[34] In more exact terms it was a liver ailment which killed her, complicated in the end by peritonitis and pleurisy.

The prosaic rites for the dead followed. Caterina's possessions were divided.[35] Giovanni (dalle Bande Nere) received the lion's share, which included the Florentine possessions and even Caterina's exotic slave Mona Bona, while the children by Girolamo had to be satisfied with other Riario estates and funds. The granddaughters Julia (Galeazzo's daughter) and Cornelia (illegitimate daughter of Ottaviano Riario) each received the key to a good marriage—a formidable dowry.[36] Carlo (formerly Bernardino) Feo was another beneficiary, and so were a host of religious institutions. The funeral was in keeping with the status of Caterina as a noble woman, no more and no less. The welfare of her soul was to be assured by a marathon of two thousand masses read during the following two months and thirty on every anniversary of her death.

Then life went on, as always unperturbed by the death of any single person. At first there were still concrete reminders of Caterina. Her sons were influential personages in Renaissance society: an archbishop (Cesare), a bishop (Ottaviano), a nobleman (Galeazzo), and later, a second bishop (Francesco),[37] and a brilliant military hero (Giovanni dalle Bande Nere).[38] Another memento was the devotion and the hatred she had evoked in those with whom she had been involved. But eventually sons, admirers, and detractors faded away. Now the Caterina of flesh and blood was replaced by the heroine of a legend. In songs, ballads, and stories she fired the imagination of many. In them, little was left of that Caterina who had ridden effortlessly to glory which she earned only later by courage, skill, and finally, by suffering; who had been an enigma composed of devout reading and donations, of bloody and boundless vengeance, of dedicated love, of unrestrained sexuality, of rough soldiering, and of deep concern for bodily beauty; and who had behaved like a man only to be more intensely a woman.

NOTE ON THE ALTENBURG PORTRAIT

THE PICTURE CHOSEN is from the collection of early Italian paintings of the Staatliches Lindenaumuseum, Altenburg, Thuringia. As shown, the picture portrays St. Catherine, but X-rays have revealed that the coat now green was formerly red with a flowery belt, and that the halo and the wheel are later additions too. Originally the picture was thus just a portrait. Although there is no inscription on the picture there are good reasons, aside from the distinct Sforza profile, for assuming the depicted lady to be Caterina Sforza. The leading expert in Renaissance art of Romagna, A. Schmarsow, was the first to suggest that the picture shows Caterina Sforza (see *Festschrift zu Ehren des Kunsthistorischen Institutes in Florenz* [Leipzig, 1897], p. 182). His conclusion was derived from the analysis of medals. These medals are among the few likenesses which were created by contemporaries of Caterina. Another scholar of Renaissance art, A. Gottschewski, later agreed with Schmarsow's ground for the identification of the portrait and further suggested the likeness of the Altenburg picture to a terra-cotta head inscribed "CIS" and ascribed to the sculptor Vincenzo Onofri (see A. Gottschewski, *Ueber die Portraets der Caterina Sforza und ueber den Bildhauer Vincenzo Onofri* [Strassburg, 1908]).

After careful analysis, Schmarsow identified Botticelli as the painter of the picture. Botticelli did indeed work in Rome from spring, 1481, to fall, 1482. Caterina Sforza, who also resided in Rome in those years, was at that time about nineteen years old, an age which fits that of the depicted lady. In addition, Botticelli worked for Sixtus IV, who quite likely commissioned the picture of his relative Caterina. Other art historians have furthermore pointed out a number of stylistic elements which speak in favor of Botticelli's authorship (see F. Schmidt, *Mensch, Raum, und Farbe in der fruehitalienischen Tafelmalerei* [Altenburg, 1956], pp. 41–43). Gottschewski suggested Piero di Cosimo as the painter, which is an objective possibility although less probable.

Note on Other Portraits of Caterina Sforza

THERE EXIST A NUMBER of other paintings which supposedly depict Caterina Sforza. Yet some of them have no ascertainable or even probable link with Caterina while others were painted long after her death and have thus no real value for the historian of Caterina's life.

The authenticity of the woodcut found in Filippo Foresti di Bergamo's *De claris selectisque mulieribus* (Ferrara, 1497) is hard to ascertain. It shows a portrait of Caterina Sforza which bears some resemblance to Caterina as depicted on the medals (see below). The considerable differences could be attributed equally well to a lack of real familiarity with Caterina's bodily features as to a lack of technical finesse.

Medals are the only other source for our knowledge of Caterina's likeness. The following medals exist:

1) Lisippo "the Younger" *ca.* 1480   Victoria and Albert Museum

2) Niccolò Fiorentino shortly   Berliner Muenzkabinett
   (probable)   after 1488   and Museo Nazionale, Florence

3) Niccolò Fiorentino   ?
   (probable)

(This is probably a redesigned version of the earlier Fiorentino medal. The widow's veil is omitted and the hair rearranged, which suggests that the medal was issued after the period of official mourning for Girolamo Riario had ended.)

4)   ?   after Caterina's Muenzkabinett, Vienna
                  death

5)   ?   after Caterina's Museo, Parma
                  death

(The last two are both impressions of the same commemorative medal for "Diva Catherina Sfortia." They have no value as witnesses for Caterina's likeness.)

NOTE ON THE MELOZZO DA FORLÌ
PAINTING: SIXTUS IV AND PLATINA

THE PERSON STANDING to the right of Sixtus IV is usually identified as Raffaello Riario (e.g. A. Schmarsow and F. Buscaroli). I suggest that an identification as Piero Riario is even more likely. Schmarsow (*Melozzo da Forlì,* p. 1) ruled out Piero Riario because the latter had died in 1474 while the picture was painted between 1475 and 1477. Against such an argument stand these counter-arguments that the representation in a family portrait need not mean actual presence at the time of painting; that Piero had been the favorite nephew of Sixtus IV and his omission seems unlikely; that Raffaello Riario was about thirteen to fifteen years old at the given dates and the depicted man is considerably older; and that the similarity between the depicted man and later portraits of Raffaello Riario is at best remote.

List of Abbreviations
for Frequently Cited Sources

1 FOR ARCHIVAL MATERIAL:

AS Bologna, AC	*Archivio di Stato,* Bologna, Archivio del Comune di Bologna
ASF	*Archivio di Stato,* Firenze
ASF, MAIP	*Archivio di Stato,* Firenze, Archivio Mediceo avanti il Principato
ASF, S, XdB, OdP, Legazioni e Commissarie-Missive Responsive	*Archivio di Stato,* Firenze, Signoria, Dieci di Balia, Otto di Pratica—Legazioni e Commissarie-Missive Responsive
ASM	*Archivio di Stato,* Milano
ASM, PE	*Archivio di Stato,* Milano, Potenze Estere
ASM, PS	*Archivio di Stato,* Milano, Potenze Sovrane
ASM, RD	*Archivio di Stato,* Milano, Registri Ducali
ASM, MD	*Archivio di Stato,* Milano, Registri delle Missive
ASMa,	*Archivio di Stato,* Mantova
ASMa, AG	*Archivio di Stato,* Mantova, Archivio Gonzaga
ASMo,	*Archivio di Stato,* Modena
ASMo, ASE	*Archivio di Stato,* Modena, Archivio Segreto Estense
ASVa	*Archivio Segreto Vaticano*
ASVa, Arm.	*Archivio Segreto Vaticano,* Armarium
ASVe	*Archivio di Stato,* Venezia
ASVe, SS	*Archivio di Stato,* Venezia, Senato Secreti
BNP, FI	*Bibliotheque Nationale,* Paris, Fonds Italien

2 FOR PERIODICALS:

AMR	*Atti e Memorie* della Deputazione di storia patria per le provincie di Romagna
ASI	*Archivio Storico Italiano*

ASL	*Archivio Storico Lombardo*
AV	*Archivio Veneto*
P	*La Piè*
R	*La Romagna*
RIS	*Rerum Italicarum Scriptores*
	o.s. Edited by L. Muratori (25 vols.; Milan, 1723–51)
	n.s. Various editors (34 vols.; Città di Castello, 1900——)
SR	*Studi Romagnoli*

3   FOR DOCUMENTS PRINTED IN VOLUME III OF PIER DESIDERIO PASOLINI, *Caterina Sforza* (3 vols.; Rome, 1893) :

PP	stands for Volume III of Pasolini's work.
py.	means that the document in question is partially printed.
fy.	means that the document in question is fully printed.
printed as *PP*	refers to documents which could not be located in the archives and for which the author had therefore to rely on Pasolini's rendering of the text.

4 *PP, ND,*	refers to Pier Desiderio Pasolini, "Nuovi documenti su Caterina Sforza (1469–1506)," *AMR*, s. 3a, XV (1896–97), pp. 72–209 and documents. The number given in the reference is always the number of the document.

NOTES

1. For Milan's role in the league and the ensuing diplomatic maneuvers involving the Sforza family, see V. Ilardi, "The Italian League, Francesco Sforza and Charles VIII (1454–1461)," *Studies in the Renaissance*, VI (1959), 129–66, and Treccani, *Storia di Milano* (16 vols.; Milan, 1953–62), VII, 64–157.

2. The *Aurea Repubblica Ambrosiana* was the republican state which existed between the demise of the Visconti (1447) and the installation of Francesco Sforza as duke of Milan (1450).

3. Among the tutors were Francesco Filelfo, Guinforte Barzizza, Bartolomeo Petroni, Cola Montana, and Giorgio Valagussa; C. Violini, *Galeazzo Maria Sforza* (Turin, 1943), p. 47.

4. For the most complete account of the Gonzaga affair see L. Beltrami, *Gli sponsali di Galeazzo Maria Sforza, 1450–1468* (Milan, 1893).

5. Letters, Galeazzo Maria Sforza to Duke Francesco Sforza, July–September, 1457 (in special folder), *ASM, PS, Galeazzo Maria Sforza,* c. 1461.

6. Galeazzo Maria to Duke Francesco, April 5 and 30, and May 26, 1459, *ASM, PS, ibid.*

7. See letters of Galeazzo Maria, *ASM, PS, Galeazzo Maria Sforza* to Duke Francesco, March 3, 1460, c. 1461, March 12, Aug. 30, and Oct. 7, 1460, c. 1462; to Duchess Bianca Visconti-Sforza, March 6, 1460, c. 146.

8. Letters of Galeazzo Maria to Duke Francesco show him staying in February and early March in Lodi, during the summer in Pavia, in October in Pigliano, Lodi, Piacenza, and returning for the winter to Milan, *ibid.,* c. 1462.

9. Cecco Simonetta to Duchess Bianca Visconti-Sforza, Aug. 27, 1460, *ibid.,* c. 1461.

10. The Landriani family, with their possessions centered around Landriano and Vidigulfo, already had provided trusted advisors and prominent supporters to the Visconti. They maintained their prominence under the Sforza rule. Evidence for that family's influence shows in the many positions they held in the 1460's and 1470's: Andrea L (andriani), *luogotenente* in Cremona, *ASM, MD,* n. 97, pp. 191–92; Melchiore L., *castellane Doizone, ASM, RD, Castellani,* n. 171, pp. 143–45; Giovanni Antonio de L., *castellane Arcis Cassani, ibid.,* pp.

235–38; Arcorsino de L., *Sindaco del Comune di Milano, ASM, RD*, n. 3, pp. 157 and 157 vo. Yet, Giampietro Landriani seems not to have been an important representative of the family. *ASM, Famiglia*, pp. 260–62, gives family charts for Mareschus, Ubertus, Marcus (only from 1500), and Jacobus Landriani. None of them show a Giampietro L. (The Landriani family charts of the Archivio Storico Civico, Milan, *Famiglie*, b. 824–827, are of no assistance in this case since they are all of dates later than 1500). One Giovanni Pietro Landriani is well authenticated, but he was a nephew of Filippo Maria Visconti's chamberlain, Donato Landriani, and thus cannot have been Lucrezia Landriani's husband (Treccani, *Storia di Milano*, VI, 531). Another person sometimes suggested to have been the husband, the *sescalco* of Bona of Savoy, Piero (or Pietro) Landriani, is in my opinion not the same person as Giampietro Landriani. Pietro Landriani is assumed to be Caterina's stepfather by Z. Arici, *Bona di Savoia* (Turin, 1935), and A. Burriel, *Vita di Caterina Sforza* (3 vols.; Bologna, 1795). He is listed first in Bona's escort for the trip to Florence, 1471, as *sescalco* on the draft dated Feb. 14, 1471, *ASM, Archivio Sforzesco, Milano Città*, c. 898, and then on the list of persons who accompanied the duchess to Mantua, July 8, 1471, *ASM, PE, Firenze*, c. 282. But a document granting exemption mentions the same Pietro Landriani together with Antonio L. (*tesoriero*), implying clearly that he resided in Milan; Aug. 14, 1497, *Archivio Storico Civile*, Milano, *RD*, n. 7, c. 29–30 vo.; printed in C. Santoro (ed.), *I registri delle lettere ducali del periodo sforzesco* (Milan, 1961), p. 284 (henceforth cited as Santoro). At that time, Giampietro was faithfully serving Caterina in Romagna.

The family of Giampietro and Lucrezia Landriani:

(Galeazzo Maria)—			—Lucrezia Landriani—			—Giampietro Landriani
Carlo (1461–83)	Caterina (1462?–1509)	Ales-sandro (1465–1523)	Chiara (1467–1531)	Pietro (castellan of Forlimpopoli 1490– ?)	Stella (m. to Andrea Ricci)	Bianca (1473–96) (m. to Tommaso Feo castellan of Ravaldino 1487–90 governor of Imola 1493–95 governor of Forlì 1495–?)

11. The exact date of Caterina Sforza's birth cannot be ascertained. The suggestion of a late 1462 birth date rests on conjecture based on fragmentary evidence. Galeazzo Maria's letters of, and actions during, the late spring and the early summer of

1462 show him unusually contrite and subservient to his parents. His changed behavior could easily be interpreted as an embarrassment of the young man over the second pregnancy of Lucrezia. Also, the naming of the baby girl does not follow either a Sforza or a Landriani tradition. It could be suggested, therefore, that the girl was either born or named on the day of Saint Catherine, November 25. As for definite references to her birth, they all place it somewhere in late 1462 or early 1463. The marriage contract of January 17, 1473, *ASM, RM,* 111a, pp. 18–19, gives Caterina's age as "de anni X." The *Instrumentum Confessionis Dotis Mag.*"*Domine Catherine,* etc., *ASM, RD,* n. 34, p. 20 vo., states "decem vel circa." In a letter of Galeazzo Maria Sforza to the cardinal of San Sisto, Jan. 17, 1473, he states "puella est annos non pluris nata quam decem," and in another to his orator in Rome (same date), "la putta è de anni decem"; both letters are in *ASM, PE, Roma,* c. 72.

12. Hyeronimo de Bursellis, *Cronica gestorum ac factorum memorabilium Bononiae,* ed. Albano Sorelli, *RIS,* n.s., XXIII, Pt. II, 103 (henceforth cited as Bursellis). B. Paolucci, *Historia di Forlì,* Biblioteca Comunale, Forlì, MS 300 (henceforth cited as Paolucci), entry under *anno 1480,* less politely calls Lucrezia "one of Galeazzo Maria's whores."

13. Galeazzo Maria to Cecco Simonetta, July 23, 1462, *ASM, PS, Galeazzo Maria Sforza,* c. 1461.

14. Galeazzo Maria to Duke Francesco, July 27, 1462, *ibid.*

15. See letters of Galeazzo Maria to his parents, July 28, 29, 30, 31, and Aug. 1, 2, 4, 5, 7 (2 letters), 1462, *ibid.*

16. Galeazzo Maria to his parents, Aug. 10, 1462, *ibid.*

17. Dorotea seems to have been a pretty girl, "beautiful beyond the common, nicely formed, with good coloration, and a good figure," A. Guidobone (Milanese orator in Mantua) to Duke Francesco, Aug. 10, 1457, *ASM, PE, Mantova,* c. 394. Galeazzo saw her in 1458, 1461, 1462, and 1463.

18. He referred to his betrothed as "Dorotea mia" and was concerned when she was ill; June 15 and 17, 1463, *ASM, PS, Galeazzo Maria Sforza,* c. 1062.

19. L. Beltrami, "L'annullamento del contratto di matrimonio fra Galeazzo Maria Sforza e Dorotea Gonzaga (1463)," *ASL,* s. 2, XVI (1889), 126–32. It is reported that Galeazzo Maria cried when the break became final. V. Scalona (Mantuan orator in Milan) to Marchesa Barbara, Dec. 17, 1463, *ASMa, AG,* E, XLIX, 2, *Milano,* c. 1622.

20. See *Epistolario di Galeazzo Maria Sforza (relativo alla spedizione sforzesca in Francia),* ASM, PE, Francia, c. 530; see also P. Ghinzoni, "Spedizione sforzesca in Francia (1465–1466)," *ASL,* s. 2, VII (March, 1890), 314–45.

21. The only Landriani ladies mentioned are the wives of Francesco de Landriani (born a Trivulzio) and of Antonio

Landriani. L. Beltrami, *Dame Milanesi invitate alle nozze di Galeazzo Maria Sforza con Bona di Savoia* (Milan, 1920), pp. 14–20.

22. For an example, see the extensive list dated November, 1471, *ASM, Archivio Sforzesco, Milano Città e Ducato*, c. 902.

23. Galeazzo Maria to Bianca Visconti-Sforza, Aug. 2, 1467; reprinted, *PP*, 13.

24. The marriage is a good example of Galeazzo Maria's free-wheeling foreign policy during his early ruling years. E. Pontieri (*Per la storia del regno di Ferrante I d'Aragonia, re di Napoli* [Naples, 1947], p. 122) points out the resentment of Naples and other powers.

25. For details of the marriage, see L. Beltrami, *Gli sponsali di Galeazzo Maria Sforza, 1450–1468;* see the same author's *Dame Milanesi invitate alle nozze di Galeazzo Maria Sforza con Bona di Savoia*.

26. Tristano Sforza, who represented his brother Galeazzo Maria in the negotiations, flattered Bona in describing her as ". . . a good person to bear sons, not tall, not short, with beautiful eyes, nose, mouth, teeth, and hair, and with graceful manners." Tristano Sforza to Galeazzo Maria, March 23, 1468, *ASM, PE, Francia*, c. 534.

27. For conflicts between Bianca and her son, see Treccani, *Storia di Milano*, VII, 250–51.

28. Bianca Visconti-Sforza, a lady "di animo più che virile," must have liked Caterina, since the girl showed signs of a similar disposition, *ibid.* p. 227.

29. Such a purchase is reflected in an exchange of letters: Cecco Simonetta to Gottardo Panigarola, March 11, 1469, *ASM, RM*, n. 85 (c. 48), f. 196 (fy., *PP, ND*, 1), and March 23, 1469, n. 89 (c. 61), f. 210. Gottardo Panigarola to Galeazzo Maria, July 27, 1469, reprinted fy., *PP*, 17.

30. For a description of education at the Sforza court, refer to C. Santoro, "L'educazione dei principi alla corte sforzesca," *Popoli*, II (1942), No. 5, and C. Magenta, *I Visconti e gli Sforza nel castello di Pavia* (2 vols.; Milan, 1883), I, 593.

31. A. Giulini, "Un probabile progetto matrimoniale per Caterina Sforza," *ASL*, s. 4, XL (1913), 220–23 and documents. For further information on Galeotto del Caretto, see C. Bricherius, *Tabulae genealogicae gentis Carettensis* (Vienna, 1741), Table XIV.

32. The contract is mentioned in Anonimo Veronese, *Cronaca 1446–88*, ed. G. Soranzo (Monumenti storici— R. Deputazione veneta di storia patria, s. 3, Vol. IV), p. 295, and in a testament by Galeazzo Maria Sforza dated May 18, *ASL*, s. 2, V (1888), 105, n. 1. U. Caleffini asserts in his *Diario* (*di Ugo Caleffini*), ed. G. Pardi ("Monumenti—R. Deputazione di storia patria per l'Emilia e la Romagna" [Ferrara,

1938]), I, Pt. I, 32, that the Torelli were a Ferrara family with branches in Naples and Milan. The latter was highly regarded at the Sforza court. Among those who headed Milanese contingents for the league forces in 1469, for example, the Torelli brothers are given as leading six hundred men on horseback (second only to Corradino Fogliano, a Sforza relative), *BNP, FI,* cod. 1592, ff. 24–25. The faithful service of the Torelli continued beyond the abortive marriage contract. The counts Torelli are in the forefront of those who welcome dignitaries for the Sforza dukes; visit of cardinal San Sisto, Sept. 12, 1473, *ASM, RM,* 111a, p. 267. Their service is furthermore documented in letters of acknowledgment and renewal of service contracts; see *ASM, RD,* n. 32, pp. 186–88 (Jan. 5, 1482) ; n. 34, pp. 274–77 (Jan. 25, 1484) ; and n. 34, pp. 320–23 (March 20, 1483).

33. Galeazzo Maria to Filippo Sagramoro (Milanese orator in Florence), Jan. 10, 1471, *ASM, PE, Firenze,* c. 281. With Venice and Naples standing together, the relationship between Milan and Florence was even more essential.

34. For a detailed description of that trip see B. Corio, *Storia di Milano* (3 vols.; Milan, 1855–57), III, 260–62.

35. See Galeazzo Maria's order to Ambrogino da Longhinana, castellan in Milan, March 1, 1471, printed in C. Violini, *Galeazzo Maria Sforza* (Turin, 1943), p. 148, n. 1 (original could not be located in *ASM* and Archivio Storico Civico, Milan). Further documentation for Caterina's absence from the traveling party is found, however, in four consecutive lists of those persons who would make the trip to Florence, dated Jan. 4, 1471, in *BNP, FI,* cod. 1592, ff. 52–54; and Jan. 21, Feb. 14, and March 4, 1471 (final), *ASM, Archivio Sforzesco, Milano Città e Ducato,* c. 898. Although all of them are detailed down to the last stableman, none lists either Caterina or any of the other children.

36. List of participants of a Parma trip, 1470 (?), *ASM, PS, Bona di Savoia,* c. 1463 *(PP, ND, 3).*

37. P. Litta, *Famiglie celebri d'Italia* (Milan, 1819–85), IX, 147, calls him "un povero uomo" and a "cimatore di panni" in Albisola.

38. B. Fregoso, *Battistae Fulgosi Opus Incomparabile* (Basel, 1541), pp. 689–90.

39. L. Cobelli, *Cronache forlivesi,* ed. G. Carducci, E. Fanti, and F. Guarini (Monumenti Istorici—Romagna [Bologna, 1874]), III, Pt. I, 349 (henceforth cited as Cobelli).

40. For the best description of Francesco della Rovere's (Sixtus IV) career see L. Pastor, *The History of the Popes* (12 vols.; St. Louis, 1923), IV, 204–8. A contemporary account is B. Platina, *Vita Sixti IV, RIS,* o.s., III, 1053–57.

41. A. Bernardi (Novacula), *Cronache forlivesi dal 1476 al*

1517, ed. G. Mazzatinti (2 vols.; Bologna, 1895–97), I, 52–53 (henceforth cited as Bernardi). Paolo Riario, the father of the boys, even loaned Francesco a goodly sum of money.

42. For all data on the appointment of cardinals, refer to F. Cristofori, *Cronotassi dei Cardinali* (Rome, 1857), and *Hierarchia Catholica*, ed. C. Eubel *et al.* (5 vols.; Regensburg, 1898).

43. Pastor, *History of the Popes*, IV, 201.

44. Litta, *Famiglie celebri d'Italia*, IX, Tables i–iv.

45. As early as Aug. 28, 1471, Nicodemo Tranchedini (orator in Rome) notified the duke of Milan of Piero Riario's prominent position and imminent elevation to the cardinalate, *ASM, PE, Roma*, c. 68. Bernardi, p. 53, states that Piero Riario had become the *chiergo* of Francesco della Rovere early in the latter's career. See also Pastor, *History of the Popes*, IV, 235–36 and 238–39.

46. Girolamo lived in the shadow of the pope's two favorite nephews—Piero Riario and Giuliano della Rovere. Bernardi, p. 53.

47. S. Infessura, *Roemisches Tagebuch*, trans. H. Hefele (Jena, 1913), p. 63 (henceforth cited as Infessura).

48. The elevation of the archbishop of Milan to the cardinalate was designed to obligate the Sforza; N. Tranchedini to Duke Galeazzo Maria on his confidential discussions with Piero Riario, Dec. 3, 1471, *ASM, PE, Roma*, c. 68.

49. He had held it as a vicar of the Church since 1458; bull of investiture, *ASVa, Arm.* XXXVI, 26, n. 33.

50. P. Zama, *I Manfredi* (Faenza, 1954), pp. 238–41. Reference is made here to the Imola line of the Manfredi. Another branch of the same family governed Faenza and stayed in power there until defeated by Cesare Borgia in 1501. See also G. Filippini, *Taddeo Manfredi, signore d'Imola, e le sue relazioni con gli Sforza* (Urbania, 1913), pp. 20–34, and B. Azzurrini, *Chronica breviora*, ed. A. Messeri, *RIS*, n.s., XXVIII, Pt. III, 240–41.

51. A condition of the pensioning was the promise not to return to Imola. *Annales Forolivienses*, ed. G. Mazzatinti, *RIS*, n.s., XXII, Pt. II, 231.

52. Piero Riario, cardinal of San Sisto, to Duke Galeazzo Maria, Jan. 16, 1472, *ASM, PE, Roma*, c. 69.

53. Piero Riario to Duke Galeazzo Maria, Jan. 17, 1472, *ibid.*

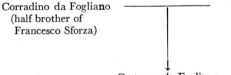

Corradino da Fogliano
(half brother of
Francesco Sforza)

Gabriella Gonzaga
(illeg. daughter of
Lodovico III,
marquis of
Mantua)

Costanza da Fogliano

54. The sale was to be handled "with the discretion necessary in such matters." N. Tranchedini to Duke Galeazzo Maria, Feb. 21, 1471, *ASM, PE, Roma,* c. 69. The same Bosco d'Alessandria had been promised to Taddeo Manfredi as compensation for Imola; Azzurrini, *Chronica,* p. 241.

55. Contract, June 15, 1472, *ASM, RD,* n. 24, 123–123 vo. A letter from the duke of Milan to N. Tranchedini, June 12, 1472, gives that day as the date of the marriage contract; *ASM, PE, Roma,* c. 70. Duplicate letter to Sixtus IV, *ibid.*

56. *"Creatio in Familiam," ASM, RD,* n. 7, p. 491.

57. This reason is given in the papal bull dated Feb. 26, 1473; copy in *ASM, RD,* I, n. 24, ff. 238 vo.–239 (fy., *PP,* 62). See also P. Ghinzoni, "Usi e costumi nuziali principeschi," *ASL,* s. 2, XV (1888), 101–11. Girolamo saw in the marriage a guarantee for his access to the world of nobility and in consummation a guarantee for its eventual realization.

58. Ghinzoni, "Usi e costumi . . . ," *ASL,* s. 2, XV, 104. The procedure was no legal substitute for an actual consummation.

59. Piero Riario to Duke Galeazzo Maria, Jan. 4, 1473, *ASM, PE, Roma,* c. 72. Nothing indicates that the cardinal was aware of the difficulties.

60. Galeazzo Maria's motivations are given in his letter to Giovanni Arcimboldi (Milanese orator in Rome), Jan. 17, 1473, *ASM, PE, Roma,* c. 72 (fy., *PP,* 55). Galeazzo Maria states both the fact of, and the reason for, the marriage contract: ". . . havemo facto un altro pensiero più honorevole et giá mandatolo ad executione, videlicet che questa matina de domenicha, ad hore XVIII, havemo dato nostra figliola Caterina per legitima sposa al dicto conte Hieronjmo et lui per anulum et osculum l'ha desponsata. . . . Tutto havimo facto volontere et de bona voglia . . . che la sanctità de nostro signore et lo reverentissimo monsignore de Sancto Sisto vedano manifestamente che la devotione ed amore nostro verso loro. . . ." Letter also printed in Ghinzoni, *ASL,* s. 2, XV, 105–7.

61. Record of the marriage contract in Cecco Simonetta's diary, *ASM, RM,* 111a, pp. 18–19. Published as *I diarii di Cecco Simonetta,* ed. A. R. Natale (Milan, 1962), I, 5; also fy., *PP,* 54. Actual *Istrumento* in *ASM, RD,* I, n. 24, ff. 123–123 vo., 137–38.

62. See letter, Pt. I, n. 60. Galeazzo Maria wrote in the same vein to the marquis of Mantua, but was reassured diplomatically by Lodovico Gonzaga that since he, Galeazzo Maria, had decided on the marriage contract, the match must have been perfectly proper, Jan. 23, 1473, *ASM, PE, Mantova,* c. 395.

63. Galeazzo Maria to Piero Riario, Jan. 17, 1473, *ASM, PE, Roma,* c. 72.

64. Galeazzo Maria to Pope Sixtus IV, Jan. 17, 1473, *ibid.*

65. Document, Jan. 20, 1473, *ASM, RD* (Cecco's diary), 111a, pp. 21–23. Also, *I diarii di Cecco Simonetta,* p. 6, and fy., *PP,* 59 and 60.

66. He left in the evening of Jan. 23, 1473, with some escorts. Entry in Cecco Simonetta's diary, *ASM, RM,* 111a, p. 24. Also *I diarii di Cecco Simonetta,* p. 7.

67. Galeazzo Maria Sforza to Giovanni Arcimboldi, Jan. 23, 1473, *ASM, PE, Roma,* c. 72 (fy., *PP,* 61). In the light of preceding events it was probably a sleeping together *senza altramente venire ala copula* ("without actual consummation").

68. See the papal bull cited in Pt. I, n. 57.

69. The population figure is an estimate based on the only figure available prior to the sixteenth century. In Cardinal Anglic Grimoard's *Descriptio provincie Romandole facta anno 1371,* Imola and its *districtus* (the immediate surroundings) are listed with 1,624 *fumantes;* see A. Theiner, *Codex Diplomaticus Dominii Temporalis S. Sedis* (Rome, 1861–62), II, 490–516. As the tax (*fumanteria,* "hearth tax") was levied on the basis of the number of hearths, no population figures are attached to the data. In using the *fumanteria* figures everything depends on their accuracy and on the assumed average family size. For estimates see K. J. Beloch, *Bevoelkerungsgeschichte Italiens* (2 vols.; Berlin, 1939), p. 85, and in J. Larner, *The Lords of Romagna* (Ithaca, N.Y., 1965), pp. 210–15. My own estimate takes into account that the population of Imola stayed, even in 1800, around the eight thousand mark (upper limit), and that no smaller than a four to five head "family" could rightfully be assumed (lower limit).

70. Azzurrini, *Chronica,* pp. 241–42, describes the bitterness over the ruthless Milanese power play.

71. See friendly exchange of letters, April 15 and 25, 1472, *ASM, PE, Romagna,* c. 173.

72. For one hundred thousand florins, according to a petition of the city of Imola (against the sale) to Galeazzo Maria, May 21, 1473, Azzurrini, *Chronica,* pp. 241–42. The Florentines already owned the upper regions of the Santerno, d'Amone, Montone, and Savio valleys.

73. *Promissio,* April, 1473, *ASM, PE, Romagna,* c. 180.

74. Sagramoro (Milanese orator in Rome) to Galeazzo Maria, May 17, 1473, *ASM, PE, Roma,* c. 72. At that time the Milanese orators in Florence and Rome were both members of the Sagramoro family of Rimini. Filippo Sagramoro served in Florence (referred to in the notes as F. Sagramoro) and his uncle Sagramori Sagramoro, bishop of Parma, in Rome (referred to in the notes as Sagramoro).

75. Sixtus IV to the king of Naples, May 16, 1473 (copy ?), *ibid.*

76. Galeazzo Maria to Sagramoro, May 28 and 29, 1473, *ibid.* The official Milanese version of the Imola affair (Taddeo a voluntary exile and Galeazzo Maria a benevolent protector) is best stated in a document dated Jan. 18, 1473, which has been preserved in two copies, one sent to F. Maletta (Milanese orator in Naples), *ASM, PE, Naples,* c. 223.

77. An excellent source for Piero's visit to Milan is Cecco Simonetta's diary, *ASM, RM,* 111a, pp. 267–75 (also *I diarii di Cecco Simonetta,* pp. 48–53). See also C. Magenta, *I Visconti e gli Sforza,* I, 492–93.

78. Piero Riario had requested an opportunity to hear him play; E. Motta, *Musici alla corte degli Sforza* (Milan, 1887), p. 59.

79. Galeazzo Maria was more than satisfied with the results of the negotiations; see his letter to Sagramoro upon Piero Riario's departure, Sept. 20, 1473, *ASM, PE, Roma,* c. 73.

80. Pontieri, *Per la storia del regno,* pp. 131–33.

81. The Venetians understood quite well that the proposed league was a means for Galeazzo Maria to escape his present diplomatic isolation. For the issues discussed and the determination to defer a decision on the part of Venice, see two entries in *ASVe, SS,* Oct. 7, 1473, reg. 26, pp. 47–47 vo.

82. F. Sagramoro (Milanese orator in Florence) to Galeazzo Maria, Oct. 18, 1473, *ASM, PE, Firenze,* c. 285.

83. For Piero Riario's indignation over the Medici refusal to finance the transaction and for Lorenzo de'Medici's bitterness over Imola and the Pazzi financing of the purchase, see letter by Sagramoro to Galeazzo Maria, Nov. 9, 1473, *ASM, PE, Roma,* c. 73.

84. Galeazzo Maria to Piero Riario on final arrangements, late October, 1473, *ibid.* See also note on delayed payment, Dec. 30, 1473, *I diarii di Cecco Simonetta,* p. 159.

85. *Giuramento,* Nov. 6, 1473, *ASVa, Arm.* XXXVI, 26, n. 34. Also on margin of bull, see below, 88 vo., Bull of Investiture, Nov. 8, 1473, *ASVa, Arm.* XXXV, 37, 85–88 (109–12).

86. No record of census payments shows for Imola during Girolamo's vicariate in *ASVa, Archivio della Camera Apostolica, Acta Camerarii, Introitus et Exitus,* nos. 498 and 499.

87. The city and *contado* were taken over by Girolamo's officials, Giovanni d'Armeria and Francesco de Salviati; see *Procura,* Dec. 6, 1473, *ASM, PE,* c. 180.

88. Galeazzo Maria to Lorenzo de'Medici, Nov. 16, 1473, *ASM, PE, Firenze,* c. 285.

89. Infessura, p. 65; he also speaks of poisoning, but evidence

for such an accusation is lacking. The report of Sagramoro to the duke speaks of a stomach ailment (*postema,* "an abscess"), Dec. 30, 1474, *ASM, PE, Roma,* c. 74.

90. Treccani, *Storia di Milano,* VII, 292–93. This league lasted only until 1476 and was effective even less long.

91. *Ibid.,* pp. 307–9. Corio, *Storia di Milano,* III, 303–15; F. Malaguzzi-Valeri, *La corte di Lodovico il Moro* (2d ed.; Milan, 1929), pp. 1–3.

92. Corio, *Storia di Milano,* III, 315.

93. Petition, Bona of Savoy to de'Mafeis, early 1477, *BNP, FI* cod. Ital. 1592, ff. 95–96; (fy., *PP,* 70). There seems to have been a discussion of the issues by some theologians; no disposition is recorded, f. 97 (fy., *PP,* 71).

94. Bona of Savoy to Girolamo Riario, Jan. 29, 1477, *ASM, RD,* n. 133, f. 9 (fy., *PP,* 73). Girolamo is told that "la magnifica vostra Consorte et la dote è ad vostro requesta et arbitrio."

95. Instructions, April 2, 1477, *ASM, PE, Genova,* c. 968. See also, S. de'Conti, *Le storie de'suoi tempi (1475–1510)* (2 vols.; Rome, 1883), I, 17–18 (henceforth cited as de'Conti). Giovanni Battista Mellini was the successor of Piero Riario as the cardinal of San Sisto; Cristofori, *Cronotassi dei Cardinali,* p. 29.

96. Sagramoro conveys Girolamo's words to Bona of Savoy, March 7, 1477, *ASM, PE, Roma,* c. 83. It may be well to point out here that after the murder of Galeazzo Maria the orators address their reports in various forms, e.g., *Principi* or "Duke of Milan" (Gian Galeazzo) or *Duchessa.* Actually the reports were meant for Duchess Bona and the chancellor Cecco Simonetta.

97. The composition of the traveling party is given in a list dated April 15, 1477, marked *ASM, Archivio Sforzesco, Milano Città e Ducato,* deposited in *PE, Romagna,* c. 186. Printed with some variations as *PP,* 71.

98. Instructions, Bona of Savoy to Gianluigi Bossi, April 26, 1477; printed as *PP,* 86.

99. Stay in Bologna: April 15 and 16, 1477; Count Carolus (ducal orator in Bologna) to duke of Milan, April 15, 1477, *ASM, PE, Romagna,* c. 186.

100. Costs at Bologna: seventy *lire bolognesi; AS Bologna, AC, Riformatori,* IX, *Libri Partitorum,* VIII, ff. 106 and 106 vo. Costs at Castelbolognese: forty-six lire; *Libri Mandatorum,* XIX, ff. 135 vo. and 136. Carolus thanks the city and the Bentivoglio for the extraordinary courtesy, May 12, 1477, *ASM, PE, Romagna,* c. 186. During the second half of the *quattrocento,* Bolognese money prevailed in Romagna: 1 *lire bolognese* = 20 *soldi* (also called *bolognino* or *baiocco*) = 120 *quattrini* = 240 *denari.* As for the purchasing power of the men-

tioned 116 *lire* (or 2,320 *soldi*) , some appreciation can be gained from the following (always being aware of the impossibility of complete accuracy) .

Cobelli gives for the 1470's in Forlì (*Cronache forlivesi*, pp. xiii and xv):

1 capon	*soldi* 5	1 lb. of beef	*soldi* 6
1 chicken	*soldi* 2	1 lb. of veal	*soldi* 8
12 eggs	*soldo* 1	1 lb. of *castrone*	*soldi* 10

Bernardi, *Cronache forlivesi*, I, 217–18 for 1477:
1 *staio* (*Forlivese*) of grain = 72,16 liters = *ca.* two bushels.......*soldi* 29–35
(depending on season)
1 *staio* (*Forlivese*) of beans.................................*soldi* 20–24
(depending on season)

The modern equivalent for a Forlivese *staio* is derived from U. Santini, "I dazii egidiani in Forlì nel 1364," *AMR*, s. 4, IV (1913–14) , p. 11. For further information on the Romagnol money system, see *Enciclopedia Italiana* (henceforth cited as *EI*) under *"staio";* see also G. A. Zanetti, *Delle monete forlivesi* (Bologna, 1778) ; G. Carlo Rubbi, *Delle monete e dell'instituzione delle zecche d'Italia* (Mantua-Lucca, 1754–60) , Table I, p. 287; G. B. Salvioni, *Il valore della lira bolognese dalla sua origine alla metà del secolo XVII* (Turin, 1961) .

101. For the Imola phase of Caterina's journey see Caterina to Chiara Sforza, May 3, 1477, *ASM, PE, Romagna*, c. 186 (fy., *PP*, 90) . For the same, a description, by companions of travel (*aulici e consoci*) for Bona of Savoy, May 3, 1477, *BNP, FI*, cod. 1592, ff. 110–111 (moisture damaged) , (fy., *PP*, 91) ; Gianluigi Bossi to *Principi* of Milan, May 4, 1477, *ASM, PE, Romagna*, c. 186 (fy., *PP*, 92) .

102. Imola, one of the towns along the Via Emilia, never quite developed to the same degree as did Faenza, Forlì, or Cesena. This was probably due to two facts: the Santerno Valley did not offer as good a passage across the Apennines to Florence as the other river valleys did, and the nearness of powerful Bologna tended to stifle the development of Imola during the *trecento*.

103. Sagramoro to Bona of Savoy, May 14, 1477, *ASM, PE, Roma*, c. 83; and Girolamo Riario to the Milanese court, May 17, 1477, *ibid.*

104. Official companions of Caterina Sforza to Bona of Savoy, May 20, 1477, *ASM, PE, Roma*, c. 81 (fy., *PP*, 105) . It offers a minute report on the happenings from the departure from Imola to the festive banquet at Pentecost in Rome.

105. Sagramoro to ducal court, May 18 and 25, 1477, *ASM, PE, Roma*, c. 81 (fy., *PP*, 100 and 103) .

106. Caterina Sforza to Bona of Savoy, May 28, 1477, *ASM, PE, Roma,* c. 83. She wrote a similar letter to Chiara on the same day, *ibid.* (fy., *PP,* 104).

II

1. Infessura, p. 69.

2. The position he had held is best expressed by Volaterranus' phrase, "vir apud pontificam primarius"; J. Volaterranus (Jacopo Gherardi da Volterra), *Diario Romano,* ed. E. Carusi, *RIS,* n.s., XXIII, Pt. III, 21 (henceforth cited as Volaterranus).

3. De'Conti, I, 26-27.

4. Forgiving of dowry (i.e., Girolamo will not use it), May 31, 1477, printed as *PP,* 106.

5. The Riario had added a sum of money to the dowry. On investing, Girolamo Riario to the duke of Milan, May 31, 1477, *ASM, PE, Roma,* c. 83.

6. Girolamo Riario to Bona of Savoy, July 3, 1477, *ibid.* In most other letters, however, Girolamo does not even attach any of the standard expressions of affection to the phrase "mia consorte," e.g., letters to the duke of Ferrara, in *ASMo, ASE, Carteggio con principi esteri, Imola,* b. 1177, reaching from Jan., 1478, to July, 1486.

7. The bulk of the correspondence between Caterina Sforza and her stepmother is preserved in *ASM, PE, Roma,* c. 83-96, and *Romagna,* c. 190, *ASM, RD,* various numbers, *ASM, RM,* c. 142, and in Biblioteca Comunale, Forlì, c. 609.

8. The last known letter to Chiara is one dated April 23, 1478, *ASM, PE, Roma,* c. 85.

9. Most of these letters went to the courts of Milan and Ferrara and to influential persons in Florence.

10. No direct documentation of the birth could be found. The date is inferred from references to Bianca's age in later years.

11. For the development of the antagonism see R. Palmarocchi, *La politica italiana di Lorenzo de'Medici* (Florence, 1933), pp. 80-83.

12. Nominated Oct. 14, 1474, *ibid.,* 83-84. Girolamo Riario's pleading with Lorenzo de'Medici not to misinterpret the appointment was in vain; Oct. 26, 1474, *ASF, MAIP,* f. 21, n. 429.

13. Infessura, pp. 83-84. Discussion of Sixtus IV's part in the conspiracy, with text of papal pronouncements, Pastor, *History*

of the Popes (12 vols.; St. Louis, 1923), IV, 304–6, and Palmarocchi, *La politica italiana,* pp. 87–91.

14. The increasing certainty about Girolamo's authorship is well reflected in three letters, Sagramoro to the Milanese court, April 28 and 30, and May 3, 1478 (the latter mostly in ciphers), *ASM, PE, Roma,* c. 85.

15. Caterina Sforza to Bona of Savoy, July 8, 1478; printed as *PP,* 128.

16. Palmarocchi claims that the war had been planned long before the hanging of the archbishop and the arrest of Raffaello Riario (*La politica italiana,* pp. 94–95).

17. Francesco was the son of the famous Italian *condottiere,* Niccolò da Tolentino; de'Conti, I, 23.

18. Girolamo Riario to Bona of Savoy, Feb. 27, 1478, *ASM, PE, Roma,* c. 85. The removal was without prejudice to Domenico who had always been close to Girolamo and who was married to Girolamo's sister, Valentina. In September he could be found as governor in Spoleto, a position he most certainly owed to Girolamo; Sixtus IV, *Epistolae 1481–82,* Bib. Naz., Florence, MS II/III, 256, Sept. 17, 1481, pp. 94–96 vo.

19. Taddeo's machinations had already become worrisome to the Milanese court and to Girolamo in 1477. On May 15, 1477, Bona asked Girolamo to threaten Carlo Manfredi, who then was engaged in fighting off the claims to Faenza of Galeotto Manfredi and in doing so found his old enemy Taddeo very useful, with the revocation of the papal vicariate for Faenza, *ASM, PE, Roma,* c. 83. Taddeo justified his agitations in a letter to Bona, June 1, 1477, *ASM, PE, Romagna,* c. 188; and see reports of F. Casate (Milanese orator in Bologna), June 27 and July 13, 1479, *ibid.*

20. Tolentino had had the task of securing the northern approach to Florence during and after the Pazzi conspiracy; see letters to Carolus, April 24 and 25, 1478, *ASM, PE, Romagna,* c. 187.

21. For peace moves in general, see L. Pastor, *History of the Popes,* IV, 327–28. According to Sagramoro, Girolamo and the pope considered all talk of peace to be outright treason, letter to duke of Milan, Feb. 15, 1479, *ASM, PE, Firenze,* c. 297. Naples was willing to make peace if it could be done with honor and security for the Rovere-Riario; Giovanni Bentivoglio to Duke Ercole d'Este, March 24, 1479, *ASMo, ASE, Carteggio con principi esteri, Bologna,* b. 1.

22. She approached Bona of Savoy on the subject and elicited a favorable response, April 7, 1479, *ASM, RM,* c. 142, p. 344.

23. Caterina Sforza to Bona of Savoy, Sept. 1, 1479, *ASM, PE, Roma,* c. 86 (fy., *PP,* 135).

24. Treccani, *Storia di Milano* (16 vols.; Milan, 1953–62), VII, 334–38.

25. Caterina Sforza to B. Calchi *(secretario ducale)*, Sept. 18, 1479, *ASM, PE, Roma,* c. 86 (fy., *PP,* 137). See also letter to Bona of Savoy, Sept. 18, 1479, *ASM, PE, Roma,* c. 86 (fy., *PP,* 138).

26. The degree of risk involved in the trip has been extensively discussed. Palmarocchi *(La politica italiana,* pp. 98–100) is inclined to view the journey as a risky enterprise while E. Pontieri *(Per la storia del regno di Ferrante I d'Aragonia, re di Napoli* [Naples, 1947], pp. 171–73) discredits excessive claims to this regard by pointing out that the diplomatic relations between the two powers never were completely interrupted. There is, however, common agreement that the journey was an act of inventiveness and some courage.

27. The alliance was concluded on April 16, 1480; for details see *ASVe, Libri Commemoriali,* XVI, 156 vo. Suspicions about a change in papal policies had already been uttered by F. Casate on Feb. 14, 1480, in connection with the visit to Romagna of Jacopo da Pistoia, Girolamo's seneshal, *ASM, PE, Romagna,* c. 189. For a discussion of the alliance see E. Piva, "Origine e conclusione della pace e dell'alleanza tra i Veneziani e Sisto IV," *AV,* s. 3, II (1901), 35–70.

28. Sixtus IV to Doge Mocenigo, April 16, 1480, *ASVe, Libri Commemoriali,* XVI, c. 162 vo. See also a similar letter by Girolamo Riario, May 1, 1480, *ibid.,* c. 163.

29. *Condotta* conditions are included in the agreement between Cardinal Pietro Foscari (Venice) and Girolamo Riario, June 10, 1480, *ibid.,* 163–64.

30. See F. Fossati, *Per l'alleanza di 25 luglio 1480* (Mortara-Vigevano, 1907). For a general discussion see L. Simeoni, *Le signorie* (2 vols.; Milan, 1950), I, 545, and Treccani, *Storia di di Milano,* VII, 348.

31. Cobelli, pp. 247–55; A. Padovani, *Istoria di Forlì,* Bibl. Com., Forlì, *MS* 276, pp. 183–87 (henceforth cited as Padovani). The conspirators included Andrea Orsi, Tommaso Pansecco, and Giovanni Serughi—all of them to appear in Caterina's life about twenty years later. See also G. Pecci, *Gli Ordelaffi* (Faenza, 1955), Chap. VII.

32. Pino's rule was confirmed by Pope Paul II even before Cecco's death. Bull, Feb. 5, 1466, *ASVa, Arm.* XXXVII, 297–302.

33. For the transition of power from the Ordelaffi to the Riario see Bernardi, I, 36–55; M. Vecchiazzani, *Historia di Forlimpopoli* (2 vols.; Rimini, 1647), II, 144–50 (henceforth cited as Vecchiazzani); de'Conti, I, 382; D. Malipiero, "Annali Veneti dall'anno 1457 al 1500," ed. F. Longo, *ASI,* VII

(1843), 669 (henceforth cited as Malipiero) ; Padovani, pp. 200–10; Paolucci, entry under *anno* 1480; see also Pecci, *Gli Ordelaffi*, Chap. IX; M. Fuzzi, *L'ultimo periodo degli Ordelaffi in Forlì* (Forlì, 1937), pp. 125–39, and C. Grigioni, "Pino III Ordelaffi," in *R,* VII (1910), pp. 118–23.

34. The Ordelaffi:

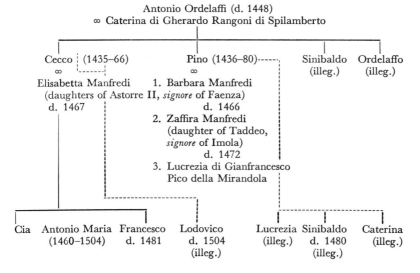

Antonio Ordelaffi (d. 1448)
∞ Caterina di Gherardo Rangoni di Spilamberto

Cecco (1435–66)
∞
Elisabetta Manfredi
(daughters of Astorre II, *signore* of Faenza)
d. 1467

Pino (1436–80)
∞
1. Barbara Manfredi
d. 1466
2. Zaffira Manfredi
(daughter of Taddeo, *signore* of Imola)
d. 1472
3. Lucrezia di Gianfrancesco Pico della Mirandola

Sinibaldo
(illeg.)

Ordelaffo
(illeg.)

Cia   Antonio Maria   Francesco   Lodovico   Lucrezia   Sinibaldo   Caterina
(1460–1504)   d. 1481   d. 1504   (illeg.)   d. 1480   (illeg.)
(illeg.)   (illeg.)

35. With regard to the name of the last Ordelaffi regent of Forlì there exist two traditions. Bernardi, de'Conti, Padovani, and Malipiero call her Lucrezia, while Vecchiazzani uses Costanza. The first version seems better substantiated, although L. Simeoni, *Le signorie,* I, 546, also uses Costanza.

36. Padovani, p. 200 vo.; Vecchiazzani, II, 144. The Ercolani were an old Forlivese family whose family tree can be traced into the 1200's. I. Gardini, *Tavole genealogiche delle famiglie patrizie di Forlì* (2 vols.), Forlì, Bibl. Com., *MSS* 1 and 2, I, 30–31.

37. Bernardi, p. 164; Padovani, p. 200 vo. Cause of death was most likely some digestive illness, although Vecchiazzani (II, 143) speaks of quartan fever. The sometimes uttered suspicion that Pino was poisoned is incorrect, since as early as the winter of 1479/80, G. Cerruto (Milanese orator in Bologna) had reported on Pino's repeated attacks "di dolor colico," *ASM, PE, Romagna,* c. 188, reg. 1 (*delle lettere di G. Cerruto*), pp. 7–8.

38. The papal bull of March 4, 1480, gave Lucrezia Ordelaffi the right to govern until Sinibaldo should take over at the age of twenty-five; *ASVa, Arm.* XXXV, 37, ff. 198 vo.–201. Lucrezia

was assisted in her rule by her brother Antonio Maria Pico della Mirandola, who had been in Forlì since 1479, when Pino's health had declined rapidly; Giovanni Bentivoglio to duke of Ferrara, March 2, 1479, *ASMo, ASE, Carteggio con principi esteri, Bologna*, b. 1.

39. On Caterina's role, F. Sagramoro to duke of Milan, June 7, 1480, *ASM, PE, Firenze*, c. 299, and duke of Milan to N. Tranchedini, June 15, 1480, *ASM, PE, Roma*, c. 87. It may be well to point out here that all letters from and to Milan were initiated or received by Lodovico il Moro, although officially they continued to be addressed to or be marked as coming from the duke of Milan and/or the duchess.

40. The subterfuge is given in various letters (all of them in *ASM, PE*), Milanese orators to duke of Milan, July 21, 1480, *Roma*, c. 87. Duke of Milan to F. Sagramoro, July 9, 1480, *Firenze*, c. 300.

41. The Venetians advised Girolamo Riario that in matters of Forlì they were "his servants," July 21, 1480, *ASVe, SS, Deliberazioni Segreti*, reg. 29, 129 vo. Even Milan recognized the Venetian obligations to the pope in matters of Forlì, but urged prudence in the Pesaro question; duke of Milan to the Doge, Aug. 21, 1480, *ASM, PE, Venezia*, c. 1063.

42. Cristoforus to Roberto Sanseverino, July 9, 1480, *ASM, PE, Romagna*, c. 190; and duke of Milan to F. Sagramoro, July 14, 1480, *ASM, PE, Firenze*, c. 299.

43. Trouble was not long in coming. On May 19, 1480, Casate reported to Milan that Forlì was filled with armed Ordelaffi partisans, *ASM, PE, Romagna*, c. 189.

44. The often-mentioned Lodovico Ordelaffi was indeed present in Forlì, but as an illegitimate son of Cecco he had no succession rights.

45. The detested Antonio Maria Pico della Mirandola was a relative of the famous philosopher, Giovanni Pico della Mirandola. Antonio Maria Pico della Mirandola was related to the Bentivoglio by his marriage to Costanza Bentivoglio.

46. The leaders were Andrea Deddo Orsi and Graziolo Orsi. The Orsi were a well-known Forlivese family, who, later on, played a significant part in the life of the Riario couple. For their status see Vecchiazzani, II, 143, and family chart in I. Gardini, *Tavole genealogiche*, Forlì, Bibl. Comunale, II, 77. R. Zazzeri, *Storia di Cesena* (Cesena, 1890), p. 146, calls them "con la plebe."

47. Vecchiazzani, II, 149.

48. Padovani (p. 208) puts it more bluntly: "this Madonna who is possessed of the devil himself."

49. The marriage plans did not stay secret for long; Cristoforus to Roberto Sanseverino, July 10, 1480, *ASM, PE, Romagna*,

c. 190; also, duke of Milan to F. Sagramoro, July 14, 1480, *ASM, PE, Firenze,* c. 299. Account given in Vecchiazzani, p. 178.

50. Petrus Andreas (Inviziati ?, document torn) to Milanese court, Aug. 1, 1480, *ASM, PE, Romagna,* c. 190; and F. Sagramoro to duke of Milan, Aug. 15, 1480, *ASM, PE, Firenze,* c. 300.

51. Antonio Maria had humbled himself in vain before the duke of Urbino, Federico da Montefeltro. He had promised to be a faithful servant of the Church. Antonio Maria's report to Galeotto Manfredi, Aug. 2, 1480, *ASM, PE, Romagna,* c. 190. Antonio Maria's bombarding and besieging of a fortress held by a properly installed papal official (the fortress of Ravaldino held by Lucrezia) was given as the legal obstacle to his obtaining Forlì; see Bull of Investiture (of Girolamo Riario), Sept. 10, 1480, *ASVa, Arm.* XXXV, 37, ff. 177–184.

52. *Giuramento,* Aug. 23, 1480, *ASVa, Arm.* XXXV, 37, f. 184 vo. Bull of Investiture, Sept. 10, 1480, *ASVa, Arm.* XXXV, 37, ff. 177–184.

53. Scholars have had reason to regret the generosity, since Lucrezia took along all the Ordelaffi papers, which subsequently disappeared.

54. Padovani, p. 210 vo.; Bernardi, I, 57–58; G. Fantaguzzi, *Caos, Cronache cesenati del sec. XV,* ed. D. Bazzocchi (Cesena, 1915), p. 12, adds that Lucrezia went to Rome, had a good time, and married the son of the *signore* of Piombino.

55. Caterina to Bona of Savoy, Aug. 25, 1480, *ASM, PE, Roma,* c. 87 (fy., *PP,* 146). Same date, to Duke Gian Galeazzo, *ibid.*

56. The embassy went to Rome on Aug. 27 and returned Sept. 17; Bernardi, II, 54–55.

57. Actually, the reductions granted by Girolamo were only a reaffirmation of those agreed upon by Federico da Montefeltro and the officials of Forlì in the capitulations for that city. Padovani (p. 211) speaks of reductions of "gabelle della macina, doti, divisioni, usuali di vitto." The reductions were thus granted on some of the most burdensome levies.

58. *Ibid.,* p. 210 vo.

59. Bernardi, I, 203–7; Cobelli, pp. 259–61.

60. The name of that obscure man is variously given as Marchionne Zocheio da Savona (Bernardi, I, 186) and Marchionne da Genova (Cobelli, p. 296). I follow the spelling of the name in official papal documents (cited Pt. III, n. 64).

61. Caterina's love for hunting is attested by her interest in hunting dogs (particularly bloodhounds, setters, and greyhounds). She solicited them from Bona of Savoy and Eleonora d'Este, duchess of Ferrara. Caterina's participation in a great

chase (January, 1484) is noted by A. de Vascho, *Diario Romano (1480–1492)*, ed. G. Chiesa, *RIS,* n.s., XXIII, Pt. III, 505.

62. Tutelage arrangements for Gian Galeazzo and administrative provisions in favor of Lodovico il Moro, Nov. 3, 1480, *ASM, RD,* n. 34, pp. 193–99.

63. Infessura, p. 71. For recent treatments of the whole incident, Simeoni, *Le signorie,* I, 546–48, and Pontieri, *Per la storia del regno,* pp. 189–93.

64. Pontieri, *Per la storia del regno,* pp. 189–96, gives a full account of the king's predicament.

65. Pastor, *History of the Popes,* IV, 343.

66. Otranto retaken, September, 1481; Infessura, p. 72.

67. Sixtus IV advocated an attack on Valona, the principal base for the Turks against Italy; Pontieri, *Per la storia del regno,* p. 208.

68. Duke of Milan to the Milanese orators in Naples, P. de Galerate and G. Angelus da Tolentino, May 24, 1480, *ASM, PE, Napoli,* c. 230.

69. Late that year Galeotto Manfredi had succeeded in ousting Carlo Manfredi, *signore* of Faenza, and Federico Manfredi, Carlo's brother and bishop of Faenza (who had been governing badly for the ailing Carlo). Description of events, P. Zama, *I Manfredi* (Faenza, 1954), pp. 246–55. A partial, contemporary description by F. Sagramoro, Nov. 23, 1477, *BNP, FI,* cod. 1592, n. 131.

70. Investiture, June 8, 1481, *ASVa, Arm.* XXXV, 35, ff. 201–207 vo. *Giuramento ASVa, Arm.* XXXV, 35, ff. 207–07 vo. Prior to that, Galeotto had governed without formal papal approval.

71. Caterina's successful intervention was on behalf of a nephew of Fra Silvestro, the powerful advisor of Galeotto Manfredi. Girolamo wanted to hang the culprit for spreading false rumors about the Riario. Caterina intervened as a favor to the Milanese court; see the appreciative note, Aug. 22, 1481, duke of Milan to Antonio Appiani, *ASM, PE, Romagna,* c. 192.

72. Malipiero, II, 25, states clearly the purpose of all the maneuvering as "to oust the Este from Ferrara." U. Caleffini, *Diario,* p. 198, speaks of a deep hatred between Ferrara and Venice.

73. *ASVe, SS, Deliberazioni Segreti,* reg. 30, pp. 25–25 vo.

74. Milanese orators in Rome to duke of Milan, July 2, 1481, *ASM, PE, Roma,* c. 89. The route the Riario family preferred for their travels to and from Romagna was: Rome—Viterbo—Orvieto—Todi—Perugia—Gubbio—Cagli—Urbino—Rimini—Cesena—Forlì.

75. Bernardi, I, 55–57. Volaterranus (p. 52) refers to Troilo as "Anconitanus."

76. The powers of Romagna had feared that Girolamo, using the Troilo affair as a pretext, would concentrate strong military forces in the area. Ercole, duke of Ferrara, to Giovanni Bentivoglio, May 28, 1481, in U. Dallari, "Carteggio tra i Bentivoglio e gli Estensi dal 1491 al 1542 esistente nell Archivio di Stato in Modena," *AMR*, XVIII (1899–1900), n. 102.

77. The best descriptions of the event are given by Bernardi, I, 58–60; Cobelli, pp. 263–67; Padovani, pp. 212 vo.–214; Antonio Appiani to the Milanese court, July 15, 1481, *ASM, PE, Romagna,* c. 192 (fy., *PP,* 162), and by an unknown Florentine agent (Matteo Menghi of Forlì ?), July 15, 1481, reprinted as *PP,* 163.

78. The potentates of Romagna understood that completely. The duke of Milan, who himself felt uneasy about the political plans of Girolamo, nevertheless assured the duke of Ferrara that the infantrymen were merely employed as a security and ceremonial force. Letter, July 26, 1481, *ASMo, ASE, Carteggio con principi esteri, Milano,* b. 1213.

79. The right of coinage had been granted to Forlì by Frederick II (in 1241) but apparently had never been used by the Ordelaffi. The coins which Girolamo and Caterina put into circulation on the occasion of their visit were struck on the basis of the imperial privilege (renewed in the bull of investiture of Sept. 10, 1480), but not in Forlì. The Roman mint produced the coins; see document printed by G. Zanetti, *Delle monete forlivesi* (Bologna, 1778), pp. 11–12. The coin with King Philip's picture carried no date and had the value of a *carlino* (or *paolo*), according to E. Gnecchi, "Un quattrino di Caterina Sforza," *Rivista Italiana di Numismatica,* XVIII (1905), 493–98. One *paolo* = 2 *baiocchi* (a silver coin of the Papal States), equal in value to 2 *soldi* or *bolognini.* One *lira bolognese* was thus equal to 10 *paoli* (see also Pt. I, n. 100).

80. Cobelli, p. 263, and Padovani, p. 213.

81. She never wore the same dress twice and changed her attendants every time she appeared in public; Padovani, p. 214 vo.

82. G. Alberghetti, *Compendio della storia della città d'Imola* (2 vols.; Imola, 1810), I, 250. It should be mentioned that in 1480, when the Forlivesi received their tax concessions, the Imolesi had also been granted lower bridge and road tolls and a reduction of the flour tax.

83. A. Appiani to duke of Milan, Aug. 13, 1481, *ASM, PE, Romagna,* c. 192 (fy., *PP,* 178).

84. A. Appiani to Milanese court, Aug. 8, 1481, *ASM, PE, Romagna,* c. 192.

85. Same persons, Aug. 4, 1481, *ibid.*

86. For a clear indication of how Caterina was to be used, see instructions from Branda Castiglione (ducal counselor) to

Leonardo Botta (new Milanese orator in Rome). The pro-Milanese sentiments of Caterina were to be strengthened and she was to be persuaded to speak in favor of Milanese policies to her husband; May 24, 1481 (shortly before the trip to the Romagna), *ASM, PE, Roma,* c. 89.

87. An invitation to visit Milan had been extended as early as the middle of July; duke of Milan to Francesco Casate in Bologna, *ASM, PE, Romagna,* c. 192. At that time the mission was entrusted to A. Appiani who became the general agent of the Sforza to deal with Girolamo and Caterina and to spy on them as much as possible. Appiani usually resided in Faenza. He had once before fulfilled a similar mission during the Forlì crisis of 1480.

88. The crucial conference came on July 19, 1481, *ASM, PE, Romagna,* c. 192 (fy., except for minor omissions, *PP,* 167).

89. The invitation came late in July and expressly included Caterina in order to prevent her from going to Milan; *ASVe, SS, Deliberazioni Segreti,* reg. 30, p. 36 vo.

90. Letter, Matthaeus Archdiaconus Forlivensis to Lorenzo de'Medici, Sept. 23, 1481, *ASF, MAIP,* f. 38, n. 330; printed in A. Fabronio, *Laurentii Medicis Magnifici Vita* (2 vols.; Pisa, 1784), "Adnotationes et Monumenta," Vol. II, pp. 226–27, doc. 120. Matteo gives as the reason for his spying ". . . per satisfare al debito mio me parso dare adviso ad Vostra Magnificentia delle cose accorse in parte. . . ." Menghi cannot be blamed for his eventual negative assessment of the visit since the vote on the alliance between the pope and Venice was taken only after the party's departure.

91. Deliberation and vote: *ASVe, SS, Deliberazioni Segreti,* reg. 30, pp. 43 vo. For general description of the Venetian stay, see de'Conti, I, 120, and Volaterranus, pp. 65–66, pp. LXXI and LXXII.

92. Bernardi, I, 201–10; Padovani, pp. 214 vo. and 215; Volaterranus, p. 79.

93. Galeotto Manfredi's role in the conspiracy is shown in a letter from the Milanese orators in Rome to the duke of Milan, Nov. 9, 1481, *ASM, PE, Roma,* c. 90.

94. A. Appiani to the duke of Milan, Oct. 14, 1481, *ASM, PE, Romagna,* c. 192.

95. Milanese orators to the duke of Milan, Oct. 26, 1481, *ASM, PE, Roma,* c. 90.

96. The birth is referred to in a letter of the Milanese orators to the duke of Milan, Oct. 30, 1481, *ASM, PE, Roma,* c. 192, and in a congratulatory letter from the duke to Caterina, Nov. 8, 1481, *ibid.*

97. Francesco Ordelaffi was slain in the course of a private feud on Jan. 25, 1481; Bernardi, I, 61–62.

98. Order to Roberto Malatesta, *ASVe, SS, Deliberazioni Segreti,* reg. 30, p. 47; to the *podestà* of Ravenna, *ibid.,* pp. 47–47 vo. Both documents are dated Oct. 23, 1481.

99. For the first phase of the Ferrara war, see R. Cessi, "Per la storia della guerra di Ferrara, 1482–1483," *AV,* s. 5, LXXIX (1950), 57–76; Treccani, *Storia di Milano,* VII, 354–60.

100. The decision to decline transit was an easy way to declare war without long consultations with the cardinals. For details, see duke of Ferrara to Giovanni Bentivoglio, April 29, 1482; printed in U. Dallari, "Carteggio . . . ," *AMR,* XIX (1900–1901), n. 154.

101. Volaterranus, p. 102. According to Malipiero (II, 261) they were accused of plotting against Girolamo.

102. Infessura, p. 78. Volaterranus (pp. 102 and 105) rightfully characterized that phase of the war around Rome as a period of inaction as far as large-scale warfare was concerned. Palmarocchi, *La politica italiana,* p. 106, argues that the inaction was due to the suddenness of the Neapolitan attack which found the papal camp unprepared.

103. The situation was so desperate that a revolt was feasible; de'Conti, I, 137.

104. The pope's distrust of the Venetians was well known. The Venetian orator, Gian Zaccaria Barbaro, warned that Girolamo was the only tie that held the alliance together, May 24, 1481, *ASVe, SS, Deliberazioni Segreti,* reg. 30, p. 15. Late in May, 1482, Sixtus IV spoke out openly against the Venetian alliance; Francesco Diedo, Venetian orator (Rome) to the marquis of Mantua, May 31, 1482, *ASMa, AG,* E XXV, 3, *Roma,* c. 846 (fy., *PP, ND,* 8). By Aug. 20, 1482, Sixtus IV feared the worst from the Venetians; Branda Castiglione, orator in Naples, to the duke of Milan, *ASM, PE, Napoli,* c. 240 (py., *PP,* 8).

105. At that time artillery was in its early stages of development and the variety of artillery pieces resembled a maze. Terms for guns also changed their connotations. During the late *quattrocento* the terms meant, in general, the following: *bombarda*—a heavy gun for siege operations; *cannone*—a medium-weight gun; *cerebottana* and *spingarda*—both light artillery pieces. The term *passavolante* refers to two weapons: (1) a siege machine which could throw large stones against fortifications, and (2) an artillery piece which at first was designed as one of medium to big caliber and only during the following centuries developed into a light artillery piece. References to *passavolante* in this work are always in accordance with the second meaning. For a contemporary analysis of early artillery see F. DiGiorgio Martini, *Trattato di architettura civile e militare del sec. XV,* ed. C. Saluzzo (Turin, 1841), and the *EI* under *"artiglieria"* and further references.

106. Sixtus IV to Roberto Malatesta, Aug. 24, 1482, *Epistolae,* 1481–84, Bibl. Naz., Florence, MS II/II, pp. 310–10 vo. (heavily damaged).

107. Caterina Sforza to the Sienese government, Aug. 21, 1482; printed, *PP,* 205.

108. In the ensuing siege the Riario position became extremely precarious. Cobelli, pp. 271–76; Bernardi, I, 91–100.

109. Giovanni Bentivoglio mentioned the siege as a maneuver to help the Neapolitans by diverting some of Girolamo's troops to the north. Giovanni Bentivoglio to the duke of Ferrara, Aug. 17, 1482, *ASMo, ASE, Carteggio con principi esteri, Bologna,* b. 1. Vecchiazzani II, 157–58, states that Tolentino brought fourteen *squadre* of men-at-arms and four *squadre* of crossbowmen.

110. Cobelli, p. 280. Vecchiazzani, I, 155, gives the full name as Giacomo d'Antonio Magnani da Marcato Sarazino.

111. Volaterranus, p. 112. Papal diplomats worked so hard to get the peace that A. Arcamone (Milanese orator in Naples) spoke of Girolamo and Sixtus IV as if they were beggars; letter to the Milanese court, Nov. 22, 1482, *ASM, PE, Napoli,* c. 241.

112. Vecchiazzani, II, 189–90.

113. The provisions of the league included a forty thousand ducat stipend for Girolamo Riario; de'Conti, I, 195, n. 6.

114. The league occasioned the first noteworthy contact between Girolamo Riario and Lorenzo de'Medici since the Pazzi conspiracy. While prior to 1478 Girolamo had occasionally written to Lorenzo on minor political matters (five letters, September, 1472–February, 1478, all in *ASF, MAIP:* f. 28, n. 545; f. 29, n. 157; f. 32, n. 370; f. 36, n. 336), there followed a four-year pause until November–December, 1482, when the league occasioned an exchange of letters, *ibid.,* f. 38, nn. 499, 523, 536, 546.

115. Milanese orators in Rome to duke of Milan, Feb. 17, 1483, *ASM, PE, Roma,* c. 92 (py., *PP,* 207). Quartan fever is a type of malaria in which the highpoints of the attacks occur every fourth day.

116. Columbino to marquis of Mantua, Dec. 4, 1482, *ASMa, AG,* E XXV, 3, *Roma,* c. 846. The incident shows how little the new allies trusted each other.

117. For departure, see Milanese orators to duke of Milan, May 27, 1483, *ASM, PE, Roma,* c. 93. Girolamo stayed in Forlì, June 6–22; Imola, June 22–July 10; Forlì, July 10–October 31.

118. Malipiero, II, 279. He also records the interesting fact that two daughters of Pino III had sought refuge in Venice (II, 284).

119. The military preparations were extensive; see Infessura,

pp. 91–92; B. Corio, *Storia di Milano* (3 vols.; Milan, 1855–57), III, 365–66.

120. Otherwise the relations with Milan were friendly during August, 1483, as thirteen letters from and to the duke of Milan attest. Most of them concern the war against Venice and all of them are preserved in *ASM, PE, Romagna,* c. 194.

121. Despite only minor damages, the psychological impact was overwhelming. Bernardi, I, 112; Cobelli, p. 281. G. Fantaguzzi, *Caos,* p. 17, described the earthquake as a major one (Aug. 11, 1483) affecting the whole area between Ancona and Bologna.

122. Bernardi, I, 211–14.

123. Milanese orators to duke of Milan, Nov. 6, 1483, *ASM, PE, Roma,* c. 94, on the return of Girolamo and Caterina.

124. *Cronaca Anonima di Forlì,* Bibl. Com., Forlì, MS 275, entry under 1483. The chronicler adds that Giacomo was "worse than the bishop" and that there was constant enmity between Giacomo and Tolentino. Milan, however, was satisfied with the new governor since he had connections with the Sforza stemming from prior service to that family; see duke of Milan to F. Sagramoro, Jan. 24, 1472, *ASM, PE, Firenze,* c. 283.

125. Bernardi, I, 116–17.

126. Infessura, p. 93.

127. The cardinal of San Giorgio had become papal chamberlain on Jan. 25, 1483, according to G. Pontani (*notaio* di Nantiporto), *Il Diario Romano (1481–1492),* ed. D. Toni, *RIS,* n.s., III, Pt. II, 24, and Volaterranus, p. 114.

128. For subsequent developments see Infessura, pp. 95–102; Volaterranus, pp. 132–35; Pontani, *Il Diario Romano,* pp. 30–41; and Pastor, *History of the Popes,* IV, 380–83.

129. His *condotta* already had been renewed by the league, Feb. 23, 1484 (until Dec. 15), *ASM, RD,* n. 32, pp. 278–81.

130. J. Burchard, *Diarium 1483–1506* (3 vols.; Paris, 1883–85), I, 16–17; Infessura, pp. 123–25.

131. The campaign of Girolamo Riario: July 2, departure for Marino and Rocca di Papa; July 7, camp before Cave; July 27, surrender of Cave; Aug. 8, camp before Paliano; beginning of the siege.

132. Infessura, pp. 131–32.

133. The negotiations in 1483 between the Republic of Venice and France were quite serious and well advanced, judging from the reports of G. Vespucci, Florentine orator in Rome; see *ASF, Riformagioni, Responsive,* cl. X, d. 3, f. 17 (Sept. 6 and 10); d. 4, f. 29 (July 4, 18, 19, and 26) and f. 30 (Aug. 17, 23, 27, 31, and Sept. 1, 2, 7, and 11). The death of Louis XI on Aug. 30, 1483, handicapped the negotiations. Nevertheless,

Milan and Florence were concerned over this Venetian policy and welcomed the peace. Naples too was eager to see the war end; B. Castiglione (orator in Naples) to Milanese court, Aug. 20, 1484, *ASM, PE, Napoli,* c. 244.

134. Corio, *Storia di Milano,* III, 402.

135. Bursellis (p. 106) wrote laconically, "when he heard the word peace, Sixtus gave up his spirit and died." The harshest, but, from the Florentine standpoint, justified verdict on Sixtus IV came from Pierfilippo Pandolfini to Lorenzo de'Medici, Aug. 15, 1484, *ASF, Riformagioni, Responsive,* cl. X, d. 2, f. 27, c. 102. "Praised be the Lord for having rescued us from so great a threat. . . . as long as Sixtus IV lived, neither we nor the rest of Italy could have lived in peace."

136. The main sources for the fate of the Riario from the death of Sixtus IV to the election of Innocent VIII are: Infessura, 139–53; Burchard, *Diarium,* I, 9–11; the reports written by Guidantonio Vespucci, Florentine orator in Rome. These are deposited in the *ASF;* those addressed to Lorenzo de'Medici in the *ASF, MAIP,* f. 39, and those sent to the *Dieci di Balia* in *ASF, Riformagioni, Responsive,* cl. X, d. 4. A selection of them is also printed in Burchard, *Diarium,* I, 493–524. Another excellent source are the reports by S. Guidotti to the marquis of Mantua during August, 1484, all in *ASMa, AG,* E XXV, 3, *Roma,* b. 847.

137. S. Guidotti to the marquis of Mantua, Aug. 13, 1484, two letters, *ASMa, AG,* E XXV, 3, *Roma,* b. 847.

138. G. Guidotti to the marquis of Mantua, Aug. 14, 1484, *ibid.* G. Vespucci to the *Dieci di Balia,* Aug. 14, 1484, in Burchard, *Diarium,* I, 497. Pontani, *Il Diario Romano,* p. 38.

139. G. Vespucci to the *Dieci di Balia,* Aug. 13, 1484, *ASF, Riformagioni, Responsive,* cl. x, d. 4, f. 32, c. 24.

140. The same, Aug. 15, 1484, *ibid.,* c. 28.

141. S. Guidotti to the marquis of Mantua, Aug. 15, 1484, *ASMa, AG,* E XXV, 3, *Roma,* b. 847. G. Vespucci to *Dieci di Balia,* Aug. 15, 1484, Burchard, *Diarium,* I, 500–501. Infessura, p. 148. Pontani, *Il Diario Romano,* p. 38.

142. S. Guidotti to marquis of Mantua, Aug. 15, 1484, stated that Caterina had occupied the castle the day before and had been staying there since. *ASMa, AG,* E XXV, 3, *Roma,* b. 847.

143. Vespucci to Lorenzo de'Medici, Aug. 18, 1484, in Burchard, *Diarium,* I, 504–5; Girolamo was still captain general of the Church and also castellan of Sant'Angelo. By stretching the terms of his authority, Caterina could be considered his substitute.

144. G. Vespucci to *Dieci di Balia,* Aug. 23, 1484, in Burchard, *Diarium,* I, 568–69; Infessura, pp. 150–51.

145. G. P. Arrivabene in his report to the marquis of Man-

tua states that the Castel Sant'Angelo was handed to the cardinal of San Giorgio and that Caterina left the same day, *ASMa, AG*, E XXV, 3, *Roma*, b. 847. See also Pontani, *Il Diario Romano*, p. 41, for note on Caterina leaving the castle on Aug. 25, 1484.

146. De'Conti, I, 135.

147. Pastor, *History of the Popes,* V. 239.

III

1. Cobelli, p. 1.

2. The general comments made in connection with the population figure of Imola apply here too. As in the case of Imola (Pt. I, n. 69) the figure chosen relies on the passages of Cardinal Anglic's *Descriptio* which concern Romagna (A. Theiner, *Codex Diplomaticus Dominii Temporalis S. Sedis* [Rome, 1861–68] II, 490–516), and their assessment by K. J. Beloch, *Bevoelkerungsgeschichte Italiens* (2 vols.; Berlin, 1939), II, 85, and J. Larner, *The Lords of Romagna* (Ithaca, N.Y., 1965), pp. 209–19). I have again chosen the factor of 4.5 to multiply the *fumanti* figure with, since it seems to me to result in the most conservative estimate possible.

3. P. Pandolfini to Lorenzo de'Medici, early September, 1484, reprinted in A. Fabronio, *Laurentii Medicis Magnifici Vita* (2 vols.; Pisa, 1784), II, 262, doc. 130. See also Bernardi, I, 125, and Vecchiazzani, II, 159.

4. Lorenzo de'Medici would soon "advise" Galeotto Manfredi not to support any conspiracies against the Riario; Lorenzo de'Medici to Galeotto Manfredi, May 5, 1485, *ASF, MAIP,* f. 43, c. 42.

5. He could have been an excellent source of support since he was named legate to Bologna in July, 1485; Bursellis, p. 105. Ascanio Sforza, twenty-nine years old and a cardinal since March 22, 1484, was the brother of Galeazzo Maria and Lodovico il Moro and thus Caterina's uncle.

6. *Cronaca Anonima,* entry September, 1485, and Bernardi, I, 138–39.

7. See the exchange of pledges of loyalty and support, Girolamo Riario to duke of Milan, Oct. 10, 1484, and duke of Milan to Girolamo, Oct. 20, 1484; both documents, *ASM, PE, Romagna,* c. 1039.

8. On the visit, see G. F. Oliva to duke of Milan, March 22, 1485, *ibid.*

9. The difficulties concerning exports, imports (mostly food stuff), skirmishes between subjects, and confiscations of prop-

erty show in letters of Domenico Ricci (governor of Imola), *AS* Bologna, *AC Riformatori, Lettere al Comune,* b. 5, May 13 and 31, June 2 and 20, July 1 and 7, Aug. 3 and 19, and Sept. 1, 1484, and in letters from the *Riformatori, ibid., Lettere dal Comune,* b. 5, reg. 4, May 12 (44 vo.), May 29 (48 vo.), June 1 (51 vo.), Aug. 16 (89) and 30 (92), 1484.

10. Girolamo Riario in a letter to the marquis of Mantua, concerning an unpleasant incident of a private nature, said expressly that he regretted the incident so much more since the two families had such excellent relations, March 12, 1485, *ASMa, AG,* E XXV, 3, *Roma,* b. 847.

11. These families had not been affected by the Riario acquisition of Forlì. Not even the Orsi family, which had supported the Ordelaffi cause to the very end, had been harmed. Two other examples for the smooth transition are found in the Paolucci and Numai families. Pino III had held Lodovico Paolucci in high esteem; see Pino III to the duke of Ferrara, Jan. 7, and June 6, 1478, *ASMo, ASE, Carteggio con principi esteri, Forlì,* b. 1167. Girolamo wrote in nearly identical terms to the duke, June 25, 1483, *ibid., Imola,* b. 1177. The Numai were another patrician family in Forlì; see Gardini, *Tavole genealogiche,* II, 70–73. By 1488 the family had split into many branches. Luffo Numai was the son of Guglielmo Numai, member of one of the seemingly most prosperous branches. Luffo Numai had been the chancellor of Pino III. But already on October 23, 1481, he carried out an important mission to Venice for Girolamo ("secretario Luffus"), *ASVe, SS, Deliberazioni Segreti,* reg. 30, p. 47. Alessandro Numai had been bishop of Forlì from 1472 (Vecchiazzani, II, 140) to 1485 (*Cronaca Anonima,* entry under 1485). The Numai usually gave loyal support to the legal administrator of the Church's rights in Forlì.

12. Instituted by Pino III Ordelaffi and first mentioned in 1451 by Giovanni di Maestro Pedrino Dipintore, *Cronica del suo tempo,* ed. A. Pasini, G. Borghezio, and M. Vattasso (2 vols.; *Studi e Testi,* nos. 50, 62; Rome, Vol. I, 1929; Vol. II, 1934), II, 227. Incomplete copy in Bibl. Com., Forlì, MS 302, p. 245b. The *Consiglio dei Quaranta* was to replace the by then largely inactive *Consiglio Generale e Aperto,* later a council of four hundred, which had its origin in the period of the free commune. Only on rare occasions did the *Consiglio Generale* function again. The membership of the Council of Forty came from the influential families of the town, as a list dated Jan. 1, 1492, shows; *Libro Madonna* (official records of the *Consiglio dei Quaranta* and the *Consiglio degli Anziani*), pp. 20–21. On the evolution of the communal councils in Romagna, see Larner, *Lords of Romagna,* chaps. 1 and 3; for Forlì particularly, pp. 14 and 279, n. 62.

13. Each of the four quarters of the city (Porta Schiavonia, San Biagio, San Pietro, San Mercuriale) had ten representatives. The *anziani* were in charge of the routine administration of the city. Some but not all of the *anziani* were also members of the Council of Forty; see *Libro Madonna, AS* Forlì, list of members of both councils, Jan. 1, 1492, pp. 20–21.

14. Bonarello actually possessed the full confidence of Girolamo; see letters of Bonarello to Girolamo Riario, June 12 and 25, 1484, *ASF, MAIP,* f. 96, nn. 151 and 152. But in order to pacify the angry populace Girolamo had to dismiss him. Bonarello had been quick to send people to the gallows for wrongly directed sympathies. He left "under cover of darkness in fear for his safety," Cobelli, p. 284; also Bernardi, I, 148.

15. ". . . *perche era straordinaria le penuria dell'anno,"* Vecchiazzani, *Historia di Forlimpopoli,* II, 159. The years 1483 and 1484 brought the worst food crisis in Romagna during the second half of the *quattrocento.* The growing season of 1483 was first characterized by drought, then by terrible floods, and that of 1484 brought nearly no rain. Grain, flour, and beans had already been in short supply in 1482 due to the war and bad weather. In 1483 and 1484 prices for these products shot up 100 to 200 per cent. In 1483 no flour was sold for four months. The imports of grain by the Riario in 1484 brought some relief (the *staio* of imported subsidized grain 4–5 lire vs. 5–7 lire for home grown grain). For information on weather, crops, and prices in Forlì see Bernardi, *Cronache forlivesi* after each year's entries; for 1484 see I, 136–37.

16. This action was very generous since the meat tax constituted one of the best revenue sources. The tax was a twofold one, being collected upon entrance of the animals into the town and upon sale.

17. Antonello had served the pope's enemies, the Florentines, in the Pazzi war and was forced to sell his fiefs for two thousand ducats, Aug. 14, 1480. He died Jan. 27, 1484, without ever regaining his possessions; *Cronaca Anonima* entry under January, 1484. His sons continued to oppose the Riario.

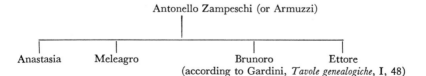

Antonello Zampeschi (or Armuzzi)

| Anastasia | Meleagro | | Brunoro | Ettore |

(according to Gardini, *Tavole genealogiche,* I, 48)

18. Formal investiture of Niccolò Riario with San Mauro and Talamello, Oct. 4, 1489, *ASVa, Arm.* XXXV, 37, 188–194 vo. Given to Girolamo Riario, Nov. 1, 1483, *ASVa, Arm.* XXXV, 37, 257–260 vo.

19. Bernardi, I, 125; Vecchiazzani, II, 159–60.

20. Taddeo Manfredi had entered the service of the duke of Ferrara and governed Borzano and Mazadella; letter, duke of Ferrara to these communities upon appointment of Taddeo, Feb. 7, 1481, *ASMo, ASE, Cancelleria, Lettere,* reg. 7 (943), p. 28.

21. Bernardi, I, 215–17. G. Alberghetti, *Compendio della storia della città d'Imola* (2 vols.; Imola, 1810), I, 252.

22. Girolamo Riario to duke of Milan, Oct. 30, 1484, "today was born by the mercy of God from whom all good comes a beautiful boy," *ASM. PE, Romagna,* c. 1039.

23. *Cronaca Anonima,* entry under Nov. 14, 1484 (baptism date). Lodovico was the most eminent of the Orsi. He had been senator of Rome in 1482; de'Conti, I, 330, n. 1. Other godfathers were the duke of Ferrara and the *signore* of Rimini; Vecchiazzani, II, 160.

24. Bernardi, I, 138; Vecchiazzani, II, 161.

25. The worst was over when the Milanese doctor arrived, Jan. 1, 1485; G. F. Oliva (Milanese emissary to Forlì) to the duke of Milan, *ASM, PE, Romagna,* c. 1039 (py., dated Jan. 2, 1485, *PP, ND,* 18). Oliva can only have arrived in Forlì a short time before Caterina fell ill.

26. G. Fantaguzzi, *Caos, Cronache cesenati del sec. XV,* ed. D. Bazzocchi (Cesena, 1915), p. 29. Judging from her wedding presents, the jewels must have been worth a multiple of the cash.

27. Only fragmentary records exist of the tax revenues which the Riario derived from Forlì and Imola. For Forlì: in November, 1499, Caterina pleaded with the Forlivesi that she could not grant any further tax reductions since the ones already conceded had diminished her Forlivese revenue to 22,000 *lire bol.;* Bernardi, II, 251. No further details or explanations are given but the context suggests that the figure must have been a low estimate. It is furthermore not clear whether Caterina referred to net or gross income. Figures which could assist in clarifying the matter are scarce. A compilation of the annual budget of Forlì during the period of 1407–9 by G. Orlandelli shows a gross income of 34,700 *lire bol.;* G. Orlandelli, "Le finanze della comunità di Forlì sotto il vicariato di Baldassare Cossa," *SR,* VII (1956), 183–92. A compilation by S. Bedolini (*Raccolta di memorie forlivesi,* Bibl. Com. Forlì, *MS* 282, pp. 49 vo.–50 vo.) for years during the middle 1500's gives a gross income of 16,202 *lire bol.* and a net income of 7,873 *lire bol.* (before payment of the census to the Church in the amount of 4,578 *lire bol.*). Because of the difference in time and accounting methods used in the data from years preceding and following 1499, comparisons prove to be of little value. Only Bernardi's wording leads one to prefer a net income interpretation

("All our income from Forlì amounts to only 22,000 *lire bolognese*," although Caterina pleads "that with it neither she nor her sons can live as *signori*"). For Imola: fragmentary evidence includes an account book in *ASF, MAIP*, f. 54, n. 12, cc. 92–101, entitled *Entrata et uscita-rocca d'Imola*, 1488, which gives the net income collected at the fortress of Imola as 3,722 *lire bol.* It cannot be ascertained which percentage of the total income and expenditure the accounting presents; for example, although the list includes expenditures for *castellani* in the *contado*, it is doubtful that the revenues represent all the revenues derived from the *contado*. The income of the Riario from taxation might be estimated to have been about 30,000 *lire bol.* Income from trade monopolies, although no documentation can be cited for the 1480's, must have been at least as important as that from taxation.

28. G. F. Oliva to duke of Milan, Aug. 11, 1485, *ASM, PE, Romagna*, c. 1039 (py., *PP, ND*, 25). The "maligni deportamenti del Tolentino" were certainly no more than urgent requests for payments. In former years he had received an annual stipend of four hundred florins plus extra payments in times of war; see records of 1479 and 1480 in *ASVa, Camera Apostolica, Introitus et Exitus*, n. 498, under *Exitus*, pp. 162, 174 vo., 188, 193, 197, 205 vo., 218, and 229.

29. G. F. Oliva to duke of Milan, Aug. 21, 1485, *ibid.* (py., *PP, ND*, 26).

30. Two letters give a good review of the negotiations: G. F. Oliva to the duke of Milan, Aug. 26, 1485, and duke of Milan to G. F. Oliva, Sept. 1, 1485, *ASM, PE, Romagna*, c. 1039 (fy., *PP, ND*, 27 and 28).

31. There was even a severe outbreak of the plague in Romagna at that time; Bursellis, p. 107.

32. Only the notice of departure, not the reason for it, is given in the letter; G. F. Oliva to the duke of Milan, *ASM, PE, Romagna*, c. 1039. Padovani (p. 224 vo.) notes that he "left without a word," during Girolamo's stay in Imola. *Cronaca Anonima*, entry for summer, 1484, has a marginal note *"a Civitella."* Tolentino was killed by irate peasants and dismembered sometime in 1487 while in Venetian service.

33. For information on Pansecco family, a family of notaries, and its role in Forlì, see Cobelli, pp. 243, 285, 290; Bernardi, I, xvi, n.

34. *Cronaca Anonima*, entry under 1485.

35. Chelini referred to the fact that in trying to revoke the tax concessions granted in 1488, Girolamo aimed at a violation of the *capitoli* he had signed in that year.

36. Padovani, p. 226; *Cronaca Anonima*, entry under 1485.

37. Cobelli, an eyewitness, gives the most dramatic account

(pp. 290-91). See also Bernardi, I, 151-53; Padovani, pp. 227-27b.

38. Cobelli, p. 290.

39. *Ibid.*, p. 291.

40. *Ibid.*, p. 292.

41. The collection of taxes was handled either by communal officials or leased to private citizens. It must have been a lucrative business since the Pansecco family received the tax collecting privilege definitely as a reward.

42. Cobelli, p. 292.

43. An ardent Ordelaffi partisan, Antonio Butrighelli had actively supported that family in 1480. He had been jailed and exiled, but was eventually pardoned by Girolamo. Antonio promptly conspired once more against the Riario. Jailed again, he benefited from Girolamo's mercy one more time. Bernardi, I, 207 and Vecchiazzani, II, 147 and 153.

44. Bernardi, I, 217-18; Vecchiazzani, II, 162-63; *Cronaca Anonima,* entry under 1486.

45. The *contado* was the countryside which surrounded a Romagnol town and was economically and politically closely connected with it.

46. Bernardi, I, 153-55 and 266-67; Vecchiazzani, II, 143. The *contadini* had a measure of self-administration in their villages (*ville*) into which the *contado* was divided. Taxes were paid by the *villa* according to the size and fertility of its soil. The *signore,* in his turn, provided the *cavalcanti,* who were a rural police for guarding the countryside and, if need be, collecting taxes.

47. Girolamo called a representative group of men from all *ville* to discuss the problem; Bernardi, I, 153. The solution was a three-year lease of the tax of *danne date* and of *balia* to the *contadini* for twelve hundred lire.

48. Bernardi I, 171; two undertakers who, clad in black, had to pick up the dead from their homes and bury them (six lire a month); a barber-surgeon (fifteen lire); a confessor (ten lire); and a physician (fifteen lire). Only thirty persons died during the epidemic.

49. Bursellis, p. 108; Treccani, *Storia di Milano* (16 vols.; Milan, 1953-62), VII, 377.

50. For fuller explanation of Roberto Sanseverino's behavior, see Treccani, *Storia di Milano,* VII, 377.

51. Bursellis, p. 108, on Bolognese position.

52. Account of Forlì incident in *Cronaca Anonima,* entry under 1486. Vecchiazzani, II, 161-62.

53. Most critical of the behavior of the Neapolitan troops are *Cronaca Anonima,* entry 1486, and Padovani, p. 228a.

54. F. Visconti to duke of Milan, Nov. 26, 1486, *ASM, PE,*

Romagna, c. 1039. Visconti filled in the fall of 1486 the role Oliva had played before, that of a quasi-permanent representative of Milan in Forlì.

55. F. Visconti gives a full account of the situation in the Riario family to the duke of Milan, Nov. 26, 1486, *ASM, PE, Romagna,* c. 1039 (fy., with minor omissions, *PP, ND, 31*).

56. Bernardi, I, 173–77. See also Bursellis, p. 108. On other occasions the standing of the Riario was more in keeping with reality. In the funeral arrangements (made according to status) for Antonio Vettori (Venetian orator in Milan) the ranking of the representatives of the Italian powers was the following: Venice (France), Naples, Florence, Milan, Ferrara, Lucca, Pesaro, Rimini, Forlì and Imola, Faenza, Bologna, etc.; March 30, 1485, *ASVe, Libri Commemoriali,* XVII, 196 vo.

57. On matrimony and mistress see P. Zama, *I Manfredi* (Faenza, 1954), pp. 267–72. Astorre was born in 1485; B. Azzurrini, *Chronica breviora,* ed. A. Messeri. *RIS,* n.s., XXVIII, Pt. III, 245.

58. The trip to Imola was Girolamo's fourth according to Bernardi, I, 177–78. See also *Cronaca Anonima,* entry under March, 1487; Cobelli, p. 298. From the correspondence it can be ascertained that the couple usually spent a few months of the warmer season in Imola. Otherwise they resided in Forlì.

59. Bernardi, I, 177. That the appointment was temporary is shown in a letter, Domenico Ricci to duke of Ferrara, June 9, 1487, which speaks of Domenico still as governor of Imola, *ASMo, ASE, Carteggio con principi esteri, Imola,* b. 1177. Bernardi, I, 178, gives Ricci's tenure as governor of Forlì as lasting from March 5 to Aug. 19, 1487.

60. *Ibid.*

61. Caterina passed through Bologna in the middle of April, 1487, *AS* Bologna, *AC, Riformatori,* IX, *Libri Mandatorum,* XX, p. 337 vo.

62. Cobelli, p. 294, "greva malattia," and *Cronaca Anonima,* entry under June, 1487, "malattia grande."

63. *Cronaca Anonima,* entry under June, 1487, "se bene gravida"; Padovani, p. 230b.

64. On his service with the papal fleet, see Sixtus IV, *Epistolae,* Bibl. Naz., Florence, MS II/III, 265, Sept. 23, 1481 (p. 49 vo.–50), Nov. 9, 1481 (p. 83 vo.), and June 6, 1482 (p. 271). See Pt. II, n. 60.

65. A ride on horseback of approximately four hours on the main road.

66. Accounts of the events in Cobelli, pp. 294–99; Bernardi, I, 186–89; *Cronaca Anonima,* entry under August, 1487; Padovani, pp. 229–31.

67. At that time Antonio Maria Ordelaffi tried hard to ob-

tain a Florentine office, preferably a castellanship in Romagna; letter to Lorenzo de'Medici, Aug. 18, 1487, *ASF, MAIP*, f. 40, n. 109.

68. Cobelli (p. 299) says merely "e l'dicto Nocente ando a Imola con madonna la contessa"; Infessura (pp. 209–10) is deeply puzzled but knows no solution; Alberghetti (*Compendio*, I, 254) speaks of poisoning. Codronchi might very well have speculated on forcing Caterina to make him once more castellan of Ravaldino. Caterina on her part had certainly no interest in another castellan to whom she was too deeply obligated. She chose instead Tommaso Feo, a Ligurian from Savona and a relative of Girolamo.

69. *Cronaca Anonima*, entry under August, 1487.

70. Investiture, *ASVa, Arm*. III, 22, p. 19.

71. Massa Lombarda situated to the northeast of Imola was one of the southernmost possessions of the Este, and as it had been variously owned by different families and cities throughout its history the territorial rights were not clearly established. Border incidents (as much as one can speak of those in a period which did not yet structure its political entities according to the principle of uniform and solid areas) were frequent.

72. Letters reflect the incidents: seizure of a necklace, May 19, 1486; settlement, May 23, 1486; seizure of jewelry and textiles, July 9, 19, and 26, 1486; settlement of a small border problem, Dec. 18, 1486; tax problem on transit jewelry, Jan. 23, 1487; same problem, March 5, 1487; all in *ASMo, ASE, Carteggio con principi esteri, Imola*, b. 1177.

73. Caterina Sforza to duke of Ferrara, July 24, 1487, *ibid*. (fy., *PP*, 249).

74. The Roffi conspiracy was the most serious threat to Riario rule in Forlì prior to 1488. The chroniclers understood that, too, and gave most detailed reports. Cobelli, p. 299–302; Bernardi, I, 218–25; *Cronaca Anonima*, entry September, 1487.

75. That conspiracy confirmed what all others already had shown. The conspirators against the Riario were usually artisans, peasants, and lower clergymen. Among these groups the Ordelaffi sympathies were strongest.

76. Bernardi, I, 191–94.

77. Bernardi, I, 194–97, not otherwise given to dramatization is gripped by the sombre quality of the event.

78. The *monte di pietà* was essentially a compromise with the hard reality of moneylending. Instead of merely repeating the century-old injunction against the taking of interest, the loan business was to be brought closer to the ideal of justice.

79. A. Monti, "Il monte di Pietà," *FL*, I (1926–27), 21–25. Only in 1511 was a *monte di pietà* erected on the foundations of the Orsi palace (destroyed by Caterina in 1488).

80. Cobelli, p. 294; *Cronaca Anonima,* entry for June, 1487.

81. At stake was the payment of taxes due on land "purchased" by the townspeople. Should the *contadino* still be held liable?

82. Cobelli, p. 305.

83. *Ibid.,* pp. 307–9.

84. *Ibid.,* p. 308.

85. *Ibid.,* pp. 311–15.

86. Girolamo's correspondence of these days betrays no uneasiness. His last letter (preserved) went to the marquis of Mantua and was written on April 12, 1488, concerning a private matter, *ASMa, AG,* E XXV, 3, *Roma,* b. 847.

87. For the assassination and the subsequent events see Cobelli, pp. 316–46; Bernardi, I, 229–74; Padovani, pp. 233b–253a; *Cronaca Anonima,* entry under 1488; Paolucci, entry under 1488, only speaks of the assassination and how Caterina "fece grandissima vendetta"; two letters from Castrocaro to Lorenzo de'Medici, April 19, 1488, *ASF, MAIP,* f. 40, c. 290 (py., *PP,* 269), and April 21, 1488, *ibid.,* c. 296 (fy., *PP,* 277). Silvestro Calandra (Mantuan orator, Urbino) to marquis of Mantua, April 20 and 26, 1488, *ASMa, AG,* E XXV, 3, *Roma,* b. 847. See also P. Bonoli, *Istorie della città di Forlì* (Forlì, 1661), pp. 257–58.

88. Cobelli, p. 316.

89. The hastily called session seems to have escaped the otherwise ubiquitous Cobelli. Padovani, pp. 240–241b; *Cronaca Anonima,* entry under 1488.

90. Savelli, canon of St. John of the Lateran and apostolic protonotary (by Pius II in 1463) had just taken over as governor of Cesena when he was faced with this major decision. He was, however, not inexperienced since he had served as papal administrator in a number of places, including Fano immediately before; de'Conti, I, 94. His position in the Savelli genealogy is unclear.

91. Bernardi, I, 241.

92. For a complete report on the situation in Imola see Giovanni Corbizzi to Lorenzo de'Medici, April 19, 1488, *ASF, MAIP,* f. 40, n. 287.

93. The Sassatelli were one of the oldest and most powerful of all Imolese families. Their possessions were south of Imola in the Santerno Valley, but the main branch of the family had long been residing in a strong fortress-like palace in Imola. The family had traditionally considered itself to be Guelphic. Under Taddeo Manfredi, Francesco Sassatelli had governed the town of Imola on a few occasions in the *signore*'s absence; Alberghetti, *Compendio,* I, 248.

94. F. Visconti to duke of Milan, April 24, 1488, *ASM, PE,*

Romagna, c. 1039. At that point, when the traditional feud between the Riario and Vaini broke out once more, Francesco Sassatelli tried to strengthen his family's position by gaining Florentine sympathies. He would bemoan the development which favored the Riario, April 26, 1488, *ASF, Otto di Pratica, Responsive,* f. 4, c. 261. Sassatelli even kept in contact with Averardo Medici, the Florentine commissioner who was in the process of taking away Piancaldoli from the Riario, *ASF, S, XdB, OdP, Legazioni e Commissarie—Missive e Responsive,* reg. 15, c. 5.

95. Cobelli, p. 321.

96. The negotiations were lengthy; Cobelli, pp. 321–22.

97. The report of Caterina's escape was exciting news in Romagna. See G. Corbizzi to Lorenzo de'Medici, April 17, 1488, *ASF, MAIP,* f. 40, n. 275; and Giovanni degli Alidosi (who kept Lorenzo informed from Castro Rivio) to Lorenzo de'Medici, April 18, 1488, *ibid.,* n. 281.

98. She made "gli quattro fichi"; an offensive gesture made with the right hand which expresses contempt and hatred; Cobelli, p. 322.

99. The earliest traces of this version appear in L. Guicciardini, *L'hore di ricreatione* (Rome, 1665), p. 208. A coarser version is found in *Estratti di lettere ai Dieci di Balia* in N. Machiavelli, *Opere,* ed. L. Passerini and G. Milanesi (6 vols.; Florence, 1874–77), II, 235 ("as far as her children were concerned she") *disse . . . che ne aveva piena la fica.* F. Oliva, *Vita di Caterina Sforza* (Forlì, 1821), pp. 48–99 (with a number of variations in different editions); P. Bonoli, *Istorie della città di Forlì,* p. 261. From then on the story has been told quite frequently.

100. The facts of another son outside of Forlì and a new pregnancy are mentioned in some letters: Silvestro Calandra (orator of Mantua in Urbino) to the marquis of Mantua, April 19, 1488, *ASMa, AG,* E XXV, 3, *Roma,* b. 847, speaks of one son in Milan and of another pregnancy; and the duke of Milan mentions a pregnancy to Matthias Corvinus, king of Hungary, May 5, 1488 (*Rerum Hungaricarum Monumenta Arpadiana,* ed. S. Endlicher [St. Gallen, 1849], year 1488, n. 253, pp. 402–4, "adhuc in utero (gravida enim est)." It is, however, very doubtful that Caterina would have used a crude ruse such as asserting that one of her sons was absent from Forlì. The people of that city knew quite well how many sons she had and that they all were held prisoner. G. Ridolfi knew it too. He wrote that "tutti figlioli e uno bastardo del Conte" were in Forlì; April 23, 1488, *ASF, Otto di Pratica, Responsive,* f. 4, c. 249 and 249 vo. The pretense of a new pregnancy is more likely to have been made, since such an assertion could be believed and de-

preciated the value of murdering Caterina's children. The reply that she could always remarry and produce more children, and also another assertion of her claim to be pregnant, are contained in two letters of G. Corbizzi to Lorenzo de'Medici, April 17 and 18, 1488, *ASF, MAIP,* f. 40, n. 275 and n. 282. Another good source is the letter from Silvestro Calandra to the marquis of Mantua, April 19, 1488, *ASMa, AG,* E XXV, 3, *Roma,* b. 847 (py., *PP, ND,* 36).

101. Bernardi, I, 240.

102. Vecchiazzani, II, 169.

103. Cobelli, pp. 322–23. Andrea Orsi must have known since he had co-operated in the deposition and murder of Cecco Ordelaffi in 1466.

104. The mistaken idea that Girolamo's assassination was due to a Florentine inspired intrigue has sometimes been voiced. For an early expression of such suspicion see *Cronaca Veneta,* Bibl. San Marco, Venice, Cl. VII, cod. CCCXXIII, p. 201.

105. Orsi brothers to Lorenzo de'Medici, April 19, 1488, *ASF, MAIP,* f. 40, n. 288, printed in J. Burchard, *Diarium, 1483–1506* (3 vols.; Paris, 1883–85), I, 520–21, and fy., *PP,* 266.

106. Actually Lorenzo de'Medici had two excellent listening posts: Faenza (Galeotto Manfredi) and the Florentine town of Castrocaro, only about ten miles southwest of Forlì (the closest Florentine possession to the Via Emilia).

107. Stefano di Castrocaro to Lorenzo de'Medici, April 21, 1488, *ASF, MAIP,* f. 40, n. 296 (printed in Burchard, *Diarium,* I, 520–21).

108. Giovanni Bentivoglio inquired about Lorenzo de'Medici's attitude on the matter. He wrote a letter explaining his support of the Milanese expedition to help Caterina and solicited Lorenzo's approval; April 18, 1488, *ASF, MAIP,* f. 40, c. 276 (fy., *PP,* 264). A similar letter was sent to the *Otto di Pratica, ASF, Otto di Pratica, Responsive,* f. 4, c. 212.

109. Cobelli, p. 321; Pier Rosichino and Antonio Baldraccani.

110. G. Lanfredini to *Otto di Pratica,* April 19, 1488, *ASF, Otto di Pratica, Responsive,* f. 4, c. 304 (fy., *PP,* 274; dated April 20).

111. B. Arlotti (orator of Ferrara in Rome) to duke of Ferrara, April 20, 1488, *ASMo, ASE, Estero, Carteggio degli oratori e corrispondenti presso le corti, Roma,* b. 6 (fy., *PP,* 276).

112. Venice, just as surprised as all the other powers by the assassination of Girolamo, persisted in a policy which favored the least change of the status quo; see G. B. Lanfredini to the *Otto di Pratica,* April 26, 1488, *ASF, Otto di Pratica, Respon-*

sive, f. 4, cc. 312–313b. Instructions for the Venetian orator in Milan at the height of the crisis, on April 27, 1488, mentioned Forlì not at all; *ASVe, SS, Deliberazioni Segreti,* reg. 33, p. 184 vo.

113. He did, however, support the Florentine operations around Piancaldoli which were clearly directed against the rights of the Riario family; G. B. Ridolfi to *Otto di Pratica, ASF, Otto di Pratica, Responsive,* f. 4, cc. 241 and 242, speaks of bombards and soldiers from Faenza.

114. G. B. Lanfredini to *Otto di Pratica,* April 23, 1488, *ASF, Otto di Pratica, Responsive,* f. 4, cc. 310–311.

115. Galeotto Manfredi to Lorenzo de'Medici, April 20, 1488, *ASF, MAIP,* f. 40, c. 289.

116. Letter, Antonio Maria Ordelaffi to Ercole, duke of Ferrara, April 22, 1488, *ASMo, ASE, Carteggio con principi esteri, Forlì,* b. 1167 (py., *PP,* 278).

117. Stefano di Castrocaro to Lorenzo de'Medici, April 24, 1488, *ASF, MAIP,* f. 40, c. 302 (py., *PP,* 281).

118. *Cronaca Anonima* under April 21 and 23, 1488. In the second letter, Cardinal Savelli wrote his relative that in a few days a papal commissioner, Domenico d'Oro, would come with soldiers and money; *Cronaca Anonima,* April 23, 1488. The chronicler remarks that the *Consiglio degli Anziani* loved the "breve." Bernardi, I, 241, mentions one letter.

119. The fortress was not strong at all—indeed, a mere gate fortification—but it was important since it guarded the western approach to Forlì. M. Trapani, "La rocchetta di Schiavonia," *Il Plaustro,* II (1912), No. 15, 127.

120. Bernardi, I, 244; Vecchiazzani, II, 170 (gives one thousand lire as purchase price).

121. Vecchiazzani (II, 170) actually says four thousand *scudi,* but that presumably is an erroneous substitution for four thousand *soldi* (or *lire bolognesi*). The *scudo* came to Romagna after 1500. See also Bernardi, I, 247; Vecchiazzani, II, 170. Note the "da Savona" in both cases, showing the trust placed in his Ligurian companions by Girolamo and confirming once more the fact that a whole group of Ligurians had followed him first to Rome and then to Forlì. Battista da Savona is called a "parente di Girolamo" by Cobelli (p. 463), but no further explanation is given.

122. Breve, Innocent VIII, April 23, 1488, reprinted as *PP,* 283.

123. B. Arlotti to duke of Ferrara, April 30, 1488, *ASMo, ASE, Estero, Carteggio degli oratori e corrispondenti presso le corti, Roma,* b. 6 (fy., *PP,* 287).

124. Orsi brothers and *Octo civitatis Status Forelivii* to Lo-

renzo de'Medici, April 29, 1488, *ASF, MAIP,* f. 40, c. 308 (fy., *PP,* 286).

125. G. B. Savelli to Lorenzo de'Medici, April 29, 1488, *ASF, MAIP,* f. 40, c. 308. His communications with Florence had been frequent. The *Otto di Pratica* had advised G. Ridolfi to stay in close contact with Savelli "et quelli di Forlì," April 26, 1488, *ASF, S, XdB, OdP,—Legazioni e Commissarie—Missive e Responsive,* reg. 15, c. 4.

126. S. Calandra reported that Florence did not do more because it did not like the course of events. Report to marquis of Mantua, April 20, 1488, *ASMa, AG,* E, XXV, 3, *Roma,* b. 847.

127. The occupation of Piancaldoli occurred on April 19, 1488. The Ubaldini family had bequeathed the fortress to Florence, and since 1373 the Florentines had held it. Tolentino took it from Florence in the course of the Pazzi war (in November, 1479, letters from Tolentino were already dated *ex castris pontificis apud Piancaldolum; ASF, MAIP,* Nov. 12 and 14, 1479, f. 96, nn. 121 and 122), and Sixtus IV gave it to Girolamo Riario. For reports on the rather ill-planned operations in 1488, see Averardo Medici to the Otto di Pratica, *ASF, Otto di Pratica, Responsive,* f. 4, April 24 (cc. 211–215), April 26 (c. 251), April 27 (c. 259), April 28 (cc. 260, 277), and April 30 (c. 320b). Giovanni Bentivoglio had warned that the action would seriously jeopardize Milanese and Florentine relations, April 24, 1488, *ASF, Otto di Pratica, Responsive,* f. 4, c. 214. It did not do so. But it did solidify the Florentine position in the upper Santerno Valley around Firenzuola.

128. The expeditionary force must have passed by Faenza on or after April 27, 1488, according to a letter of Galeotto Manfredi, *ASF, Otto di Pratica, Responsive,* f. 4, c. 246. On April 26 it was still stationed around Imola, and Savelli hoped that Faenza would prevent its advance toward Forlì; G. B. Ridolfi to *Otto di Pratica, ibid.,* c. 280.

129. Giovanni Landriani is not identical with Giampietro Landriani (Caterina's stepfather) who with his son Pietro (Caterina's stepbrother) arrived in Romagna with the military expeditionary force.

130. Piero Alamanni (Florentine orator in Milan) to Lorenzo de'Medici, April 28, 1488, *ASF, MAIP,* f. 40, c. 136 (py., *PP, ND,* 40).

131. Cobelli is mistaken when he gives two contradictory reasons for Caterina's prohibition of a sack. At one point (p. 332) he claims that Caterina acted out of good will toward her subjects, and at another he asserts that Lodovico il Moro wanted to have fire set to Forlì in order to destroy the city

completely and that Caterina could prevent such an act of destruction only by pleading that all her looted possessions would then be destroyed together with the houses (p. 331).

132. *Cronaca Anonima,* entry under April 29, 1488. Similar passage in *ibid.,* p. 326.

133. Bernardi, I, 252.

134. Dramatic accounts of the fateful night in Cobelli, pp. 328–30, and Bernardi, I, 254–55.

135. G. Ridolfi to *Otto di Pratica,* April 30, 1488, *ASF, Otto di Pratica, Responsive,* f. 4, c. 319.

136. G. Ridolfi to *Otto di Pratica,* April 30, 1488, *ibid.,* cc. 317–318.

IV

1. Cobelli, pp. 332–33, described the celebrations of Caterina's victory.

2. Bernardi, I, 257–58.

3. Although the people feared that Brambilla would take Forlì from Caterina in favor of Lodovico il Moro (Cobelli, p. 341), there is no evidence that Caterina yielded any appreciable amount of authority to Brambilla.

4. Bernardi, I, 261–62.

5. All that is left of Girolamo's tomb in the cathedral today is a plaque. The tomb was demolished in the eighteenth century.

6. Francesco Machietta to G. B. Ridolfi, May 7, 1488, *ASF, S, XdB, OdP, Legazioni e Commissarie—Missive—Responsive,* n. 15, c. 7. (The letter is really a copy of one received by Machietta from G. Corbizzi the day before.)

7. Order to illuminate and hold processions, May 2, 1488, *Archivio Storico Civile,* Milano, *RD,* n. 5, c. 260 vo.; in Santoro, p. 234.

8. Cobelli, p. 335.

9. *Ibid.*

10. For two detailed and contemporary accounts of Caterina's vengeance, see Cobelli, pp. 335–43, and Bernardi, I, 261–73. See also the report of an outsider, F. Machietta to G. B. Ridolfi, May 7, 1488, *ASF, S, XdB, OdP, Legazioni e Commissarie—Missive—Responsive,* n. 15, c. 7.

11. Cobelli, pp. 337–38; Bernardi, I, 265; Vecchiazzani, II, 174–75.

12. Bernardi, I, 286.

13. The other important prisoners, among them Giovanni Francesco, count of Bagno, and Carlo di Pian di Meleto,

must have been released at about the same time; Cobelli reports their arrest (p. 333) , but not their release.

14. G. B. Savelli to G. B. Ridolfi, June 15, 1488, *ASF, S, XdB, OdP, Legazioni e Commissarie—Missive—Responsive,* n. 15, c. 26.

15. *Bando di Caterina Sforza,* May 8, 1488, *ASM, PE, Romagna,* c. 1039 (fy., but without date, *PP,* 294) .

16. Bernardi, I, 270–71.

17. *Ibid.*

18. *Ibid.*

19. Galeazzo Sanseverino advised the marquis of Mantua of the imminent departure of the army in a letter expressing gratitude for the Mantuan assistance, May 7, 1488, *ASMa, AG, E XXV, 3, Roma,* b. 847.

20. The Cantagallo family was an Imolese family. From 1200 to 1500, members of the Cantagallo family are often mentioned in the chronicles as medics and jurists.

21. The men of the Nanni family had been arrested before, in 1487. At that time they were accused of having planned to divert the water from the city moat in order to facilitate the success of the Roffi conspiracy; Cobelli, p. 302.

22. Bernardi, I, 274; Vecchiazzani, II, 175.

23. The purpose of the visit seemed to uninitiated observers clearly to have been to help Caterina in a most difficult period of her life; Bernardi, I, 274, and Padovani, p. 252 ("per aiutare Madonna") . The diplomats knew better: e.g., Antonio Boscoli to G. B. Ridolfi, May 19, 1488, who implied clearly that the cardinal came to supervise Caterina; *ASF, S, XdB, OdP, Legazioni e Commissarie—Missive—Responsive,* n. 15, c. 10. His legal right to interfere rested on the *Instrumentum Procurae* for Cardinal Riario on behalf of the sons of Girolamo and Caterina, July 1, 1488, *ASVa, Arm.* XXV, 38, ff. 93–95.

24. At that time the *libbra* used in Romagna ranged from 361.85 grams (Bologna and trade norm) to 347.83 grams (Ravenna) ; U. Santini, "I dazii egidiani in Forlì nel 1364," *AMR,* s. 4, IV (1913–14) , p. 10, and Larner, *The Lords of Romagna* (Ithaca, N.Y., 1965) , pp. 231–32.

25. A *quartarolo* equaled a quarter of a *staio* (see Pt. I, n. 100) .

26. Bernardi, I, 278, states that the reductions were granted on Oct. 24, 1488. For details and the implications of the reductions see B. Squarzoni, "Notizie economiche romagnole in un manoscritto settecentesco della *Vita di Caterina Sforza* di Fabio Oliva," *SR,* V (1954) , 547–60.

27. The cardinal of San Giorgio and the Milanese envoy did not compete at this point, although the cardinal's sympathies were much more directed toward Florence; see letter to G. B.

Ridolfi, July 30, 1488, *ASF, S, XdB, OdP, Legazioni e Commissarie—Missive—Responsive,* n. 15, c. 56.

28. Instructions to Branda Castiglione, Milanese orator in Florence, May 13, 1488, *ASM, PE, Romagna,* c. 1039 (fy., *PP,* 1392).

29. There is an unexplainable discrepancy in dates. Bernardi (I, 277) and the *Cronaca Anonima* place the celebration on July 30, 1488, while the bull of investiture is dated Aug. 15, 1488, *ASVa, Arm.* XXV, 38, ff. 98–100.

30. For description of events see Bernardi, I, 279–91; Cobelli, pp. 346–48; narrative and interpretations: Padovani, pp. 253–53 vo.; B. Azzurrini, *Chronica breviora. RIS,* n.s., XXVIII, Pt. III, pp. 248–50. Also, more general, C. Boattini, "Galeotto Manfredi, signore di Faenza (1440–88)," in *P,* XXII (1953), 132–34, 173–76, 211–13, 297–98, and G. Donati, *La fine della signoria dei Manfredi in Faenza* (Turin, 1938), p. 13.

31. The valley of the Lamone River is referred to as the Val d'Amone. Through it ran an ancient road to Florence. More densely populated than other valleys, it seems to have had a population of ten to eleven thousand in 1371. (I agree here with the estimate made from Cardinal Anglic's *Descriptio* by A. Metelli, *Storia di Brisighella e della Valle di Amone* [4 vols.; Faenza, 1869–72] I, 270, and Table VI.) In 1410/11 the valley became a unit under the name "comites Brisighellae et vallie Amonis" (lorded over by the Manfredi of Faenza); G. Cavina, *Antichi fortilizi di Romagna: Brisighella* (Faenza, 1964), pp. 25–26 and 31. There was a keen competition between the *valligiani* and the town of Faenza for political influence, of which the 1488 development is typical.

32. G. A. Aquilano informed the *anziani* of Faenza that the Florentine intervention aimed at the "quietà e tranquilità de Italia," and that Florence had the greatest sympathy for Giovanni Bentivoglio despite the displeasure the arrest would cause, June 6, 1488, *ASF, S, XdB, OdP, Legazioni e Commissarie—Missive—Responsive,* n. 15, c. 19.

33. G. B. Ridolfi used the good services of G. B. Savelli to ask for the investiture of Astorre Manfredi; answer of G. B. Savelli, June 11 and 12, 1488, *ibid.,* cc. 22 and 23.

34. For an account of Ottaviano's activities in these days, see N. Missiroli, "Faenza e il pretendente Ottaviano Manfredi nell'anno 1488," *R,* V (1908), 250–61, 299–311, and A. Missiroli, *Astorgio III Manfredi, signore di Faenza, (1488–1501)* (Bologna, 1912). Also, P. Zama, *I Manfredi* (Faenza, 1954), pp. 296–305. Ottaviano was the son of the deposed (1477) Carlo Manfredi and Costanza Varano; he was born Aug. 6, 1472.

The Manfredi of Faenza:
Astorre II
signore of Faenza (1448–68)

Federico	Carlo	Barbara	Elisabetta	Lancelotto	Galeotto
bishop of Faenza	*signore* of Faenza	married to Pino Cecco Ordelaffi		*condottiere*	*signore* of Faenza
ousted 1477	1468–77	d. 1466 d. 1467		d. 1480	1477–88
	Ottaviano (d. 1499)				Astorre III *signore* of Faenza (under regency) 1488–1501

35. G. B. Ridolfi spelled out the reasons why Florence must prefer Astorre (greater "legitimacy," easier control) ; letter to Lorenzo de'Medici, July 12, 1488, *ASF, MAIP,* f. 5, c. 335.

36. Bernardi, I, 283. This was the beginning of the historical prominence of the Naldi family of Brisighella. Vincenzo Naldi was at that time Ottaviano's main supporter; D. Zauli-Naldi, *Dionigi e Vincenzo Naldi in Romagna, 1495–1504* (Faenza, 1925), p. 22.

37. According to Lodovico il Moro, in a letter to Lorenzo de'Medici, March 14, 1493, *ASM, PE,* Firenze, c. 939.

38. He got along well with the new representative of Milan (replacing the late "Bergamino" [or "Brambilla"] as governor of Forlì), Count Borella. The latter, who would eventually be the tutor of Lodovico's sons, came to Forlì on June 13, 1488; *Cronaca Anonima,* entry under that date; also Vecchiazzani, II, 176. There is some mystery surrounding his departure. *Cronaca Anonima* entry under August 12 gives that date as Borella's departure, while Cobelli (p. 276) states January, 1489. Both mention that a man from Savona and confidant of the cardinal stayed on. *Cronaca Anonima* is more complete in the information given and calls the man the cardinal's brother, Aldebrando de Riario da Savona. He was supposedly governor of Forlì after Borella. If that was a fact, his tenure was short, and he was certainly put in the position by the cardinal and not by Milan. A man with the similar name Benedetto Aldebrando (a Feo relative) appeared later as *podestà* of Forlì. It is almost certain that the two are identical, but it is doubtful that Aldebrando was the cardinal's brother.

39. Bernardi, I, 292–93. Vecchiazzani, II, 177, blames *"masnadieri."*

40. Letters, Feb. 12 and 19, 1489, *ASMa, AG,* E XXVI, 2, *Forlì,* b. 1065.

41. A valuable gift since one *libbra* (about 0.8 pounds Avoirdupois) of eels cost three *soldi* and six *denari,* which was about twenty-one times the price of sardines and ten times that of carp, according to Cobelli, pp. xiii and xv.

42. For the particular exchange, see Caterina Sforza to duke of Ferrara, March 11, 1489, *ASMo, ASE, Carteggio con principi esteri, Forlì,* b. 1167. Her gifts were rose apples. Similar exchanges occurred every year in Lent.

43. For Caterina's relationship with the chapter of Imola see A. Grilli, "Dieci lettere inedite di Caterina Sforza al capitolo di San Casciano d'Imola," *R,* s. 4., VIII (1911), 313–58, and doc.

44. For description see J. Graevius, *Thesaurus Antiquitatum et Historiarum Italiae* (2 vols.; Leyden, 1704), II, 499–514.

45. Both cases involved Bologna and the Bentivoglio; letters from the *Sedici Riformatori dello Stato di Libertà di Bologna,* March 17 and April 17, 1489, *AS,* Bologna, *AC, Riformatori, Registro Litterarum dal Comune,* reg. 5, cc. 429–436.

46. The Holy Virgin had appeared to a pilgrim from Cremona just south of Imola on April 17, 1489. On the approximate spot the sanctuary of Piratello was to rise and Caterina was its sponsor; Bernardi, I, 296–98, and Vecchiazzani, II, 177. A second tradition places the miracle on April 17, 1483; G. Alberghetti, *Compendio della storia civile, ecclesiastica e letteraria della città di Imola,* (2 vols.; Imola, 1810), II, 148.

47. G. B. Marconi, *Le guerre della Romagna alta e le tragedie della città di Imola,* Bibl. Com. Imola, MS 349, c. 40. *Cronaca Anonima,* entry under April–Summer, 1489. Vecchiazzani, II, 177.

48. The Riario possessed extensive estates around Bubano. The country house in question was close to the parish of Giardino and actually a small palace with a large surrounding park; see D. L. Baldisseri, *La rocca di Bubano* (Imola, 1898), p. 12.

49. Vecchiazzani, II, 177–78, still suspects the Venetians of having disturbed the idyl.

50. Ever since Antonio Maria had received Venetian support the Florentines had been cool toward him.

51. G. Lanfredini to Lorenzo de'Medici, July 29 and August 4, 1489, *ASF, MAIP,* f. 58, cc. 146 and 152 (partially ciphered) (py., *PP, ND,* 49 and 50).

52. Duke of Milan to Branda Castiglione (orator in Florence), Sept. 11, 1489, *ASM, PE, Florence,* c. 310 (py., *PP,* 338).

53. Malipiero, II, 310.

54. Cobelli's unpleasant experience is well reflected in the

long gap in his chronicle during that period. Bernardi, I, 298–99; Marconi, *Le guerre della Romagna,* cc. 40 vo.–42.

55. J. Petrus (Inviziati) to Bartolemeo Calco (ducal secretary), Sept. 26, 1489, *ASM, PE, Romagna,* c. 1040.

56. A contemporary account, Bernardi, I, 313. A full discussion of the issue is given by C. Manaresi, "Caterina Sforza e il castellano d'Imola," *R,* s. 6, XV (1924), 268–77.

57. Information on the financial issue, *ASM, Sezione Giudizaria, Senato, Miscellanea Atti avanti ai Consigli della Sapienza e Giustizia,* c. 428.

58. Bernardi, I, 302, says the cardinal came on Nov. 2, 1489. Infessura (pp. 232–33) remarks sarcastically that having won a huge sum of money at the gambling table from the pope's son, the cardinal was quite happy to leave for Romagna because of the supposed problems which had arisen there.

59. Bernardi, I, 299; *Cronaca Anonima,* entry under November, 1489. Also, Tommaso Feo to Caterina Sforza, Nov. 7, 1489, *ASF, MAIP,* f. 78, n. 2.

60. The Feo family:

Giuliano Feo   Cesare Feo
(relative of Girolamo   castellan of Tossignano
by marriage to one of   (1480's)
his cousins)
governor of Forli (1487)
castellan of Ravaldino
(1491–?)

Tommaso Feo	Giacomo Feo	Lucrezia Feo
m. to Bianca Landriani	lover of Caterina	m. to Simone Ridolfi
castellan of Ravaldino	(1489/90–95)	advisor of Giovanni
(1487–90)	castellan of Ravaldino	de'Medici
governor of Imola	(1490–91)	governor of Forlì in
(1493–95)		1499 (dismissed Octo-
governor of Forlì		ber, 1499)
(1495–?)		

Another Feo present in Forlì in the 1480's, Corradino, could not be placed in the genealogy.

61. The Jews of Forlì were merchants and pawnbrokers. Their community was large enough to maintain a synagogue in 1466 (*Archivio Notarile,* Forlì, reg. 19, c. 94 vo.). Numerous pawnshops existed in Forlì, most of them maintained by Jews because of the Church's still standing, though often violated, ban on interest taking; see E. Rinaldi, "Gli Ebrei in Forlì, nei secoli XIV e XV," *AMR,* s.4a X (1919–20), 295–323.

62. Bernardi (I, 304) says that Caterina did it in order "to help and favor the whole community and especially those desperately poor."

63. Bernardi, I, 304–5; the man's name was Guglielmo d'Aia.

64. Pawns given included hoes, spades, small knives, pickaxes, plowshares, and other utensils.

65. Caterina Sforza to B. Calco, April 21, 1490, *ASM, PE, Romagna,* c. 1040 (fy., *PP, 359*) .

66. Alberghetti, *Compendio,* I, 258–60.

67. Cobelli, p. 349 (a brief account by an observer who was too careful to write about what he knew since he had been in jail only the year before) , and Bernardi, I, 310–12; Padovani, pp. 255–255 vo.; *Cronaca Anonima,* entry under August, 1490.

68. Bernardi, I, 311.

69. Caterina Sforza to Ercole, duke of Ferrara, Aug. 30, 1490, *ASMo, ASE, Carteggio con principi esteri, Imola,* b. 1177 (*PP,* 365) ; Padovani, pp. 255–56, speaks of the affair in terms clearly attempting to be more complimentary to Caterina. Caterina could not really deceive anybody. F. Tranchedini wrote to the duke of Milan on Aug. 29, 1490, that Caterina's real motive was to gain control of her state, *ASM, PE, Romagna,* c. 1040.

70. He never did get his money despite an intervention by Lodovico il Moro. Giovanni Andrea declined to accept all offers of a nominal sum to be paid in lieu of his demand which he reduced to three thousand ducats. See Manaresi, "Caterina Sforza . . . ," *R,* s.6, XV (1924) , 275–77.

71. Giovanni Andrea left on Dec. 16, 1490; Bernardi, I, 312–13.

72. On July 30, 1490, Giampietro Landriani had still pledged his loyalty as castellan of Forlimpopoli, *ASF, MAIP,* f. 78, c. 6. On December 18, 1490, he already appears as castellan of Imola in a list of possessions consigned to him by Caterina, *ibid.,* f. 104, n. 14, cc. 121–133. Bernardi (I, 313) mentions the shift of castellans.

73. Giacomo Feo relinquished the castellanship of Ravaldino a year later in order to make his dominating position a bit less obvious; Cesare Feo, his uncle, took over the post (Oct. 1, 1491) ; Bernardi, I, 324.

74. Lodovico il Moro to Caterina Sforza, Dec. 4, 1490, *ASM, PE, Romagna,* c. 1040. B. Sfondrati had a double duty: to keep an eye on Caterina and her affairs and to help settle the Cotignola issue. The latter centered around taxes which the Cotignolesi (who were Milanese subjects) had agreed to pay in 1478 for grain grown on Faenza soil. The Cotignolesi contested the agreement and refused to use the barge provided by Faenza for

the transport of their grain. Although in retrospect the issue seems minor, it disturbed the relations between Faenza and Milan from 1490 to 1492; see B. Castiglione to duke of Milan, June 14, 1490, *ASM, PE, Firenze,* c. 311.

75. Copy of the whole book in Pasolini, III, 599–807. For an explanation of some of the prescriptions see R. C. Storti, "Le frivolezze di una grande donna. Gli esperimenti di Caterina Sforza." *Lettura,* XLII (1942), 657–63; V. Nigrisoli, "Cenni sul ricettario di Caterina Sforza," *P,* IX (1928), 178–82; and by the same author, "Spigolature dal ricettario di Caterina Sforza," *P,* X (1929), 34–36 and 38–39.

76. Lodovico Albertino, *speziale di Forlì,* to Francesco Fortunati, Sept. 8, 1509, *ASF, MAIP,* f. 69, c. 95 (py., *PP,* 1364).

77. Lorenzo de Mantechitis to Caterina Sforza, n.p., n.d., *ASF, MAIP,* f. 125, n. 202.

78. Her stepmother, Bona of Savoy, like most ladies of the Renaissance, had had her own *speziale.* Cristoforo da Brugora kept his own botanical garden which Bona began to visit soon after her marriage. Caterina may have learned about botanical gardens on one or more of those visits; A. Laghi, *Cristoforo de Brugora, speziale della duchessa Bona e della corte sforzesca* (Pavia, 1959).

79. While it is impossible to estimate the accurate value of Caterina's wardrobe it definitely was considerable. Wives of even well-to-do patricians had only one or two dresses of the kind which Caterina possessed by the dozens. See *Inventario della guardaroba di Madonna (Caterina Sforza) fatto da Antonio Melozzo,* n.d., *ASF, MAIP,* f. 104, cc. 336–341. While the inventory seems to stem from a later period, it still gives a good account of Caterina's wardrobe.

80. Cobelli, p. 350.

81. The strange mixture of liberality and brutality in Romagnol politics can be seen if one contrasts the bloody vengeance on everybody who had opposed the Riario after the assassination of Girolamo (1488) and the interesting fact which appears at that point. Niccoló Tornielli, who in 1488 had counseled for the surrender of the city to the Church, became one year after restoration of the councils, once more *primus consilii* (January, 1492); *Libro Madonna, AS,* Forlì, *MS,* p. 20.

82. *Libro Madonna,* pp. 5–5 vo., for actual letting of building contracts, entry March 22, 1491, *ibid.,* pp. 8–9; summary of proceedings in Bernardi, I, 317–21.

83. Although one finds in the testament of Caterina, May 28, 1509, the phrase "secundo viro legiptimo," a marriage appears highly unlikely. *ASF, MAIP,* f. 99, c. 12 (fy., *PP,* 1355). The phrase protected Caterina from the onus and status of Bernardino being an illegitimate child. But the treatment he received

in the will suggests that he was just that. The child was later renamed Carlo (in honor of the French king).

84. Cobelli, p. 413.

85. Such titles were purely honorific and awarded as means to influence persons. In Giacomo's case the title was badly needed because he was actually a nobody. The Milanese named Giacomo a *cavaliere* (Jan. 23, 1491). *Ibid.*, pp. 348 and 350.

86. *Ibid.*, p. 350.

87. For details on the conspiracy see Bernardi, I, 324–28; Cobelli, pp. 352–43; and Padovani, p. 258 vo., who states that the Vaini were the actual originators of the conspiracy. F. Mancini and W. Vichi, *Castelli, rocche, e torri di Romagna* (Bologna, 1959), p. 21, state that the fortress of Tossignano was remodeled during the rule of Caterina Sforza.

88. Cobelli, p. 353.

89. Caterina Sforza to duke of Ferrara, July 4, 1491, *ASMo, ASE, Carteggio con principi esteri, Imola,* b. 1177.

90. Request for ouster of Enea Vaini to duchess, Aug. 3, 1491, *ibid.*

91. Caterina Sforza to duke of Ferrara, Jan. 5, 1491, *ASMo, ASE, Carteggio con principi esteri, Imola,* b. 1177. She was afraid that her denial of the request would be misunderstood and was unusually apologetic. Something the Este must have known, too, should be pointed out here, namely that Caterina, while usually hard pressed for funds, did have ample silverware and finery in her possession. Inventory of possessions consigned to Giampietro Landriani, Dec. 18, 1490, *ASF, MAIP,* f. 104, n. 14, cc. 121–146 (133–46 are empty pages).

92. The marriage contract had been signed and celebrated years before, June 4, 1477, *Archivio Storico Civile,* Milano, *RD,* n. 4, c. 159; also Santoro, n. 165.

93. Bernardi, I, 382. Pride in one's city, which was an important factor in the life of people was, however, no reason for not trying to escape the payment of taxes.

94. Vecchiazzani, II, 192–93. The actual murderer was Brunoro. Meleagro reappeared in Venetian service in 1499.

95. The first letter to that regard was addressed to F. Tranchedini (ducal orator in Bologna), Nov. 1, 1491, *ASM, PE, Romagna,* c. 1041; later to duke of Milan, Nov. 14 and Dec. 7, 1491, *ibid.* She demanded that she should not be forced to pay the installation fee a second time.

96. Bernardi, I, 328–31; also Cobelli, p. 353; Padovani, pp. 258 vo–259 vo.

97. Bernardi, I, 329.

98. Padovani, pp. 258 vo.–259 vo. says that Solombrino was a shoemaker, which fact once more confirms the already stated opposition from the side of the artisans.

99. F. Tranchedini to duke of Milan, April 27, 1492, *ASM,*

PE, Romagna, c. 1042 (py., *PP,* 1398). Cobelli (p. 353) considered such an action to betray a lack of common sense.

100. Cobelli, p. 353; Padovani, p. 258 vo., *"fondo di torre."*

101. F. Tranchedini to the duke of Milan, Dec. 4, 1492, *ASM, PE, Romagna,* c. 1042 (py., *PP,* 446).

102. The *rastelli* ("checkpoints") had been established in February, 1491, at two Ronco bridges at Ronco and at Bagnolo. The *pedaggi* ("tolls") levied were supposed to pay for a rebuilding of the dilapidated main Ronco bridge. Guards on foot and horseback made sure that the *pedaggi* were paid. No bridge was ever built from the revenue received; Bernardi, I, 316–17.

103. F. Tranchedini to duke of Milan, May 4, 1492, *ASM, PE, Romagna,* c. 1042. Bolognese protest, *Riformatori dello Stato* to Caterina Sforza, March 17, 1492, *AS* Bologna, *AC, Riformatori, Registro Litterarum dal Comune,* reg. 5, c. 63.

104. F. Tranchedini to duke of Milan, Aug. 21, 23, and 24, 1492, *ASM, PE, Romagna,* c. 1042 (py., *PP,* 439–41). Tranchedini speaks of an attack of "double" tertian fever. The term could not be clarified.

105. Caterina Sforza to duke of Milan, May 31, 1492, *ASM, PE, Romagna,* c. 1042 (py., *PP,* 426).

106. The same, March 10, 1492, *ibid.* (fy., *PP,* 410).

107. Giovanni Bentivoglio to Lorenzo de'Medici, Sept. 7, 1489, *ASF, MAIP,* f. 41, n. 308. Although no answer is known, Lorenzo de'Medici did probably temporize since he could hardly see any need to strengthen the position of Caterina Sforza and Milan in pro-Florentine Faenza.

108. Caterina Sforza and Ottaviano Riario to Lorenzo de'Medici, Jan. 4, 7, and 21, 1490, *ASF, MAIP,* f. 41, nn. 429, 435, 461.

109. Lodovico il Moro to F. Visconti, March 16, 1490, *ASM, PE, Romagna,* c. 1040.

110. F. Visconti to Lodovico il Moro, March 20, 1490, *ASM, PE, Romagna,* c. 1040.

111. Isabella herself acquired a rival when Lodovico il Moro married Beatrice d'Este of Ferrara (January, 1491). For the dissension between Milan and Naples, see Treccani, *Storia di Milano,* VII, 391–92.

112. G. Priuli, *I Diarii (1494–1512),* ed. A Segre, *RIS,* n.s. XXIV, Pt. III, 115. (Appears as *Chronicon Venetum* ascribed to M. Sanuto in *RIS,* o.s. XXIV; henceforth cited as Priuli.) P. de Commines, *Memorien,* trans. and ed. F. Ernst (Stuttgart, 1952), p. 292, calls him clever but timid, and sly but not trustworthy.

113. Pact concluded Jan. 24, 1492. See. F. Delaborde, *L'expédition de Charles VIII* (Paris, 1888), p. 228.

114. Treccani, *Storia di Milano,* VII; 388–89.

115. Caterina Sforza to Piero de'Medici, April 10, 1492, *ASF, MAIP,* f. 47, n. 465, and Dionisio Pucci to Piero de'Medici, April 11, 1492, *ibid.,* n. 134 (fy., *PP,* 417).

There is good evidence for asserting that during his late years Lorenzo de'Medici supported Caterina fully in her endeavor to rule Forlì and Imola; see the use made by Caterina of the Florentine representative in Rome, Piero d'Alamanni, and Lorenzo de'Medici's recommendation of Caterina to Piero; two letters, July 7 and 8, 1491, Baker Library, Harvard University, Selfridge Collection, n. 210 and n. 212 (heavily damaged).

116. Dionisio Pucci to Piero de'Medici, Sept. 25, 1492, *ASF, MAIP,* f. 54, n. 156; Dec. 13, 1492, n. 161.

117. Piero de'Medici to Dionisio Pucci, March 1493, *ASF, Carte Strozziane,* s. la, f. 310, c. 162. Other families considered Astorre to be a more valuable marriage prospect, as e.g., the Gonzaga and the Este; G. Donati, *La fine della signoria dei Manfredi,* pp. 85–86.

118. For three years with a stipend of twenty thousand florins (6666⅔ fl. a year); see B. Castiglione (Milanese orator in Florence) to Lodovico il Moro, March 9, 1493, *ASM, PE, Firenze,* c. 939.

119. Changes in the papal regime always brought anxious moments for the *signori* of the Papal States. Thus an elaborate delegation was dispatched to the new pope to show the loyalty of the Forlivesi and Imolesi and to bring back the reaffirmation of the Riario in their positions. The members of the delegations were: Giovanni dalle Selle (jurist) and Antonio Baldraccani (jurist) of Forlì; Pier Paolo Calderini (jurist) and Michaele Machiello of Imola; Cobelli, pp. 354–55; Padovani, pp. 259 vo.–260.

120. Not only was "Ascanio Sforza first and closest to His Holiness," but he was standing just about as high as the pope; Ambrogio Mirabilia to B. Calco, Aug. 13, 1492, *ASM, PE, Roma,* c. 106.

121. "then she, Caterina, decided to dedicate one of her sons to God"; Bernardi, I, 324.

122. Caterina paid the considerable tailor bills. Giacomo preferred clothing made of black and red velvet; see list of clothing made by a tailor named Jacopo for Giacomo Feo, *ASF, MAIP,* n.d., f. 104, n. 31, c. 347, and also an inventory of Giacomo's possessions, *ibid.,* n.d., n. 34, cc. 378–383. In the latter document Giacomo is referred to as "maggiordomo di Caterina Sforza." It showed that Giacomo possessed about one hundred and ten pieces of expensive clothing and some one hundred and thirty pieces of silverware. One year after his death Giacomo's possessions were assigned to his mother, Dec. 18, 1496, *ibid.,* n. 35, cc. 384.

123. Neither Cobelli nor Bernardi were very sympathetic to Giacomo Feo, although his behavior was just that of a young fellow who suddenly found himself in possession of a fortune without having had to exert himself for it. The motive might shine through in Cobelli's sneering at Giacomo's low origin (p. 413).

124. Puccio Pucci to Piero de'Medici, May 23, 1493, *ASF, MAIP,* f. 54, n. 165 (fy., *PP,* 468).

125. Duke of Milan to Caterina Sforza, April 24, 1493, *ASM, PS,* c. 1110; also Treccani, *Storia di Milano,* VII, 399–401. In this and many other cases important information came to Caterina from Milan. As she could not afford a diplomatic service of her own, she was forced to rely on the services of other rulers and on her own occasional special emissaries. Milan represented the outstanding source of information, followed at a long distance by Florence, Bologna, and Ferrara.

126. Treccani, *Storia di Milano,* VII, 406–7.

127. Actually most of the troops were destined for the protection of Pesaro during the absence of Giovanni Sforza's troops, which went to Rome for his wedding to Lucrezia Borgia. The troops were under the command of Gaspare Sanseverino (Fracasso), Francesco Quartieri, and Francesco Casate, each of them operating for himself either from Cotignola (the old Sforza home) or from Pesaro.

128. Puccio Pucci to Piero de'Medici, May 10, 1493, *ASF, MAIP,* f. 54, n. 165. The *Otto di Pratica* showed themselves less worried, since they saw in Lodovico's trip merely a return visit to Ferrara, but they still told Pucci to watch events with great prudence; May 13, 1493, *ASF, S, XdB, OdP, Legazioni e Commissarie—Missive—Responsive,* reg. 15, c. 63.

129. Contained in a letter from Puccio Pucci to Piero de'Medici, May 25, 1493, *ASF, MAIP,* f. 54, n. 167.

130. Puccio Pucci to Caterina Sforza upon his assuming office as Florentine commissioner, May 11, 1493, *ASF, MAIP,* f. 54, n. 138. She answered the letter immediately, May 11, 1493, *ibid.,* n. 137. See also Caterina Sforza to P. Pucci, May 23, 1493, *ASF, S, XdB, OdP, Legazioni e Commissarie—Missive—Responsive,* reg. 15, c. 71.

131. Caterina Sforza to Puccio Pucci, May 25, 1493, *ibid.* c. 78. Lodovico il Moro, irked by Casate's exclusion, impressed upon Caterina that the Milanese troops had the purpose of protecting Giovanni Sforza's territory and of helping the pope in his campaign against the *signori* of Perugia and Città di Castello, but that she had nothing to fear from them. Discussion between Fracasso and Caterina in the fortress of Ravaldino of Forlì, June 3, 1493; P. Pucci to Piero de'Medici, *ASF, MAIP,* f. 54, n. 174.

132. The same, May 23, 1493, *ASF, MAIP,* f. 54, n. 139.

133. Puccio Pucci conveys to Piero de'Medici Caterina's wish to stay out of all alliances; July 2, 1493, *ASF, MAIP,* f. 54, n. 186.

134. After the treaty had been signed, Charles VIII had turned to Count Belgioso, Milan's ambassador, and remarked that now the road was open for the Neapolitan campaign and that Lodovico would become a leading figure in it; L. Simeoni, *Le signorie* (2 vols.; Milan, 1950), II, 729. On the consequences of the peace for Italy, see Delaborde, *L'expédition de Charles VIII,* p. 266.

135. P. de Commines, *Memoiren,* pp. 293–94.

136. *Ibid.,* p. 295.

137. For the details on the marriage see M. Sanuto, I *diarii* (58 vols.; Venice, 1879–1902), I, 353–55 (Sanuto quotes always refer to columns) ; Treccani, *Storia di Milano,* VII, 403. Investiture was promised on June 24, 1493.

138. King Ferrante of Naples had already made plans for a quick invasion of Lombardy and Genoa; L. Simeoni, *Le signorie,* II, 731.

139. Sources for the figures given are: Cobelli, p. 360 (approximately twenty thousand troops) ; P. Giovio, *Elogi* (Venice, 1558), pp. 81–84 (gives a detailed description of the French army after its arrival in Rome) ; E. Gagliardi, *Der Anteil der Schweizer an den italienischen Kriegen, 1494–1516* (Zurich, 1919), p. 151; and Piero Pieri, *Il Rinascimento e la crisi militare italiana* (Turin, 1952), Pt. II, chap. 4.

v

1. Letter, Sept. 17, 1488, *ASF, MAIP,* f. 58, n. 73.

2. P. Pieri, *Il Rinascimento e la crisi militare italiana* (Turin, 1952), pp. 325–26.

3. The visit took place on June 30, 1494 and "parole inzuriose" were spoken; Bernardi, II, 73. Caterina herself reported on the quarrels with the cardinal to the ducal orators in Bologna, Aug. 3, 1494, *ASM, PE, Romagna,* c. 1044.

4. The investiture instrument speaks of a census of two pounds and six ounces of silver, April 6, 1494, *ASVa, Arm.* XXXV, 41, ff. 32–36. If these were figures based on the *libbra mercantile,* the amount of silver equaled approximately 905 grams (*ca.* 2 lbs. avoirdupois) .

5. Padovani, p. 260 vo.

6. The prescription against depressing spirits relied mainly on the burning of a mixture of nine different kinds of incense

and the reading of the Bible; prescription in P. D. Pasolini, *Caterina Sforza* (3 vols.; Rome, 1893), III, 755, MS page n. 444.

7. Caterina Sforza to Lodovico il Moro, Feb. 8 and 10, 1494, *ASM, PE, Romagna,* c. 1043. (The middle part of both documents is damaged; fy., *PP*, 500 and 501.)

8. The Martinelli-Tiberti feud kept Cesena at the edge of turmoil all through the pontificate of Innocent VIII. In 1494 the feud was once more begun. At that point, the *consiglio* of the Commune voted fifty to twenty to oust both families, but without significant result; G. Fantaguzzi, *Caos* (Cesena, 1915), pp. 36–48.

9. P. Pucci to Piero de'Medici, June 16, 1494; printed as *PP*, 521. For Bologna's position in the summer of 1494, see G. B. Picotti, "La neutralità bolognese nella discesa di Carlo VIII," *AMR*, s. 4, IX (1919), 165–246, and "Caterina Sforza Riario e la Romagna alla calata di Carlo VIII," *AMR*, n.s., XV–XVI (1963–65; ed. 1966), (in press).

10. Bernardi, II, 13–14, reports Tranchedini's arrival on Sept. 14. On his return trip he was promptly arrested by the Neapolitans, but set free upon request by Caterina.

11. Lodovico il Moro to Caterina Sforza, June 3, 1494, *ASM, PE, Romagna,* c. 1043.

12. Instructions to Francesco Quartieri, special Milanese envoy to Caterina Sforza, Aug. 8, 1494, *ASM, PE, Romagna,* c. 1044 (fy., *PP,* 531).

13. Lodovico il Moro to Caterina Sforza, Aug. 13, 1494, *ASM, PE, Romagna,* c. 1044.

14. The strength of the Neapolitan–papal contingent was "sessanta squadre" according to Priuli, p. 3. A detailed account of the ensuing events, based on contemporary documents, is found in G. L. Moncallero, "Documenti inediti sulla guerra di Romagna del 1494," *Rinascimento,* IV (1953), 233–61; V (1954), 45–79; VI (1955), 3–74.

15. Montemauro, Riolo, Monte Battaglia, Tossignano, Dozza, Mordano, Bagnara, Bubano, and, of course, Imola and Ravaldino of Forlì.

16. Bernardi, II, 13. Vecchiazzani, II, 181 and 196, calls Zuntini "tesoriero del Riario."

17. Caterina must have shared the general confidence in the duke of Calabria's military brilliance. This trust seemed to have been justified by a series of initial skirmishes he had won.

18. Bernardo Dovizi (later Cardinal Bibbiena) to Piero de'Medici, Sept. 23, 1494, *ASF, MAIP,* f. 18, n. 294 (fy., *PP,* 536).

19. Antonio Colenuccio (Florentine orator in Rome) to Piero de'Medici, Aug. 29, 1494, *ASF, MAIP,* f. 18, n. 273.

20. B. Dovizi to Piero de'Medici, Sept. 3 and 18, 1494, *ibid.,*

f. 18, nn. 269 and 283. In addition, his attention was diverted by a love affair.

21. For military operations on Sept. 1, 1494, around Imola and Forlì, see Pieri, *Il Rinascimento,* pp. 327–29.

22. Bernardi, II, 12; Cobelli, pp. 355–57. Description of the October phase of the campaign, Pieri, *Il Rinascimento,* pp. 330–31.

23. Bernardi, II, 17–19; Cobelli, pp. 357–58; *Cronaca Anonima,* entry Oct. 20, 1494; Padovani, p. 261 b; B. Dovizi to Piero de'Medici, Oct. 21, 1494, *ASF, MAIP,* f. 18, nn. 347 and 348. Also J. L. de La Pilorgerie, *Campagne et bulletins de la grande armeé d'Italie commandée par Charles VIII, 1494–1495* (Nantes and Paris, 1866), p. 87. He estimates the strength of the siege detachment to have been sixteen to seventeen hundred men and the duration of the assault about an hour.

24. On the Taverna mission see reports of B. Dovizi to Piero de'Medici, Oct. 9 and 11, 1494, *ASM, MAIP,* f. 18, cc. 322 and 327 (fy., *PP,* 540 and 541). Lodovico il Moro had protested Taverna's arrest to Caterina, Oct. 16, 1494, *ASM, PE, Romagna,* c. 1044. See also G. B. Picotti, "La neutralità bolognese . . . ," *AMR,* s. 4, IX (1919), p. 233.

25. All through the difficult period Caterina had been staying in well-fortified and well-provisioned Imola. B. Dovizi to Piero de'Medici, Oct. 21, 1494, *ASF, MAIP,* f. 18, n. 347.

26. It was such behavior that Commines referred to when he regretfully stated that "the people adored us like saints when we came. . . . but this delusion did not last long with all our disorder and pillage"; P. de Commines, *Memoiren,* trans. and ed. F. Ernst (Stuttgart, 1952), p. 304.

27. *Libro Madonna, AS* Forlì, entry under Nov. 19, 1494 (fy., *PP,* 560).

28. B. Corio, *Storia di Milano* (3 vols.; Milan, 1855–57), III, 574.

29. Lodovico il Moro to Caterina, Oct. 21, 1491, *ASM, PS,* c. 1110 (fy., *PP,* 547). For three days Milan celebrated on orders of Lodovico il Moro, Oct. 22, 1494, *Archivio Storico Civile, Milano, RD,* reg. 6, c. 176, printed in Santoro, p. 265.

30. Vecchiazzani, I, 186, for Caterina's elaborate delegation in May, 1495. Lodovico, who had called himself *Lodovico Maria Sforza Visconti, duca di Bari, governatore dello stato di Milano, amministratore e luogotenente generale,* assumed the title of *duca di Milano,* pending imperial approval half a year later; Corio, *Storia di Milano,* III, 514 and 640.

31. Cobelli, pp. 361–62.

32. F. Quartieri's numerous reports show how closely he watched Caterina. All of them (dated November and Decem-

ber) in *ASM, PE, Romagna*, c. 1044. In addition the envoy was charged with strengthening Milanese influence in Faenza.

33. P. Pucci to Piero de'Medici, May 21, 1493, *ASF, MAIP*, f. 54, n. 144 (fy., *PP*, 467).

34. Even P. Pucci, who was sympathetic to Giacomo Feo because Giacomo supported Caterina's pro-Florentine policy, called Caterina's condition one of servitude. P. Pucci to Piero de'Medici, July 13, 1494, *ASF, MAIP*, f. 18, n. 267 (fy., *PP*, 528).

35. P. Pucci to Piero de'Medici, May 25, 1493, *ibid.*, f. 54, n. 167 (fy., *PP*, 471).

36. F. Tranchedini to Lodovico il Moro, May 27, 1494, *ASM, PE, Romagna*, c. 1043 (py., *PP*, 1402).

37. F. Quartieri to Lodovico il Moro, Dec. 2, 1494, *ibid.*, c. 1044.

38. Bernardi, II, 80–81; Caterina announced the marriage to the marquis of Mantua on Feb. 1, 1495, *ASMa, AG*, E XXVI, 2, *Forlì*, b. 1065. In the letter she states that the marriage contract "is the work of the most illustrious and excellent duke of Milan, my uncle." G. Donati, *La fine della signoria dei Manfredi in Faenza* (Turin, 1938), pp. 85–86, gives a review of prior marriage projects for Astorre and Bianca. According to that account, Caterina had once sought for Bianca a marriage contract with the *signore* of Pesaro, Giovanni Sforza. For Astorre there had been three suggestions: a Gonzaga girl, a daughter of Sigismondo d'Este, and the girl born to Giulia Farnese (mistress of Pope Alexander VI).

39. Lodovico il Moro to F. Quartieri, Sept. 5 and 7, 1494, *ASM, PE, Romagna*, c. 1044. Soon Astorre was to be given a Milanese *condotta*. By the time the marriage contract was published, Lodovico and Astorre (actually those governing for the young Astorre) were on excellent terms; Astorre Manfredi to Lodovico il Moro, Feb. 22, 1495, *ASM, PE, Romagna*, c. 1045; see also Lodovico's letter to Astorre, May 1, 1495, *ibid.*

40. Pictured in Zanetti, (*Delle monete . . .* , Appendix, T.I., picture x. For a general description of festivities see G. Ballardini, *Fidanzamento di Astorgio III con Bianca Riario* (Faenza, 1907).

41. Caterina Sforza to Lodovico il Moro, April 23, 1495, *ASM, PE, Romagna*, c. 1045.

42. Cobelli, pp. 374–81; Bernardi, II, 83–89; Vecchiazzani, II, 186.

43. Guido da Bagno alias Guido "Guerra" was the son of the late Count Gianfrancesco di Bagno (a onetime associate of Girolamo and Caterina). Guido "Guerra" was a fitting nickname.

44. Cobelli, pp. 380–81.

45. For the story of the assassination see Cobelli, pp. 381–84; for subsequent events see Padovani, pp. 266–71; Bernardi, II, 97–99.

46. Cobelli, p. 382.

47. Padovani (p. 267) sees in Giacomo Feo's death a penalty for his "cattivi portamenti." Cobelli, although he exclaims "Oh compassione granda! Oh pietate! Oh crodelitate!" (p. 383) at the terrible sight of the corpse of Giacomo Feo, cannot suppress his feelings when he quotes an old proverb, "one who is handsome *and* virtuous cannot perish," leaving the obvious conclusion about Giacomo to the reader.

48. An auditor was a judicial official with the most varied functions, very often including purely administrative details.

49. For vendetta see Cobelli, pp. 384–90; Bernardi, II, 99–112.

50. Her vendetta in 1495 was much more severe than that in 1488. Cobelli lists for Forlì:

	1488	1495
killed	12	46
exiled	26	5
long-term imprisonment	5	?

(pp. 343–45) (pp. 390–92)

51. *Ibid.*, p. 392.

52. *Ibid.*, p. 388.

53. *Ibid.*, p. 384.

54. *Ibid.*

55. Scipio (ne) soon escaped the supervision of Paolo Vitelli under which he at first had been put. He tried to gain a position with the Bentivoglio, but that family decided that a permission for Scipio to stay in Bologna would disturb relations with Caterina. Scipio went to Venice, where he was welcome, as most disgruntled exiles of potential value were.

56. Bernardi, II, 134–35.

57. The park was in line with the pronounced interest Caterina showed for nature and with the general love for parks at that time. Caterina could draw on the examples of the parks in Mantua, Pavia, and Ferrara. See J. Cartwright, *Italian Gardens of the Renaissance* (New York, 1914), for the Este Gardens, pp. 31–48, and Gonzaga gardens, pp. 53–58. Other gardens closer to Forlì were at Gubbio and Urbino.

58. Bernardi, II, 115.

59. Cobelli, pp. 394–97; Bernardi, II, 90–97; 115–45; R. Zazzeri, *Storia di Cesena* (Cesena, 1890), pp. 152, 381–400. Castelnuovo, the main aim, is located south-southeast of Meldola and had at various times belonged to the archbishop of

Ravenna, the Commune of Forlì, and the Malatesta family. Later the counts of Giaggiolo took it from the Ordelaffi; F. Mancini and W. Vichi, *Castelli, rocche, e torri di Romagna* (Bologna, 1959), p. 157.

60. Infessura, p. 215: "Caterina Sforza loots Church property but nobody talks much about it."

61. Bernardi, II, 113–14.

62. Caterina estimated their strength at three hundred. *Stradioti* were light cavalry men who had proved their value in the fight against the Turks in Greece and Albania. Used for the first time in Italy during the Ferrara war, they soon were dreaded for their speed and murderous behavior.

63. She pretended not to understand why the *podestà* of Ravenna got so excited about Castelnuovo. F. Tranchedini to duke of Milan on discussions with Caterina, Dec. 6, 1495, *ASM, PE, Romagna,* c. 1045.

64. Castelnuovo was lost on Nov. 31, 1496; Cobelli, p. 396.

65. Lodovico il Moro's relief over the end of the Castelnuovo occupation shows in a letter to F. Tranchedini, Dec. 18, 1495, *ASM, PE,* c. 1045.

66. The Martinelli had even hired five hundred German mercenaries. Cobelli, p. 379. For a fuller account of the events, see Fantaguzzi, *Caos,* pp. 60–62.

67. She freely admits her joy over the Tiberti's victory to Lodovico il Moro, May 3, 1496, *ASM, PE, Romagna,* c. 1046.

68. Cobelli, p. 398; also Vecchiazzani, II, 188–89. The stones were probably meteorites since Vecchiazzani speaks of five pieces of metal.

69. Cobelli, p. 387.

70. This event of interest for medical history is recorded by Bernardi, II, 162.

71. Bernardi, II, 126.

72. The issue was once more the *danne date* sale. Bernardi, II, 130–32, states that Caterina decided to sell it for twenty-two hundred *lire bol.,* to be paid in three installments, with sixteen hostages as a guarantee of payment, and with stiff penalties for non-payment. See also Padovani, p. 273.

73. The incident is illuminating for the position of near monopoly held by Cervia salt. Forlì at that point bought four hundred bags of salt from a region called Apole (Apulia). The salt arrived Oct. 27, 1496, was very rough in texture, and sold for twice and one-half as much as Cervia salt. The *quartarolo* cost 30 *soldi* as against 13 *soldi* and 4 *denari* for Cervia salt; and in retail the price was raised even more sharply: 1 *soldo* per pound (at 361.85 g.) as compared to 5 *denari* per lb.; see Bernardi, II, 143–44, and an ordinance concerning salt management from Nov. 14, 1496, to Oct. 30, 1497, *ASF, MAIP,* f.

150, n. 50. One *quartarolo* equals one-fourth of a *staio* (about one-half bushel grain measure) according to Larner's tabulation of the measures in use in Romagna (*The Lords of Romagna,* pp. 231–33).

74. F. Tranchedini to Lodovico il Moro, Sept. 4, 1496, *ASM, PE, Romagna,* c. 1046 (py., *PP,* 586).

75. Caterina to Lodovico il Moro, March 27, 1496, *ASM, PE, Romagna,* c. 1046 (py., *PP,* 645).

76. The exact purpose of Baldraccani's mission is nowhere stated, but from the context in which it occurred it must have concerned the cardinal's attitude toward Caterina. See credentials for A. Baldraccani, Jan. 3, 1496, *ASM, PE, Romagna,* c. 1046, and announcement of his coming, to Lodovico il Moro, Jan. 31, 1496, *ibid.*

Antonio Baldraccani, who appears to have entered Caterina's service sometime prior to the mission, was a descendant of an old Forlivese family which can be traced back in Forlì to about 1363 (I. Gardini, *Tavole genealogiche delle famiglie patrizie di Forlì* [2 vols.; Bibl. Com. Forlì, MSS 1 and 2], I, 9–10). Many members of the family were jurists like Antonio. He is described by Cobelli as "un discreto huomo" (p. 321) and had been on good terms with the Riario family for quite some time. For example, Antonio and his brother Francesco had been favored in a breve by Sixtus IV concerning a private matter, *ASVa, Arm.* XXXV, 37, pp. 255 vo.–256 vo. That he had been one of the men who delivered the pledge of loyalty to the pope during the revolt of 1488 was never held against Antonio. He became a member of two high-level delegations, one of which congratulated Alexander VI upon his election in 1492, and another of which went to Milan, May 26, 1495, in order to bring Lodovico il Moro the good wishes of Caterina upon his formal investiture as duke of Milan. By 1496, Antonio Baldraccani and Caterina were close associates, with the degree of closeness open to speculation.

77. Ascanio Sforza to Lodovico il Moro, Feb. 22, 1496, *ASM, PE, Roma,* c. 115 (py., *PP,* 634).

78. This step, practical although lacking in taste, is described in Caterina's letters to Lodovico il Moro, Sept. 5, Oct. 31, and Nov. 12, 1494, *ASM, PE, Romagna,* c. 1047. She assumed that the cardinal would not object to a request on behalf of her sons even though he was on bad terms with her.

79. Caterina Sforza to Lodovico il Moro, March 27, 1496, *ASM, PE, Romagna,* c. 1046 (py., *PP,* 645).

80. F. Tranchedini to Lodovico il Moro, July 26, 1496, *ASM, PE, Romagna,* c. 1047.

81. The marriage contract had been concluded in August,

1488, when relations between the Riario and the Bentivoglio had been excellent.

82. A gap in Bernardi's chronicle obscures the name of the lady. The daughter was named Cornelia and eventually entered a monastery.

83. Bernardi (II, 157) mentions a second child born in September, 1498, but it died soon after birth.

84. The *valligiani* supported Ottaviano because of his age advantage over Astorre. Defeated in 1488, the *valligiani* battled all through 1489 for proper representation in Faenza; G. Cavina, *Antichi fortilizi di Romagna: Brisighella* (Faenza, 1964), pp. 72–73. Now in 1495 their grievances made them once more rally around Ottaviano; Malipiero, II, 416.

85. For the role of the Naldi family (whose services Caterina would soon use) see D. Zauli-Naldi, *Dionigi e Vincenzo Naldi in Romagna (1495–1504)* (Faenza, 1925), p. 27.

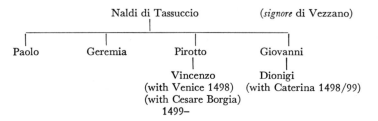

Genealogical table of the Naldi family according to Cavina, *Brisighella*, pp. 176 and 221.

86. On Dec. 18, 1495, the Venetian *provveditore*, Bernardino Contarini, backed up by about fourteen hundred armed men, threatened Ottaviano with an attack; Malipiero, II, 416, and Zauli-Naldi, *Naldi in Romagna*, p. 27. After Ottaviano had withdrawn, the Venetians moved south, destroyed houses of the Naldi and their partisans, and executed some of the Naldi (Zauli-Naldi, pp. 33–34).

87. Milan and Caterina looked helplessly on as Venice established a new Romagnol base; F. Tranchedini to Lodovico il Moro, Dec. 8, 1495, *ASM, PE, Romagna*, c. 1045.

88. The *condotta* was signed on Dec. 15, 1495. See Malipiero, II, 416, and Priuli, pp. 47–48, on conditions. Malipiero adds the significant remark that Astorre was a small boy in poor health. Priuli (p. 46) sums up the purpose of the *condotta*: "to offer the territory of Faenza and its very young *signore* for protection to the Republic." For events in Faenza during the winter of 1495/96, see also P. Zama, "Caterina Sforza e gli ultimi Manfredi, signori di Faenza (1488–1500)," *AMR*, n.s., XV–XVI (1963–65; ed. 1966), (in press).

89. The first *provveditore,* Bernardo Contarini, had left after the December crisis because his harshness had made him unpopular.

90. Caterina to Lodovico il Moro, July 18, 1496, Bibl. Com., Forlì, c. 609. Also Malipiero, II, 230.

91. Letter, April 10, 1496, *ASM, PE, Romagna,* c. 1046. Astorre Manfredi complained to Caterina about the Venetian arrogance, Aug. 18, 1496, Bibl. Com., Forlì, c. 609.

92. Lodovico il Moro defended the Venetians and accused the Florentines of expansionism in a letter to Caterina, April 17, 1496, *ASM, PE, Romagna,* c. 1046. Caterina answered firmly that such accusations against the Florentines were unfounded and that the Venetians were more dangerous than he thought, April 24, 1496, *ibid.*

93. Bernardi, pp. 144–45. The Orsi had established themselves rather successfully in Camerino. Cecco had become "capo di squadre," Padovani, p. 273; Lodovico was highly esteemed and when he died was buried "in duomo con grandissimi honori," Padovani, p. 273 b.

94. The pieces coined were: 1 *quattrino,* 4 *quattrini,* 2 *soldi;* Bernardi, II, 122; Padovani, p. 273. These coins were actually the first to be minted in Caterina's territories. The mint was in Forlimpopoli (Vecchiazzani, II, 186) and Caterina employed a Spanish mintmaster (Padovani, p. 273). Why did she go into the minting business? One suspects that prestige was the main factor. The *quattrino* was a coin which came into use when the *denaro's* value had diminished to the extent that its use as more than a bookkeeping unit became impractical. The *quattrino* in question was equal to 2 *denari;* see G. Zanetti, *Nuova raccolta delle monete e zecche d'Italia* (Bologna, 1775–86), pp. 463–64, and Squarzoni, "Notizie economiche . . . ," *SR,* V (1954), 549–51. For a special essay on Caterina's *quattrino,* see Gnecchi, "Un quattrino . . . ," *Rivista Italiana di Numismatica,* XVIII (1905), 493–98.

95. On May 10, 1496, Caterina directed a formal inquiry to Lodovico il Moro on what she should do in case the expected French invasion took place, *ASM, PE, Romagna,* c. 1046.

96. Letter, Ascanio Sforza to duke of Milan, May 31, 1496, *ASM, PE, Roma,* c. 146 (py., *PP,* 668).

97. A peace which the Venetian Priuli (p. 36) clearly labeled as treason against the league; see also p. 34, n.

98. Letters from Lorenzo il Moro on that subject, *ASM, PE, Romagna,* c. 1046, June 2 (py., *PP,* 669), June 6, and June 28; c. 1047, Nov. 8 and 12, 1496. In all of them he reproached her for supporting the Florentines by enabling them to buy provisions in her territories.

99. Lodovico il Moro disregarding her wishes had named the

Riario as his allies in the league instrument, April 23, 1495, *Libri commemoriali*, VI, 18.

100. Caterina Sforza to Lodovico il Moro, June 16, 1496, *ASM, PE, Romagna,* c. 1046. A similar request was made on Sept. 24, 1496, *ibid.*

101. The same, Aug. 22, 1496, *ibid.,* c. 1047 (fy., *PP,* 686). The Gianfrancesco Gonzaga mentioned here was the brother of the marquis of Mantua, Gianfrancesco II. He had been count of Sabbioneta, Viadana, and Bozzolo (d. 1490).

102. The same, Aug. 21, 1496, *ibid.,* c. 1047.

103. F. Tranchedini to Lodovico il Moro, Oct. 10, 1496, *ibid.* (py., *PP,* 695).

104. Simplified genealogy of the Medici family:

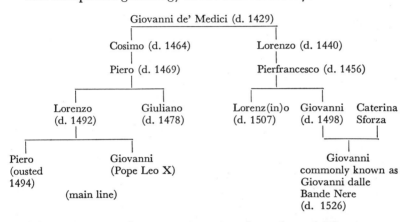

105. "Some say he came as an ambassador of Florence to conclude a league," Cobelli, p. 413. Bernardi, II, 412–13, just notes Giovanni's coming. There is no evidence for an official mission in *ASF, Signori—Carteggi—Missive—Legazioni e Commissarie, Elezioni e Istruzioni,* XXIII, and *Dieci di Balia, Deliberazioni, Condotte e Stanziamenti,* XXXV, both covering the critical period.

106. F. Tranchedini to Lodovico il Moro, Jan. 5 and 6, 1497, *ASM, PE, Romagna,* c. 1047 (fy., *PP,* 710; py., *PP,* 711). G Pampaloni in "La crisi annonaria fiorentina degli anni 1496–1497 e le importazioni di grano dalla Romagna," *AMR,* n.s., XV–XVI (1963–65; ed. 1966) (in press), points out the openly admitted antagonism between Giovanni and the Florentine government in a letter of Dec. 5, 1496, in *ASF, Archivio dell'Abbondanza,* f. IX.

107. Receipt signed by Lorenzo and Giovanni de'Medici for a loan in the amount of 1,320 ducats extended by Caterina Sforza for four years (Feb. 14, 1495, *ASF, MAIP,* f. 83, n. 40, c. 210, and f. 137, n. 1009).

108. Giovanni de'Medici to Caterina Sforza, May 25 and July 6, 1496, *ASF, MAIP*, f. 78, n. 5. The troops (twenty men-at-arms and ten crossbowmen for three hundred ducats) were under the command of a certain Achille Cavalcaro, but their purpose is obscure.

109. For information on the situation in Florence at that time see G. Pampaloni, *AMR*, n.s., XV–XVI (1963–65; ed. 1966) (in press).

110. *Ibid.* (in press), and purchase order for two hundred florins worth of grain, Ufficiali dell'Abbondanza to Neri Venturi, Aug. 8, 1496; *ASF, Archivio dell'Abbondanza*, f. 9.

111. Padovani, p. 175. These were the quarters Giacomo Feo had occupied formerly. Giovanni must soon have lived in the fortress for long periods, since Bernardi (II, 113) remarks, "he who lives in the fortress like our *signore.*"

112. *"i secreti deli magnati sono molte deficile da intendre";* Bernardi, II, 212, 213.

113. Cobelli, pp. 412–13.

114. F. Tranchedini to Lodovico il Moro, Jan. 5, 1497, *ASM, PE, Romagna,* c. 1047 (fy., *PP,* 710). *Corba* was a dry measure equal to three Forlivese *staia* (about six bushels). The amount given is equal to approximately thirty-six thousand bushels. According to the high market prices for grain in Forlì the value of the grain in question was: December, 1496, 54,000 *lire bol.;* March, 1497, 72,000 *lire bol.* (Bernardi, II, 163 and 169).

115. For records of the grain deal, see *ASF, MAIP*, f. 83, n. 83, cc. 251–56 vo. and *ASF, MAIP*, f. 86, n. 47, cc. 354–56.

116. The grain was collected by Caterina's *fattori:* in Imola by Giulio degli Albizzi (see *ASF, MAIP*, f. 86, c. 352) and in Forlì by Ser Lucchino (see f. 86, c. 354). Once in Castrocaro, the grain became Florentine responsibility and was transported from there to Firenzuola, Borgo San Lorenzo, and Florence.

117. The year 1496 was a rather humid one in Romagna. Toward the end of the year and in early 1497 grain and flour prices rose more than usual, most certainly also influenced by the large exports of grain. The *staio* grain cost 60 *soldi,* late in 1496, 80 *soldi* early in 1497, and 120 *soldi* in early summer, 1497; Bernardi, II, 163 and 169.

118. The exact profits made by Caterina and Giovanni cannot be determined. It is known that of the 64,944¾ *staia,* 61,048 were sold at 70 to 80 *soldi* per *staio* and the rest at 30 to 32 *soldi* per *staio* (early in 1498). The shrinkage losses amounted to 1,017 *staia.* As the purchase price is not known, no profit accounting can be made. Giovanni and Lorenzo de'Medici were paid 2,600 florins as an import premium by the Florentine government; *ASF, MAIP*, f. 86, c. 359.

119. Battista Sfondrati (Milanese orator in Venice) to duke

of Milan, Dec. 19, 1496, *ASM, PE, Venezia,* c. 1274 (py., *PP,* 708). Sfondrati knew Caterina from his stay in Forlì as a special envoy in the winter of 1490/91.

120. The first reports on the new *amatore* of Caterina reached Lodovico il Moro from Bologna. Letter, F. Tranchedini to duke of Milan, Oct. 10, 1496, *ASM, PE, Romagna,* c. 1047 (py., *PP,* 695).

121. The agent also had an interview with Benedetto Aldrovando, a relative of Giacomo Feo and, then, *podestà* of Forlì (he may have been the man who followed Count Borella as governor of Forlì in 1488; see Pt. IV, n. 38). It was hoped that resentment of Caterina's new lover would make Benedetto tell all. He did not. F. Tranchedini to Lodovico il Moro, Dec. 2, 1496, *ASM, PE, Romagna,* c. 1047.

122. Two reports on the discussions, Jan. 5 and 6, 1497, *ASM, PE, Romagna,* c. 1047 (py., *PP,* 710; fy., *PP,* 711).

123. His mission is referred to in a Tranchedini letter to Lodovico il Moro, Jan. 6, 1497, *ibid.*

124. These assertions are repeated over and over by Caterina to Tranchedini and Lodovico il Moro. See letter, F. Tranchedini to Lodovico il Moro, Nov. 20, 1496, *ASM, PE, Romagna,* c. 1047 (py., *PP,* 704) ; Caterina Sforza to Lodovico il Moro, Jan. 3 and March 20, 1497, *ibid.,* c. 1047, and in her discussions with Tranchedini, see Pt. V, n. 122.

125. Caterina Sforza to Lodovico il Moro, Aug. 3, 1497, *ASM, PE, Romagna,* c. 1047.

126. No marriage record exists and the date given is based on inference. Caterina was awarded the Florentine citizenship on July 23, 1498, which strongly suggests a prior marriage. Vecchiazzani, II, 192, states that she had been married quietly the same year, 1498, in which Lodovico, better known under his later name Giovanni (delle Bande Nere) had been born. I, however, suggest that September, 1497, is the most likely month. At that time Giovanni's brother Lorenzo came for a visit which seemingly had no purpose. Rumors then circulating in Forlì spoke of a planned marriage between Ottaviano and Lorenzo's daughter. Milanese observers reported these rumors to Milan. Lauro Bossi to Lodovico il Moro, Sept. 25, 1497, *ASM, PE, Romagna,* c. 1047 (py., *PP,* 730) , and F. Tranchedini to Lodovico il Moro, Sept. 28, 1497, *ibid.,* c. 1047. The rumors may have been purposely disseminated to veil the actual marriage of Giovanni and Caterina. There never was a marriage project between Ottaviano and Lorenzo's daughter.

Guido Pampaloni, "La crisi annonaria . . . ," *AMR,* n.s., XV–XVI (1963–65; ed. 1966) , (in press) , suggests December, 1497, as the month in which the wedding took place. He bases his suggestion on the change in address from the informal *tu* to the more formal *voi* in the letters of Florentine officials to Giovanni. As the husband of Caterina, who was Lady of Forlì and Imola, he presumably commanded greater respect. I still would argue for the earlier date.

127. F. Tranchedini to Lodovico il Moro, Jan. 23, 1497, *ASM, PE, Romagna,* c. 1047 (py., *PP,* 714) .

128. Savonarola to Caterina Sforza, June 18, 1497, reprinted in R. Ridolfi, *Le lettere di Girolamo Savonarola* (Florence, 1933) , pp. 135–36, letter No. LV.

129. Cobelli, p. 414.

130. The reason for the destruction of the old fortress of Bubano is unknown. For the fortress of Bubano see L. Baldisseri, *La rocca di Bubano* (Imola, 1898) , pp. 1–18, and F. Mancini and W. Vichi, *Castelli,* pp. 23–34.

131. No documentation of his death is available. The years given are based on conjecture.

132. Caterina Sforza to duke of Ferrara, Dec. 9, 1497, *ASMo, ASE, Carteggio con principi esteri, Imola,* b. 1177.

133. Caterina to Lodovico il Moro, Jan. 5 and 23, 1498, *ASM, PE, Romagna,* c. 1048, and "Brief on the conflict of the sons of Girolamo Riario with Pandolfo over rights in San Mauro," *ibid.*

134. The name of the son was originally Lodovico and only at the death of Giovanni de'Medici changed to Giovanni; Bernardi, II, 212. Exact birth date: April 6, 1498.

135. The idea of a marital tie between Ottaviano and the eighteen-year-old Lucrezia Borgia was one of a number tried out by the Borgia family and was probably instigated by Caterina's uncle, Ascanio Sforza. Ascanio Sforza did inquire, on July 5, 1498, about the outcome, which betrays his interest in the plan; *ASM, PE, Roma,* c. 126 (py., *PP,* 777) . The best description of the negotiations is found in Caterina's letter to Cristoforo Risorboli (one of the Florentines who was serving both Giovanni de'Medici and Caterina) , May 31, 1498, *ASF, MAIP,* f. 79, cc. 59–59 vo. (fy., *PP,* 772) .

136. For Caterina's answer to this second Gonzaga proposal, see her letter to Lodovico il Moro, Jan. 18, 1498, *ASM, PE, Romagna,* c. 1048. See Pt. V, n. 101, for first proposal.

137. For summary treatments of the Pisan war see Pieri, *Il Rinascimento,* pp. 368–77, and L. Simeoni, *Le signorie* (2 vols.; Milan, 1950) , II, 743–45.

138. Bursellis, p. 114.

139. This important change in the direction of Milanese foreign policy is reflected in the letters arriving from Milan during the summer of 1497. They contain no reproaches directed at Caterina for her pro-Florentine policy.

140. Caterina to Lodovico il Moro, May 16, 1498, *ASM, PE, Romagna,* c. 1048.

141. F. Tranchedini to Lodovico il Moro, May 17, 1498, *ibid.* (py., *PP,* 770).

142. The attempt had to be abandoned because of the general easing of the food shortage. See letters by Giovanni de'Medici to Niccolò di Alessandro degli Strozzi (Giovanni's main representative in Florence), particularly May 18, 1498, *ASF, MAIP,* f. 86, c. 354. See also G. Pampaloni, "La crisi annonaria . . . ," *AMR,* n.s., XV–XVI (1963–65; ed. 1966), (in press).

143. Vincenzo Naldi had made his peace with the Venetians who only a few years before, in 1495, had brutally killed some of his relatives in the fight between Astorre and Ottaviano.

144. A proud Caterina notified the Milanese court of the negotiations for a *condotta;* Caterina Sforza to Lodovico il Moro, June 4, 1498, *ASM, PE, Romagna,* c. 1048. The *condotta* was formally issued on June 9, 1498; see *Atti relativi alla condotta di Ottaviano Riario nella guerra sostenuta contro Pisa dalla Republica Fiorentina, ASM, MAIP,* f. 78, n. 56, cc. 180–185.

145. Caterina Sforza to Lodovico il Moro, June 12 and 17, 1498, *ASM, PE, Romagna,* c. 1048; also Vecchiazzani, II, 194, and Priuli, p. 80. Sanuto, I, 1038, states that the restitution of Ordelaffi rule in Forlì had been agreed upon.

146. Letter, June 14, 1498, *ASM, PE, Romagna,* c. 1048.

147. Ottaviano left around June 20, 1498; Cobelli, p. 414. Priuli (p. 80) says with one hundred men-at-arms and one hundred *cavaleggeri.* Ottaviano made a good initial impression on the Florentines; see Landucci, *Florentinisches Tagebuch,* II, 1: "he came in fine mettle." As for the political repercussions of the *condotta,* in her letter to Lodovico il Moro, June 22, 1498, Caterina spoke defiantly of the Venetians and was full of enthusiasm for the Florentines, who through the device of the *condotta* had given her political and financial support.

148. Venetian mercenaries under Manfroni helped in this expedition against Caterina under the pretext of her "giving shelter to some deserters from the Manfroni company," Padovani, p. 274 b.

149. In 1498 Fracasso was forty-eight years old, a well-known soldier, lord of Piadena, Calvatone, and Spineda. See C. Clough, "Gaspare Sanseverino and Castiglione's *Il Cortegiano," Philological Quarterly,* XLIII (April, 1964), 276–80, and the expanded version of that article in *AMR,* n.s., XV–XVI (1963–65; ed. 1966), (in press).

150. Bernardi, II, 191.

151. Document of citizenship, July 23, 1498; reprinted in A. Burriel, *Vita di Caterina Sforza* (3 vols.; Bologna, 1795) , III, lxxiii–lxxv. She was awarded the citizenship for her service to the Florentine republic (but one suspects that the fact of being married to Giovanni de'Medici had just as much to do with it) . All her natural and legitimate children participated in the privilege.

152. Fracasso had just participated in a tournament at Innsbruck and was on his way to Pisa when he was ordered to Forlì; Priuli, p. 81. For arrival date, *ibid.,* p. 94.

153. The castellan, Niccolò Castagnino, had never gotten along with the Venetians, since he had been the actual power in Faenza before the Venetians interfered. He had controlled the regents of Astorre in the absence of the Venetians.

154. They had sent four hundred *stradioti* into the city.

155. In order to gain Lodovico il Moro's support she wrote him about her machinations. Her letters plead with him to render support. Caterina must have expected Lodovico to offer Astorre a *condotta* and to ready Milanese troops to assist the castellan in his struggle with the Venetians; July 18 and 21, 1498, *ASM, PE, Romagna,* c. 1048.

156. For Antonio Maria Ordelaffi's participation, see Malipiero, II, 504.

157. His arrival there was one of the gravest pieces of news Caterina received during 1498. Combined with the constant re-enforcements of the Venetian troops it produced the major crisis described; see Fracasso to Lodovico il Moro, Aug. 21, 1498, *ASM, PE, Romagna,* c. 1048.

158. Caterina Sforza to Lodovico il Moro, Aug. 24, 1498, *ASM, PE, Romagna,* c. 1048.

159. During the middle of August, 1498, Giovanni de'Medici visited Ottaviano Riario in the latter's camp and must have fallen ill there judging from his early return to Romagna; Padovani, 275 b. Bagno di Romagna is located in the upper Savio valley (south of Cesena) . The waters of that area have borolithic-bromo-bicarbonate-sodic ingredients which have been considered beneficial to sufferers from the gout and other rheumatic disorders. Giovanni went to S. Piero in Bagno (2.6 miles from Bagno) .

160. Caterina Sforza to Lodovico il Moro, *ASM, PE, Romagna,* c. 1048, Aug. 27, 1498 (fy., *PP,* 840) .

161. The same, Sept. 4, 1498; *ibid.,* c. 1049 (fy., *PP,* 850) .

162. M. Sanuto, *I diarii* (58 vols.; Venice, 1879–1902) , I, 1100; Priuli, p. 99; Malipiero, I, 512. Caterina had succeeded in persuading Lodovico il Moro to offer Astorre a *condotta* with generous terms; Donati, *La fine della signoria dei Manf-*

redi, p. 126, states that on Sept. 3, 1498, Caterina and Fracasso were officially empowered to negotiate with Faenza officials on such a contract.

163. Caterina Sforza to Lodovico il Moro, Sept. 26, 1498, *ASM, PE, Romagna,* c. 1049. Answer of Lodovico il Moro in instructions to an unknown envoy, Oct. 22, 1498, *ibid.* (py., *PP,* 926).

164. Giovanni de'Medici to Caterina Sforza, Sept. 2, 1498, *ASF, MAIP,* f. 78, n. 63 (py., *PP, 848*). For the other last letters from Giovanni de'Medici to Caterina Sforza, concerned with politics (news from France), pleasantries shown to Caterina (gifts of wine and cooked trout), and expressions of optimism about Giovanni's health, see Aug. 29, 1498, *ASF, MAIP,* f. 78, n. 62 (py., *PP,* 842); Sept. 2, n. 67 (py., *PP,* 857); Sept. 5, printed in C. Clough "The Sources for the Biography of Caterina Sforza and for the History of the State during her Rule," *AMR,* n.s., XV–XVI (1963–65; ed. 1966), Appendix II, doc. 5i; Sept. 7, *ASF, MAIP,* f. 78, n. 66 (also C. Clough, II, doc. 5ii), and Sept. 9, n. 65 (C. Clough, II, doc. 5iii).

165. Notice of the death of Giovanni de'Medici, F. Tranchedini to Lodovico il Moro, Sept. 16, 1498, *ASM, PE, Romagna,* c. 1049. Death must have come to Giovanni during the night of Sept. 14 or the early morning of Sept. 15. Bernardi, II, 212–13 states that it was Sept. 14.

166. Since the marriage had never been formally acknowledged no condolences came from Milan. On Sept. 16, 1498, she blamed Lodovico il Moro for the final loss of Faenza to the Venetians, and a day later she wrote to Milan about military operations as if nothing had happened; *ASM, PE, Romagna,* c. 1049.

167. Simone Ridolfi had been one of Giovanni de'Medici's and Caterina's close associates. He was married to Lucrezia Feo; Vecchiazzani, II, 188. Bernardi, II, 113, calls her Ginevra Feo. Giovanni had arranged the marriage.

168. Sanuto, *I diarii,* II, 9 and 12.

169. Caterina Sforza to Lodovico il Moro, Sept. 24, 1498, *ibid.* (fy., *PP,* 881).

170. Landucci, *Florentinisches Tagebuch,* II, 5–6.

171. He had come to Forlì on Oct. 2, 1498 (Bernardi, II, 196); also, Sanuto, *I diarii,* I, 1098, and Priuli, p. 98. Galeazzo had brought with him two hundred men and a Mantuan contingent, as can be seen from a note of gratitude penned by Galeazzo to the marquis of Mantua, Sept. 5, 1498, *ASMa, AG,* E XXVI, 2, *Forlì,* b. 1065.

172. For the development of that strategy see Sanuto, *I diarii,* II, 1, 12, 14, and 20, and Bernardi, II, 194.

173. On the siege see Sanuto, *I diarii*, II, 9–16. Venier had been named *provveditore* in Romagna and had left Venice on Aug. 25. His appointment had been one of the earliest signs of the coming offensive; Priuli, p. 94.

174. One of them was Antonio Giacomini (1453–1517), a well-known Florentine captain.

175. Sanuto, *I diarii*, II, 9.

176. These significant early troop movements to the east occurred about Oct. 12, 1498, according to Sanuto, II, 33. See also Bernardi, II, 197, who says Oct. 14.

177. Sanuto, *I diarii*, II, 9. The raids lasted all through November; Bernardi, II, 199–200.

178. Bernardi, II, 198–99.

179. He was the successor to Carlo Malatesta, count of Sogliano, who had died in 1486. Bernardi, I, 168.

180. For conquest see Landucci, *Florentinisches Tagebuch*, II, 8–14; see also Bernardi, II, 198–99, who states that the Casentino campaign was an idea of Piero de'Medici, at that time a protégé of Venice. Priuli, pp. 104–5.

181. Caterina Sforza to Lorenzo de'Medici, Oct. 28, 1498, *ASF, MAIP, Minute di lettere dalla Madonna di Forlì al Lorenzo de'Medici nel 1490–1499*, f. 79, c. 26 (py., *PP*, 934).

182. The same, Oct. 30, 1498, *ibid.* (fy., *PP*, 936).

183. Caterina had advocated such a campaign earlier; Caterina to Lorenzo, Oct. 12, 1498, *ASF, MAIP, Minute . . .*, f. 79, cc. 7–7 vo.

184. Galeazzo Sanseverino had once been bound by contract (January, 1490) to marry Bianca Giovanna Sforza (illegitimate daughter of Lodovico il Moro). She had then been eight years old and died before the marriage could be consummated; F. Malaguzzi-Valeri, *La corte di Lodovico il Moro* (2d ed.; Milan, 1929), p. 428.

185. Caterina Sforza to Lorenzo de'Medici, Oct. 18, 1498; *ASF, MAIP, Minute . . .*, f. 79, cc. 16–17 vo. (fy., *PP*, 919).

186. The same, Oct. 14, 1498; *ibid.*, cc. 12–13 vo. and *Estratti di lettere ai Dieci di Balia* in Niccolò Machiavelli, *Opere*, ed. L. Passerini and G. Milanesi (6 vols.; Florence, 1874–77), II, 146, 208, 211, and 212.

187. Bernardi, II, 194. The incident serves as a telling comment on the decay of the once so effective communal militia.

188. *Opere di Baldassare Castiglione, Giovanni della Casa, Benvenuto Cellini*, ed. C. Cordié (La letteratura Italiana, Storia e Testi; Milan-Naples, n.d.), XXVII, 37–38. For an interesting attempt to link Fracasso and Caterina to the episode found in *Il Cortegiano*, see C. Clough, "Gaspare Sanseverino . . . ," *Philological Quarterly*, XLIII (April, 1964), 276–80.

VI

1. Caterina Sforza to Lodovico il Moro, Jan. 10, 1499, *ASM, PE, Romagna,* c. 1050.

2. From Oct. 23 to Dec. 31, 1498, there was hardly a letter which does not show her concern, *ASF, MAIP, Minute . . . ,* f. 79, from cc. 22 to 42–42 vo.

3. She even sent some troops to Bagno in support of the Florentines; Caterina Sforza to Francesco Fortunati, Jan. 3, 1499, *ASF, MAIP,* f. 70, c. 84.

4. Vecchiazzani, II, 195.

5. As late as Feb. 25, 1499, Caterina tried to make use of Malatesta de'Malatesta, an opponent of Ramberto of Sogliano. Nothing came of it; Caterina Sforza to Lodovico il Moro, Feb. 25, 1499, *ASM, PE, Romagna,* c. 1050. The fury of Caterina's attack can be measured by Ramberto's urgent appeal to Venice for four hundred men; M. Sanuto, *I diarii* (58 vols.; Venice, 1879–1902), II, 193.

6. Sanuto, *I diarii,* II, 354; Malipiero, I, 530.

7. L. Landucci, *Ein Florentinisches Tagebuch, 1450–1516,* trans. M. Herzfeld (2 vols.; Jena, 1913), II, 32; Padovani, p. 276b; Priuli, pp. 115–19, gives Ercole d'Este credit for his mediation.

8. Polidoro Tiberti to Caterina Sforza, Nov. 13, 1498, *ASF, MAIP,* f. 78, n. 78 (fy., *PP,* 941).

9. That purpose is clearly stated in Caterina's letter to Lodovico il Moro, Jan. 9, 1499, *ASM, PE, Romagna,* c. 1050. Due to the deterioration of relations between the Bentivoglio and Caterina, Cesare was advised to avoid Bologna territory on his return trip; Caterina protested to F. Tranchedini about it, Feb, 15, 1499, *ASM, PE, Romagna,* c. 1050 (fy., *PP,* 989).

10. Lodovico il Moro to Alessandro Orpheo, March 4, 1499, *ASM, PE, Romagna,* c. 1050.

11. Caterina Sforza to Lodovico il Moro, Jan. 8 and 13, and May 8, 1499, *ASM, PE, Romagna,* c. 1050.

12. Sanuto, *I diarii,* III, 56, mentions Achille Tiberti (and Giovanni da Casale later).

13. Records indicate that F. Fortunati must have been the main business agent in Giovanni de'Medici's and Caterina's service since 1496. The important final accounting by Lionardo Strozzi for Caterina on the grain deal of 1497/98 was handed over to F. Fortunati on Oct. 28, 1498; see *ASF, MAIP,* f. 83, n. 83, cc. 251–56 vo.

14. She even went so far as to appeal to the duke of Milan to

help Ottaviano in regaining Faenza. Caterina Sforza to Lodovico il Moro, Jan. 19, 1499, *ASM, PE, Romagna,* c. 1050.

15. P. de Commines, *Memoiren,* trans. and ed. F. Ernst (Stuttgart, 1952), pp. 387, and 404–5, describes the fateful collision of Charles VIII with a bulkhead.

16. Priuli, pp. 87–88.

17. *Ibid.,* p. 96.

18. The event is recorded by Sanuto, *I diarii,* I, 1054, with the regretful comment "and thus went everything to ruins in the Church of God." The final permission must have come later, on Nov. 26, 1498, according to an entry concerning a consistory on that day in *ASVa, Fondo consistoriale, Acta Vicecancellarii,* I, 8.

19. J. Burchard, *Diarium 1483–1506* (3 vols.; Paris, 1883–85), II, 495–96, calls Cesare still "cardinalis Valentinus" and says he left "per mare." Although Cesare arrived with pomp at the French court, he left Rome very quietly.

20. Ascanio Sforza prudently noted the wedding in his official record (*ASVa, Fondo consistoriale, Acta Vicecancellarii,* I, 55) as a "pleasant piece of news," although he must have known of its perilous nature for the Sforza family.

21. Bernardi, II, 215–16. Caterina's complicity in the murder is highly unlikely despite F. Tranchedini writing to Lodovico il Moro that a secret confidant had told him of Caterina's share in the crime; Feb. 25, 1499, *ASM, PE, Romagna,* c. 1050 (fy., *PP,* 997). There never were apparent any signs of disagreements between Corbizzi and Caterina during their long association, which seemed to have begun in 1489 according to some private letters; Caterina Sforza to Corbizzo Corbizzi, June 3, 1489, *ASM, MAIP,* f. 18, n. 205, and Dec. 27, 1489, f. 42, n. 414. Machiavelli interrupted his trip to Forlì to do some detective work in the Corbizzi case; see letter, Machiavelli to *Dieci di Balia,* July 24, 1499, in *Opere* (ed. A. Panella), II, 861–62.

22. Bernardi, II, 220–21.

23. At first the Manfredi had even blocked the transit of Caterina's personal belongings. Later, they limited the restrictions to war material. Caterina Sforza to Lodovico il Moro, Feb. 23, 1499, *ASM, PE, Romagna,* c. 1050 (py., *PP,* 994).

24. The same; Feb. 27, 1499, *ibid.,* c. 1050. Sanuto, *I diarii,* II, 489.

25. Sanuto, *I diarii,* II, 550, speaks of a "confermation del matrimonio" on March 20, 1499. He also reports secret attempts by Piero de'Medici to reconcile Caterina with Venice in an obvious attempt to make a continuation of the Pisan war more attractive to Venice (II, 521).

26. See letter in Pt. VI, n. 24.

27. The chronicler Cobelli, old and sick, cried out against

the "arrogant Venetians": "Oh, can't you see how our Mother Italy suffers . . . ," and condemned the *signori* as the "new pharaohs . . . whose greed steeps Italy in misfortune," pp. 416–17. For modern assessments see L. Simeoni, *Le signorie* (2 vols.; Milan, 1950), II, 750–51; R. Cessi, *Storia della Repubblica di Venezia* (2 vols.; Milan, 1944–46), II, 38–39.

28. *ASVa, Arm.* XXXV, 41, pp. 86–89 vo. It cannot be ascertained when the decision to depose Caterina and her sons and to invest Cesare was reached. The consistory closest to the date of the bull seems to have been held on March 6, 1499. Yet in the *Acta Vicecancellarii*, I, 40, in *ASVa, Fondo consistoriale,* Ascanio Sforza had remarked about the consistory on March 6, 1499, "in quo nihil fuit factus." Ascanio Sforza and Raffaelle Riario did not, of course, sign the bull which deposed their relatives.

29. The census which was to be deposited with the papal *camera* every year *in vigilia* of (i.e., the day before) the feast of Saints Peter and Paul had never been paid. At least none is recorded in the *ASVa, Archivio della Camera Apostolica, Introitus Exitus,* Nos. 504–31, and in the records of the *Camera Apostolica* deposited in the *AS Roma.*

30. Even so strong a papal partisan as de'Conti admitted that the non-payment of the census was merely a pretext, II, 209.

Evidence for the accuracy of the papal statements on the non-payment of the census seems to be offered by a letter from Caterina Sforza to Lorenzo de'Medici, July 7, 1491; Baker Library, Harvard University, Selfridge Collection, n. 212. Since the letter is severely damaged, its interpretation is tentative. But from the remaining portion of the letter it can be deduced that Caterina had trouble because of her non-payment of the census as early as 1491. At that time, however, she suffered no ill effects from the failure to fulfil her obligations.

31. Giovanni dalle Selle is given in the *Libro Madonna,* p. 40 vo., as the *advocato communis* for 1493. He had been on important missions for Caterina before.

32. Landucci, *Florentinisches Tagebuch,* II, 5; Padovani, p. 276b. Although the compilation was talked about a good deal in Caterina's time, no such document could be located. *PP,* 231, gives as the depository the *AS Roma,* but the *registri mandati della Camera Apostolica,* cc. 57 vo., 61 vo., 62–64, show individual transactions of Girolamo with the *camera,* but no general accounting.

33. He arrived on March 7, 1499; Caterina Sforza to Lodovico il Moro, March 7, 1499, *ASM, PE, Romagna,* c. 1050.

34. Instructions to Alessandrio Orpheo on occasion of his mission to Caterina Sforza, *ASM, PE, Romagna,* c. 1050.

35. The notice once more shows the advancement of Anto-

nio Baldraccani since the days when he had been used for various missions (see Pt. V, n. 76) ; A. Orpheo to Lodovico il Moro, March 9, 1499, *ASM, PE, Romagna,* c. 1050.

36. Orpheo dismissed Achille Tiberti as a bully ("homo facinoroso") ; the same, March 12, 1499, *ibid.* (py., *PP,* 1013).

37. A. Orpheo to Lodovico il Moro, March 8, 1499, *ASM, PE, Romagna,* c. 1050 (py., *PP,* 1008).

38. Bernardi, II, 225–26.

39. *ASVa, Fondo consistoriale, Acta Vicecancellarii,* I, 55–57. Cesare had arrived in Rome the month before.

40. Bernardi, II, 221–25; A. Virgili, "L'assassinio di Ottaviano Manfredi," *ASI,* s.5, CCXXI (1901), pp. 101–13. Fortunati himself investigated the murder and reported in detail to Caterina; see letter, April, 1499, *ASF, MAIP,* f. 85, c. 265. His description of the event corresponds closely to that which F. Tranchedini gave to Lodovico il Moro, April 14, 1499, *ASM, PE, Romagna,* c. 1050 (py., *PP,* 1019). Sanuto, *I diarii,* II, 624, states that Ottaviano accompanied a Florentine commissioner to Florence and that a Corbizzi was the murderer.

41. Among the participants in the funeral procession is listed Tommaso Feo. No further mention of his presence in Forlì is made thereafter. He seems to have left Caterina before the French invasion reached Romagna; Bernardi, II, 224.

42. Dionigi Naldi, for whom Caterina had intervened when he had been imprisoned in the fortress of Urbino (see D. Zauli-Naldi, *Dionigi e Vincenzo Naldi in Romagna (1495–1504),* (Faenza, 1925), was the instrument of vengeance; A. Metelli, *Storia di Brisighella e della Valle di Amone* (4 vols.; Faenza, 1869–72), I, 498. See also G. Tonduzzi, *Historie di Faenza* (Faenza, 1675), p. 547.

43. See Pt. IV, n. 100.

44. Caterina Sforza to Lodovico il Moro, May 12, 1499; reprinted py., *PP,* 1032. From that time on every trace of Orpheo is missing. His mission had either ended or death had cut it short. Giovanni di Casale had been Girolamo's chancellor. After 1488 he left for Milan and temporarily returned with Fracasso in 1498.

45. The first confirmation of Casale's presence in Forlì appears in a letter from Lodovico il Moro to G. di Casale, June 5, 1499, *ASM, PE,* c. 1051. Sanuto soon after called him "favorito di madonna," Sanuto, *I diarii,* III, 140–41.

46. See Caterina Sforza to Lorenzo de'Medici, July 12, 1499, *ASF, MAIP,* f. 79, c. 60; G. di Casale to Lodovico il Moro, July 29, 1499, *ASM, PE, Romagna,* c. 1051 (py., *PP,* 1062). Lodovico il Moro to G. di Casale, Aug. 3, 1499, *ibid.* Sanuto chronicles the sending of troops by Caterina to Milan, II, 947, 1024, 1031, and 1188.

47. Ottaviano's company was still encamped in Tuscany. Caterina was forced to pay their services out of her own pocket.

48. In her letters to F. Fortunati she complained bitterly about the Florentine attitude toward Ottaviano's new *condotta* and the defense of her states; Caterina Sforza to F. Fortunati, June 28, 1499; printed py., *PP,* 1046.

49. Instructions and credentials in Niccolò Machiavelli, *Opere,* ed. L. Passerini and G. Milanesi (6 vols.; Florence, 1874–77), II, 8–11. The legal problem involved in the renewal of Ottaviano's *condotta* was the exercise of the *beneplacito* rights by both parties. Most *condotte* had a flexible duration with a number of firm years and an extra year optional to both parties (*anno a beneplacito*).

50. Lodovico il Moro had stated to G. di Casale that if Florence had no use for the services of Ottaviano Riario, Milan would welcome the young Riario and his company. See note of acknowledgment, Caterina Sforza to Lodovico il Moro, July 27, 1499, *ASM, PE, Romagna,* c. 1051.

51. Niccolò Machiavelli to *Dieci di Balia,* July 17, 1499, in *Opere,* ed. A. Panella (Milan-Rome, 1938–39), II, 851–56.

52. The same, July 22, 1499, *ibid.,* II, 856–58; Sanuto, II, 947.

53. The same, July 23, 1499, *ibid.,* II, 858–61.

54. The same, July 24, 1499, *ibid.,* II, 861–62. See also G. di Casale's report on the failure of Machiavelli's mission to Lodovico il Moro, July 29, 1499, *ASM, PE, Romagna,* c. 1051 (py., *PP,* 1061).

55. For examples of Caterina's far-flung business deals see records of grain transport and grain sales in Romagna, 1495–99, *ASF, MAIP,* f. 83, n. 43, cc. 214–218, and records of grain sales, n.d., *ibid.,* n. 47, cc. 261–295.

56. Inventory of the silverware owned by the late Giovanni de'Medici, Dec. 21, 1498, *ASF, MAIP,* f. 83, n. 34, c. 199. The list includes the usual assortment of plates, ornamental pieces, and chandeliers.

57. Inventory of the personal belongings of the late Giovanni de'Medici, June 21, 1499, *ASF, MAIP,* f. 83, n. 36, cc. 201–204. It contains a list of 257 pieces of clothing, which once more reveals Giovanni's affluence.

58. Records of grain sales on behalf of Giovanni de'Medici and grain stored on his estates, Feb. 9, 1499, *ibid.,* n. 38, c. 206, and list of debtors, *ibid.,* n. 39, cc. 207–209. The latter document shows particularly well the intertwining of public and private affairs when Caterina's officials C. Risorboli and Giampietro Landriani appear as guardians for private possessions.

59. Debts of Lorenzo de'Medici to Ottaviano Riario, Oct. 28, 1499, *ibid.,* n. 44, cc. 229–244. Also at stake was an old debt

from February, 1495, involving 1,320 ducats, repayable February, 1499, *ibid.*, n. 40, c. 210.

60. Caterina Sforza to Lorenzo de'Medici, Aug. 18 and Sept. 3, 1499, *ASF, MAIP, Minute* . . . , f. 79, cc. 63 and 70. P. Parenti states that in June, 1499, an envoy of Caterina told Lorenzo de'Medici that Giovanni (dalle Bande Nere) was a legitimate child and as such should inherit half of his father's estate; Bibl. Naz., Florence, *MMS*, II/II, 131, Vol. III, 160.

61. Aug. 14, 1499; Bernardi, II, 213.

62. Legal instrument dated May 29, 1499, *ASF, MAIP*, f. 87, n. 42, cc. 132–135.

63. Caterina Sforza to *Signoria* of Florence, Aug. 3, 1499, *ASF, MAIP*, f. 79, c. 62.

64. The final Florentine refusal is recorded in a letter from Giovanni di Casale to Lodovico il Moro, Aug. 20, 1499, *ASM, PE, Romagna,* c. 1051.

65. Lodovico il Moro to Caterina Sforza, Aug. 27, 1499, *ibid.*

66. Treccani, *Storia di Milano* (16 vols.; Milan, 1953–62), VII, 503–4; P. Pieri, *Il Rinascimento e la crisi militare italiana* (Turin, 1952), pp. 381–83; and L. Simeoni, *Le signorie* (2 vols.; Milan, 1950), II, 754–55. Lodovico il Moro, who prided himself on being a great statesman, had shown little political skill in 1498 and 1499. With an ill-befitting arrogance he had offended Venice, lost old friends, and won no new ones.

67. Written in the midst of the summer crisis of 1498, Caterina Sforza to Lodovico il Moro, Aug. 25, 1498, *ASM, PE, Romagna,* c. 1048.

68. Caterina Sforza to Lorenzo de'Medici, Aug. 28, 1499, *ASF, MAIP*, f. 79, c. 5.

69. The list of *aderenti et confederati* sent to the French king by Venice included the Manfredi and the Malatesta but not Caterina Sforza; Aug. 12, 1499, Sanuto, *I diarii*, II, 1140–41. Caterina's attempts to be added to the list failed; Sanuto, II, 1227 and 1259.

70. Bernardi, II, 218; Padovani, p. 276.

71. S. Ridolfi, one of the holdovers from the Giovanni de'Medici era, was dismissed on Oct. 19, 1499; Bernardi, II, 224.

72. Reported by Priuli, p. 190; and letter, N. Machiavelli to Caterina Sforza, Oct. 16, 1499, in *Scritti inediti riguardanti la storia e la milizia,* ed. G. Canestrini (Florence, 1857), pp. 250–51. The attempt must have been made by the Florentines around Oct. 20.

73. Rumors spoke of another league between Ferrara, Bologna, Florence, and the "madonna di Furlì" against the French and Cesare; Priuli, p. 190.

74. The earliest proof of Vincenzo Calmeta's serious inten-

tion of assisting Caterina appears in a letter from Calmeta to Giovanni Castranovo, Oct. 26, 1499, *ASF, MAIP,* f. 98, c. 552 (printed in V. Calmeta, *Prose e lettere edite e inedite,* ed. Cecil Grayson [Bologna, 1959], pp. 81–82). On Oct. 29, 1499, Calmeta assured Caterina of his devotion and his willingness to help her; *ASF, MAIP,* f. 78, n. 117 (printed in Calmeta, *Prose e lettere* . . . , p. 82). The Calmeta letters are also printed in C. Clough, "Sources for the Biography of Caterina Sforza and for the History of the State during her Rule," *AMR,* n.s., XV–XVI (1963–65; ed. 1966), (in press).

75. V. Calmeta to Caterina Sforza, Oct. 31, 1499, *ASF, MAIP,* f. 78, n. 118 (fy., *PP,* 1090; a more accurate transcription is found in Calmeta, *Prose e lettere* . . . , pp. 83–85).

76. Begin of march toward Romagna in early November, 1499; Bernardi, II, 227; Sanuto, *I diarii,* III, 49, states Nov. 5.

77. Bernardi, II, 227. She probably died of the plague.

78. Bernardi, II, 242, in describing the occupation of Imola bemoans the fact that such a little town had to give shelter to 14,500 people (without supplying further details). Vecchiazzani, II, 198, gives a similar summary figure. Cesare's army is given by R. Zazzeri, *Storia di Cesena* (Cesena, 1890), p. 408, as having arrived at Cesena on Jan. 23, 1500, in the following strength:

Fanti pagati	7,000	*Cavalli per artigleria*	400
Venturieri	1,000	*Carri*	60
Spagnoli	300	*Cannoni grossi*	5
Soldati del duca a cavallo	400	*Colubine*	1
		Falconetti	1
Soldati di Enrico Bentivoglio	400	*Femine*	200
Soldati del Re di Francia a cavallo	2,500		

Fantaguzzi, *Caos,* p. 102, differs in the number of guns mentioned; 17 instead of 7. Padovani, p. 279, puts the number of prostitutes at 2,000 and adds "2,000 altra canaglia." Priuli, pp. 250 and 270, puts the papal contribution to the Imola and Forlì campaign at 20,000 ducats and mentions 6,000 papal soldiers. Pieri, *Il Rinascimento,* p. 391, speaks of 15,000 soldiers but says that only the 4,000 Swiss and 1,800 French soldiers were of real value. His total figure seems to have been derived from Bernardi, II, 242, and Vecchiazzani, II, 198.

79. The *lancia francese* consisted of six men: a heavily armed warrior, one *coustillier* (an equerry who supported the lord in battle), two crossbowmen or archers, one valet, one page boy; see Pieri, *Il Rinascimento,* p. 232.

80. The poisoning attempt is recorded by Bernardi, II,

295–96, Burchard, *Diarium,* II, 578–79, and Priuli, p. 234. Fantaguzzi, *Caos,* p. 103, states that on Nov. 27, 1499, a papal breve came from Rome telling of Caterina's attempt to poison the pope.

81. Burchard, *Diarium,* II, 578.

82. The letter is reprinted by Burchard, *Diarium,* II, 579–80, and fy., as *PP,* 1096.

83. The cardinal had made strong representations at the papal court in favor of the Riario sons by pointing at the sixty thousand ducat credit which Girolamo had accumulated before he had left Rome. Girolamo Sacrati, Este orator in Rome, Nov. 1, 1499, *ASMo, ASE, Estero, Carteggio degli oratori e corrispondenti presso le corti, Roma,* b. 6 (py., *PP,* 1091). Raffaello Riario left Rome on Nov. 21, 1499, for an Orsini possession and proceeded from there to Sienese territory and finally by boat to Savona; G. Lucido Cataneo to marquis of Mantua, Dec. 6, 1499, *ASMa, AG,* E XXV, 3, *Roma,* c. 853. Venice offered the cardinal asylum for himself and his family; Priuli, p. 227, and Sanuto, *I diarii,* III, 49 and 51. It is not clear whether that did include the Riario of Forlì.

84. Caterina Sforza to Lodovico il Moro, Nov. 14, 1498, *ASM, PE, Romagna,* c. 1049 (py., *PP,* 942).

85. For the events in Imola and Forlì from November, 1499, to January, 1500, see Bernardi, II, 238–85; *Cronaca Anonima,* entries of that period; Padovani, pp. 276b–82; Paolucci, entries for that period; Fantaguzzi, *Caos,* pp. 102–6; Vecchiazzani, II, 195–204. Cobelli had little to say about these months as he must have been rather ill and died shortly after the end of the campaign (May 14, 1500).

86. Bernardi, II, 249.

87. Report on session: *ibid.,* pp. 239 and 245–48. That council was at that point composed of the Council of Forty and additional patricians and some *contadini.*

88. The family of Tarchionata Marullus of Constantinople had arrived in Italy during the aftermath of the conquest of Constantinople. Marullo (Italian form), who wrote Latin verse well and tried his hand at soldiering, had come to Forlì with three fugitive Sforza brothers from Milan. He perished during the following year in the Cecina River near Volterra.

89. Bernardi, II, 245.

90. Dionigi Naldi, returned from the Lombard campaign, entered Caterina's services with six hundred men; Sanuto, *I diarii,* II, 1251.

91. Nicknamed "il Cagnazzo" or "il Cagnaccio." Giovanni was the son of Francesco Sassatelli (murdered in December, 1488). He had been in Milanese service and had distinguished himself as a brave and alert soldier. The nickname "il Cagnac-

cio" means "snarling dog" and was given to Giovanni by a French opponent; see G. C. Cerchiari, *Ristretto storico della città d'Imola* (Bologna, 1847–48) , p. 173, n. 14.

92. Bernardi, II, 250–51.

93. *Ibid.,* p. 251.

94. *Ibid.*

95. *Ibid.,* pp. 249–51.

96. *Ibid.,* pp. 252–53.

97. Gianotto's coming appalled even the loyal Bernardi (II, 253) .

98. Bernardi, II, 254. The hostages were requested from families with relatives in Cesare's camp, e.g., the son of Caterina's banker because he was married to a Tiberti.

99. Caterina Sforza to F. Fortunati, Nov. 2, 1499, *ASF, MAIP,* f. 70, n. 87.

100. Caterina Sforza to marquis of Mantua, Nov. 4, 1499, *ASMa, AG,* E XXVI, 2, *Forlì,* b. 1065 (fy., *PP,* 1094) .

101. For Caterina's connections with the Murate monastery see Landucci, II, 253; and letters, Caterina Sforza to abbess of the monastery, July 18 and Sept. 25, 1499, reprinted as *PP,* 1056 and 1084. On the transfer of her children see S. di Branca Tedallini, *Diario Romano 1485–1524,* ed. P. Piccolomini, *RIS,* n.s., XXIII, Pt. iii, 293.

102. Priuli, p. 227.

103. *Ibid.,* p. 236. Priuli reports that the Venetian government held long and secret meetings before they arrived at the negative conclusion.

104. In April, 1499, Achille Tiberti had been an honored guest in Forlì at the funeral for Ottaviano Manfredi; Bernardi, II, 224. Then in October, Tiberti had been in Rome and had been won over by the papal party. In return for lofty promises he betrayed Caterina and fielded 100 crossbowmen and 100 retainers against her; Fantaguzzi, *Caos,* p. 98. The troops were less important than the support of Cesare in the city of Cesena, which it was hoped would be increased by Tiberti's change of alignment. A papal breve, which called for the support of Cesare, aimed at the same objective; *ibid.,* p. 100.

105. Priuli reports some dissension in Imola on the decision of surrender (p. 233) . He blames the eventual surrender on the "viltà del magistrato imolese" (p. 234) .

106. Alberghetti, *Compendio,* I, 268. A delegation of citizens, including Piero (da) Sassatello and Piero (da) Cantagallo, went to Rome to pledge the loyalty of the city; Bernardi, II, 245.

107. Priuli, p. 234, "they chased them from their houses and slept with their women."

108. Bernardi, II, 238–45.

109. The name of the traitor is concealed by an interesting gap in Bernardi's chronicle, II, 243.

110. Bernardi, II, 240. Dionigi Naldi, after having recovered from his headwound, tried hard to be of service to Cesare. He offered to deliver Faenza to Cesare, but failed in the attempt on the city, which was protected by the Venetians; Vecchiazzani, II, 204–5.

111. Venice kept a close and armed watch over her interest sphere, including Faenza, Rimini, and Urbino. Great numbers of soldiers were stationed around Ravenna; Priuli, pp. 227–28, and Sanuto, III, 50. Six hundred men were stationed in Faenza, according to Bernardi, II, 254. For more details on the Venetian measures see A. Bonardi, "Venezia e Cesare Borgia," *AV*, XX (1910), 381–433.

112. Bernardi, II, 254, states that coins were silver *quattrini* and *grossi Lucchesi;* see also Padovani, p. 277; Vecchiazzani, II, 196.

113. These names are known from a list of prisoners made by Cesare after the fall of Ravaldino; Bernardi, II, 258–59.

114. On Nov. 13, Scipio, for reasons only known to him, had returned to Forlì in order to stand by the side of Caterina; Bernardi, II, 252.

115. Priuli, p. 230, and Sanuto, *I diarii*, III, 58, mention cryptically that at one time Fracasso, sent by Lodovico il Moro, came with some soldiers in order to help her. Supposedly Caterina made impossible demands and thus he left again. I doubt that such an episode ever took place.

116. Bernardi, II, 254.

117. *Ibid.,* II, 255–56. There were approximately four hundred persons in attendance, mostly from the town, together with some representatives from the *contado*. The question on the agenda was what kind of war effort should be undertaken and who would pay for it, the city or Caterina.

118. Vecchiazzani, II, 197.

119. Bernardi, II, 257. Even Cesare Riario, *electus pisanus,* was in Florence. See Cesare Riario to Caterina Sforza, Nov. 7, 1499, *ASF, MAIP,* f. 71, n. 42.

120. Bernardi, II, 259.

121. *Ibid.,* 259–60.

122. This was the last political maneuver by Luffo Numai. A few years later he died in Ravenna.

123. Bernardi, II, 260–61.

124. Bernardi, II, 261–62.

125. Bernardi, II, 262, "le nostre contadini se levone in arme." The incident once more points out the severe tensions between city dwellers and the *contadini*. When Caterina heard the noise she sent soldiers into the city expecting hopefully that the turmoil was caused by her partisans; Padovani, 278 b.

126. A. Desjardins, *Négociations diplomatiques de la France avec la Toscane* (4 vols.; *Paris, 1859*), II, 33–34.

127. With that she showed quite a different attitude than another Sforza, Giovanni, *signore* of Pesaro. Upon news of the fall of the city of Forlì, he would flee Pesaro.

128. On Dec. 17, Cesare accepted the *capitoli;* Bernardi, II, 262.

129. Padovani, p. 279.

130. Bernardi, II, 263.

3	*soldi*	for	1 lb of bread
20	*soldi*	for	barrel of wine
20	*soldi*	for	*staio* (2 bushels) of beans
25	*soldi*	for	*staio* of oats
20	*soldi*	for	*staio* of spelt

In 1499 the price of grain had ranged from 35 *soldi* (early in the year) to 24 to 25 *soldi* before the fighting started, and that of beans from 20 to 24 *soldi; ibid.,* pp. 217–18. The prices which Cesare prescribed as *signore* were thus generally lower than those under Caterina's rule; one has the suspicion that he wished to impress the populace as benevolent and also wanted to secure cheap provisions for his troops. The price soon rose as the occupation forces depleted food stocks. At the turn of the year grain was sold for 35 to 40 *soldi* (the *staio*) and beans for 25 *soldi*. Meat, oil, and other food were just not available.

131. *Ibid.,* p. 264; Padovani, p. 279; *Cronaca Anonima,* entry Dec. 19, 1499.

132. Actually the *capitoli* prescribed that the main body of the army would not enter the city, but with the freezing weather the soldiers decided that the Forlivese houses were a more comfortable place than their camp; Priuli, p. 243. See also Sanuto, *I diarii,* III, 74, and Malipiero, p. 599, for the ensuing destruction and pillage.

133. Quoted in G. Sacerdote, *La vita di Cesare Borgia* (Milan, 1950), p. 351.

134. Bernardi, II, 270; Padovani, p. 280. He was the son of the Forlivese *speziale,* Antonio Folfi.

135. There were three Giovanni Borgia: the "Greater," archbishop and cardinal, died 1503; the "Lesser," who did all the diplomatic maneuvering in Romagna prior to the coming of Cesare's expeditionary force and who is referred to here; the third was an obscure infant. Giovanni Borgia the "Lesser" had in a secret consistory, Aug. 9, 1499, been named *Legato ad dominationem Venetorum et ad alios potentates* to prepare the campaign of Cesare diplomatically; Priuli, p. 159, n. Sanuto, *I diarii,* II, 1075, reports on the visit of the legate to Bologna (Sept. 1), Ferrara (Sept. 9), Padua (Sept. 10), and Venice

(Sept. 11–25). Venice vetoed Cesare's attack on Rimini and discouraged one on Ferrara.

136. Bernardi, II, 268. The Roverse family had in 1469 received the right to carry "l'impresa del leone col cimiero e il motto io spero"; Vecchiazzani, II, 199. The incident sheds light on the uneasy relations between Venice and Cesare.

137. On discussions, Bernardi, II, 268. The kidnapping plan is reported by Paolucci, entry under December, 1499; Priuli, p. 47; and Vecchiazzani, II, 199–200 (who also reports the discussions).

138. Cristoforo Poggio (secretary of Giovanni Bentivoglio) to marquis of Mantua, Dec. 26, 1499, *ASMa, AG,* E XXX, 3, *Bologna,* b. 1144 (py., *PP, ND,* 63). Ulisse Dolfi to marquis of Mantua, Dec. 29, 1499, *ibid.* (py., *PP, ND,* 64). Priuli (p. 244) states that Ottaviano was promised the cardinal's hat and Caterina an annual pension of three thousand ducats. Sanuto (*I diarii,* III, 72) errs when he speaks of a visit to Forlì by the cardinal of San Giorgio himself.

139. Cristoforo Poggio to marquis of Mantua (see n. 138 above).

140. The original building years of Ravaldino are unknown but the construction of the fortress must have occurred during the late 1300's. About a hundred years later Pino III Ordelaffi entrusted the reconstruction of Ravaldino to the well-known Florentine architect, Giorgio Fiorentino. Girolamo Riario added a wider moat and Caterina the structure called the *paradiso.* Although the fortress by 1499 was a much more comfortable place to live in, it was outdated as a military stronghold. For a detailed description see F. Mancini and W. Vichi, *Castelli, rocche, e torri di Romagna* (Bologna, 1959), pp. 133–36, and plans of the fortress in L. Marinelli, "Caterina Sforza alla difesa dei suoi domini nella Romagna," *AMR,* s. 4a, XXII (1931–32), 95–112.

141. In addition, Cesare now had a plentiful supply of gunpowder; see *Diario Ferrarese (1409–1509),* unknown author, in *RIS,* o.s. XXIV, c. 375.

142. Sanuto, *I diarii,* III, 77.

143. On the situation in Milan and Lodovico il Moro's return, Treccani, *Storia di Milano,* VII, 502–6.

144. Ottaviano Riario did not share that optimistic feeling. He complained to Lorenzo de'Medici about the total lack of help for his mother, Jan. 3, 1500, *ASF, MAIP,* f. 77, n. 8.

145. Sanuto, *I diarii,* III, 72–73, and Priuli, p. 244.

146. Cristoforo Poggio to marquis of Mantua, Dec. 31, 1499, *ASMa, AG,* E XXXV, 3, *Bologna,* b. 1144.

147. Sanuto, *I diarii,* III, 74–75.

148. Bernardi, II, 272.

149. For the last phase of the siege, see *ibid.,* 272–77.

150. Priuli, p. 250.

151. The relatively quick fall of what contemporaries considered a strong fortress provoked numerous accusations, particularly against Caterina's right-hand man, Giovanni di Casale. He repudiated all accusations of treachery and cowardice in a long document, 1500, *ASF, MAIP,* f. 99, n. 81 (*PP,* 1139). In subsequent years his correspondence with Caterina, his former lover and employer, also shows that she at no time thought much of the allegations against Casale (letters to Caterina, *ASF, MAIP,* f. 78, May 4, 1501, n. 205; Oct. 9, 1503, n. 311; both letters are polite in tone and private in substance and are part of a correspondence otherwise lost). One is inclined to agree with the sound and sober assessment of the affair by Machiavelli, in his *Dell'Arte della Guerra,* in *Opere,* ed. A. Panella (2 vols.; Milan-Rome, 1938–39), II, 640–41, who ascribes the debacle to outdated defense structures, an inept leadership, and the hopelessness of relying on any one fortress for one's whole fortune. Marinelli, "Caterina Sforza . . . ," *AMR,* s.4a, XXII (1931–32), pp. 111–12, blamed poor preparation, lack of an integrated defense system between *cittadella* and *rocca,* lack of sufficient modernization, insufficient men and artillery, and an unco-ordinated command structure for the failure of the defense.

152. Bernardi, II, 276.

153. On the capture, see *ibid.,* 276–77; also Priuli, p. 253; Burchard, *Diarium,* III, 10; Vecchiazzani, II, 200–201; Padovani, 280b; de'Conti, II, 209–10.

154. Bernardi, II, 277–82; Sanuto, *I diarii,* III, 84.

155. Bernardi, II, 356, "injustices committed to our unfortunate *madonna,* Caterina Sforza, who had such a beautiful body."

156. *Ibid.,* II, 264.

157. Priuli, p. 253; Sanuto, *I diarii,* III, 84–85; de'Conti, 209–10; Padovani, 280b.

158. Letter, Louis XII to Commune of Bologna, Nov. 5, 1499, quoted in Sacerdote, *La vita di Cesare Borgia,* p. 340.

159. Cesare reported to the pope that Caterina was in good hands (with some ladies in waiting) but that she was in "un animo terribile"; G. Lucido Cataneo to marquis of Mantua, Jan. 23, 1500, *ASMa, AG,* E XXV, 3, *Roma,* b. 854.

160. Bernardi, II, 284–85; Priuli, pp. 258–59, "Madonna fu venduta al Valentino." Padovani, p. 281b.

161. Priuli, pp. 234–35.

162. Bernardi, II, 301, gives May 24, 1500, as the day of death.

163. Cobelli, pp. 417–18.

164. The recreated Council of Forty is mentioned by Bernardi, II, 283, and by Vecchiazzani, II, 202. It included many of the same families who had served as members under Caterina's rule, among them the Numai, Lambertelli, Todelli, and Muratini.

165. Vecchiazzani, II, 209 ("Ramiro dell'Lorqua, tenente generale") ; Sacerdote, *La vita di Cesare Borgia,* pp. 598–99.

166. Vecchiazzani, II, 203–4.

167. Fantaguzzi, *Caos,* p. 107; Sanuto, *I diarii,* III, 84. The latter also reports (III, 118) that Caterina was six months pregnant, an erroneous piece of information.

168. Sanuto, *I diarii,* II, 92; Fantaguzzi, *Caos,* p. 108, says that the French marched west late in January, 1499.

169. Burchard, *Diarium,* III, 19–22, "I have never seen such pomp before"; Priuli, p. 260; Sacerdote, *La vita di Cesare Borgia,* pp. 367–68.

170. Sanuto, *I diarii,* III, 141.

171. G. Lucido Cataneo to marquis of Mantua, Feb. 27, 1500, *ASMa, AG,* E XXV, 3, *Roma,* b. 854; also S. di Branca Tedallini, *Diario Romano,* p. 293.

172. G. Lucido Cataneo to marquis of Mantua, as in Pt. VI, n. 171.

173. Since Fortunati had not been one of the defenders of Ravaldino he must have joined Caterina in her prison of his own accord. He had been in Florence during the dramatic days of 1499.

174. Letter, Ottaviano Riario to Caterina, May 27, 1500, *ASF, MAIP,* f. 78, n. 126.

175. Capitoli approved (Bernardi, pp. 291–92) : for grain "6 dinari a gabella per centonare," no tax on property division of relatives, no marriage tax, no soldier tax levied on peasants, and reservation of all bridge tolls from the Ronco bridge for the commune of Forlì, so that it could eventually build a new bridge. Also Sanuto, *I diarii,* III, 266.

176. Sacerdote, *La vita di Cesare Borgia,* p. 376.

177. The best source for the conspiracy is a letter from Alessandrio Braccio, who at that time negotiated with the *curia* on the Riario's behalf, to Ottaviano and Cesare Riario, May 26, 1500, *ASF, MAIP,* f. 78, n. 125 (fy., *PP,* 1129) . Sanuto notes the affair briefly, III, 403. Another hint of the plot appears in a letter from Caterina to Lauro Bossi in which she obligated herself to pay him four hundred ducats; May 23, 1500, *ASF, MAIP,* f. 72, n. 520. The money was certainly intended to permit the bribing of a guard. The plot itself has never been completely clarified. It involved Lauro Bossi and a bribed servant of Cesare Borgia, and possibly a man named Corvarano and Giovanni Battista of Imola. At the time of the plot negotia-

tions were carried on to free Caterina. As for Bossi, he most certainly was a relative of the Bossi family which had served Duke Galeazzo Maria Sforza and Bona of Savoy (see Pt. I, n. 98). Lauro Bossi himself had lived for a while in Bologna and at that time (1497) had served Lodovico il Moro as an observer of matters in Forlì and Imola.

178. Bernardi, II, 295.

179. A number of letters show the eagerness of the sons for an accommodation with the pope. Ottaviano and Cesare Riario to Caterina, May 27, 1500, *ASF, MAIP,* f. 77, n. 10. Ottaviano Riario to Caterina, May 27, 1500, *ibid.,* f. 78, n. 126.

180. Printed as a note in P. D. Pasolini, *Caterina Sforza* (3 vols.; Rome, 1893), III, 255–56.

181. Letter, Giovanni Lucido, orator, to marquis of Mantua, July 30, 1500, *ASMa, AG,* E XXV, 3, *Roma,* b. 854.

182. The bitterness of their relationship shows in three letters of Caterina to Lorenzo di Pierfrancesco de'Medici (Popolano) of July, 1500, *ASF, MAIP,* f. 78, nn. 128, 129, and 326.

183. Sacerdote, *La vita di Cesare Borgia,* pp. 393–95.

184. For Cesare's campaign see *ibid.,* pp. 398–433. For general political picture during the campaign, see Simeoni, *Le signorie,* II, 770–72.

185. An implicit complaint about Cesare's excesses is contained in *Anziani* of Imola to marquis of Mantua, July 19, 1500, *ASMa, AG,* E XXV, 3, *Roma,* b. 854. The same, Aug. 3, 1500, *ibid.* See also Sacerdote, *La vita di Cesare Borgia,* pp. 434–40.

186. Cesare relied on a mixed form of government. On one side were the trusted lieutenants who had over-all control; on the other, panels of local jurists *(rota),* who saw to strict law enforcement, and the old representative assemblies with limited functions. Peace was enforced on all factions according to the principle "indulgenzia per i piccoli, rigori contro i grandi." A measure of Cesare's popularity is the fact that as late as three years after his death the *anziani* of Imola voted him the flattering description of a "minister divinae justitiae"; Sacerdote, *La vita di Cesare Borgia,* pp. 807–10.

187. P. Zama, *I Manfredi* (Faenza, 1954), pp. 319–20.

188. G. Donati, *La fine della signoria dei Manfredi di Faenza* (Turin, 1938), pp. 179–80.

189. Bernardi, II, 311.

190. Ottaviano Riario to Caterina Sforza, April, 1501, *ASF, MAIP,* f. 85, nn. 328–29.

191. Francesco de'Pepi, Florentine orator, to *Dieci di Balia,* June 20, 1501, *ASF, Riformagioni, Responsive,* cl. X, d. 4, n. 63, c. 293. A letter which Caterina received a few months later from King Louis XII of France attests to the interest the

French took in her release. Although the letter contains little more than an expression of happiness on the king's part over Caterina's having taken up residence in Florence, it would indicate that d'Allegre had at least the strong support of the French court for his action. Louis XII to the Dame of Imola (Caterina Sforza), Sept. 6 (1501?), *ASF, MAIP*, f. 45, n. 59.

192. Sanuto, *I diarii*, IV, 61.

193. Cesare's opposition is stated in a later letter by F. Fortunati to Ottaviano and Cesare, July 8, 1502, *ASF, MAIP*, f. 77, n. 92.

194. Bernardi, II, 297; Burchard, *Diarium*, III, 146; letter from Francesco de'Pepi, orator, to *Dieci di Balia*, June 30, 1501, *ASF, Riformagioni, Responsive*, cl. X, d. 4, n. 63, c. 313.

195. F. Fortunati to Ottaviano and Cesare Riario, July 8, 1501, *ASF, MAIP*, f. 138, n. 619 (fy., *PP*, 1147).

196. On the French army in Rome and the passage through Rome see Sanuto, *I diarii*, IV, 61–64.

197. Florence was the obvious city to go to, and Francesco de'Pepi reports to his superiors that Caterina had asked him to recommend her to them; July 10, 1501, *ASF, Riformagioni, Responsive*, cl. X, d. 4, n. 66, c. 20.

198. Alexander VI to *Signoria* of Florence, July 13, 1501, fy., *PP*, 1149.

199. The exact date cannot be ascertained. The most reliable notice seems to be the one contained in G. Lucido Cataneo's letter to the marquis of Mantua, July 20, 1501, *ASMa, AG*, E XXV, 3, *Roma*, b. 854. The departure probably occurred around July 20.

200. The pope must have been unaware of Caterina's choice of the sea route; at least such is indicated by a papal recommendation to a Sienese citizen. It shows that Alexander expected her to travel along the usual route via Orvieto and Siena to Florence. The letter is reprinted as *PP, ND*, 79. Caterina's choice was certainly motivated by concern for her safety.

VII

1. The complexity of the property question is suggested by the *Atti* of Caterina Sforza's and Lorenzo de'Medici's legal quarrels before the *Tribunale della Mercanzia* between 1502 and 1506, *ASF, MAIP*, f. 127, cc. 1–57; *Atti frammentari*, n.d., *ibid.*, f. 128, c. 467–472; *Atti relativi Caterina Sforza . . . ,* Jan. 31, 1502–March 23, 1502, *ibid.*, f. 129, cc. 363–379; decision on one suit, March 22, 1502, *ibid.*, f. 84, n. 23, cc. 51–52.

The intervening war period with Caterina's subsequent imprisonment and Lorenzo's constant use of some of the funds had confused the accounts to such an extent that even good friends could have found an amicable settlement only with difficulties.

2. Although there exists a letter from G. Tornadello of Imola to Caterina dated as early as Nov. 1, 1496, *ASF, MAIP,* f. 28, n. 28, the exact nature of the connection between the two persons is not known.

3. Tornadello even shed some doubt on the loyalty to Cesare of the castellan of Imola when he told Caterina that he could go in and out of the fortress at will and had confidential discussion with the castellan. G. Tornadello to Caterina Sforza, Oct. 9, 1501, *ASF, MAIP,* f. 78, n. 164. Tornadello must have visited Caterina soon after the writing of that letter; letter to Caterina, Feb. 22, 1503, *ibid.,* n. 217.

4. Vecchiazzani, II, 207; for detailed description see C. Errera, "Il passaggio per Forlì di Lucrezia Borgia sposa di Alfonso d'Este," *ASI,* s. 5, X (1892) , 280–301, doc.

5. Except for the cordial regards for Caterina relayed by Domenico Campana (a member of the Predicant order) whom Caterina had dispatched with high hopes to the imperial court; D. Campana to Caterina Sforza, March 24, 1502, *ASF, MAIP,* f. 125, n. 231.

6. For a detailed account of the political situation in Romagna in the turbulent half of 1503, see G. Soranzo, "Il clima storico della politica Veneziana in Romagna e nelle Marche nel 1503 (agosto–dicembre) ," *SR,* V (1954) , 513–46. For the return of the *signori,* see p. 517.

7. G. Tornadello to Caterina Sforza, Sept. 9, 1503 (two letters) , *ASF, MAIP,* f. 78, cc. 252 and 253. On Sept. 29, Tornadello called for a quick attack with infantry and light horsemen. The result would be as desired, especially so since the fortress could be had for four thousand ducats. G. Tornadello to Caterina Sforza, Sept. 29, 1503, *ASF, MAIP,* f. 78, c. 253.

8. Letter, Giovanni Battista Ridolfi to *Dieci di Balia,* Sept. 12, 1503, *ASF, Riformagioni, Responsive,* cl. X, d. 4, n. 74, c. 135: "maybe if she were dead he would be welcome."

9. Cesare and Galeazzo Riario to Ottaviano Riario, Sept. 15, 1503, *ASF, MAIP,* f. 77, n. 129 (fy., *PP,* 1189) .

10. Aloisio Ciocha to Caterina Sforza, Oct. 17, 1503, *ASF, MAIP,* f. 78, n. 168.

11. G. F. de Cichi to Caterina Sforza, *ASF, MAIP,* Oct. 8, 1503, f. 78, n. 263; Nov. 7, 1503, n. 334; Dec. 15, 1503, n. 341.

12. This position was clearly stated in the message sent to the Venetian officials and partisans of Venice in Romagna, dated Sept. 7, 1503, *ASVe, SS, Deliberazioni Segreti,* reg. 39, p. 110.

By the end of 1503 Venice had succeeded in taking over all the fortresses which once belonged to Faenza, together with the Val d'Amone; see list in *Libri commemiorali*, XVI, c. 223 vo.

13. Two letters from Ottaviano Riario to Caterina Sforza reveal the financial insufficiency of the Riario; *ASF, MAIP,* f. 78, cc. 288 and 293.

14. G. Tornadello to Caterina Sforza, Oct. 22, 1503, *ASF, MAIP,* f. 78, n. 284 (fy., *PP,* 1197). Imola was at that time thinking of asking for the "protection" of Venice; G. Soranzo, "Il clima . . .," *SR,* V (1954), p. 537.

15. Sanuto, *I diarii,* V, 128, 210-11, 237, 239; Priuli, pp. 310-11; Paolucci, entry under 1503; Soranzo, "Il clima . . . ," *SR,* V (1954), 526. This episode ushered in the last period of Ordelaffi rule in Forlì. Venice soon succeeded in driving a wedge between the Ordelaffi and Florence by frightening Antonio Maria Ordelaffi with the possibility of Florentine support for the Riario; Sanuto, V, 205-6, 214.

16. G. Tornadello to Caterina Sforza, Oct. 23, 1503, *ASF, MAIP,* f. 77, n. 188 (py., *PP,* 1198).

17. At one time Caterina offered a marriage contract between Ottaviano and a Venetian noble lady in addition to Ottaviano's military service for Venice; Sanuto, *I diarii,* V, 223.

18. Ottaviano Riario to F. Fortunati, Dec. 15, 1503, *ASF, MAIP,* f. 69, n. 35; and G. B. Catano to Caterina on Ottaviano's unwillingness to resign, Jan. 16, 1504, *ASF, MAIP,* f. 75, n. 13.

19. On Nov. 4, 1504, Pope Julius II revoked the vicariate of Imola in favor of direct Church rule; *ASVa, Arm.* II, *Con.* 9, n. 2. This bull came at the end of a bitter fight in Imola. Ever since Cesare Borgia's fall from power two factions had been fighting for control of the city. Guido Vaini led the so-called Ghibellines who favored Caterina's son Galeazzo, and Giovanni Sassatello ("il Cagnaccio") was the head of the Guelphs who stood for direct Church rule. The Ghibellines lost and were exiled; G. Cerchiari, *Ristretto storico della città d'Imola* (Bologna, 1847-48), pp. 59-67. Also G. Alberghetti, *Compendio della storia della città d'Imola* (2 vols.; Imola, 1810), I, 274.

20. The delegation included Niccolò Tornielli and Giovanni dalle Selle; Vecchiazzani, II, 214-15.

21. *Ibid.,* 217.

22. Lodovico had been in the service of Venice until his coming to Forlì on Nov. 7, 1503, *ibid.,* p. 214.

23. *Ibid.,* p. 224, and Paolucci, entry under 1504.

24. The vicariate over Forlì was formally revoked.

25. The *ASF, MAIP,* contains letters from Giampietro Landriani to Caterina which show that during the early 1500's he

lived in Milan and occasionally in Landriano. The relationship between the two was cordial but it remained rather superficial. The letters do not clarify the question of why there exists no correspondence between Lucrezia Landriani and Caterina. They are contained in f. 75 (3), f. 77 (1), and f. 78 (9). The last letter received by Caterina from her stepfather dates from May 13, 1507 (f. 75, n. 149). It does not explain the cessation of correspondence afterward. Death may well have cut both exchanges short.

26. L. Bossi to Caterina Sforza, April 11, 1502, *ibid.,* f. 78, n. 200.

27. A. Baldraccani to Caterina Sforza, Dec. 6, 1502, *ibid.,* f. 78, n. 183.

28. Lodovico Albertini to Caterina Sforza, *ibid.,* f. 75, March 9, 1505, n. 98, and April 22, 1505, n. 257. The letters, which contain mainly personal matters (e.g., the story of Lodovico's severe illness) suggest, however, that Caterina's former associates were still in contact with each other (mentioned are Lodovico's connections with Baldraccani and S. Ridolfi).

29. List of jewels pawned with Pierantonio Soderini, Feb. 17, 1505, *ibid.,* f. 83, n. 92, c. 532.

30. His appointment must already have been a fact in June, 1507, because from then on he signs many of his letters *Electus Viterbiensis;* letter to F. Fortunati, June 20, 1507, *ibid.,* f. 70, n. 239. Ordination occurred on Sept. 16, 1508.

31. While her brothers frantically maneuvered, Bianca Riario married (probably in 1502; a letter written to Caterina on June 5, 1501, *ASF, MAIP,* f. 85, n. 330 is still signed Bianca Riario, while in August, 1503, she signs Bianca de'Rubeis; *ibid.,* f. 77, n. 118) and then gave birth to two children; see letter to Caterina Sforza on the birth of the second child, July 9, 1507, *ibid.,* f. 125, n. 162 (from Sancto Secundo where she apparently lived). Her older boy, Pietro Maria, was with Caterina in Florence at that time.

32. The final settlement came on June 5, 1505, with an arbitration ruling to which Caterina and Lorenzo de'Medici had given their consent; *ibid.,* f. 137, n. 1035 (py., *PP,* 1271).

33. Vincenzo da Monferra, Niccolò Sarristori, Fra Zenobic, and Ser Bartolomeo Massaconi.

34. She probably died in the Palazzo Medici; see D. Morsiani-Quadalti, *Del luogo dov'è morta la contessa Caterina Sforza signora d'Imola e di Forlì* (Bologna, 1880).

35. Testament of Caterina Sforza, May 28, 1509, *ASF, MAIP,* f. 99, n. 38, cc. 112–142 (fy., *PP,* 1355).

36. A smaller sum was to be paid in case any of them should enter a monastery. That Cornelia must have done so is indi-

cated by a letter dated Sept. 7, 1524, in *ASF, MAIP,* f. 69, n. 242, which originated in a convent in Parma.

37. He was ordained bishop of Lucca, Nov. 12, 1517.

38. Of Scipio Riario we know little more than that he survived the conquest of Ravaldino and still was alive in 1515 (see Scipio to Giovanni dalle Bande Nere, *ASF, MAIP,* f. 112, n. 20).

BIBLIOGRAPHICAL NOTE

THE FIRST BIOGRAPHY of Caterina Sforza was written by Fabio Oliva in the sixteenth century and eventually printed in Forlì in 1821 as *Vita di Caterina Sforza*. An abbreviated version of Oliva's biography appeared in serialized form in the April, 1701, issues of Giovanni Pellegrino Dandi's "Il Gran Giornale dei Letterati." Although it is therefore not an original work, the *Estratto della vita di Caterina Sforza* nevertheless represents the first printed biography of Caterina Sforza.

It was the Spanish Jesuit Antonio Burriel who produced the first major biography of Caterina. His three volume *Vita di Caterina Sforza* (Bologna, 1795) was a respectable achievement, considering the state of historical scholarship and the limitations under which he worked. It provided the image of Caterina Sforza until the late 1800's, when other efforts to understand the great Renaissance lady appeared. Vittorio Cian's *Caterina Sforza* (Turin, 1893) never achieved the prominence, expected of it, since in the same year Pier Desiderio Pasolini published his three volumes on the life of Caterina (*Caterina Sforza*, [Rome, 1893]; two volumes of text and one volume of documents). Based on extensive research, Pasolini's work became the basis of our knowledge of Caterina Sforza for decades. It brought in its wake a great number of popularizations, the best known of which are: Margherita Cerato, *Caterina Sforza* (Rome, 1903); Aldo Randi, *Caterina Sforza* (Ravenna, 1935); Bruna Bondi-Solieri, *Madonna Caterina da Forlì* (200 copies; Faenza, 1955); and Angelo Braschi, *Caterina Sforza* (Rocca da Casciano, 1965). These biographies are all based solely on Pasolini's research (although Braschi's work contains a few revisions derived from periodical literature).

BIBLIOGRAPHY

A SOURCES

1 Archival Sources

Archivio di Stato, Bologna	Archivio del Comune di Bologna, Riformatori dello stato —Libri Partitorum—Libri Mandatorum
Archivio di Stato, Firenze	Archivio Diplomatico—Riformagioni—Atti Publici
	Archivio Mediceo avanti il Principato
	Carte Strozziane
	Dieci di Balia—Missive—Legazioni e Commissarie—Responsive
	Otto di Pratica—Lettere e Istruzioni a Oratori—Responsive
	Signoria, Dieci di Balia, Otto di Pratica—Legazioni e Commissarie—Missive e Responsive
	Signori—Missive—Prima Cancelleria—Carteggi—Missive —Legazioni e Commissarie —Elezioni e Istruzioni
Archivio di Stato, Forlì	Miscellaneous material
Archivio di Stato, Mantova	Archivio Gonzaga—Series E XXV, 3 Roma—Series E XXVI, 1–3 Pesaro, Urbino, Forlì—Series E XXX, 3 Bologna—Series E XXXI, 3 Ferrara—Series E XLIX, 2 Milano
Archivio di Stato, Milano	Archivio Notarile
	Archivio Visconteo-Sforzesco —Potenze Estere—Potenze Sovrane
	Famiglia
	Lettere di Giustizia
	Registri Ducali
	Registri delle Missive

350

Archivio di Stato, Modena	Archivio Segreto Estense— Estero—Dispacci Estere— Dispacci degli Ambasciatori —Registri di Lettere—Carteggio con principi esteri
Archivio di Stato, Venezia	Libri Commemoriali Senato Secreti
Archivio Segreto Vaticano	Registri Vaticani Fondo consistoriale—Acta Camerarii—Acta Vicecancellarii Archivium Arcis Archivio della Camera Apostolica—Introitus et Exitus— Collectoriae
Archivio Storico Civile, Milano	Registri Ducali
Biblioteca Comunale, Forlì	Miscellaneous archival material
Bibliotheque Nationale, Paris	Fonds Italien

2   Other Sources

Annales Forolivienses. Edited by G. Mazzatinti. *RIS,* n.s., XXII, Pt. II.

Anonimo Veronese. *Cronaca 1446–88.* Edited by G. Soranzo (Monumenti storici—R. Deputazione veneta di storia patria, s. 3, Vol. IV), Venice, 1915.

Azzurrini, B. *Chronica breviora.* Edited by A. Messeri. *RIS,* n.s., XXVIII, Pt. III.

Bernardi, A. *Cronache forlivesi dal 1476 al 1517.* Edited by G. Mazzatinti. 2 vols. Bologna, 1895–97.

Burchard, J. *Diarium, 1483–1506.* 3 vols. Paris, 1883–85.

Bursellis, H. *Cronica gestorum ac factorum memorabilium civitatis Bononiae.* Edited by Albano Sorelli. *RIS,* n.s., XXIII, Pt. II.

Caleffini, U. *Diario.* Edited by G. Pardi. (Monumenti istorici —R. Deputazione di storia patria per l'Emilia e la Romagna, Vol. I, Pt. I.) Ferrara, 1938.

Calmeta, V. *Prose e lettere edite e inedite.* Edited by Cecil Grayson. Bologna, 1959.

Castiglione, B., della Casa, G., and Cellini, B. *Opere.* Edited by C. Cordié (La letteratura Italiana, Storia e Testi, Vol. XXVII.) Milan-Naples, n.d.

Cobelli, L. *Cronache forlivesi.* Edited by G. Carducci, E. Fanti, and F. Guarini. (Monumenti Istorici—Romagna, Vol. III, Pt. I.) Bologna, 1874.

Commines, P. de. *Memoiren*. Translated and edited by F. Ernst. Stuttgart, 1952.

Conti, S. de'. *Le storie de'suoi tempi (1475–1510)*. 2 vols. Rome, 1883.

Cronaca Anonima di Forlì. Biblioteca Comunale, Forlì, MS 275.

Cronaca Veneta. Unknown author. Biblioteca San Marco, Venice, *MS*, cl. VII, cod. CCCXXIII.

Desjardins, A. *Négociations diplomatiques de la France avec la Toscane*. 4 vols. Paris, 1859.

Diario Ferrarese (1409–1502). Unknown author. *RIS*, o.s., XXIV.

Fantaguzzi, G. *Caos. Cronache cesenati del sec. XV*. Edited by D. Bazzocchi. Cesena, 1915.

Filippo Foresti di Bergamo. *De claris selectisque mulieribus*. Ferrara, 1497.

Ghirardacci, C. *Historia di Bologna*. Bologna, 1605.

Guicciardini, F. *Storia d'Italia*. 4 vols. Milan, 1884.

I Diarii di Cecco Simonetta. Edited by A. R. Natale. Milan, 1962.

I libri commemoriali della Repubblica di Venezia, Regesti. Edited by R. Predelli. Venice, 1876–1914.

Infessura, S. *Roemisches Tagebuch*. Translated by H. Hefele. Jena, 1913.

I registri delle lettere ducali dal periodo sforzesco. Edited by C. Santoro. Milan, 1961.

Landucci, L. *Ein Florentinisches Tagebuch, 1450–1516*. Translated by M. Herzfeld. 2 vols. Jena, 1913.

Luenig, J. H. *Codex Italiae Diplomaticus*. Frankfurt-Leipzig, 1725–32.

Machiavelli, N. *Opere*. Edited by L. Passerini and G. Milanesi. 6 vols. Florence, 1874–77.

———. *Opere*. Edited by A. Panella. 2 vols. Milan-Rome, 1938–39.

———. *Scritti inediti riguardanti la storia e la milizia*. Edited by G. Canestrini. Florence, 1857.

Malipiero, D. "Annali Veneti dall'anno 1457 al 1500." Edited by F. Longo. *ASI*, VII (1843), Pts. I and II.

Monumenti ravennati de'secoli di mezzo. Edited by M. Fantuzzi. 6 vols. Venice, 1801–4.

Morbio, C. *Codice visconteo-sforzesco, 1390–1497*. Milan, 1846.

Pedrino Depintore, G. di. *Cronica del suo tempo*. Edited by A. Pasini, G. Borghezio, and M. Vattaso. 2 vols. (Studi e Testi, nos. 50 and 62.) Vatican City, 1929–34.

Platina, B. (Bartolomeo Sacchi). *Vita Sixti IV. RIS*, o.s., III.

Pontani, G. (*notaio* di Nantiporto). *Il Diario Romano*

(1481–1492). Edited by D. Toni. *RIS,* n.s., III, Pt. II.

Priuli, G. *I Diarii (1494–1512)*. Edited by A. Segre *RIS,* n.s., XXIV, Pt. III.

Rerum Hungaricarum Monumenta Arpadiana. Edited by S. Endlicher. St. Gallen, 1849.

Ridolfi, R. *Le lettere di Girolamo Savonarola*. Florence, 1933.

Sanuto, M. *Commentarii della guerra di Ferrara tra li Veneziani e il duca Ercole nel 1482*. Venice, 1829.

————. *I diarii*. 58 vols. Venice, 1879–1902.

————. *La spedizione di Carlo VIII in Italia*. Edited by R. Fulin. Venice, 1873–82.

Tedallini, S. di Branca. *Diario Romano, 1485–1524*. Edited by P. Piccolomini. *RIS,* n.s., XXIII, Pt. III.

Theiner, A. *Codex Diplomaticus Dominii Temporalis S. Sedis*. Rome, 1861–62.

Vascho, A. de. *Diario Romano, 1480–92*. Edited by G. Chiesa. *RIS,* n.s., XXIII, Pt. III.

Volaterranus, J. (Jacopo Gherardi da Volterra). *Diario Romano (1479–84)*. Edited by E. Carusi. *RIS,* n.s., XXIII, Pt. III.

B OTHER WORKS

1 Manuscripts and Books

Ady, C. *The Bentivoglio of Bologna*. London, 1937.

Alberghetti, G. *Compendio della storia civile, ecclesiastica e letteraria della città d'Imola*. 2 vols. Imola, 1810.

Alberti, F. L. *Descrittione di tutta Italia*. Venice, 1577.

Allodoli, E. *Giovanni dalle Bande Nere*. Florence, 1929.

Alvisi, E. *Cesare Borgia, duca di Romagna*. Imola, 1878.

Ammirato, S. *Albero e istoria della famiglia de'Conti Guidi*. Florence, 1640.

Arici, Z. *Bona di Savoia*. Turin, 1935.

Armand, A. *Les Médailleurs Italiens de quinzième et seizième siècles*. 3 vols. Paris, 1883–87.

Baldisseri, L. *La rocca di Bubano*. Imola, 1898.

Ballardini, G. *Fidanzamento di Astorgio III con Bianca Riario*. Faenza, 1907.

Bazzocchi, D. *Cesena nella storia*. Cesena, 1915.

Bedolini, S. *Raccolta di memorie forlivesi*. Biblioteca Comunale, Forlì, *MS* 282.

Beloch, K. J. *Bevoelkerungsgeschichte Italiens*. 2 vols. Berlin, 1939.

Beltrami, L. *Dame Milanesi invitate alle nozze di Galeazzo Maria Sforza con Bona di Savoia*. Milan, 1920.

————. *Gli sponsali di Galeazzo Maria Sforza (1450–1468)*. Milan, 1893.

Beltrami, L. *La vita nel Castello di Milano al tempo degli Sforza.* Milan, 1900.

Benacci, G. *Memorie storiche intorno alla terra di Tossignano.* Imola, 1840.

———. *Compendio della storia di Imola.* Imola, 1810.

Biondo da Forlì, F. *Roma ristaurata et Italia illustrata.* Venice, 1543.

Bondi-Solieri, B. *Madonna Caterina da Forlì.* Faenza, 1955.

Bonoli, G. *Della Storia di Cotignola.* Ravenna, 1880.

Bonoli, P. *Istorie della città di Forlì.* Forlì, 1661.

Braschi, A. *Caterina Sforza.* Rocca da Casciano, 1965.

Bricherius, C. *Tabulae genealogicae gentis Carettensis.* Vienna, 1741.

Brissio, C. *Relatione dell'antica e nobile città di Cesena.* Ferrara, 1598.

Burriel, A. *Vita di Caterina Sforza.* 3 vols. Bologna, 1795.

Buscaroli, R. *Melozzo da Forlì.* Rome, 1938.

Buser, B. *Die Beziehungen der Mediceer zu Frankreich waehrend der Jahre 1434–1494 in ihrem Zusammenhang mit den allgemeinen Verhaeltnissen.* Leipzig, 1879.

Cartwright, J. *Italian Gardens of the Renaissance.* New York, 1914.

Cavina, G. *Antichi fortilizi di Romagna: Brisighella.* Faenza, 1964.

Cerato, M. *Caterina Sforza.* Rome, 1903.

Cerchiari, G. *Ristretto storico della città d'Imola.* Bologna, 1847–48.

Cessi, R. *Storia della Repubblica di Venezia.* 2 vols. Milan, 1944–46.

Cian, V. *Caterina Sforza.* Turin, 1893.

Cipolla, C. *Storie delle signorie Italiane dal 1300 al 1530.* Milan, 1881.

Ciuffulotti, E. *Faenza nel Rinascimento.* Bagnacavallo, 1922.

Corio, B. *Storia di Milano.* 3 vols. Milan, 1855–57.

Cristofori, F. *Cronotassi dei Cardinali.* Rome, 1857.

Davari, S. *Il matrimonio di Dorotea Gonzaga con Galeazzo Maria Sforza.* Genoa, 1890.

Delaborde, F. *L'expédition de Charles VIII.* Paris, 1888.

DiGiorgio Martini, F. *Trattato di architettura civile e militare del sec. XV.* Edited by C. Saluzzo. Turin, 1841.

Donati, G. *La fine della Signoria dei Manfredi in Faenza.* Turin, 1938.

Fabriczy, C. von. *Italian Medals.* Translated by Mrs. Gustavus W. Hamilton. London, 1904.

Fabrionio, A. *Laurentii Medicis Magnifici Vita.* 2 vols. Pisa, 1784.

Fanti, I. *Imola sotto Giulio II.* Imola, 1882.

Filippi, G. *Il matrimonio con Bona di Savoia di Galeazzo Maria Sforza.* Turin, 1890.

Filippini, G. *Taddeo Manfredi, signore d'Imola, e sue relazioni con gli Sforza.* Urbania, 1913.

Floerke, H. *Die Moden der Renaissance.* Munich, 1924.

Fossati, F. *Sulle cause dell'invasione turca in Italia del 1480.* Vigevano, 1901.

———. *Per l'alleanza del 25 luglio 1480.* Mortara-Vigevano, 1907.

Fregoso, B. *Battistae Fulgosi Opus Incomparabile.* Basel, 1541.

Friedlaender, J. *Die Italienischen Schaumuenzen des 15. Jahrhunderts.* Berlin, 1882.

Fueter, E. *Geschichte des Europäischen Staatensystems, 1493–1559.* Munich, 1919.

Fuzzi, M. *L'ultimo periodo degli Ordelaffi in Forlì.* Forlì, 1937.

Gagliardi, E. *Der Anteil der Schweizer an den italienischen Kriegen, 1494–1516.* Zurich, 1919.

Gardini, I. *Tavole genealogiche delle famiglie patrizie di Forlì.* 2 vols. Biblioteca Comunale, Forlì, *MSS* 1 and 2.

Garner, L. *Cesare Borgia.* London, 1912.

Geiger, L. *Alexander VI. und sein Hof.* (Memoirenbibliothek IV/3.) Stuttgart, 1912.

Giovio, P. *Elogi.* Venice, 1558.

Gottschewski, A. *Ueber die Portraets der Caterina Sforza.* Strassbourg, 1908.

Graevius, J. G. *Thesaurus Antiquitatum et Historiarum Italiae.* 2 vols. Leyden, 1704.

Gregorovius, F. *Geschichte der Stadt Rom im Mittelalter.* 8 vols. Stuttgart, 1889–1903.

———. *Lucrezia Borgia.* Stuttgart, 1895.

Guicciardini, F. *Storia d'Italia.* 4 vols. Milan, 1884.

Guicciardini, L. *L'hore di ricreatione.* Rome, 1665.

Habich, G. *Die Medaillen der Renaissance.* Stuttgart-Berlin, 1923.

Hierarchia Catholica. Edited by C. Eubel *et al.* 5 vols. Regensburg, 1898.

Hill, G. F. *A Corpus of the Italian Medals of the Renaissance.* 2 vols. London, 1930.

Kretschmayr, H. *Geschichte von Venedig.* 2 vols. Gotha, 1920.

Laghi, A. *Cristoforo de Brugora; speziale della duchessa Bona e della corte sforcesca.* Pavia, 1959.

La Pilorgerie, J. L. de. *Campagne et bulletins de la grande armée d'Italie commandée par Charles VIII, 1494–95.* Nantes-Paris, 1866.

Larner, J. *The Lords of Romagna.* Ithaca, N.Y., 1965.

Litta, P. *Famiglie celebri d'Italia.* Milan, 1819–85; 2a series, 1902–23.

Magenta, C. *I Visconti e gli Sforza nel castello di Pavia*. 2 vols. Milan, 1883.

Malaguzzi-Valeri, F. *La corte di Lodovico il Moro*. 2d ed. Milan, 1929.

Mancini, F., and Vichi, W. *Castelli, rocche, e torri di Romagna*. Bologna, 1959.

Mansuelli, G. *Caesena, Forum popili, Forum Livi*. Rome, 1928.

Marchesi, S. *Supplemento historico dell'antica città di Forlì*. Forlì, 1678.

———. *Compendium historiae celeberrimae civitatis Forolivi*. Forlì, 1722.

———. *Vitae virorum illustrium foroliviensium*. Forlì, 1726.

Marconi, G. B. *Le guerre della Romagna alta e le tragedie della città di Imola*. Biblioteca Comunale, Imola, MS 349, c. 40.

Marinelli, L. *Le antiche fortezze di Romagna*. Imola, 1938.

Matteini, N. *Romagna: personaggi, luoghi, fatti e leggende*. Bologna, 1954.

Mattingly, G. *Renaissance Diplomacy*. Boston, 1955.

Maulde la Claviere, R. de. *The Women of the Renaissance*. Translated by G. H. Ely. New York, 1901.

Messeri, A., and Calzi, A. *Faenza nella storia e nell'arte*. Faenza, 1909.

———. *Galeotto Manfredi, signore di Faenza*. Faenza, 1904.

Metelli, A. *Storia di Brisighella e della Valle di Amone*. 4 vols. Faenza, 1869–72.

Missiroli, A. *Astorgio III, signore di Faenza*. Bologna, 1912.

Morsiani-Quadalti, D. *Del luogo dov'è morta la contessa Caterina Sforza, signora d'Imola e di Forlì*. Bologna, 1880.

Motta, E. *Musici alla corte degli Sforza*. Milan, 1887.

Nissim, Rossi L. *I Malatesta*. Florence, 1934.

Oliva, F. *Vita di Caterina Sforza*. Forlì, 1821.

Padovani, A. *Istoria di Forlì*. Biblioteca Comunale, Forlì, MS 276.

Palmarocchi, R. *La politica italiana di Lorenzo de'Medici*. Florence, 1933.

———. *Lorenzo de'Medici*. Turin, 1941.

Palmieri, A. *La montagna bolognese nel periodo dei comuni*. Bologna, 1931.

Paolucci, B. *Historia di Forlì*. Biblioteca Comunale, Forlì. MS 300.

Pasolini, P. *I tiranni di Romagna e i papi del medio evo*. Imola, 1888.

———. *Caterina Sforza*. 3 vols. Rome, 1893.

———. *Caterina Sforza*. Translated and abridged by Paul Sylvester. New York, 1898.

Pastor, L. *The History of the Popes*. 12 vols. Vols. IV–VI. St. Louis, 1923.

Pecci, G. *Gli Ordelaffi*. Faenza, 1955.

Pelissier, L. G. *Louis XII et Lodovico Sforza*. Paris, 1896.

Pieri, P. *Il Rinascimento e la crisi militare italiana*. Turin, 1952.

Pontieri, E. *L'eta dell' equilibrio politico in Italia (1454–1494)*. Naples, 1962.

———. *Per la storia del regno di Ferrante I d'Aragonia, re di Napoli*. Naples, 1947.

Portigliotti, G. *Some fascinating Women of the Renaissance*. Translated by B. Miall. London, 1929.

Randi, A. *Caterina Sforza*. Ravenna, 1935.

Rosetti, G. *Vite degli uomini illustri forlivesi*. Forlì, 1858.

Rossi, G. *Vita di Giovanni de'Medici*. Milan, 1833.

Rubbi, G. C. *Delle monete e dell'instituzione delle zecche d'Italia*. Mantua-Lucca, 1754–60.

Sabatini, R. *Life of Cesare Borgia*. London, 1926.

Sacerdote, G. *La vita di Cesare Borgia*. Milan, 1950.

Salvioni, G. *Il valore della lira bolognese dalla sua origine alla metà del secolo XVII*. Turin, 1961.

Schmarsow, A. *Melozzo da Forlì*. Berlin, 1886.

Schmidt, F. *Mensch, Raum und Farbe in der Fruehitalienischen Tafelmalerei*. Altenburg, 1956.

Silvagni, L. *Guelfi e Ghibellini in Forlì*. Forlì, 1911.

Simeoni, L. *Le signorie*. 2 vols. Milan, 1950.

Soranzo, G. *La Lega Italica, (1454–1455)*. Milan, n.d.

Sorbelli, A. *Il comune rurale dell'Apennino emiliano nei sec. XIV e XV*. Bologna, 1910.

Tonini, L. *Storia di Rimini*. Rimini, 1862.

Treccani. *Storia di Milano*. 16 vols. Milan, 1953–62.

Tonduzzi, G. *Historie di Faenza*. Faenza, 1675.

Ulmann, H. *Kaiser Maximilian I*. Stuttgart, 1884–91.

Valeri, N. *Signorie e principati*. Milan, 1949.

Vasina, A. *Cento anni di studi sulla Romagna, 1861–1961. Bibliografia storica*. 3 vols. Faenza, 1962.

Vecchiazzani, M. *Historia di Forlimpopoli*. 2 vols. Rimini, 1647.

Violini, C. *Galeazzo Maria Sforza*. Turin, 1943.

Winker, W. *Kaiser Maximilian I*. Munich, 1950.

Wolff, V. *Die Beziehungen Kaiser Maximilian I zu Italien, 1495–1508*. Innsbruck, 1909.

Yriarte, C. *Cesare Borgia*. 2 vols. Paris, 1930.

Zama, P. *I Malatesti*. 2d rev. ed. Faenza, 1965.

———. *I Manfredi*. Faenza, 1954.

Zanetti, G. *Delle monete forlivesi*. Bologna. 1778.

Zanetti, G. *Nuova raccolta delle monete e zecche d'Italia.* Bologna, 1775–86.

Zauli-Naldi, D. *Dionigi e Vincenzo Naldi in Romagna (1495–1504)*. Faenza, 1925.

Zazzeri, R. *Storia di Cesena.* Cesena, 1890.

2 Periodical Literature

Ballardini, G. "La costituzione della contea di Brisighella e della Val d'Amone," *Valdilamone,* VII (1927), nn. 1–2, 23–40.

Bauer, C. "Studi per la storia delle finanze papali durante il pontificato di Sisto IV," *Archivio della R. Società Romana di storia patria,* I (1927), 319–400.

Beltrami, L. "L'annullamento del contratto di matrimonio fra Galeazzo Maria Sforza e Dorotea Gonzaga (1463)," *ASL,* s. 2, XVI (1889), 126–32.

Boattini, C. "Galeotto Manfredi signore di Faenza (1440–88)," *P,* XXII (1953), 132–34, 173–76, 211–13, 297–98.

Bonardi, A. "Venezia e Cesare Borgia," *AV,* XX (1910), 381–433.

Bottari, S. "La pittura in Romagna nel tempo di Caterina Sforza," *AMR,* n.s., XV–XVI (1963–65; ed. 1966), (in press).

Cencetti, G., and Fasoli, G. "Gli studi storici sulle signorie romagnole," *AMR,* IV (1938–39), 239–63.

Cessi, R. "Per la storia della guerra di Ferrara, 1482–1483," *AV,* s. 5, LXXIX (1950), 57–76.

Cicognani, A. "Riolo: La rocca sforzesca—le Terme," *P,* XXVII (1958), 124–25.

Clough, C. "Gaspare Sanseverino and Castiglione's *Il Cortegiano,*" *Philological Quarterly,* XLIII (April, 1964), (in press).

——. "Caterina Sforza, Gaspare Sanseverino e *il Cortegiano* del Castiglione," *AMR,* n.s., XV–XVI (1963–65; ed. 1966), (in press).

——. "The Sources for the Biography of Caterina Sforza and for the History of the State during her Rule," *AMR,* n.s., XV–XVI (1963–65; ed. 1966), 45–108.

Dallari, U. "Carteggio tra i Bentivoglio e gli Estensi dal 1491 al 1542 esistente nell' Archivio di Stato in Modena," *AMR,* XVIII (1899–1900), 1–88, 285–332; XIX (1900–1901), 245–372.

Errera, C. "Il passaggio per Forlì di Lucrezia Borgia sposa di Alfonso d'Este," *ASI,* s. 5, X (1892), 280–301.

Franceschini, G. B. "Caterina Sforza e il tramonto della Signoria su Imola e Forlì," *AMR,* n.s., XV–XVI (1963–65; ed. 1966), 1–14.

Garzanti, "Un banco ebreo in Forlì," *R*, V (1908), 266–79.

Ghinzoni, P. "Spedizione sforzesca in Francia (1465–66)," *ASL*, s. 2, VII (1890), 314–45.

———. "Usi e costumi nuziali principeschi," *ASL*, s. 2, XV (1888), 101–11.

Giulini, A. "Un probabile progetto matrimoniale per Caterina Sforza," *ASL*, s. 4, XL (1913), 220–23.

Gnecchi, E. "Un quattrino di Caterina Sforza signora di Forlì," *Rivista Italiana di Numismatica*, XVIII (1905), 493–98.

Grigione, C. "Pino III Ordelaffi," *R*, VII (1910), 118–23.

Grilli, A. "Dieci lettere inedite di Caterina Sforza al capitolo di San Casciano d'Imola," *R*, s. 4, VIII (1911), 313–58, and doc.

Ilardi, V. "The Italian League, Francesco Sforza and Charles VII (1454–1461)," *Studies in the Renaissance*, VI (1959), 129–66.

Mambelli, A. "Un estratto settecentesco della *Vita di Caterina Sforza*," *AMR*, n.s., XV–XVI (1963–65; ed. 1966), (in press).

Manaresi, C. "Caterina Sforza e il castellano d'Imola," *R*, s. 6, XV (1924), 268–77.

Manzoni, L. "Storia dei castelli di Romagna e specialmente di Mordano dal 1401 al 1470," *AMR*, s. 3a, II (1883–84), 90–91 and 260–61.

Marinelli, L. "Caterina Sforza alla difesa dei suoi domini nella Romagna," *AMR*, s. 4a, XXII (1931–32), 95–112.

———. "Ricostruzione al tempo di Caterina Sforza della rocca di Meldola," *AMR*, s. 4a, XVI (1925–26), 124.

Mazzatinti, G. "Il principato di Pino III Ordelaffi," *AMR*, s. 3a (1894–95), 1–56.

Missiroli, N. "Faenza e il pretendente Ottaviano Manfredi nell'anno 1488," *R*, V (1908), 250–61, 299–311.

Moncallero, G. L. "Documenti inediti sulla guerra di Romagna del 1494," *Rinascimento*, IV (1953), 233–61; V (1954), 45–79; VI (1955), 3–74.

Monti, A. "Il monte di Pietà," *FL*, I (1926–27), 21–25.

Morandini, F. "Il conflitto fra Lorenzo il Magnifico e Sisto IV dopo la congiura de'Pazzi. Dal Carteggio di Lorenzo con Girolamo Morelli, ambasciatore fiorentino a Milano," *ASI*, CVII (1949–50), 113–54.

Nigrisoli, V. "Cenni sul ricettario di Caterina Sforza," *P*, IX (1928), 178–82.

———. "Spigolature dal ricettario di Caterina Sforza," *P*, X (1929), 34–36, 38–39.

Novaga, P. "Brunoro I il fratricida," *Forum Popili*, I (1961), 77–79.

Orlandelli, G. "Le finanze della communità di Forlì sotto il vicariato di Baldassare Cossa," *SR*, VII (1956), 183–92.

Pampaloni, G. "La crisi annonaria fiorentina degli anni 1496–1497 e le importazioni di grano dalla Romagna," *AMR,* n.s., XV–XVI (1963–65; ed. 1966), (in press).

Pasolini, P. D. "Nuovi documenti su Caterina Sforza (1469–1506)," *AMR,* s. 3a, XV (1896–97), 72–209, and documents.

Pecci, G. "Antonio Maria Ordelaffi e Caterina Sforza," *AMR,* n.s., XV–XVI (1963–65; ed. 1966), (in press).

Pelissier, L. "Alcuni documenti sconosciuti su Caterina Sforza," *ASI* s. 5, I (1898), 322–31.

Picotti, G. B. "La neutralità bolognese nella discesa di Carlo VIII," *AMR,* s. 4, IX (1919), 165–246.

———. "Caterina Sforza Riario e la Romagna alla calata di Carlo VIII," *AMR,* n.s., XV–XVI (1963–65; ed. 1966), (in press).

Piva, E. "Origine e conclusione della pace e dell'alleanza tra i Veneziani e Sisto IV," *AV,* s. 3, II (1901), 35–70.

Ricci, C. "Il ritratto di Caterina Sforza," *FL,* III (1928), 5–12.

Rinaldi, E. "Gli Ebrei in Forlì nei secc. XIV e XV," *AMR,* s. 4a, X (1919–20), 295–323.

Santa, G. della. "Benedetto Soranzo, Patrizio Veneto, Archivescovo di Cipro, e Girolamo Riario," *AV,* s. 3, XXVIII (1914), 308–87.

Santini, U. "I dazii egidiani in Forlì nel 1364," *AMR,* s. 4, IV (1913–14), 1–122.

Santoro, C. "L'educazione dei principi alla corte Sforzesca," *Popoli,* II (1942), No. 5.

Sassi, A. "Il castello di Dovadola," *Il Plaustro,* III (1913), 284–85.

Storti, R. C. "Le frivolezze di una grande donna. Gli esperimenti di Caterina Sforza," *Lettura,* XLII (1942), 657–63.

Soranzo, G. "Il clima storico della politica veneziana in Romagna e nelle Marche nel 1503 (agosto–dicembre)," *SR,* V (1954), 513–46.

Squarzoni, B. "Notizie economiche romagnole in un manoscritto settecentesco della *Vita di Caterina Sforza* di F. Oliva," *SR,* V (1954), 547–60.

Torre, A. "Caterina Sforza," *AMR,* n.s., XV–XVI (1963–65; ed. 1966), (in press).

Trapani, M. "La rocchetta di Schiavonia," *Il Plaustro,* II p. 468 (1912), 127, n. 15.

Vasina, A. "Caterina Sforza all'opera di Pier Desiderio Pasolini," *AMR,* n.s., XV–XVI (1963–65; ed. 1966), (in press).

Virgili, A. "L'assassinio di Ottaviano Manfredi," *ASI,* s. 5, CCXXI (1901), 101–13.

Zama, P. "Caterina Sforza e gli ultimi Manfredi," *AMR,* n.s., XV–XVI (1963–65; ed. 1966), (in press).

INDEX